Comprehensive English

REVIEW TEXT

FOURTH EDITION

HAROLD LEVINE *Author of*

Vocabulary for the High School Student
Vocabulary for the College-Bound Student
Vocabulary Through Pleasurable Reading, Books I and II
Vocabulary and Composition Through Pleasurable Reading, Books III, IV, V, VI
English Alive (Grammar)
English Alive (Complete Edition)

Dedicated to serving

AMSCO

our nation's youth

AMSCO SCHOOL PUBLICATIONS, INC.
315 Hudson Street   New York, N.Y. 10013

When ordering this book, please specify:
either **R 224 P** *or* COMPREHENSIVE ENGLISH

ISBN 0-87720-390-3

ABOUT THIS BOOK

To the Student

This book was written to give you practical help and guidance as you review high school English and prepare for the New York State Comprehensive Examination. Here you will find abundant, easy-to-understand explanations and practice exercises to improve your skills as a user of English and broaden your understanding and appreciation of the subject. These materials can help you pass the examination with distinction.

You will find that this book uses a two-step approach to each part of the examination. First it helps you analyze typical questions so that you may know what will be expected of you. Then it provides you with the necessary instruction and practice materials for improving your knowledge and skill in answering similar questions.

If, like many other students, you sometimes feel uneasy about your answers to listening and reading comprehension questions, you will be glad to know that this book teaches logical, reliable procedures for answering such questions. Also, it shows you how to check your answers so that you may be confident that they are indeed correct.

To improve your composition ability, this book guides you in discovering the strengths and weaknesses in numerous pieces of student writing, and it shows you how to remedy many typical weaknesses.

For the other areas of the examination—vocabulary, spelling, usage, library and research skills, parliamentary procedure, the newspaper, magazines, propaganda techniques, letter-writing skills, etc.—this book offers similarly thorough instruction and preparation.

The *Guide to Good Literature* (Chapter 9) provides brief annotations on more than six hundred widely read works, including short stories, poems, essays, novels, plays, biographies, and books of true experience. The *Guide* may help you recall some of the literature you have already read, and it can suggest to you some worthwhile titles for additional reading.

A high score on the Comprehensive Examination is, of course, one of your goals. Another, and even more important, goal is your growth in over-all competence in the most vital of all subjects—English. To both of these goals this book is dedicated.

To the Teacher

Comprehensive English Review Text, Fourth Edition, reflects the changes that have been made in the New York State Comprehensive Examination since the publication of the last edition. The necessary additional instructional material and practice exercises have been incorporated into the text. As in the past editions, several of the most recent examinations are reprinted at the back of the book.

—HAROLD LEVINE

CONTENTS

> **IMPORTANT NOTICE TO STUDENTS**
> Skip Chapter 8 and go directly to Chapter 9.
> *Question C is no longer a part of the test.* Use
> Chapter 8 only if you wish to review tests given
> before 1982 reprinted at the back of this book.

AN OVERVIEW OF THE COMPREHENSIVE EXAMINATION IN ENGLISH

At the examination, you will receive an examination booklet containing a detachable answer sheet. On this sheet you are to write your answers to the short-answer questions. For your answers to the essay questions, you will be provided with essay paper. You will have three hours to complete the examination.

The examination is divided into three parts.

PART I IS THE SHORT-ANSWER TEST
VALUE: 50 CREDITS

It consists of the following:

QUESTIONS	TOPICS	CREDITS
1–10	Listening	10
11–30	Vocabulary	10
31–40	Spelling	5
41–60	Reading Comprehension	20
61–65	Correct Usage or	
	Related Areas	5
	Value of Part I	50 credits

PART II IS THE LITERATURE TEST
VALUE: 20 CREDITS

It measures your understanding and appreciation of the literature you have read in and out of class. Part II offers you the choice of answering questions *A* or *B*, each worth twenty credits.

Both *A* and *B* are essay-type questions. One of them (either *A* or *B*) asks you to discuss *two full-length works,* such as novels, biographies, books of true experience, and full-length plays. The other asks you to write about *four short works,* such as short stories, poems, essays, and one-act plays.

Value of Part II .... **20 credits**

PART III IS THE COMPOSITION TEST
VALUE: 30 CREDITS

It requires you to write a composition of 250–300 words, either on one of several suggested topics, or in reply to a specific question.

Value of Part III .... **30 credits**

PART I OF THE EXAMINATION

Chapter 1 The Listening Test (Questions 1-10)

THE IMPORTANCE OF LISTENING

Listening is one of the principal ways by which we learn. Through listening, we get facts, information, and ideas, and we form opinions and judgments. Listening is a vital part of every conversation and discussion we participate in; we cannot make good contributions as speakers unless we are good listeners. Listening also gives us pleasure. We enjoy music, drama, films, the talk of stimulating people, and our favorite radio and TV programs through listening. It is a fact that people spend more time listening than reading, speaking, or writing.

You are more likely to do well in your chosen occupation or career, in making and keeping friends, and in college, where the lecture method is heavily used to impart knowledge, if you are a skillful listener.

TYPICAL REGENTS LISTENING TEST

The listening test measures your ability to get and interpret information from a passage that will be read to you by the teacher. You will not see the passage. Only the teacher will have a copy. Here are the instructions for the test as they appear on page 1 of the examination booklet:

3

DIRECTIONS FOR THE LISTENING SECTION

(1) The teacher will read a passage aloud. Listen carefully. DO NOT WRITE ANYTHING.

(2) After the first reading of the passage, the teacher will tell you to turn over this page and to read all the questions on page 2.

(3) Then the teacher will read the passage aloud a second time. <u>As you listen to the second reading</u>, choose the best answer to each question and write its <u>number</u> in the appropriate space on the answer sheet.

(4) After you have listened to the passage the second time, you will have up to five minutes to look over your answers.

(5) The teacher is not permitted to answer questions about the passage.

(6) After you have answered the listening questions on page 2, go right on to the rest of the examination.

The following passage was read to students in a Regents listening test. Bear in mind that they did not see this passage. It is reprinted here solely to help us analyze the listening test.

LISTENING PASSAGE

Bulgaria's Communist Party leader makes a speech lasting six hours. In Washington, they're shorter . . . but maybe only because nobody will listen that long.

The Bulgarian Communist Party is having its annual party congress in
5 Sofia. It's a time when the party leaders come in from the provinces . . . get a look at such bright lights as Sofia has . . . get a few free meals . . . and get treated for a few days as if they were important . . . vote as they're told to vote . . . and go home. It's a standard ritual in the Communist world . . . a week or so of public sweetness and agreement . . . and private
10 bickering. You never see their party leaders having a public argument, as ours always do. They settle differences in private and then announce the result in public. Everyone says yes, that's fine . . . and it's all over.

When the leader of the Bulgarian Communist Party made his speech to the congress, he started talking . . . and didn't stop for six hours. Six
15 hours. And his audience sat through it because it had to. The Communist states have made remarkable progress in some areas, but obviously not in this one. The Bulgarian leader still holds . . . as do some of Russia's leaders . . . that a speech isn't truly important unless it runs for hours and hours.

And so they drone away for hours to an audience that must listen, or at
20 least sit there and stay awake, or appear to.

The U.S. Senate has in the past had a few members afflicted with this
disease—voxophilia, or something like that—whose symptom is a love of
hearing one's own voice. But here nobody has to listen. Senators can walk
out, and do. Often, speeches on the Senate floor are delivered before an
25 audience of one or two, out of a membership of 100. And the speaker
does not complain . . . because next week somebody will make a speech
he doesn't want to sit through . . . and he will walk out on that. It's a
pretty amiable arrangement. Everybody gets to talk . . . but nobody has
to listen. It has to be that way in a town like Washington . . . where we
30 have a vast oversupply of talkers . . . and a critical shortage of listeners.

In Washington . . . brief remarks generally run 10 to 20 minutes. A
speech runs an hour or more . . . but seldom much more. In the House
of Representatives, there are so many members . . . 435 . . . they have a
one-minute rule for speakers. One-minute speeches usually run from two
35 minutes up to five, or ten. Except for filibusters, nobody here to my knowledge has ever equalled or even approached the Bulgarian chairman's six
hours. Because we lack one essential agreement found only in the police
state . . . the power to force anybody to listen. We have talkers, all right,
including some who might be willing to go six hours. But, fortunately,
40 we don't have the listeners.

After the first reading of the above passage by the teacher, the students
were asked to read silently the following ten questions, which were printed
on page 2 of their examination booklets:

1 Bulgarian party leaders gather in Sofia primarily in order to
  1 enjoy the bright lights
  2 secretly meet other politicians
  3 vote as they are told to vote
  4 receive treatment due such important people

2 According to this passage, one experience common to politicians in both
  Sofia and Washington is
  1 listening to speeches   3 flattering treatment
  2 free meals   4 bright lights and parties

3 What does the author suggest about Bulgarian politicians?
  1 They are more polite than American politicians.
  2 They make more important speeches than American politicians.
  3 They have great confidence in their party leaders.
  4 They are afraid to walk out on their leaders' speeches.

4 According to this passage, the activities of the Bulgarian Party Congress are typical of those found in
  1 both Bulgaria and the United States
  2 all Communist countries
  3 Bulgaria, only
  4 many European countries

5 From the passage, the listener can most safely conclude that the arguments among American political leaders
  1 take place in public
  2 are settled in private
  3 occur infrequently
  4 are settled in a friendly manner

6 In the United States Congress, Senators may talk longer than Representatives do because
  1 Senators have more to say
  2 the Senators have to pass more bills
  3 there is no limit upon the length of their speeches
  4 Representatives will not listen to long speeches

7 According to this passage, which idea does the author suggest about the United States Senate?
  1 There are few Senators who like to speak.
  2 There is a shortage of Senators willing to listen to long speeches.
  3 There are many opportunities to listen and learn before voting.
  4 The Senate benefits from the use of the filibuster.

8 The House of Representatives has a rule that members can speak for
  1 one minute
  2 two minutes to four minutes
  3 five minutes to ten minutes
  4 one hour

9 The author most likely believes that Congressional rules concerning speeches should
  1 force more members of Congress to listen
  2 allow only party leaders to speak
  3 forbid filibusters
  4 be kept as they are now

10 The author feels that the major difference between customs in Sofia and in Washington regarding politicians is that

1 Washington is more efficient than Sofia
2 Bulgarian political leaders never disagree
3 a free country has politicians who do not listen to speeches
4 the Sofia Congress meets for a longer time than the Washington Congress

Then the teacher read the passage aloud a second time. As they listened, the students recorded the answers to the above questions on their answer sheets. After the second reading, the students had up to five minutes to look over their answers before proceeding to the next part of the examination.

SUGGESTIONS FOR ANSWERING LISTENING TEST QUESTIONS

1. Base your answers solely on the evidence you will hear *in the passage read by the teacher.* Do not answer any question on the basis of knowledge about the subject that you may have acquired previously.

2. The proof for the answer to every question is stated or implied *in the passage.* If you listen carefully, you will hear it.

The following analysis shows the proof you could have heard in the passage to help you answer all of the questions correctly.

QUESTIONS	ANSWERS (WITH PROOF)
1 Bulgarian party leaders gather in Sofia primarily in order to 1 enjoy the bright lights 2 secretly meet other politicians 3 vote as they are told to vote 4 receive treatment due such important people	*3* is the correct answer. Lines 5–8 in the passage contain a series of things the party leaders do before going home. The fact that *vote as they are told to vote* comes last in this series suggests it is the most important, or PRIMARY, item: not until the party leaders *vote as they are told to vote* can they go home. *2, secretly meet other politicians,* is not supported. Lines 9–11 show the discussions are private, but this does not mean the meetings are secret. Nothing in the passage suggests an attempt to conceal the fact that the meetings are taking place.

2 According to this passage, one experience common to politicians in both Sofia and Washington is
1 listening to speeches
2 free meals
3 flattering treatment
4 bright lights and parties

3 What does the author suggest about Bulgarian politicians?
1 They are more polite than American politicians.
2 They make more important speeches than American politicians.
3 They have great confidence in their party leaders.
4 They are afraid to walk out on their leaders' speeches.

4 According to this passage, the activities of the Bulgarian Party Congress are typical of those found in
1 both Bulgaria and the United States
2 all Communist countries
3 Bulgaria, only
4 many European countries

1 is the correct answer. There is no evidence *in the passage* that *free meals, flattering treatment,* or *bright lights and parties* are part of the experience of politicians in Washington. On the other hand, lines 19–20 and 23–25 show that *listening to speeches* is an experience politicians in both Sofia and Washington have in common—even though the listening is compulsory in the first place and voluntary in the second.

Caution: You may have knowledge from sources other than the passage that some Washington politicians get free meals, flattering treatment, or invitations to parties. Such knowledge is dangerous at this time, as it may trap you into wrong answers. Remember to base your answers only on what you hear in the passage.

4 is the correct answer. Lines 19–20 state that the audience of Bulgarian politicians "must listen, or at least sit there and stay awake, or appear to." This evidence suggests *they are afraid to walk out on their leaders' speeches.*

2 is the correct answer. In describing some Bulgarian Party Congress activities, lines 8–9 state: "It's a standard ritual in the Communist world." Lines 15–20, which identify these activities with practices followed by "the Communist states" and "some of Russia's leaders," reinforce the idea that they are typical of those to be found in *all Communist countries.*

5 From the passage, the listener can most safely conclude that the arguments among American political leaders
1 take place in public
2 are settled in private
3 occur infrequently
4 are settled in a friendly manner

1 is the correct answer. Lines 10–11, which state that "you never see their party leaders having a public argument, *as ours always do*," indicate that arguments among American political leaders *take place in public.*

6 In the United States Congress, Senators may talk longer than Representatives do because
1 Senators have more to say
2 the Senators have to pass more bills
3 there is no limit upon the length of their speeches
4 Representatives will not listen to long speeches

3 is the correct answer. According to lines 32–35, there is a limit on the length of speeches in the House because it has "so many members . . . 435." But the passage makes no mention whatsoever of any limit in the Senate where, as line 25 indicates, there are only 100 members. The passage therefore implies that the reason Senators may talk longer is that *there is no limit upon the length of their speeches.*

The passage does not support the idea that Senators have more to say or have to pass more bills, and it makes no distinction whatever between Senators and Representatives in the matter of willingness to listen to long speeches.

7 According to this passage, which idea does the author suggest about the United States Senate?
1 There are few Senators who like to speak.
2 There is a shortage of Senators willing to listen to long speeches.
3 There are many opportunities to listen and learn before voting.
4 The Senate benefits from the use of the filibuster.

2 is the correct answer according to lines 38–40: "We have talkers, all right [in the Senate and the House], including some who might be willing to go six hours. But, fortunately, we don't have the listeners." Note, also, that lines 1–3 state that "nobody [in Washington] will listen that long [six hours]."

1, There are few Senators who like to speak is not supported. *Few* means "almost no." It should not be confused with *a few,* which means "some, but not many." Lines 21–23 state that there had been *a few* (not *few*) Senators in the past who liked to talk.

The passage makes no reference to *opportunities to listen and learn before voting* or to *benefit from the use of the filibuster.*

8 The House of Representatives has a rule that members can speak for
1 one minute
2 two minutes to four minutes
3 five minutes to ten minutes
4 one hour

1 is the correct answer according to lines 32–34: "In the House of Representatives . . . they have a *one-minute* rule for speakers."

9 The author most likely believes that Congressional rules concerning speeches should
1 force more members of Congress to listen
2 allow only party leaders to speak
3 forbid filibusters
4 be kept as they are now

4 is the correct answer. The author nowhere in the passage states that Congressional rules should *force more members of Congress to listen,* or *allow only party leaders to speak,* or *forbid filibusters.* On the other hand, the positive remarks he makes about the present system—"It has to be that way in a town like Washington (line 29)" and "fortunately, we don't have the listeners (lines 39–40)"—suggest that he believes the rules should *be kept as they are now.*

10 The author feels that the major difference between customs in Sofia and in Washington regarding politicians is that
1 Washington is more efficient than Sofia
2 Bulgarian political leaders never disagree
3 a free country has politicians who do not listen to speeches
4 the Sofia Congress meets for a longer time than the Washington Congress

3 is the correct answer. The author repeatedly makes the point that *a free country has politicians who do not listen to speeches.* Note the following:

"In Washington, they're [the speeches] shorter . . . but maybe only because nobody will listen that long (lines 1–3)."

"But here [in the U.S. Senate] nobody has to listen (line 23)."

"Everybody [every Senator] gets to talk . . . but nobody has to listen (lines 28–29)."

". . . we have a vast oversupply of talkers [in Washington] and a critical shortage of listeners (lines 29–30)."

"... we lack ... the power to force any-body to listen (lines 37–38)."

And note, especially, the conclusion, where an author customarily stresses his major point: "We have talkers, all right. ... But, fortunately, we don't have the listeners (lines 38–40)."

1, Washington is more efficient than Sofia is not supported. The passage shows that Washington is more democratic.

2, Bulgarian political leaders never dis-agree is disproved by the reference to their "private bickering (lines 9–10)."

4, the Sofia Congress meets for a longer time than the Washington Congress is disproved by line 9, which indicates that the Sofia Congress lasts only "a week or so." The fact that the Washington Con-gress meets for a longer time can be in-ferred from the statement in lines 26–27: "because next week somebody will make a speech he [the Senator] doesn't want to sit through."

SUGGESTIONS FOR MAKING THE BEST USE OF YOUR TIME DURING THE LISTENING TEST

I. During the first reading by the teacher:

Listen for the topic, usually stated in the opening sentence or two, and for the supporting details that develop it. Pay particular attention, also, to the conclusion, which often stresses the main idea or makes an important point.

If something is unclear, remember that you will soon get further clues from reading the questions and from listening to the second reading of the passage by the teacher.

II. During your reading of the questions:

Your primary goal at this time is to become as aware as possible of *all* the questions, so that you will know the specific information to listen for in the second reading by the teacher. If a particular question tantalizes you, do not try to work it out at this time unless you have carefully read *all* the questions, and there is time remaining.

III. During the second reading by the teacher:

The two things you are asked to do at this time are to listen to the passage and to write the answers. Of the two, the listening is the more important. You must keep listening.

It is advisable, as the teacher reads, to make a quick check next to those answers you are sure of, but do not stop listening to work on a troublesome question. Skip it for the time being, and keep listening.

Remember that you are going to have five minutes after the teacher stops reading to work on your answers. If you stop listening at this time, you may miss important clues.

IV. During the five minutes for recording the answers:

During this five-minute period, look over your answers and enter them on the answer sheet. If a question continues to puzzle you, pass it up, take care of the others, and then return to it, entering the answer that seems best on the basis of what you have heard in the passage.

Answer all ten of the questions; do not leave any answer space blank.

FORMER REGENTS LISTENING TESTS

CAUTION: Do *not* read the listening passage that follows. To do so is to defeat the purpose of this material. Instead, use the following procedure:

1. Give the listening passage to a person who reads well. Ask that person, first, to read the passage silently to become familiar with it and, second, to read the passage aloud to you.

2. Read to yourself the ten questions based on the listening passage.

3. Have the person read the passage aloud to you a second time.

4. Record the answers in the next five minutes.

If you follow the above procedure with each former Regents Listening Test here reprinted, you will be better prepared to deal with this part of the examination successfully.

LISTENING PASSAGE: TEST 1

Richard Burton and Laurence Olivier are great actors. They obviously respect each other.

Burton tells this story of Laurence Olivier's acting genius: Larry, as Richard Burton called him, was starring in a Shakespearean play. There is a famous scene during which the King is compelled to chop off his own left hand with a hatchet. Burton speaks, telling how realistically Olivier played the scene.

"The King says a fond and rueful farewell to his hand; that's what it amounts to. As you know, the speech takes place *before* the removal of the hand, and there was Larry—crooning and mooning and kissing his dear hand as though it were a lost, pathetic child. It was brilliant! I had never seen him so truthful, so real. There was a freshness, a newness, an illusion of the first time, a spontaneity unlike anything I've ever seen from Larry. It brought me bolt upright in my seat, my eyes and ears wide open.

"Up to this moment, he had been the same old Larry—expert and crisp—but now he began to moon and whimper and kiss the hand he was about to lose. He brought each finger to his lips, he pressed the palm to his cheek, he turned it this way and that and held the wrist with his right hand as though to memorize the thumb, the wrinkles in the knuckles, each tiny blue vein, each fingernail. He murmured to it longingly, like some passionate Casanova. The effect of the scene was overwhelming. It was so *intimate,* like something played out behind closed doors. At one point, he all but turned his back on the audience for several lines, several kisses, as though he too was aware that this was all too private. I was absolutely hypnotized by the way he moved his mouth about the hand while his other hand caressed it, stopping here to pinch—and there to touch—it was as though the whole business had been choreographed! A beautiful dance of the hands! Such an artistic pattern; such a moving design. . . .

"Well, indeed it was a design—as we soon found out. For when he finally came to the end of the speech, he stopped his crooning and caressing; he straightened his shoulders and placed his beloved hand flat against a table top; then he accepted the hatchet from a soldier, swung it a great round-house whack through the air, brought it down into that butcher's block as though he were chopping firewood, let out one of his hair-raising shrieks, and bounded across the stage—leaving—his own hand, dismembered, sitting all alone on that mad little table. I tell you, the audience was thunderstruck. We gasped as one person—a few ladies fainted! And I swear to you that, for one awful moment, I believed it! Truly, I thought he had gone round the bend and chopped off his own left hand: the last and most spectacular of all his effects!

"Well, do you begin to smell out the sordid facts of all this business? Method? Sincere feeling? Psychological drama? Nothing of the kind. He had to do the speech in just that way. He needed all the pauses to give himself time to undo the artificial hand which was attached to his arm and his costume. The bent shoulders, the passionate-looking hunch came from having to withdraw his own true hand carefully up his sleeve. The kissing and caressing and back-turning and touching with the other hand were all necessary to conceal the nuts and bolts and ratchets, the springs and screws he was putting carefully into place. He didn't choose to play the scene that way—it was thrust upon him. It was inevitable! Method indeed—it was a magic act! And beautiful, too. He's the Harry Houdini of the stage—the greatest trickster of them all."

LISTENING QUESTIONS: TEST 1

1 In the passage, what clue most clearly indicates that Burton and Olivier know each other well?
1 Burton praises Olivier.
2 Burton calls Olivier by his nickname.
3 Both have acted in plays by Shakespeare.
4 Burton went to the theater to watch Olivier act.

2 Burton compares Olivier's emotional attitude toward his hand to that which would occur in a
1 murder mystery   3 love drama
2 musical comedy   4 medieval tragedy

3 The speech most impressed Burton because it was
1 the first time he had ever heard it
2 the first time Olivier had said it
3 as though Olivier had just made it up
4 as though Olivier were reading it

4 As used in the passage, the word "choreographed" refers to
1 drawing   3 transportation
2 engineering   4 dancing

5 Burton gives the listener the impression that Olivier's acting *usually* is
1 skillful and concise   3 emotional and flashy
2 deceptive and smooth   4 acrobatic and dynamic

6 At what point in the scene did Olivier act out the chopping off of his hand?
   1 just before he ended his speech
   2 immediately at the end of his speech
   3 in the middle of his speech
   4 before he began his speech

7 After Olivier chopped off his hand, a loud shriek came from
   1 Olivier   3 Burton
   2 a few ladies   4 the audience

8 For a moment Burton thought that Olivier had
   1 dropped the hatchet
   2 chopped off both his hands
   3 insanely chopped off his hand
   4 accidentally chopped off his hand

9 Burton says that Olivier played the scene the way he did in order to
   1 make the audience pity him
   2 follow an acting method
   3 add psychological excitement
   4 have time to take off his artificial hand

10 What tone of voice would Richard Burton most probably use in telling this story?
   1 amazed   3 humorous
   2 sarcastic   4 angry

LISTENING PASSAGE: TEST 2

. . . We have also come to this hallowed spot to remind America of the fierce urgency of now. This is no time to engage in the luxury of cooling off or to take the tranquilizing drug of gradualism. Now is the time to make real the promises of democracy. Now is the time to rise from the dark and desolate valley of segregation to the sunlit path of racial justice. Now is the time to lift our nation from the quicksand of racial injustice to the solid rock of brotherhood. Now is the time to make justice a reality for all of God's children.

It would be fatal for the nation to overlook the urgency of the moment. This sweltering summer of the Negro's legitimate discontent will not pass until there is an invigorating autumn of freedom and equality. Nineteen sixty-three is not an end, but a beginning. Those who hope that the Negro needed to blow off steam and will now be content will have a rude awakening if the nation returns to business as usual. There will be neither rest nor tranquility in America until the Negro is granted his citizenship rights. The whirlwinds of revolt will continue to shake the foundations of our nation until the bright day of justice emerges.

But that is something that I must say to my people who stand on the warm threshold which leads into the palace of justice. In the process of gaining our rightful place we must not be guilty of wrongful deeds. Let us not seek to satisfy our thirst for freedom by drinking from the cup of bitterness and hatred.

We must forever conduct our struggle on the high plane of dignity and discipline. We must not allow our creative protest to degenerate into physical violence. Again and again we must rise to the majestic heights of meeting physical force with soul force. The marvelous new militancy which has engulfed the Negro community must not lead us to a distrust of all white people, for many of our white brothers, as evidenced by their presence here today, have come to realize that their destiny is tied up with our destiny. And they have come to realize that their freedom is inextricably bound to our freedom. We cannot walk alone.

As we walk, we must make the pledge that we shall always march ahead. We cannot turn back. There are those who are asking the devotees of civil rights, "When will you be satisfied?" We can never be satisfied as long as the Negro is the victim of the unspeakable horrors of police brutality. We can never be satisfied as long as the Negro's basic mobility is from a smaller ghetto to a larger one. We can never be satisfied as long as our children are stripped of their selfhood and robbed of their dignity by signs stating "For Whites Only." We cannot be satisfied as long as a Negro in Mississippi cannot vote and a Negro in New York believes he has nothing for which to vote. No, no, we are not satisfied, and we will not be satisfied until justice rolls down like waters and righteousness like a mighty stream.

I am not unmindful that some of you have come here out of great trials and tribulations. Some of you have come fresh from narrow jail cells. Some of you have come from areas where your quest for freedom left you battered by the storms of persecution and staggered by the winds of police brutality. You have been the veterans of creative suffering. Continue to work with the faith that unearned suffering is redemptive.

Go back to Mississippi, go back to Alabama, go back to South Carolina, go back to Louisiana, go back to the slums and ghettos of our Northern cities, knowing that somehow this situation can and will be changed. Let us not wallow in the valley of despair. . . .

LISTENING QUESTIONS: TEST 2

1 According to this passage, the speaker implies that the struggle for racial justice can best be won through
  1 marching on Washington
  2 civil disorder
  *3 creative protest
  4 challenging unjust laws in the courts

2 The speaker's attitude toward white people appears to be based on
  1 noncommitment
  2 contempt for authority
  3 mutual distrust
  * 4 respect for individual worth

3 The speaker's response to those who ask "When will you be satisfied?" can be characterized as
  *1 assertive   3 casual
  2 defensive   4 appeasing

4 The speaker's remarks indicate that he considers the racial problem a national problem because
  1 all white Americans are prejudiced
  2 American blacks are moving to the suburbs
  * 3 all areas of American life are affected
  4 the United States Constitution supports segregation

5 What does the speaker say about unearned suffering?
  1 It brings brutality.
  2 It redeems people.
  3 It insures equality.
  4 It brings persecution.

6 In this passage, the speaker's attitude is generally
  1 prejudiced   3 fearful
  2 cynical   4 optimistic

7 In this speech, the speaker argues for
  *1 nonviolent resistance   3 Communist ideals
  2 faith in God   4 social turmoil

8 The intent of this speech is apparently to
  1 expose a social problem
  2 persuade its listeners to action
  3 narrate the trials of blacks in America
  4 suggest alternatives to democracy

9 The speaker's tone of voice in this speech most probably was
  1 inspirational   3 defiant
  2 boastful   · 4 sad

10 Which quotation best suggests the main idea of the speech?
  1 "... we must not be guilty of wrongful deeds."
  2 "We cannot walk alone."
  3 "We cannot be satisfied as long as the Negro's basic mobility is from a smaller ghetto to a larger one."
  4 "... this situation can and will be changed."

LISTENING PASSAGE: TEST 3

The energy crunch, which is being felt around the world, has dramatized how the reckless despoiling of the earth's resources has brought the whole world to the brink of disaster. The overdevelopment of motor transport, with its spiral of more cars, more highways, more pollution, more suburbs, more commuting, has contributed to the near-destruction of our cities, the disintegration of the family, and the pollution not only of local air, but also of the earth's atmosphere. The catastrophe has arrived in the form of the energy crunch.

Our present situation is unlike war, revolution, or depression. It is also unlike the great natural catastrophes of the past. Worldwide resource exploitation and energy use have brought us to a state where long-range planning is crucial. What we need is not a continuation of our present perilous state, which endangers the future of our country, our children and our earth, but a movement forward to a new norm in order to work rapidly and effectively on planetary problems.

This country has been reeling under the continuing exposures of loss of moral integrity and the revelation that lawbreaking has reached into the highest places in the land. There is a strong demand for moral reinvigoration and for some commitment that is vast enough and yet personal enough to enlist the loyalty of all. In the past it has been only in a war in defense of their own country and their own ideals that any people have been able to invoke a total commitment.

This is the first time that we have been asked to defend ourselves and what we hold dear in cooperation with all the other inhabitants of this planet, who share with us the same endangered air and the same endangered oceans. There is a common need to reassess our present course, to change that course, and to devise new methods through which the world can survive. This is a priceless opportunity.

To grasp it, we need a widespread understanding of the nature of the crisis confronting us—and the world—a crisis that is no passing inconvenience, no byproduct of the ambitions of the oil-producing countries, no figment of environmentalists' fears, no byproduct of any present system of government. What we face is the outcome of the inventions of the last four hundred years. What we need is a transformed lifestyle. This new lifestyle can flow directly from science and technology, but its acceptance depends on an overriding commitment to a higher quality of life for the world's children and future generations.

LISTENING QUESTIONS: TEST 3

1 The speaker feels that the energy crisis has brought the entire world close to

   1 cooperation   3 destruction
   2 revolution   4 transformation

2 Which word does the speaker frequently repeat in the introduction of the speech to emphasize the overdevelopment of several countries?

   1 "more"   3 "disaster"
   2 "transport"   4 "brought"

3 Which condition does the speaker feel has nearly destroyed our cities?

   1 lack of financial planning
   2 the breakup of the family
   3 natural disasters in many regions
   4 the excessive growth of motor transportation

4 According to the speaker, what is one example of our loss of moral integrity?

   1 disregard for law
   2 lack of loyalty
   3 lack of cooperation
   4 exploitation of resources

5 Which words does the speaker repeat when speaking of her concern for the air and oceans?

1 "first time"   3 "there is"
2 "same endangered"   4 "this polluted"

6 Why is the speaker's repetition of the word "no" effective in the conclusion of the speech?
1 It reinforces the audience reaction.
2 It parallels her introduction.
3 It emphasizes that there are no easy answers.
4 It emphasizes her discouraged attitude.

7 By comparing past problems with present ones, the speaker draws attention to the
1 significance of this crisis
2 inadequacy of governments
3 similarity of the past to the present
4 hopelessness of the situation

8 What commitment does the speaker feel people must now make?
1 Search for new energy sources.
2 Outlaw motor transportation.
3 Accept a new lifestyle.
4 Adopt a new form of government.

9 What transitional device does the speaker most frequently use?
1 pronoun references
2 connecting words
3 repetition of consonant sounds
4 repetition of words and phrases

10 Which order does the speaker follow in this speech?
1 comparison and contrast of past and present
2 statement of problem, history and development, appeal for solution
3 chronological order of the events leading to the problem
4 appeal to all nations, history, statement of problem, solution

Chapter 2 The Vocabulary Test
(Questions 11-30)

THE IMPORTANCE OF VOCABULARY

A good vocabulary identifies you as a superior student. It indicates that you have probably done considerable reading. It strongly suggests that you have the word power to function on a high level in thinking, understanding others, and expressing your own ideas.

Quite properly, the New York State Regents Comprehensive Examination in English places heavy emphasis on vocabulary. The vocabulary test (ten points) is not the only measure of your word power. Other parts of the examination that test your vocabulary are the reading test (twenty points), the literature-discussion test (twenty points), and the composition test (thirty points).

The following examinations, in which you are likely to have a personal stake, also test vocabulary:

> Preliminary Scholastic Aptitude Test/National Merit Scholarship
> Qualifying Test (PSAT-NMSQT)
> Scholastic Aptitude Test (SAT)
> American College Test (ACT)
> Aptitude Test of the Graduate Record Examination (GRE)
> Civil Service Tests

SAMPLE REGENTS VOCABULARY QUESTIONS

The vocabulary test measures your ability to select the synonym of a word from a group of several choices. It is a challenging test, as you will discover by answering the sample questions that follow. But first cover the answers that have been inserted on the lines at the right.

Directions (11–30): In the space provided on the separate answer sheet, write the *number* of the word or expression that most nearly expresses the meaning of the word printed in heavy black type.   [10]

11 **prune** (verb)
  1 cut off   3 put away   5 remind
  2 expect   4 lay waste   11 ...*1*...

12 **amiable**
  1 active   3 religious   5 absentminded
  2 good-natured   4 changeable   12 ...*2*...

13 **improvise**
  1 object loudly   3 refuse support   5 translate
  2 predict   4 prepare offhand   13 ...*4*...

14 **connive**
  1 cooperate secretly   3 pause slightly   5 need greatly
  2 enter quickly   4 push unexpectedly   14 ...*1*...

15 **gait**
  1 turning over and over   3 manner of walking
  2 passing in review   4 fundamental attitude
          5 crowd of spectators   15 ...*3*...

16 **bumble**
  1 weep   3 resent   5 complain
  2 rebel   4 blunder   16 ...*4*...

17 **devoid of**
  1 accompanied by   3 without   5 despite
  2 in the care of   4 behind   17 ...*3*...

18 **pang**
  1 feeling of indifference   3 fatal disease
  2 sense of duty   4 universal remedy
          5 spasm of pain   18 ...*5*...

19 **tedium**
  1 bad temper   3 warmth   5 musical form
  2 boredom   4 abundance   19 ...*2*...

20 **intimate** (adjective)
  1 hospitable   3 familiar   5 forgiving
  2 well-behaved   4 plainly seen   20 ..*3*..

21 **delve**
  1 hope for   3 set upon   5 dig into
  2 believe in   4 take into account   21 ..*5*..

22 **shrouded**
  1 found   3 stoned   5 rewarded
  2 torn   4 wrapped   22 ..*4*..

23 **exploit** (verb)
  1 annoy   3 use   5 set free
  2 join   4 mix up   23 ..*3*..

24 **robust**
  1 bragging   3 sincere   5 sturdy
  2 huge   4 upright   24 ..*5*..

25 **piecemeal**
  1 on the spur of the moment
  2 by degrees
  3 over and over
  4 as a matter of course
  5 from first to last   25 ..*2*..

26 If Jan has **ambivalent** feelings toward Rick,
she feels both
  1 attracted to and repelled by him
  2 angry with and ashamed of him
  3 unhappy with and jealous of him
  4 pity and concern for him
  5 friendship for and interest in him   26 ..*1*..

27 In the sentence "Don't be deceived by his
lugubrious appearance; he's really quite a
jolly person," the word "lugubrious" most
nearly means
  1 peaceful   3 sarcastic   5 ugly
  2 mournful   4 conservative   27 ..*2*..

28   Inasmuch as Mike's Halloween "trick" was
       innocuous, he did not get into trouble.
       1   harmless   3   clever
       2   evil   4   secretive   28 ..*1*...

29   They approved the plan in spite of its
       shortcomings.
       1   hasty preparation   3   defects
       2   harsh terms   4   provisions   29 .*3*...

30   Rheumatism **plagued** her during her
       childhood.
       1   retarded   3   changed
       2   tormented   4   weakened   30 .*2*..

ANALYSIS OF THE SAMPLE VOCABULARY QUESTIONS

Analysis shows that the vocabulary questions are difficult, except for the student who has read widely and is precise in his thinking. They are difficult because:

1. Some of the words you have to define are offered in isolation, not in context. How much easier it would be if in question 11, for example, you were to be confronted with "prune the dead branches of a rosebush," instead of merely "prune"!

2. The choices offered usually contain traps for the unwary. There are two principal ways in which you may be misled:

a. Associated Words. Example 1: In question 23, the careless student may hastily choose "annoy" or "mix up" as the answer because he may associate these words with "exploit." After all, is it not true that people who "exploit" us (*use* us for their own advantage) usually "annoy" us or "mix us up" in the process? These words, however, are not synonyms for "exploit." We must be precise in our thinking. The answer is "use."

Example 2: In question 24, the correct synonym for "robust" (*strong and vigorously healthy*) is "sturdy." Yet, wouldn't it be likely for a careless student to choose "huge" as the answer because we so often associate size with sturdiness?

These examples should lead you to see that, even if you know the meaning of the test word, you may sometimes choose the wrong synonym. You must carefully weigh each alternative and select the one "that most nearly expresses the meaning," as the directions state.

b. Sound Traps. Example 1: In question 15, a student may offer "crowd of spectators" for "gait" because of confusion with "gate," a word that sounds exactly alike. One of the meanings of "gate" is a *"crowd of spectators* admitted to a sports event." But "gait" means "manner of walking."

Example 2: In question 16, "complain" is a sound trap. It suggests "grumble," which sounds so much like "bumble" that a student may offer "complain." The correct answer is "blunder."

Example 3: In question 12, "changeable" is a sound trap because its last two syllables are identical with the last two of "amiable." But "amiable" means "good-natured."

The vocabulary test is rife with sound traps.

Caution: Do not assume from the foregoing that any similarity in sound is necessarily a trap. Note that the synonym for "delve" in question 21 is "dig into," and the synonym for "bumble" in question 10 is "blunder."

HOW TO CHOOSE THE CORRECT SYNONYM

1. Since some of the test words are presented without context, your first step, if you are unsure of the meaning of a test word, should be to *recall a context in which you have seen or heard or used that word.* Examples:

> Plan your speech, don't *improvise* (question 13) as you go along.
> I felt a sharp *pang* (question 18) in my left shoulder.
> Did you finish your reading all at once, or did you do it *piecemeal* (question 25)?

If a question asks for the meaning of a word as a particular part of speech, as in question 11, *prune* (*verb*), think of a context in the same part of speech:

> *not*........I ate a *prune* (noun).
> *but*........*Prune* (verb) some of the new growth from the shrubs.

2. If the test word is presented in a context, as in questions 26–30 (pages 23–24), examine the context for a clue to the meaning of the test word. There are three principal kinds of context clues:

a. An opposite word or expression in the context. The word "jolly" in question 27 (page 23) suggests that it is an *antonym* (opposite word) for "lugubrious." To find the meaning of "lugubrious," we ask ourselves, "Which of the choices is the opposite of 'jolly' and, therefore, a synonym for 'lugubrious'?" The answer, of course, is "mournful."

b. A similar word or expression in the context. For example, it is easy to learn the meaning of "dispense with" from the context of the following: "We can *dispense with* a coffee break but we cannot do without lunch." The meaning of "dispense with" is the similar expression "do without."

c. A common-sense clue in the context. The word "rheumatism," a painful stiffness of the joints, is a common-sense clue to the meaning of "plagued" in question 30 (page 24). By using common sense, we can tell that "tormented" is a synonym for "plagued."

3. Be precise. A related or approximate definition will not do. Make sure that your choice "most nearly expresses the meaning" of the test word.

4. Should you find that a word is completely unfamiliar, try breaking it down into its component parts—prefix, root, and suffix.

PREFIXES, ROOTS, SUFFIXES

You should memorize the meanings of common prefixes, roots, and suffixes because they form countless words in our language. Notice how a knowledge of prefixes, roots, and suffixes can help you to answer these typical Regents vocabulary questions:

QUESTION: **amiable**
1 active   3 religious
2 good-natured   4 changeable
                  5 absentminded

ANSWER: good-natured

EXPLANATION: *amiable* contains the following:

ami—a root meaning "like" or "love"
able—a suffix meaning "capable of being"

Therefore, *amiable* means "capable of being liked," or *good-natured.*

QUESTION : **revocation**

1 certificate	3 animation	5 plea
2 repeal	4 license	

ANSWER: repeal

EXPLANATION: *revocation* contains the following:

re—a prefix meaning "back"
vocat—a root meaning "call"
ion—a suffix meaning "act or result of"

Therefore, *revocation* means "act or result of calling back," or *repeal*.

LATIN PREFIXES

PREFIX	MEANING	SAMPLE DERIVATIVES
a, ab	away, from	avert (turn away), abhor (shrink from)
ad	to	adhere (stick to), adjoin (be next to)
ante	before	anteroom (room before), antedate (come before in date)
bene	good, well	benefactor (one who does some good for another), benevolent (well-wishing)
bi	two	bilateral (having two sides), bisect (cut in two)
circum	around	circumnavigate (sail around), circumvent (go around)
co (com, con, col)	together	coherent (sticking together), compatible (able to exist together), convoke (call together), collaborate (work together)
contra, contro	against	contravene (go against; violate), controversy (a "turning against"; quarrel)
de	down	demote (move down), depreciate (go down in value)
dis	apart, differently	dissect (cut apart), dissent (feel differently)
e, ex	out	emit (send out), exclusive (shutting out others)

LATIN PREFIXES (continued)

PREFIX	MEANING	SAMPLE DERIVATIVES
extra	outside	extracurricular (outside the curriculum), extravagant (outside the bounds of reason)
in (il, im, ir)	not	inflexible (not easily bent), illegible (not able to be read), immaculate (not spotted), irrelevant (not pertinent)
in, im	in, on	inhibit (hold in), immerse (dip in)
inter	between	intercede (go between), interurban (between cities)
intra	within	intraparty (within a party), intravenous (within the veins)
mal, male	evil, badly	malefactor (evildoer), maladjusted (badly adjusted)
ob	in the way	obstacle (something standing in the way), obstruct (be in the way)
per	through	perennial (continuing through the years), permeate (pass through)
post	after	posterity (generations that will come after), posthumous (occurring after one's death)
pre	before	preclude (put a barrier before), premature (before the proper time)
pro	forward, forth	propel (drive forward), provoke (call forth)
re	again, back	renovate (make new again), repel (drive back)
retro	backward	retrogress (move backward), retrospect (backward look)
se	apart	secede (go apart; withdraw), segregate (set apart)
semi	half	semicircle (half circle), semiconscious (half-conscious)
sub	under	submerge (put under water), subterranean (underground)

LATIN PREFIXES (continued)

PREFIX	MEANING	SAMPLE DERIVATIVES
super	above	superlative (above all others), supersonic (above the speed of sound)
trans	across, over	transgress (step across; violate), transcribe (write over)
ultra	exceedingly	ultraconservative (exceedingly conservative)

LATIN ROOTS

ROOT	MEANING	SAMPLE DERIVATIVES
ag, act	act	agent (one who acts for another), react (act back; respond to a stimulus)
am(i), amor	like, love	amiable (likable, good-natured), amorous (loving)
cad, cas	fall	cadaver (body of one who has fallen; corpse), casualty (one who has fallen victim to accidental injury or death)
cap, cept	take, hold	captor (one who takes or captures), receptacle (something that holds smaller objects; container)
ced, cess	go	secede (go apart; withdraw), recessive (tending to go back)
cid, cis	kill, cut	suicide (killing of oneself), incision (act of cutting into)
clud, clus	shut	exclude (shut out), recluse (one who lives shut off from the world)
cred, credit	believe	credible (believable), discredit (refuse to believe)
cur(r), curs	run	concurrent (running together; happening simultaneously), precursor (forerunner)
dict	tell	predict (tell beforehand; prophesy)
duc, duct	lead, conduct	induce (lead on), aqueduct (artificial channel for conducting water)
fact	make	artifact (thing made by human skill)

LATIN ROOTS (continued)

ROOT	MEANING	SAMPLE DERIVATIVES
fer	bear	odoriferous (bearing an odor; fragrant)
flect, flex	bend	genuflect (bend the knee), flexible (capable of being bent; not rigid)
grad, gress	step, go	gradual (by steps), progressive (going forward to something better)
here, hes	stick	adhere (stick to; cling), cohesion (act of sticking together)
ject	throw	projectile (anything thrown forward)
junct	join	junction (place where things join)
leg, lect	read, choose	legible (easy to read), select (chosen as the best; superior)
loqu, locut	talk, speak	loquacious (talkative), elocution (art of speaking)
mit(t), miss	send	emit (send out; give off), emissary (person sent on a mission)
mov, mot, mob	move	immovable (incapable of being moved), remote (moved back in place or time), mobile (movable)
ped	foot	pedestrian (foot traveler)
pel(1), puls	drive	expel (drive out), repulse (drive back)
pend, pens	hang	pendant (hanging ornament), suspense (condition of being left "hanging" or in doubt)
pon, posit	put	postpone (put off), imposition (a "putting on"; burdensome demand)
port	carry	portable (able to be carried)
rupt	break	abrupt (broken off; sudden)
scrib, script	write	scribe (person who writes), inscription (something written on a monument, coin, etc.)
sect	cut	dissection (act of cutting apart)
sent, sens	feel	sentiment (feeling), sensitive (having a capacity for feeling)

LATIN ROOTS (continued)

ROOT	MEANING	SAMPLE DERIVATIVES
sequ, secut	follow	sequel (something that follows), consecutive (following in regular order)
spect	look	prospect (thing looked forward to)
sta, stat	stand	stable (able to stand; not changing; enduring), status (standing)
tang, tact	touch	intangible (incapable of being touched), tactile (pertaining to the sense of touch)
termin	end	terminate (bring to an end)
tract	draw, pull	tractor (vehicle used for drawing or pulling)
ven, vent	come	convene (come together; meet), advent (coming; arrival)
vert, vers	turn	invert (turn upside down), versatile (able to turn with ease from one thing to another)
vid, vis	see	provident (foreseeing; making provision for the future), invisible (not able to be seen)
vinc, vict	conquer	invincible (not conquerable), victor (conqueror)
voc (voke), vocat	call	vocal (pertaining to the voice), revoke (call back; annul), vocation (calling)
volv, volut	roll, turn	evolve (unroll or work out; develop gradually), revolution (a turning around)

Exercise A. Each of the italicized words below is made up of a prefix and a root discussed previously. Define each word and then check your definitions with the dictionary.

1. a *circumspect* person
2. Don't *involve* me.
3. an *abject* beggar
4. *Repel* the attack.
5. a *disruptive* force
6. to *intercede* in a quarrel
7. an *eloquent* speaker
8. *Eject* that rowdy.
9. an *incisive* reply
10. a vicious *obloquy*

Exercise B. Construct word families (at least five words to a family) with each of the following italicized roots. Then check your results with the dictionary. Example:

ag, act (do): agent, actor, inactive, agency, transaction

1. cap, cept (take)
2. cur(r), curs (run)
3. duc, duct (lead)
4. mit(t), miss (send)
5. mov, mot, mob (move)

6. ped (foot)
7. pel(l), puls (drive)
8. port (carry)
9. scrib, script (write)
10. vid, vis (see)

GREEK PREFIXES AND ROOTS

PREFIX OR ROOT	MEANING	SAMPLE DERIVATIVES
a, an	not, without	atypical (not typical), anonymous (without a name)
anthropo	man	anthropology (science dealing with facts about man)
anti	against	antipathy (feeling against; repugnance)
aster, astro	star	asterisk (star-shaped mark), astronaut ("star sailor"; traveler in space)
auto	self	autonomous (self-governing)
biblio	book	bibliophile (lover of books; book collector)
bio	life	biography (story of a person's life written by another person)
chrom	color	polychromatic (showing a variety of colors)
chron, chrono	time	synchronize (cause to agree in time), chronological (arranged in order of time)
cosmo	world	cosmopolitan (composed of persons from many parts of the world)
cracy	government	bureaucracy (government by bureaus)
dem	people	epidemic ("among the people"; widespread)
eu	good, well	euphonious ("good" or pleasing in sound), eulogize (speak "well" or in praise of someone)

GREEK PREFIXES AND ROOTS (continued)

PREFIX OR ROOT	MEANING	SAMPLE DERIVATIVES
geo, gee	earth	geophysics (science of forces that modify the earth), apogee (farthest point from earth in orbit of a satellite)
gram, graph	write	cryptogram (something written in secret code), graphic (written or told in a vivid manner)
hydr	water	dehydrate (remove the water from)
hyper	over	hypercritical (overcritical)
hypo	under	hypodermic (injected under the skin)
log	speech	monolog (long monopolizing speech by one person)
logy	science, study	bacteriology (science dealing with bacteria)
meter	measure	odometer (instrument for measuring distance traveled)
micro	small	microfilm (film of very small size)
mis	hate	misanthropy (hatred of mankind)
mono	one	monosyllabic (having but one syllable)
onym	name, word	pseudonym (fictitious name; pen name), synonym (word having same meaning as another word)
pan	all	panacea (cure-all)
path	feeling	apathy (lack of feeling; indifference)
peri	around	perimeter ("around" or outer measurement of a closed plane figure)
phil	love	philanthropy (love of mankind)
phob	fear	claustrophobia (fear of confined spaces)
phon	sound	cacophony (harsh or clashing sound)
poly	many	polyphonic (having many sounds or voices)
pseudo	false	pseudoscience (something falsely or erroneously considered as a science)
psycho	mind	psychology (science or study of the mind)

GREEK PREFIXES AND ROOTS (continued)

PREFIX OR ROOT	MEANING	SAMPLE DERIVATIVES
scope	see	fluoroscope (instrument for seeing objects exposed to X rays)
soph	wisdom	philosopher (lover of wisdom)
syn, sym	together	synthesis (putting together), symbiosis (living together of two dissimilar organisms)
tele	at a distance	telecommunication (communication at a distance)
theo	God	theology (study of God or religion)
therm	heat	diathermy (generation of heat in body tissues for medical purposes)

Exercise C. Test your skill. First define each word below, using your knowledge of Greek prefixes and roots. (Each of the words has two such components.) Then check your definitions with the dictionary.

1. monolog
2. psychology
3. perimeter
4. democracy
5. anonymous

6. bibliophile
7. hydrophobia
8. monotheism
9. geology
10. philanthropy

SUFFIXES

SUFFIX	MEANING	SAMPLE WORDS
-able, -ible	capable of being	lovable, reversible
-ance, -ence, -cy, -ty	act of or state of being	appearance, independence, infancy, novelty
-ary, -ic, -ical	having to do with	revolutionary, democratic, musical
-ate, -ize, -fy	to make	liberate (make free), pauperize (make poor), magnify (make big)
-er, -or, -ant, -ent, -ian, -ist	one who	teacher, editor, servant, resident, comedian, pianist
-ion, -age, -(a)tion, -ment	act or result of	rebellion, marriage, conversation, judgment

-ish, -like	resembling a	clownish, childlike
-itis	inflammation of	sinusitis, tonsillitis
-less	without	senseless
-ous, -y	full of	perilous, risky
-ship	office, skill	kingship, penmanship

Exercise D. In this final exercise, make use of your knowledge of suffixes, as well as of prefixes and roots. Define each of the following words by giving the meaning of each of its component parts. Then check your results with the dictionary.

Example: The word "eruption" is made up of "e" (out), "rupt" (break), and "ion" (act of). It means "the act of breaking out."

1. incredible
2. convocation
3. porter
4. terminate
5. psychologist

6. victor
7. inscription
8. psychopathic
9. visualize
10. polychromatic

HOW TO BUILD A GOOD VOCABULARY

1. Read Widely. As you read for pleasure or information in literary works and good newspapers and magazines, you encounter unfamiliar words. Many of these you may be able to define by using the two methods we have already discussed:

a. Using the Context. This means getting the definition of a strange word from the words that surround it (the context). The context may help by providing a *synonym,* an *antonym,* or a *common-sense clue.* Examples:

In the following sentence, a *synonym* provides the clue to the meaning of *version.*

Now that you have heard his version of the accident, listen to my *account.*

The context tells us that *version* means *account.*

Next, in the following sentence, an *antonym* provides the clue to the meaning of *hostile.*

Are the natives hostile or *friendly?*

The context tells us that *hostile* means *unfriendly.*

Finally, in the following sentence, there is a *common-sense clue* to the meaning of *volition*.

Were you fired, or did you leave of your own volition?

The context tells us that *volition* means *will*.

b. Using Word Analysis. This is the process of getting the meaning of the unfamiliar word by breaking it down into its component parts (prefix, root, suffix).

2. Develop the Dictionary Habit. There will, of course, be many words that will yield to neither of the above methods; in these cases you must refer to the dictionary. By all means develop the habit of consulting the dictionary. In later years you will come to realize that few habits are so important and rewarding.

a. Purchase a Dictionary. You should own a good desk dictionary. The following dictionaries are listed alphabetically, without indication as to relative merit.

Funk & Wagnalls Standard College Dictionary. Funk & Wagnalls.
Random House Dictionary of the English Language (College Edition). Random House.
Thorndike-Barnhart High School Dictionary. Scott, Foresman.
Webster's New World Dictionary (College Edition). World.
Webster's Seventh New Collegiate Dictionary. G. & C. Merriam.

b. Use Newly Acquired Words. Don't make the mistake of looking up a new word, putting its meaning down in your vocabulary notebook, and letting it go at that! You will never make much progress if that is all you do. You must consciously, deliberately, *use* the new word in your speaking and writing as soon as possible in appropriate situations—in chats with friends, in classroom discussions, in letters and compositions. If a new word remains unused in your notebook, it is soon forgotten; only by "exercising" the new word will you succeed in making it part of your active vocabulary.

c. Learn to Differentiate Between Commonly Confused Words. In the following pairs of words, one is frequently mistaken for the other. Eliminate the confusion by looking up the meaning of each word and using it in a complete (written) sentence:

1. soliloquy, monolog
2. allusion, illusion
3. continual, continuous
4. disinterested, uninterested
5. effect, affect
6. hypercritical, hypocritical
7. ingenious, ingenuous
8. ancestor, descendant
9. respectfully, respectively
10. translucent, transparent

d. Trace Word Histories. This can be one of the most fascinating ways of building your vocabulary. Do you know, for example, that "boycott" was actually the name of a land agent in Ireland, Captain Charles C. Boycott? Because he refused to lower the rents and evicted many tenants, the inhabitants organized a campaign of retaliation. They would have no dealings with him, and they prevented him from dealing with anyone, even to purchase food. Since that time (1880), to "boycott" has meant to follow a policy of refusing to deal in any way (with a person, group, or nation) as a punitive measure.

Using an unabridged dictionary, record in your notebook the origin and meaning of the following words:

1. stentorian	4. iridescent	7. congregation
2. hector	5. laconic	8. curfew
3. mentor	6. solon	9. Pyrrhic victory

VOCABULARY NOTEBOOK EXERCISE

In your notebook write (1) the definition and (2) a short illustrative sentence for each of the words in the list that follows.

WORD	DEFINITION	ILLUSTRATIVE SENTENCE
impartial	just	A judge should be *impartial*.
import	meaning	I did not get the *import* of your remark.

1. fictitious	13. prerogative	25. insurgent	37. posterity
2. proximity	14. pensive	26. tremulous	38. arrogance
3. siphon	15. allot	27. celerity	39. enmesh
4. placid	16. impeach	28. facade	40. vivacious
5. intern	17. glib	29. scrutinize	41. deft
6. fluctuate	18. prevaricate	30. dexterous	42. coalition
7. dilemma	19. utilitarian	31. cardiac	43. prudent
8. writhe	20. jargon	32. instigate	44. garrulous
9. rudiment	21. condole	33. rescind	45. genial
10. invariable	22. chaotic	34. maudlin	46. evasive
11. consensus	23. irate	35. volition	47. pomp
12. annals	24. appraisal	36. immunity	48. jostle

MATCHING TESTS IN VOCABULARY

Match the words in column *A* with their definitions in column *B*.

Test 1

Column A	Column B
a. traditional	1. imprison
b. compulsion	2. penetrate
c. sinister	3. close watch
d. nullify	4. force
e. longevity	5. customary
f. surveillance	6. destroy
g. rendition	7. interpretation
h. permeate	8. long life
i. innocuous	9. harmless
j. incarcerate	10. evil

Test 2

Column A	Column B
a. inflexible	1. stern
b. salvage	2. dismay
c. succumb	3. unyielding
d. precision	4. praise
e. cult	5. save
f. integrity	6. honesty
g. docile	7. yield
h. relentless	8. accuracy
i. consternation	9. obedient
j. commend	10. sect

Test 3

Column A	Column B
a. ethics	1. customers
b. zealousness	2. exaggeration
c. clientele	3. destructive
d. chronology	4. earnestness
e. articulation	5. fixed idea
f. autocratic	6. moral principles
g. obsession	7. time sequence
h. vestige	8. enunciation
i. hyperbole	9. trace
j. subversive	10. dictatorial

Test 4

Column A	Column B
a. deteriorate	1. doctrine
b. adolescent	2. frank
c. antagonist	3. weakened
d. diluted	4. agree
e. abridge	5. shorten
f. candid	6. youthful
g. concur	7. sagacity
h. capitulate	8. opponent
i. dogma	9. surrender
j. acumen	10. depreciate

Test 5

Column A	Column B
a. resilient	1. suffocation
b. melancholy	2. fashion
c. vogue	3. universe
d. massive	4. elastic
e. asphyxia	5. pithy saying
f. accelerate	6. quicken
g. cosmos	7. gloomy
h. epigram	8. weighty
i. prophylactic	9. voluble
j. loquacious	10. preventive

Test 6

Column A	Column B
a. felony	1. departure
b. decoy	2. crime
c. dazing	3. grip
d. enthusiastic	4. ardent
e. grapple	5. wickedness
f. aggravate	6. understand
g. exodus	7. intensify
h. fathom	8. stunning
i. laconic	9. lure
j. iniquity	10. concise

FORMER REGENTS VOCABULARY TESTS

The following tests have been assembled from questions that appeared in past Comprehensive English Examinations.

Directions: In the space provided on the separate answer sheet, write the *number* of the word or expression that most nearly expresses the meaning of the word printed in heavy black type.   [10]

Test 1

1. **dynamic**
   1 specialized
   2 active
   3 fragile
   4 magical
   5 comparative

2. **Achilles' heel**
   1 source of strength
   2 critical test
   3 hereditary curse
   4 vulnerable point
   5 base conduct

3. **ad lib**
   1 cheerfully
   2 freely
   3 carefully
   4 literally
   5 wisely

4. **decry**
   1 baffle
   2 weep
   3 trap
   4 belittle
   5 imagine

5. **ravage**
   1 ruin
   2 tangle
   3 delight
   4 scold
   5 crave

6. **rendezvous**
   1 surrender
   2 appointment
   3 souvenir
   4 hiding place
   5 mutual exchange

7. **skulk**
   1 trail
   2 shadow
   3 ambush
   4 lurk
   5 race

8. **cliché**
   1 formal farewell
   2 exclusive group
   3 trite remark
   4 conclusive argument
   5 good taste

9. **nuptial**
   1 moonlike
   2 blunted
   3 ritualistic
   4 matrimonial
   5 blessed

10. **balked**
    1 swindled
    2 thwarted
    3 enlarged
    4 waved
    5 punished

11. **crescendo**
    1 increasing volume
    2 decreasing tempo
    3 abrupt ending
    4 discordant note
    5 musical composition

13. **unwieldy**
    1 stubborn
    2 unhealthy
    3 monotonous
    4 shameful
    5 clumsy

15. **interim**
    1 go-between
    2 meantime
    3 mixture
    4 hereafter
    5 period of rest

17. **crystallize**
    1 glitter
    2 give definite form to
    3 chill
    4 sweeten
    5 polish vigorously

19. **lacerated**
    1 unconscious
    2 stitched
    3 slender
    4 raveled
    5 mangled

12. **indiscreet**
    1 unpopular
    2 embarrassing
    3 disloyal
    4 unwise
    5 greatly upset

14. **envisage**
    1 plot
    2 conceal
    3 wrinkle
    4 contemplate
    5 sneer

16. **resolute**
    1 determined
    2 vibrating
    3 irresistible
    4 elastic
    5 demanding

18. **regime**
    1 ruler
    2 military unit
    3 form of government
    4 contagion
    5 guardian

20. **amiss**
    1 friendly
    2 faulty
    3 tardy
    4 central
    5 purposeless

Test 2

1. **indolence**
   1 poverty
   2 laziness
   3 danger
   4 truth
   5 attention

2. **precarious**
   1 trustful
   2 early
   3 previous
   4 cautious
   5 uncertain

3. **connoisseur**
   1 investigator
   2 government official
   3 pretender
   4 critical judge
   5 portrait artist

5. **emit**
   1 overlook
   2 adorn
   3 discharge
   4 encourage
   5 stress

7. **extricate**
   1 disentangle
   2 die out
   3 praise
   4 purify
   5 argue with

9. **coerce**
   1 coincide
   2 strengthen
   3 accompany
   4 compel
   5 seek out

11. **cumbersome**
   1 habitual
   2 clumsy
   3 hasty
   4 blameworthy
   5 uneducated

13. **zealous**
   1 serious
   2 speedy
   3 flawless
   4 necessary
   5 enthusiastic

15. **retrospect**
   1 careful inspection
   2 reversal of form

4. **hilarity**
   1 wittiness
   2 disobedience
   3 mirth
   4 heedlessness
   5 contentment

6. **ad infinitum**
   1 to a limit
   2 from eternity
   3 occasionally
   4 endlessly
   5 to the finish

8. **squalid**
   1 dirty
   2 unresponsive
   3 wasteful
   4 stormy
   5 congested

10. **inter**
   1 bury
   2 stab
   3 change
   4 make peace
   5 emphasize

12. **captivate**
   1 charm
   2 dictate terms
   3 overturn
   4 find fault
   5 hesitate

14. **aromatic**
   1 shining
   2 precise
   3 ancient
   4 fragrant
   5 dry

16. **whet**
   1 bleach
   2 exhaust

3 review of the past
4 respect for authority
5 special attention

17. contusion
1 puzzle
2 shrinkage
3 bruise
4 uncleanness
5 fraud

19. callous
1 secretive
2 unruly
3 gloomy
4 unfeeling
5 hotheaded

3 harden
4 stimulate
5 question

18. compatible
1 eloquent
2 adequate
3 overfed
4 comfortable
5 harmonious

20. repudiate
1 reject
2 revalue
3 repay
4 forget
5 forgive

Test 3

1. unwilling
1 undignified
2 unintentional
3 slack
4 obstinate
5 unaccustomed

3. scrupulous
1 scornful
2 clean
3 frightening
4 doubting
5 conscientious

5. cessation
1 witnessing
2 stopping
3 strain
4 leave-taking
5 unwillingness

7. evict
1 summon
2 excite
3 force out

2. attribute
1 quality
2 tax
3 desire
4 law
5 final sum

4. usurp
1 lend money
2 replace
3 murder
4 surrender
5 seize by force

6. colossal
1 ancient
2 influential
3 destructive
4 dramatic
5 huge

8. mischance
1 omission
2 ill luck
3 feeling of doubt

4 prove
5 draw off

9. felon
1 criminal
2 fugitive
3 traitor
4 coward
5 loafer

11. implicit
1 unquestioning
2 rude
3 relentless
4 sinful
5 daring

13. extraneous
1 familiar
2 unprepared
3 foreign
4 proper
5 utmost

15. absolve
1 forgive
2 reduce
3 mix
4 deprive
5 detect

17. requisite
1 desirable
2 ridiculous
3 liberal
4 necessary
5 majestic

19. scintillate
1 whirl
2 wander
3 scorch
4 sharpen
5 sparkle

4 unlawful act
5 distrust

10. deplore
1 empty
2 regret deeply
3 spread out
4 take an oath
5 pour

12. slovenly
1 sleepy
2 tricky
3 untidy
4 moody
5 cowardly

14. impasse
1 command
2 stubbornness
3 crisis
4 deadlock
5 failure

16. proletariat
1 revolutionists
2 intellectuals
3 slaves
4 laboring classes
5 landowners

18. tenacious
1 violent
2 given to arguing
3 slender
4 holding fast
5 menacing

20. propriety
1 success
2 cleverness
3 nearness
4 security
5 suitability

Test 4

1. **debris**
   1 sadness
   2 decay
   ③ ruins
   4 landslide
   5 hindrance

3. **stamina**
   1 flatness
   2 clearness
   3 hesitation
   ④ vigor
   5 reliability

5. **inanimate**
   1 emotional
   2 thoughtless
   ③ lifeless
   4 inexact
   5 silly

7. **enhance**
   1 sympathize
   2 act out
   3 weaken
   ④ make greater
   5 fascinate

9. **sedate**
   1 sober
   2 seated
   3 buried
   ④ drugged
   5 timid

11. **ascertain**
   1 hold fast
   2 long for
   3 declare
   ④ find out
   5 avoid

13. **oscillate**
   1 please
   ② swing

2. **consolidate**
   1 show pity
   ② strengthen
   3 restrain
   4 infect
   5 use up

4. **facet**
   ① phase
   2 humor
   3 story
   4 discharge
   5 assistance

6. **callous**
   1 frantic
   2 misinformed
   3 youthful
   4 impolite
   ⑤ unfeeling

8. **disreputable**
   ① impolite
   2 bewildered
   3 debatable
   4 unavailable
   ⑤ shameful

10. **lucrative**
   1 lazy
   2 coarse
   ③ profitable
   4 brilliant
   ⑤ amusing

12. **literal**
   1 flowery
   ② matter-of-fact
   3 sidewise
   4 well-educated
   5 firsthand

14. **concise**
   ① accurate
   ② brief

3 purify
4 saturate
5 harden

15. consternation
1 restraint
2 close attention
3 dismay
4 self-importance
5 acknowledgment

17. impediment
1 obstacle
2 base
3 spice
4 mechanism
5 footstool

19. shackle (verb)
1 hide
2 glide
3 anger
4 quiet
5 hamper

3 sudden
4 similar
5 painful

16. heedless
1 unfortunate
2 expensive
3 careless
4 happy
5 weatherbeaten

18. quaver
1 launch
2 quicken
3 sharpen
4 tremble
5 forget

20. lowly
1 idle
2 silent
3 humble
4 sorrowful
5 solitary

Test 5

1. afflict
1 promise
2 injure
3 send
4 profit
5 menace

3. eject
1 expose
2 exceed
3 extend
4 expel
5 excite

5. whack
1 cough
2 ruin
3 chop
4 point
5 swell

2. pandemonium
1 wild uproar
2 diseased state
3 contempt
4 luxury
5 mild manner

4. tally (verb)
1 load
2 record
3 hunt
4 play
5 move

6. maul
1 trap
2 cuddle
3 carve
4 throw
5 beat

7. animation
   1 liveliness
   2 automation
   3 carelessness
   4 dispute
   5 exchange

8. smolder
   1 show suppressed anger
   2 grow up quickly
   3 find easily
   4 report back
   5 become weary

9. protrude
   1 make a fool of
   2 fall into
   3 put down
   4 thrust out
   5 steer clear of

10. benevolent
   1 profitable
   2 sociable
   3 wealthy
   4 receptive
   5 charitable

11. unobtrusive
   1 annoying
   2 unquestionable
   3 inconspicuous
   4 united
   5 healthy

12. scrutiny
   1 signal
   2 plot
   3 delay
   4 investigation
   5 announcement

13. heinous
   1 evil
   2 permanent
   3 unreasonable
   4 open
   5 timid

14. garrulous
   1 confused
   2 eager
   3 panting
   4 talkative
   5 informal

15. converse (noun)
   1 junction
   2 poetry
   3 ancestor
   4 follower
   5 opposite

16. A person who is **diminutive** is
   1 scholarly
   2 shy
   3 small
   4 bossy
   5 tired

17. If Mary voted by **proxy,**
   she
   1 voted by absentee
     ballot
   2 voted twice
   3 authorized another to
     vote for her
   4 voted for an independent
     candidate
   5 voted with the majority

18. Which person would be
   most likely to behave
   surreptitiously?
   1 a marksman
   2 a young child
   3 a busdriver
   4 a shoplifter
   5 an athlete

19. If Jan has **ambivalent** feelings toward Rick, she feels both
  1 attracted to and repelled by him
  2 angry with and ashamed of him
  3 unhappy with and jealous of him
  4 pity and concern for him
  5 friendship for and interest in him

20. In the sentence "Don't be deceived by his **lugubrious** appearance; he's really quite a jolly person," the word "lugubrious" most nearly means
  1 peaceful
  2 mournful
  3 sarcastic
  4 conservative
  5 ugly

Test 65

1. **ingenuity**
  1 sincerity
  2 trustworthiness
  3 distinguishing feature
  4 inventiveness

2. **muzzle** (verb)
  1 caress
  2 avoid
  3 gag
  4 divert

3. **strut** (verb)
  1 educate for life
  2 parade with pride
  3 scatter around
  4 hide from view

4. **oligarchy**
  1 government by a few
  2 government by the people
  3 government by women
  4 home of the gods

5. **admonish**
  1 approach
  2 gain
  3 warn
  4 arrive

6. **vehement**
  1 able
  2 violent
  3 tailored
  4 coughing

7. **palatable**
  1 appetizing
  2 deficient
  3 fluttering
  4 smooth

8. **fidelity**
  1 sound
  2 loyalty
  3 interest
  4 meaning

9. **formidable**
  1 easy
  2 unpleasant
  3 well-educated
  4 awe-inspiring

10. **veritable**
  1 actual
  2 complicated
  3 enjoyable
  4 rhythmical

11. Mary had a **penchant**
for pretty things.
1 jewel box
2 special fund
3 secret container
④ great liking

12. Ralph decided that the good
life he led would **refute** the
predictions of his relatives.
1 restrain
2 lead to
3 prove false
④ reward

13. Rheumatism **plagued** her
during her childhood.
1 retarded
② tormented
3 changed
4 weakened

14. Nothing so pleases an aspir-
ing politician as an appre-
ciative **throng**.
1 vote
② contribution
3 family
④ crowd

15. The soldier's **prowess** in
combat came as a surprise
to those who had known
him as a shy boy.
1 rebellious behavior
2 excited reactions
③ superior bravery
4 overconfidence

16. The search for the Northwest
Passage turned out to be a
fiasco.
1 complete failure
2 popular cause
3 impossible goal
④ moral victory

17. John's **aversion** to corruption in government
influenced his decision
to become an investi-
gative reporter.
① experience with
2 fascination with
3 involvement with
4 dislike of

18. When Pat was caught with
her hand in the cookie jar,
a look of **chagrin** came over
her face.
1 fear
2 defiance
③ embarrassment
4 pleading

19. From earliest childhood
Joan had shown **inherent**
sensitivity.
① inborn
2 acute
3 effortless
4 inappropriate

20. The new manager soon learned
that **mundane** activities such
as scrubbing floors and polish-
ing the display cases were
part of good business.
1 disgusting
2 ordinary
3 physical
④ small

Chapter 3   The Spelling Test
(Questions 31-40)

THE IMPORTANCE OF SPELLING

If you think that spelling is not too important because the spelling test (questions 31–40) is worth only five points, you are making a serious mistake. Don't forget that your spelling is tested also in your composition and literature-essay answers, which together are worth fifty points. When you receive your test booklet, you will notice the following statement on page 1 in bold type:

> **"No paper seriously deficient in English composition will be accepted for Regents credit."**

One of the reasons for which the examiners may consider your paper "seriously deficient in English composition" is a marked spelling deficiency.

Looking beyond the examination, you will find that in your career as a student, and later in your social and business activities, the ability to spell correctly will spare you needless pain and embarrassment and earn you respect.

TYPICAL REGENTS SPELLING TEST

The Regents spelling test measures your ability to recognize misspelled words and to rewrite them correctly. Try this typical test, checking your spellings with the correct answers in parentheses.

Directions (31–40): In each of the following groups of words, only one of the words is misspelled. In *each* group, select the misspelled word and spell it correctly in the space provided on the separate answer sheet.   [5]

31 argueing
   baggy
   contagious
   knives
   shepherd
   (argueing)

32 civillian
   primeval
   uncanny
   trigonometry
   bewitches
   (civilian)

33 thousandth
   unreleived
   canine
   vengeful
   obituary
   (unreleived)

34 dissapprove
   apologetic
   truancy
   theologian
   statuesque
   (dissapprove)

35 cadence
   millinery
   lonliness
   caramel
   burglarize
   (lonliness)

36 perpetuate
   colleague
   familiar
   mannerism
   ajournment
   (adjournment)

37 publicity
   promontory
   bureaucracy
   patriarch
   sacrafice
   (sacrifice)

38 abandonment
   righteous
   wiry
   critisize
   usefulness
   (critisize)

39 loosely
   breakage
   symtom
   angrily
   bridle
   (symptom)

40 vindictive
   satchel
   transferable
   preliminary
   obstinite
   (obstinate)

ANALYSIS OF THE SPELLING TEST

The words misspelled in the test fall into these categories:

a. **Words that conform to spelling rules.** Examples:

31. argueing, baggy, contagious, knives, shepherd

    ANSWER: arguing

    RULE: Drop silent *e* before a suffix starting with a vowel. (See page 58, rule 1.)

32. civillian, primeval, uncanny, trigonometry, bewitches

    ANSWER: civilian

    RULE: Do not add a letter when attaching a suffix. (See rule on top of page 56.)

33. thousandth, unreleived, canine, vengeful, obituary

    ANSWER: unrelieved

    RULE: Write *i* before *e*, except after *c*. (See pages 54–55, *ie* and *ei* rules.)

34. dissapprove, apologetic, truancy, theologian, statuesque

    ANSWER: disapprove

    RULE: Do not add a letter when attaching a prefix. (See rule on page 55.)

35. cadence, millinery, lonliness, caramel, burglarize

    ANSWER: loneliness

    RULE: Keep silent *e* before a suffix starting with a consonant. (See page 58, rule 2.)

    NOTE: *lone + ly = lonely* (Silent *e* is kept.)
    lonely + ness = loneliness (See bottom of page 56, rule 1.)

b. **Words that are misspelled because they are carelessly pronounced.** (See page 70.)

39. loosely, breakage, symtom, angrily, bridle

    ANSWER: symptom

c. **Words that are difficult to spell because they contain a silent letter.** (See page 71.)

36. perpetuate, colleague, familiar, mannerism, ajournment

    ANSWER: adjournment

d. **Words that present individual difficulties and require special study.** (See the spelling lists on pages 79–85.)

37. publicity, promontory, bureaucracy, patriarch, sacrafice

    ANSWER: sacrifice

38. abandonment, righteous, wiry, critisize, usefulness

    ANSWER: criticize

40. vindictive, satchel, transferable, preliminary, obstinite

    ANSWER: obstinate

HOW TO IMPROVE YOUR SPELLING

To make you a better speller, this chapter will provide a thorough review of spelling under these seven headings:

A. KNOW YOUR SPELLING RULES

Here are the rules for dealing with six of the most troublesome spelling problems:

1. SPELLING CERTAIN SOUNDS

1. The *-ful* rule

The sound *full* at the end of a word is spelled with only one *l*. Examples: careful, graceful, healthful, hopeful, teaspoonful, etc.

Exception: the word *full* itself.

2. The *-ceed* or *-cede* rule

There are only three verbs in the English language ending in *-ceed*. All other verbs with that sound end in *-cede*.

-ceed: succeed, proceed, exceed
-cede: secede, recede, intercede, concede, accede, cede, precede, antecede

Exception: super*sede*. This is the only verb ending in *-sede*.

Exercise 1. Rewrite each word, inserting *ceed, cede,* or *sede.*

1. ante_____nt
2. super_____d
3. inter_____s
4. suc_____ing
5. pre_____nt
6. ex_____ed
7. re_____s
8. pro_____s
9. con_____d
10. ex_____ingly

3. The *ie* and *ei* rules

In some words, the sound of $\bar{e}$ as in $\bar{e}ve$ is spelled *ie* (ach*ie*ve, bel*ie*ve). In certain other words, the same sound is spelled *ei* (c*ei*ling, rec*ei*ve).

To help yourself to recognize when *i* comes before *e* (believe, relief, grief) and when *e* comes before *i* (receive, deceit, receipt), master the following rule and its exceptions:

Write *i* before *e*

(Examples: achieve, belief, brief, chief, fiend, fierce, grief, piece, shriek, siege, yield, etc.)

Except after *c*

(After *c*, the rule is reversed; we write *e* before *i*. Examples: ceiling, conceit, conceive, deceit, deceive, perceive, receipt, receive, etc.)

Or when sounded like *ay*
As in *neighbor* or *weigh*.

(In such cases, too, we write *e* before *i*. Examples: freight, reign, sleigh, vein, weight, etc.)

Master these seven common exceptions, each of which has *e* before *i*: either, neither, foreigner, height, leisure, seize, weird.

Exercise 2. Rewrite each word, inserting *ie* or *ei*.

1. bes___ged	13. dec___tful	25. w___rd
2. misch___f	14. r___gned	26. c___ling
3. gr___vance	15. unperc___ved	27. retr___vc
4. conc___ted	16. cash___r	28. fr___ght
5. n___ther	17. s___zure	29. ___ther
6. rel___f	18. n___ghborly	30. sh___lding
7. fr___ndly	19. f___ndish	31. rel___ve
8. sl___gh	20. v___l	32. v___n
9. inconc___vable	21. n___ce	33. br___f
10. hyg___ne	22. ach___vement	34. p___rcing
11. p___ce	23. bel___f	35. unw___ldy
12. h___ght	24. rec___pt	36. l___surely

2. ATTACHING PREFIXES

Rule

Do not omit or add a letter when attaching a prefix to a word. Keep *all* the letters of the prefix and *all* the letters of the word.

PREFIX		WORD		NEW WORD
dis	+	satisfied	=	dissatisfied
dis	+	organized	=	disorganized
mis	+	spell	=	misspell
un	+	natural	=	unnatural
un	+	acceptable	=	unacceptable

Exercise 3. Write the new words formed by adding the prefixes.

1. dis + similar
2. inter + related
3. extra + ordinary
4. un + necessary
5. dis + service

6. re + election
7. with + hold
8. de + emphasize
9. mis + understand
10. pre + arrangement

3. ATTACHING SUFFIXES

Rule

Do not omit or add a letter when attaching a suffix to a word—unless the word ends in *y* or silent *e*. Keep *all* the letters of the word and *all* the letters of the suffix.

WORD		SUFFIX		NEW WORD
accidental	+	ly	=	accidentally
drunken	+	ness	=	drunkenness
ski	+	ing	=	skiing
foresee	+	able	=	foreseeable

Exercise 4. Write the new words formed by adding the suffixes.

1. possess + ing
2. govern + ment
3. book + keeper
4. radio + ed
5. sudden + ness

6. Hindu + ism
7. room + mate
8. embarrass + ment
9. total + ly
10. disagree + able

ATTACHING SUFFIXES TO WORDS ENDING IN Y

Rule 1

If the letter before final *y* is a *consonant,* change the *y* to *i* before attaching a suffix.

WORD		SUFFIX		NEW WORD
hurry	+	ed	=	hurried
sturdy	+	er	=	sturdier
costly	+	ness	=	costliness
greedy	+	ly	=	greedily

Exception A. Except before *ing*: hurry + ing = hurrying.

Exception B. Learn these special exceptions: dryly, dryness, shyly, shyness, babyish, ladylike.

Rule 2

If the letter before final *y* is a *vowel,* do not change the *y* before attaching a suffix.

$$\begin{array}{lcl}
\text{destroy} & + \quad \text{ed} \quad = & \text{destroyed} \\
\text{play} & + \quad \text{ing} \quad = & \text{playing}
\end{array}$$

Exceptions: laid, paid, said, and their compounds (mislaid, underpaid, unsaid, etc.); daily.

Exercise 5. Add the suffixes *er, est, ly,* and *ness* to each of the words below.

EXAMPLE: happy—happier, happiest, happily, happiness

1. lazy
2. heavy
3. gay
4. clumsy
5. icy

6. weary
7. stealthy
8. hearty
9. ugly
10. busy

Exercise 6. Add the suffixes *ing* and *ed* to each of the words below.

EXAMPLE: occupy—occupying, occupied

1. deny
2. stay
3. fortify
4. repay
5. delay

6. rely
7. convey
8. supply
9. say
10. satisfy

Exercise 7. Write the new words formed by adding the suffixes.

1. accompany + ment
2. mercy + ful
3. decay + ed
4. fancy + er
5. foolhardy + ness
6. pacify + ed
7. magnify + ing
8. overpay + ed
9. momentary + ly
10. controversy + al

11. deny + al
12. ceremony + ous
13. shy + ness
14. oversupply + ing
15. contrary + wise
16. disqualify + ed
17. bury + al
18. harmony + ous
19. worry + some
20. lucky + est

ATTACHING SUFFIXES TO WORDS ENDING IN SILENT *E*

Rule 1

Drop the silent *e* if the suffix begins with a *vowel*.

WORD		SUFFIX		NEW WORD
write	+	ing	=	writing
love	+	able	=	lovable
use	+	age	=	usage
produce	+	er	=	producer

Exception A. When the word ends in *ce* or *ge*, keep the *e* if the suffix begins with *a* or *o*.

notice	+	able	=	noticeable
manage	+	able	=	manageable
advantage	+	ous	=	advantageous

Exception B. Learn these additional exceptions: acreage, mileage, singeing, canoeing, hoeing, shoeing.

Rule 2

Keep the silent *e* if the suffix begins with a *consonant*.

excite	+	ment	=	excitement
care	+	ful	=	careful
fierce	+	ly	=	fiercely
complete	+	ness	=	completeness

Exceptions: argument, awful, duly, truly, wholly, ninth.

ATTACHING SUFFIXES TO WORDS ENDING IN *IE*

Rule

If the word ends in *ie*, drop the *e* and change the *i* to *y* before adding *ing*.

WORD		SUFFIX		NEW WORD
die	+	ing	=	dying
lie	+	ing	=	lying
tie	+	ing	=	tying
vie	+	ing	=	vying

Exercise 8. Write the new words formed by adding the suffixes.

1. disadvantage + ous	13. desire + ous
2. excite + able	14. service + able
3. untie + ing	15. discourage + ing
4. encourage + ment	16. dye + ing
5. true + ly	17. sense + ible
6. pursue + ing	18. whole + ly
7. mile + age	19. outrage + ous
8. believe + able	20. die + ing
9. avenge + ing	21. sincere + ly
10. hope + less	22. nine + ty
11. peace + able	23. canoe + ing
12. singe + ing	24. argue + ment

ATTACHING THE SUFFIX *LY*

Rule

To change an adjective to an adverb, we usually add *ly*.

ADJECTIVE		SUFFIX		ADVERB
brave	+	ly	=	bravely
calm	+	ly	=	calmly
usual	+	ly	=	usually

Exception A. If the adjective ends in *ic*, add *al* before attaching *ly*.

drastic	+	al	+	ly	=	drastically
scientific	+	al	+	ly	=	scientifically

Exception B. If the adjective ends in *ble*, simply change *ble* to *bly*.

ADJECTIVE	ADVERB
able	ably
noble	nobly
probable	probably

Reminders:

1. Remember: duly, truly, wholly.

2. If the adjective ends in *y* preceded by a *consonant,* remember to change *y* to *i* before adding *ly*.

$$easy + ly = easily$$

Exercise 9. Change the following adjectives to adverbs:

1. normal	6. possible	11. quiet	16. respectful
2. hasty	7. frantic	12. economic	17. specific
3. democratic	8. definite	13. annual	18. steady
4. final	9. partial	14. surprising	19. favorable
5. due	10. heroic	15. horrible	20. general

DOUBLING FINAL CONSONANTS BEFORE SUFFIXES

Why is the *r* in *defer* doubled (defe*rr*ed) when *ed* is added, whereas the *r* in *differ* is not (differed)? Why is the *n* in *plan* doubled (pla*nn*ing) before *ing*, whereas the *n* in *burn* is not (burning)? To clear up these matters, review two rules for doubling final consonants.

Rule 1

In a one-syllable word, double the final consonant before a suffix beginning with a vowel.

WORD		SUFFIXES		NEW WORDS
plan	+	ing, er	=	planning, planner
stop	+	ed, age	=	stopped, stoppage
big	+	er, est	=	bigger, biggest

Exception A. If the final consonant comes right after two vowels, do not double it.

fail	+	ed, ing	=	failed, failing
stoop	+	ed, ing	=	stooped, stooping

Exception B. If the final consonant comes right after another consonant, do not double it.

warm	+	er, est	=	warmer, warmest
last	+	ed, ing	=	lasted, lasting

Rule 2

In a word of two or more syllables, double the final consonant only if it is in an *accented* syllable before a suffix beginning with a vowel.

deFER′	+	ed, ing, al	=	deferred, deferring, deferral
resubMIT′	+	ed, ing	=	resubmitted, resubmitting

Note carefully that the rule does not apply if the final consonant is in an *unaccented* syllable.

DIF′fer	+	ed, ing, ent	=	differed, differing, different
BEN′efit	+	ed, ing	=	benefited, benefiting

Exception A. The rule does not apply if the final consonant comes right after two vowels.

obTAIN′	+	ed, ing	= obtained, obtaining
conCEAL′	+	ed, ing	= concealed, concealing

Exception B. The rule does not apply if the final consonant comes right after another consonant.

abDUCT′	+	ed, ing, or	= abducted, abducting, abductor
comMEND′	+	ed, ing, able	= commended, commending, commendable

Exception C. The rule does not apply if the accent shifts back to the first syllable.

conFER′	+	ence	= CON′ference
preFER′	+	ence	= PREF′erence
reFER′	+	ence	= REF′erence

However: exCEL′ + ence = EX′cellence.

Exercise 10. Write the new words formed by adding the suffixes.

1. concur + ing
2. entail + ed
3. abhor + ent
4. flat + er
5. retract + able
6. refer + al
7. dispel + ed
8. deter + ent
9. occur + ed
10. drum + er
11. elicit + ing
12. imperil + ed
13. absorb + ent
14. defer + ence
15. propel + ant
16. infer + ing
17. append + age
18. regret + able
19. discredit + ed
20. adapt + able
21. bar + ed
22. rebel + ion
23. slim + est
24. excel + ent

Exercise 11. Add the indicated suffixes to each word below.

1. regret + ing + ed + ful
2. sin + ing + ed + er
3. patrol + ing + ed + man
4. confer + ing + ed + ence
5. remit + ing + ed + ance
6. flip + ing + ed + ant
7. transmit + ing + ed + er
8. profit + ing + ed + able
9. defer + ing + ed + ment
10. dissent + ing + ed + er
11. protract + ing + ed + or
12. spot + ing + ed + er
13. commit + ing + ed + ment
14. excel + ing + ed + ence
15. recur + ing + ed + ent

ATTACHING SUFFIXES TO WORDS ENDING IN *IC*

Rule

Insert a **k** after the *c* before adding *ed, er, ing,* or *y.* (The *k* keeps the *c* from being pronounced as *s.*)

picnic—picnicked, picnicker, picnicking

Reminder: When adding *ly* to an *ic* word, first add *al,* and then *ly.*

magic + al + ly = magically

Exercise 12. Write the new words formed by adding the suffixes.

1. panic + ed   4. hectic + ly   7. mimic + ing
2. frolic + ing   5. traffic + ing   8. panic + y
3. mimic + ed   6. frolic + ed   9. romantic + ly

ADDING THE SUFFIX *ABLE* OR *IBLE*

Rule

An adjective usually ends in *able,* rather than *ible,* if you can trace it to a noun ending in *ation.*

NOUN	ADJECTIVE
adaptation	adaptable
alteration	alterable
commendation	commendable

Exception: sensation—sensible.

Aside from the above rule, there is no easy way to tell whether an adjective ends in *able* or *ible.* Study each word separately and consult your dictionary when in doubt. Here are some words to review:

ABLE		*IBLE*	
acceptable	excusable	accessible	indelible
believable	favorable	audible	inexhaustible
changeable	formidable	collapsible	intelligible
charitable	incurable	contemptible	invincible
comfortable	indefatigable	credible	legible
comparable	manageable	edible	negligible
debatable	memorable	eligible	permissible
dependable	perishable	feasible	sensible
desirable	preferable	flexible	tangible
despicable	profitable	forcible	visible

Exercise 13. Write the words formed by adding the suffixes *able* or *ible*.

1. uncomfort____	8. unaccept____	15. communic____
2. imagin____	9. inflamm____	16. unmanage____
3. inflex____	10. invis____	17. demonstr____
4. forc____	11. unprofit____	18. incred____
5. unchange____	12. cur____	19. exhaust____
6. illeg____	13. irrit____	20. imit____
7. present____	14. sens____	

ADDING THE SUFFIX OR OR ER

Rule

Verbs ending in *ate* usually become nouns ending in *or,* rather than *er.*

VERB	NOUN
create	creator
demonstrate	demonstrator
indicate	indicator
liberate	liberator

Exception: debate—debater.

Aside from the above rule, there is no easy way to tell whether a noun ends in *or* or *er*. Study each word separately and consult your dictionary when in doubt. Here are some words to review:

OR		*ER*	
aggressor	monitor	consumer	organizer
ambassador	possessor	coroner	philosopher
censor	professor	defender	pretender
contributor	prosecutor	dissenter	purchaser
creditor	tailor	interpreter	subscriber
debtor	traitor	invader	supporter
governor	vendor	laborer	sympathizer

Exercise 14. From each verb below, form a noun ending in *or* or *er.*

1. own	8. debate	15. labor
2. regulate	9. buy	16. arbitrate
3. report	10. originate	17. print
4. generate	11. legislate	18. contribute
5. advertise	12. manufacture	19. administrate
6. liberate	13. send	20. sing
7. possess	14. elevate	

ADDING THE SUFFIX *ANT* OR *ENT*

Rule 1

Spell an adjective with *ant*, rather than *ent*, if you can trace it to a noun ending in *ance* or *ancy*.

NOUN	ADJECTIVE
brilliance	brilliant
vacancy	vacant

Rule 2

Spell an adjective with *ent*, rather than *ant*, if you can trace it to a noun ending in *ence* or *ency*.

independence	independent
decency	decent

Study the following:

ANCE, ANCY		*ENCE, ENCY*	
abundance	nonchalance	adherence	frequency
assistance	observance	adolescence	imminence
attendance	poignancy	coherence	incompetence
compliance	relevance	convalescence	negligence
defiance	reliance	correspondence	permanence
extravagance	repentance	currency	pertinence
fragrance	resistance	decadence	potency
hesitancy	truancy	eloquence	recurrence
ignorance	vagrancy	eminence	urgency
inconstancy	vigilance	fluency	vehemence

Exercise 15. Rewrite each word, supplying the missing letter.

1. perman__nt	9. vagr__nt	17. nonchal__nt
2. ignor__nt	10. inconst__nt	18. extravag__nt
3. adolesc__nt	11. adher__nt	19. resist__nt
4. impot__nt	12. impertin__nt	20. infrequ__nt
5. tru__nt	13. correspond__nt	21. repent__nt
6. irrelev__nt	14. hesit__nt	22. eloqu__nt
7. unobserv__nt	15. poign__nt	23. self-reli__nt
8. decad__nt	16. urg__nt	24. vigil__nt

4. FORMING CONTRACTIONS

Rule

When contracting two words, insert an apostrophe in the space where a letter (or letters) has been lost.

does	+	not	=	doesn't
it	+	is	=	it's
they	+	will	=	they'll
you	+	have	=	you've
I	+	am	=	I'm
we	+	are	=	we're
she	+	would	=	she'd
can	+	not	=	can't

Notice this special contraction: will + not = won't.

Exercise 16. Write each of the following as a contraction:

1. we have
2. has not
3. let us
4. would not
5. he will
6. were not
7. there is
8. it is
9. must not
10. they are
11. I have
12. could not
13. it will
14. who is
15. you are
16. will not
17. she will
18. we would
19. was not
20. we will

5. FORMING PLURALS

Rule 1

(*a*) Add *s* to form the plural of most nouns.

bird—birds lamp—lamps
tree—trees desk—desks

(*b*) Add *es* if the noun ends in *s, sh, ch,* or *x.*

class—classes inch—inches
dish—dishes box—boxes
Jones—the Joneses

Rule 2

(*a*) If the noun ends in *y* preceded by a *consonant,* change the *y* to *i* and add *es.*

city—cities lady—ladies
liberty—liberties melody—melodies

(*b*) If the noun ends in *y* preceded by a *vowel*, add *s*.

essay—essays   journey—journeys
monkey—monkeys   survey—surveys

Exception: words ending in -*quy*, as soliloquy—soliloquies.

Rule 3

(*a*) If the noun ends in *o* preceded by a *vowel*, add *s*.

cameo—cameos   folio—folios
radio—radios   ratio—ratios
studio—studios   patio—patios

(*b*) If the noun ends in *o* preceded by a *consonant*, the situation is as follows:

(1) Some nouns take *es*.

potato—potatoes   Negro—Negroes
tomato—tomatoes   echo—echoes
hero—heroes   veto—vetoes

(2) Some nouns take *s* only.

piano—pianos   solo—solos
dynamo—dynamos   soprano—sopranos
silo—silos   alto—altos

(3) Some nouns take either *s* or *es*.

cargo—cargos, cargoes   domino—dominos, dominoes
motto—mottos, mottoes   tornado—tornados, tornadoes
buffalo—buffalos, buffaloes zero—zeros, zeroes

Rule 4

Add *s* to most nouns ending in *f*.

brief—briefs   staff—staffs
proof—proofs   sheriff—sheriffs
belief—beliefs   chief—chiefs

Exceptions. Change *f* or *fe* to *v* and add *es* in the following:

leaf—leaves   half—halves
knife—knives   thief—thieves
life—lives   wolf—wolves
wife—wives   self—selves

But not in the case of a name: Mr. Wolf—the Wolfs.

Exercise 17. Write the plural of each word below.

1. spy	8. turkey	15. potato
2. wife	9. convoy	16. shelf
3. eyelash	10. yourself	17. birch
4. portfolio	11. hostess	18. fox
5. attorney	12. rodeo	19. tariff
6. handkerchief	13. Burns	20. alley
7. tomato	14. ally	21. piano

Rule 5

In compound words, make the principal word plural.

mother-in-law	mothers-in-law
passerby	passersby

Exception A. If there is no noun in the compound word, add *s* to the end of the word.

takeoff	takeoffs
mix-up	mix-ups

Exception D. If the compound ends in *ful,* add *s* to the end of the word.

cupful   cupfuls

Rule 6

(*a*) In the following, form the plural by changing the spelling, rather than by adding *s* or *es.*

foot—feet	child—children
tooth—teeth	man—men
louse—lice	woman—women
mouse—mice	ox—oxen
goose—geese	

(*b*) In the following, use the same spelling for the plural as for the singular:

deer, swine, series, sheep, moose, species
Portuguese (and other nationalities ending in *ese*)

(*c*) Study these foreign plurals:

alumnus—alumni	bacterium—bacteria
alumna—alumnae	criterion—criteria
stimulus—stimuli	

Exercise 18. Write the plural of each word below.

1. sister-in-law	6. criterion	11. louse
2. fireman	7. Vietnamese	12. frame-up
3. mouthful	8. Commander in Chief	13. attorney-at-law
4. sheep	9. hanger-on	14. alumnus
5. series	10. spoonful	15. moose

6. FORMING POSSESSIVES

Rule 1

To form the possessive of singular nouns, add an apostrophe and *s*.

SINGULAR NOUNS	POSSESSIVE CASE
boy	boy's hat
friend	friend's book
child	child's toy
James	James's mother

Rule 2

To form the possessive of plural nouns ending in *s*, add the apostrophe alone after the *s*.

PLURAL NOUNS	POSSESSIVE CASE
girls	girls' lockers
ladies	ladies' dresses
students	students' projects
players	players' averages

Rule 3

To form the possessive of plural nouns that do not end in *s*, add the apostrophe and *s*.

PLURAL NOUNS	POSSESSIVE CASE
men	men's clothes
women	women's handbags
mice	mice's tails
sheep	sheep's wool

Rule 4

To form the possessive of (*a*) a compound noun, (*b*) a business name, or (*c*) a joint owner, put the apostrophe and *s* after the last word.

(*a*) brother-in-law   brother-in-law's age
(*b*) Abraham and Straus   Abraham and Straus's prices
(*c*) Gilbert and Sullivan   Gilbert and Sullivan's operettas

Note: Possessive pronouns (*yours, his, hers, its, ours, theirs,* and *whose*) do *not* require an apostrophe.

> That boat is *ours* (not *our's*).
> That dog is *hers* (not *her's*).
> Her hair lost *its* (not *it's*) gloss.
> *But:*
> *It's* all over. (Here *it's* is correct because it means *it is*, the apostrophe standing for the missing *i*.)

Exercise 19. Reduce each of the following to fewer words by using a possessive form.

Example: the work done by Gerald: *Gerald's work*

1. the cats belonging to our neighbor
2. the mark Phyllis received
3. an experiment done by Frank and George
4. novels written by Dickens
5. the troops of the enemy
6. styles for teen-agers
7. a pen belonging to somebody
8. the sale at Lord and Taylor
9. duties of policemen
10. the business owned by her father-in-law
11. entertainment for an hour
12. the reputation of the class
13. fees charged by physicians
14. the rights that belong to everyone
15. the nest where the mice lived
16. the importance of it
17. the desk of the editor in chief
18. a trip lasting a day
19. wages earned by a laborer
20. the speech given by Charles
21. food for the babies
22. the garage owned by the Smiths
23. supplies for a week
24. the responsibilities of the pupils
25. the flight by the Wright brothers

B. WATCH YOUR PRONUNCIATION

Careless pronunciation often results in careless spelling. If you have been misspelling any of the words below, it is most likely the result of your leaving out a sound or inserting one that doesn't belong. Form the habit of pronouncing these words correctly (check with the dictionary, if in doubt) and you will have no trouble in spelling them correctly.

1. Do not carelessly omit an unstressed vowel.

bound*a*ry	lab*o*ratory	temp*e*rature
choc*o*late	min*i*ature	veg*e*table
di*a*mond	monot*o*nous	veter*i*narian
int*e*resting	orig*i*nal	visu*a*lize

2. Do not carelessly omit an unstressed syllable.

accident*al*ly	incident*al*ly	super*in*tendent

3. Do not carelessly omit a required consonant.

Ar*c*tic	Feb*r*uary	reco*g*nize
can*d*idate	gover*n*ment	represen*t*ative
dip*h*theria	lib*r*ary	su*r*prise
dip*h*thong	proba*b*ly	sym*p*tom
eig*h*th	quan*t*ity	

4. Do not carelessly insert an unnecessary vowel between the two letters in italics.

at*hl*etics	f*or*ty	pron*un*ciation
bur*gl*ar	hin*dr*ance	remem*br*ance
chi*mn*ey	jewe*lr*y	sched*ul*e
disas*tr*ous	light*n*ing	um*br*ella
encum*br*ance	mischie*v*ous	won*dr*ous

Exercise 20. Write correctly the misspelled word in each group.

1. unnoticeable, bigger, pronounciation, superseded, height
2. original, cupsful, differed, besieging, overpaid
3. benefited, pursuing, library, withheld, specificly
4. proceeded, ninety, clumsiest, government, probaly
5. fourty-four, sleigh, unforeseeable, preference, management
6. leisure, disasterous, tying, unpaid, excellence
7. skiing, barrenness, supprised, canoeing, remittance
8. eigth, ladylike, de-emphasized, pianos, boundary
9. lonelier, monkeys, argument, bacterias, disbelieved
10. candidate, awful, does'nt, denial, exceedingly

C. STUDY UNPHONETIC WORDS

An unphonetic word is one that is spelled differently from the way it sounds.

1. **Silent letters.** The following words have a letter that is not pronounced. Be sure to include that letter in your spelling.

silent *b:* clim*b*, com*b*, crum*b*, de*b*t, dou*b*t, dum*b*, plum*b*er, re-
dou*b*table, su*b*poena, su*b*tle, thum*b*, undou*b*tedly

silent *c:* a*c*quaint, a*c*quire, a*c*quit, as*c*ertain, corpus*c*le, *c*zar, de-
s*c*end, fas*c*inate, indi*c*t, mis*c*ellaneous, mus*c*le, s*c*ent, s*c*issors

silent *d:* a*d*join a*d*just (and all other *adj-* words), han*d*kerchief

silent *g:* ali*g*n, desi*g*n, diaphra*g*m, *g*narled, *g*naw, *g*nome

silent *h:* ex*h*aust, ex*h*ibit, ex*h*ilaration, fore*h*ead, *gh*astly, *gh*etto,
*gh*ost, ging*h*am, *h*eir, *h*erb, r*h*etoric, r*h*eumatism, r*h*yme,
r*h*ythm, shep*h*erd, spag*h*etti, ve*h*icle

silent *k:* ac*k*nowledge, *k*nack, *k*nob (and all other *kn-* words)

silent *l:* a*l*mond, ba*l*m, ca*l*m, fo*l*k, ha*l*f, sa*l*mon, ta*l*k, wa*l*k, wou*l*d

silent *m:* *m*nemonic

silent *n:* autum*n*, colum*n*, condem*n*, dam*n*, hym*n*, solem*n*

silent *p.* *c*orps (the *s* is silent too), cu*p*board, em*p*ty, *p*neumatic,
*p*neumonia, *p*salm, *p*seudonym, *p*sychology, *p*tomaine,
recei*p*t

silent *s:* ais*l*e, corp*s* (the *p* is silent too), debri*s*, i*s*land, li*s*le, Louis-
ville, rendezvou*s*, vi*s*count

silent *t:* bankrup*t*cy, Chris*t*mas, lis*t*en, mor*t*gage, mus*t*n't, stre*t*ch,
whis*t*le, wres*t*le

silent *u:* body*g*uard, ga*u*ge, g*u*arantee, g*u*ardian, g*u*ess, g*u*est, g*u*ide,
lifeg*u*ard

silent *w:* ans*w*er, play*w*right, s*w*ord, t*w*o, *w*hole, *w*rap, *w*rite (and
all other *wr-* words)

2. **-ain words.** Review these words, in which the sound *-in* is spelled *-ain:*

Brit*ain*	cert*ain*	curt*ain*	porcel*ain*
capt*ain*	chieft*ain*	mount*ain*	vill*ain*

3. **e, not i.** Observe that in these words there is an *e* where you might expect an *i:*

beaut*e*ous	extemporan*e*ous	met*e*or
Caribb*e*an	hid*e*ous	naus*e*ate
court*e*ous	liqu*e*fy	pit*e*ous
delin*e*ate	mall*e*able	simultan*e*ous
erron*e*ous	Mediterran*e*an	spontan*e*ous

4. *-cian* words. End the word with *-cian* (not *-tian*) if you can trace it to an *-ic* word:

electri*cian* (from electri*c*) opti*cian* (from opti*c*)
logi*cian* (from logi*c*) pediatri*cian* (from pediatri*c*)
magi*cian* (from magi*c*) physi*cian* (from physi*c*)
mathemati*cian* (from mathemati*cs*) politi*cian* (from politi*c*)
musi*cian* (from musi*c*) statisti*cian* (from statisti*c*)

5. *y*, not *i*.

ab*y*ss	h*y*pocrisy	s*y*mphony
anal*y*ze	paral*y*sis	s*y*non*y*m
anon*y*mous	s*y*llable	s*y*nopsis
c*y*linder	s*y*mmetry	s*y*nthesis
c*y*nical	s*y*mpathy	t*y*ranny

6. *-ar*, not *-er*.

begg*ar*	burs*ar*	cell*ar*
burgl*ar*	calend*ar*	li*ar*

7. Additional unphonetic words for study. If you are in doubt about the pronunciation of these words, look them up in a dictionary.

biscuit	forfeit	sergeant
bouquet	furlough	sieve
brooch	hiccough	sovereign
buoy	lieutenant	suite
bureau	naïve	surgeon
chamois	naphtha	ukelele
colonel	parliament	Wednesday
Connecticut	pigeon	yacht
draught	quay	

Exercise 21. Rewrite each word, supplying the missing letter or letters.

1. porcel____n
2. W____day
3. statisti____an
4. s____non____m
5. naus____ting
6. s____geant
7. Carib____an
8. parl____ment
9. l____tenant
10. hic____gh
11. erron____us
12. burgl____r
13. col____nel
14. pediatri____an
15. Conne____cut
16. surg____n
17. politi____ian
18. furl____gh
19. anon____mous
20. delin____te

D. KNOW YOUR HOMONYMS

Homonyms are words that are pronounced alike but are different in meaning and spelling. Be careful to use the spelling required by the context. Review the following:

already, before, previously
The train had *already* left.

all ready, everyone prepared
We are *all ready.*

all together, everyone at one time
We sang the hymn *all together.*

altogether, completely
This is *altogether* wrong.

altar, table-like structure in a place of worship
The bride was led to the *altar.*

(to) **alter,** (to) change
The captain had to *alter* the ship's course.

ascent, act of rising or mounting
The *ascent* to the 61th floor took a few seconds.

assent, act of agreeing
Indicate your *assent* by saying "aye."

bare, without any covering
They fought with *bare* fists.

(to) **bear,** 1. (to) endure
Can you *bear* the pain?
2. large shaggy animal
The zoo has a new polar *bear.*

born, brought into life
When were you *born?*

borne, endured, suffered
These burdens can no longer be *borne.*

brake, device for stopping
The driver stepped on the *brake.*

(to) **break,** (to) shatter
Don't *break* the dishes!

capital, seat of government
Washington, D.C., is our nation's *capital.*

Capitol, building where the U.S. legislature meets
Congress meets in the *Capitol.*

coarse, rough
The overalls were made of *coarse* cloth.

course, way, path
The Mississippi has often altered its *course*.

complement, full quantity
He has his *complement* of troubles.

compliment, praise
Your work deserves the highest *compliment*.

council, group that advises
Who are the members of the executive's inner *council?*

counsel, advice
Thank you for your good *counsel*.

(to) **desert,** (to) abandon
Rats *desert* a sinking ship.

dessert, last course of a meal
She had watermelon for *dessert*.

dual, double
Driver-training cars have *dual* controls.

duel, combat between two persons
The rivals fought a *duel*.

(to) **hear,** (to) perceive by ear
Did you *hear* that noise?

here, in or to this place
Please come *here*.

its, belonging to *it*
The bird hurt *its* wing.

it's, it is
It's too late.

lead, marking substance
I need *lead* for my mechanical pencil.

led, conducted
Firemen *led* the tenants to safety.

miner, worker in a mine
How much does a coal *miner* earn?

minor, 1. person under the age of legal responsibility
You are a *minor* if you are under 21.
    2. less important
The composition had one serious fault and several *minor* ones.

passed, went by
   We *passed* your house.
past, 1. gone by
   You helped us on *past* occasions.
      2. time gone by
   You helped us in the *past.*
      3. close to and then beyond
   We went *past* your house.
peace, opposite of war
   The warring nations were urged to make *peace.*
piece, fragment
   Don't step on that *piece* of glass.
principal, 1. main
   Broadway is our city's *principal* street.
      2. head of a school
   Mr. Brown is our new *principal.*
principle, rule of conduct
   He made it a *principle* never to buy what he could not afford.
shone, shined
   The moon *shone* brightly.
shown (used after a helping verb), taught
   We were *shown* how to add fractions.
their, belonging to *them*
   They returned to *their* homes.
there, in or at that place
   Have you ever been *there?*
they're, they are
   They're coming.
to, in the direction of and reaching
   Joe walks *to* school.
too, 1. also
   I agree and Fred does *too.*
      2. excessively
   The room is *too* cold.
two (the number)
   It's *two* o'clock.
who's, who is
   Who's there?
whose, belonging to *whom*
   Whose book is this?

your, belonging to *you*
 You must do *your* work.
you're, you are
 You're altogether right.

The following pairs, though not precisely homonyms, are similar enough to cause confusion:

(to) **accept,** (to) receive with approval
 He *accepted* my apology.
(to) **except,** (to) leave out
 In granting raises, he *excepted* the newest employees.

advice, recommendation; counsel
 What is your *advice?*
(to) **advise,** (to) give advice to
 What do you *advise* me to do?

(to) **affect,** (to) influence
 Absence may *affect* your mark.
effect, result, outcome
 One possible *effect* of absence is a lower mark.

formally, following established custom; conventionally
 Certain restaurants insist that their guests be *formally* attired.
formerly, previously
 Our principal was *formerly* the dean of boys.

have (helping verb)
 He might *have* become rich.
of (preposition)
 The rest *of* us went home.

loose, free; not fastened
 Who turned the dog *loose?*
(to) **lose,** (to) part with accidentally
 How did you *lose* your wallet?

quiet, silent
 When the teacher spoke, the room became *quiet.*
quite, completely
 By bedtime, the children were *quite* exhausted.

than (conjunction used in comparisons)
 My sister is younger *than* I.
then, at that time
 Chicago was *then* a small frontier town.

weather, condition of the atmosphere
The *weather* is cloudy.
whether, if it is or was true that
Find out *whether* he agrees or disagrees.

Exercise 22. Write the correct choice, and state the reason for your choice.

1. John and Mary wish to go because (their, there, they're) eager to visit the museum.
2. Is that (your, you're) jacket on the floor?
3. Have you successfully (passed, past) all your final examinations?
4. The article describes the (principal, principle) (affects, effects) of the new drug.
5. I expected a (complement, compliment)—not criticism.
6. If you drop this vase, it will (brake, break).
7. Had you listened to my (counsel, council), you would have passed.
8. (Who's, Whose) at the door?
9. In the violent storm, the boat broke (loose, lose) from its moorings.
10. We did not realize that the boys' father had forbidden them to keep (there, their, they're) puppy.
11. We want to go to the movies (to, too, two).
12. In the (passed, past) we have always held our commencement exercises in the evening.
13. A true friend will never (desert, dessert) you.
14. It's (already, all ready) past the deadline.
15. The tiny bulb (shown, shone) weakly in the dim hallway.
16. A (minor, miner) cannot vote in public elections.
17. He is taller (then, than) his brother by several inches.
18. He is the boy (who's, whose) poster was chosen for the contest.
19. I was advised to review the (principals, principles) of correct usage.
20. They have (borne, born) these hardships without complaint.
21. The weather forced us to (altar, alter) our plans.
22. (Formally, Formerly), an elderly couple lived here.
23. From the base of the mountain to the halfway point, the (assent, ascent) is not too difficult.
24. She was (quite, quiet) breathless from running upstairs.
25. Macbeth was afraid he would (loose, lose) his crown to one of Banquo's descendants.
26. There were fewer candidates (then, than) we had been (led, lead) to expect.
27. Your interpretation of the results of the test is (all together, altogether) inaccurate.

28. The (peace, piece) of string is too short.
29. Albany is the (Capitol, capital) of New York State.
30. Unfortunately, I am unable to (accept, except) your kind invitation.
31. The (dual, duel) was to have taken place at dawn.
32. How will the new tax (effect, affect) your business?
33. The reward must (have, of) pleased them very much.
34. The horse lifted (its, it's) head and snorted.
35. My English teacher gave me ample opportunity to make up for (passed, past) mistakes.
36. You have been (led, lead) astray by your own carelessness.
37. Homeowners say they are already (baring, bearing) very heavy tax burdens.
38. What (course, coarse) of action do you suggest?
39. We could not learn (weather, whether) they had arrived or not.
40. I (advice, advise) you not to do it.
41. The reply was loud enough for everyone to (hear, here).
42. Doing a task promptly is better (than, then) worrying about it.
43. It's (your, you're) turn to drive now, if you're ready.
44. The alumni have announced that (their, there, they're) sending a representative to our graduation.
45. You should (of, have) been in the assembly yesterday.
46. What is the (effect, affect) of sunlight on plants?
47. Tell me (who's, whose) on third base; I don't recognize him.
48. On his doctor's (advice, advise), he resumed a full program of physical activities.
49. The dog wagged (its, it's) tail and barked happily.
50. The merchant promised to refund my money if I were not (all together, altogether) satisfied.

E. INVENT MNEMONICS

A *mnemonic* (the first *m* is silent) is a trick of association that helps you to remember. The following mnemonics may help you to remember when the correct spelling is *principle* and when it is *principal*. (The associated or similar elements have been italicized.)

1. A princip*le* is a ru*le*.
2. A princip*al* (the head of a school) ought to be a *pal*.
3. A princip*al* street is a *main* street.

When you have unusual difficulty in spelling a word, try to invent a mnemonic. No matter how farfetched or ridiculous the association may be, if it can help you to spell correctly, it is a good mnemonic. Here are some additional mnemonics that have proved helpful:

WORD	MNEMONIC DEVICE
beginning	the be*ginning* of the *inning*
believe	Don't be*lie*ve that *lie!*
calendar	Janu*ar*y and Febru*ar*y are in the calend*ar*.
friend	a fri*end* to the *end*
parallel	*All* rails are par*all*el.
piece	a *pie*ce of *pie*
privilege	It is a pr*i*v*i*lege to have two eyes (*i*'s) and a *leg*.
pronunciation	The *nun*'s pro*nun*ciation is excellent.
stationary	Station*a*ry means st*a*nding still.
stationery	Station*e*ry is writing pap*e*r.
there	*There, here, where* all refer to place.

F. FOLLOW RECOMMENDED STUDY PROCEDURES

When you study a new word, carefully follow this step-by-step method:

1. Pronounce the word. Use it correctly in a sentence.
2. See the word. Say it by syllables. Say the letters in order.
3. Close your eyes and spell the word. Check your spelling to be sure that it is correct.
4. Write the word correctly. Form every letter carefully, especially *i*'s and *e*'s, *a*'s and *o*'s.
5. Cover the word and write it. If the spelling is correct, cover the word and write it again.
6. If you make a mistake during step 5, repeat the previous steps before repeating step 5.

G. STUDY COMMONLY MISSPELLED WORDS

1. ONE HUNDRED SPELLING DEMONS

ache	break	could	every
again	built	country	February
always	business	dear	forty
among	busy	doctor	friend
answer	buy	does	grammar
any	can't	done	guess
been	choose	don't	half
beginning	color	early	having
believe	coming	easy	hear
blue	cough	enough	heard

here	none	sugar	used
hoarse	often	sure	very
hour	once	tear	wear
instead	piece	their	Wednesday
just	raise	there	week
knew	read	they	where
know	ready	though	whether
laid	said	through	which
loose	says	tired	whole
lose	seems	tonight	women
making	separate	too	won't
many	shoes	trouble	would
meant	since	truly	write
minute	some	Tuesday	writing
much	straight	two	wrote

2. WORDS WITH TROUBLESOME CONSONANTS

DOUBLED CONSONANT FOLLOWED BY SINGLE CONSONANT

accelerate	cinnamon	innocuous
accumulate	collateral	irrelevant
alliteration	commemorate	moccasin
allotment	correlation	occasion
apparel	corridor	parallel
assimilate	corroborate	piccolo
broccoli	guillotine	scurrilous
bulletin	immaculate	vaccinate

SINGLE CONSONANT FOLLOWED BY DOUBLED CONSONANT

beginning	necessary	recurrent
Caribbean	omitted	Renaissance
dilemma	penicillin	sheriff
dilettante	Philippine	tariff
harass	professional	tomorrow
Mediterranean	rebellion	tyranny
metallic	recommend	vacillate

DOUBLED CONSONANT FOLLOWED BY ANOTHER DOUBLED CONSONANT

accessible	assessment	misspell
accommodate	committee	possession
aggression	connoisseur	reconnaissance
assassinate	embarrass	Tennessee

3. SEVEN HUNDRED WORDS FOR STUDY AND REVIEW

abbreviate
abscess
absence
absolutely
abyss
academic
acceptable
accidentally
accompanying
accuracy
achievement
acknowledge
acquaintance
acquisition
adage
adequate
adjacent
adjournment
adjustment
admittance
advantageous
adversely
advisable
affirmative
aggravate
aggregate
agitation
allocated
allotted
allowance
alphabetical
amateur
ambassador
ambiguous
amendment
ammunition
amplify
analysis
anatomy
ancestor
ancestry

anchored
anecdote
anesthetic
anniversary
announcement
annual
anonymous
anthology
anticipate
antique
antonym
anxious
apartment
apologetic
apology
apparatus
apparently
appetite
appraisal
apprehension
appropriation
approximately
aquarium
aquatic
arbitrary
architecture
arguing
argument
arouse
article
artificial
ascending
ascertain
assassination
assistance
assurance
athletic
attendant
audience
auspicious
authentic

auxiliary
average
aversion
awkward

bachelor
balloon
banana
bankruptcy
barbecue
bargain
beautifully
belief
beneficial
benefit
besieged
betrayal
biased
bibliography
bicycle
bigamy
bituminous
blizzard
bolster
bookkeeping
boulevard
boundary
boycotted
brilliance
budget
bureau
burglaries

cafeteria
calendar
callous
callus
campaign
candidacy

capacity
capsule
carburetor
career
carnival
carriage
casualty
category
cathedral
caucus
cauliflower
cavalry
ceiling
celebration
celebrity
cellar
cellophane
cemetery
certainly
challenge
champagne
chancellor
changeable
charitable
chauffeur
cholera
choosing
civilian
clearance
collegiate
combustible
comedy
commercial
commitment
committing
comparative
comparison
competent
competition
competitor
compulsory

computer	deferred	eliminate	fatiguing
concentrate	definite	elliptical	feasible
concerning	delegate	embarrass	feminine
conclusively	deliberate	embassies	fertile
condemned	delicious	emperor	fervent
confectionery	delinquent	emphasis	fickle
conferring	deluge	encourage	fictitious
confidential	descendant	encyclopedia	fiendish
congratulate	description	engagement	fierce
congressional	desirous	enormous	filial
conscientious	despise	entertaining	finally
conscious	destruction	enthusiastic	fiscal
consequently	deteriorate	entitled	flexible
conservatory	detrimental	entrance	forecast
consonant	diagnosis	envelope	forehead
conspicuous	dilapidated	environment	foreign
constant	dimension	epidemic	foremost
contemptuous	dirigible	equipment	foreshadow
continuous	disagreeable	equipping	foresight
controversial	disappeared	escapade	forfeit
convenience	disappoint	essentially	fortunately
conveyance	disapprove	evaporate	forty-fourth
copyright	discernible	exaggerate	frostbitten
cordial	disciplinary	exceedingly	
coronation	discouragement	excellent	
coroner	disease	excitement	gadget
corporal	disillusioned	exercise	gallery
corpuscle	disintegrate	exhausted	gardener
corrugated	dispatch	exhaustion	gaseous
countenance	disperse	exhibition	ghetto
courageous	dissatisfied	existence	gracefulness
criminal	dissolve	expedition	grammar
criticism	distinguished	expense	grateful
criticize	dormitory	explanation	grease
cruelty	dramatize	exquisite	greenness
curiosity	duped	extracurricular	guarantee
cylinder		extraordinary	guardian
		extravagant	
	ecstasy	extricate	
debtor	efficiency		
deceitful	eighth		handicapped
decided	elaborate	familiarize	handkerchief
defense	eligible	fascinate	handwriting
			heaviness

height	inquiry	loneliness	mystery
hemorrhage	institute	loyalty	
hereditary	instrumental	lubricant	
heritage	insurance	luxury	narrative
heroes	integrity		negative
hoping	intelligence		negligible
humiliate	intelligible	magnificent	neither
humorous	intensified	maintain	neutral
hundredth	intercede	maintenance	niece
hurricane	interchangeable	management	nineteenth
hybrid	interfered	maneuver	ninety
hypnotize	interpretation	manually	nonsense
hypocrisy	interrogative	marmalade	notary
	interrupt	marriage	noticeable
	interview	masquerade	notoriety
icing	intimate	masterpiece	nourishment
icy	intriguing	mathematics	nuclear
identity	irresistible	mattress	nucleus
illegally	irresponsible	meanness	nuisance
illegible		medallion	
illiterate		medicine	
illness	jeopardy	medieval	obliterate
illogical	journal	memorandum	obnoxious
imagination	journeying	merchandise	obstacle
imitate	juvenile	merely	obstinate
immature		metaphor	occasional
immediately		metropolitan	occupancy
immovable	keenness	microphone	occurrence
implement	kindergarten	millionaire	offense
inadequate	kindliness	minimum	offering
inaugural		misappropriate	official
inconceivable		mischievous	omitted
inconvenience	laboratory	misdemeanor	onomatopoeia
incredible	larceny	misinterpreted	opponents
indebtedness	lavender	missile	opportunity
indefinite	legend	missionary	oppression
independence	legitimate	Mississippi	optimistic
indifferent	leisure	misunderstood	orbit
individual	liability	monkeys	ordinarily
influential	librarian	municipal	organization
information	license	murderer	original
ingredients	lieutenant	murmuring	ornament
initiative	literally	musical	orphaned

outrageous	predecessor	recruit	sequence
overrule	predominant	recurring	session
	prefabricate	referee	settlement
	preface	refrigerator	severity
pageant	preference	regardless	sieges
pamphlet	preferred	regretting	sieve
papal	prejudice	rehearsal	similar
parachute	preliminary	relieve	simile
paradise	preparation	religious	simultaneous
paradoxical	pretense	relinquish	sincerity
parallel	prevalent	renewal	softening
paralysis	primarily	repetitious	soliciting
parliament	prisoner	replacement	solos
partially	privacy	resemblance	soluble
peaceable	privilege	reservoir	sophisticated
peculiarity	proceedings	resistance	sophomore
pedigree	proclamation	responsible	specific
peninsula	professor	restaurant	spectacle
pennant	proficiency	revival	spectacular
perforated	projectile	rewriting	spiral
performance	prominent	rheumatism	sponsor
permanent	promissory	rhythm	standard
permissible	promptness	ridiculous	standardize
persevere	propaganda	righteous	statistics
personnel	proprietor	routine	stretcher
physical	prosperous		stubborn
physician	psychology		stunning
pianos	publicity	sacrifice	submitting
picnicking	purchase	safety	subsidy
piercing		salaries	substantial
pleasant		sandwich	successful
poise	quizzes	saucy	suffrage
poisonous		scandal	superb
politician		scarcity	superintendent
porcelain	rabid	scenery	supremacy
postponed	rearmament	schedule	surgeon
poultice	rearrangement	scissors	surgery
poultry	rebelled	séance	surprising
practical	rebuttal	secretarial	suspense
prairie	reciprocate	seize	syllable
preceding	recognize	seizure	symbolize
precious	recommendation	seldom	symptom
precipice	reconciliation	senatorial	synonym

telegram	truthfulness	vacant	volume
television	turkeys	vacuum	voluble
temperature	twelfth	valuable	volunteer
temporary		vegetable	
tendency		vehicle	
testimony	umbrella	vengeance	warrior
tomatoes	unbearable	vertical	weird
tragedy	unconscious	vicinity	whistle
tragic	uncontrollable	victim	wield
transferred	undecided	viewpoint	windshield
transition	unmanageable	village	witnessed
transparent	unrelieved	villain	wrestling
treachery	unscheduled	vinegar	
tremendous	unveiling	virtue	
trophies	utensil	visibility	yield
troupe		visualize	

FORMER REGENTS SPELLING TESTS

Note: The Regents spelling test is a proofreading exercise. It requires you to examine words and to make corrections where necessary. It is no time for speed reading. If you are too hasty, you may fail to notice that a letter has been omitted, or added, or changed, in a word that you know how to spell. Don't let this happen. Be a good proofreader.

Directions: In each of the following groups of words, only one of the words is misspelled. In *each* group, select the misspelled word and spell it correctly in the space provided on the separate answer sheet.   [5]

Test 1

1 perform
  divide
  apologize
  occasion
  acheive

2 appreciate
  forhead
  accomplice
  dual
  withholding

3 accumulate
  endeavor
  businesslike
  labratory
  interruption

4 agreeable
  parallel
  arrouse
  conscience
  psychology

5 antagonize
reguardless
vagrancy
treacherous
unsanitary

6 consonant
symbilize
neutrality
optimistic
noticeable

7 prarie
recruiting
breathe
fatality
nourishment

8 complexion
pitifully
metropolitain
accuracy
stationery

9 appraisel
remnant
facet
nobly
playwright

10 propaganda
interpreted
slippery
triumphant
efficently

Test 2

1 absolutely
delegate
capacity
foriegner
spokesmen

2 society
disguise
fullfilling
personnel
stretcher

3 uncontrollable
surgery
furthermore
edible
paticularly

4 congenial
aptitude
soliloquy
proceedure
especially

5 mathematician
partisipate
retroactive
befriended
challenger

6 clientele
cylinder
arguement
sympathetic
gingham

7 stepfather
fireman
conclusivly
commodity
intercede

8 siege
almanac
lisence
manageable
impel

9 franchise
   alliteration
   twitching
   plaintiff
   disobediant

10 chaufeur
   encumbrance
   specialty
   sacrilege
   pulleys

Test 3

1 opposite
   fulfilled
   representative
   parallell
   congratulate

2 luxury
   heros
   nevertheless
   corridor
   unanimous

3 scarcely
   inherent
   fiscal
   illiterate
   athletics

4 semester
   occured
   dismissal
   fiery
   boulevard

5 preventive
   bankruptcy
   overwhelmed
   ingredients
   conqueror

6 chronicle
   identity
   imagination
   surname
   amiable

7 ritual
   meanness
   boycott
   visible
   privilege

8 destruction
   lightning
   appealing
   procedure
   accompanying

9 fascinating
   existence
   sophomore
   premise
   millionaire

10 satellite
   pneumatic
   conspiracy
   ominous
   misapprehend

Test 4

1 elliminate
   appendix
   luxuries
   mountainous
   pessimist

2 rewritting
   triangular
   women's
   hubbub
   identity

3 capacity
beggarly
axiom
kindred
tomatoe

5 loses
frivolous
conservatory
orniment
technique

7 abusive
practicle
threshold
contestant
ruddy

9 despair
facinate
vicinity
bisect
inaugural

4 personally
cemetary
pneumonia
slaughter
temperature

6 benefactor
referendum
discription
immortal
inadequate

8 cordially
fictitious
priority
deliverance
nuisance

10 hundreths
grasshopper
popularize
aeronautics
maintenance

Test 5

1 historical
managment   *e*
adjourned
successfully
calendar

3 deferment
appearence
familiarity
vehicle
preamble

5 environment
glistening
predicament
fervent
lazyness   *laziness*

2 communicate
foreign
pleasant
conciet   *conceit*
development

4 acquitted
philosophical
undeceided   *undecided*
criticism
wariness

6 muscle
errosion   *erosion*
extravagant
frostbitten
utterance   *U*

7 inverted
 financial
 respectibility *[H]*
 premise
 personnel

8 miscelaneous
 transparent
 businesslike
 conspiracy
 subtlety

9 surrendered
 proprietor
 circumstantial
 hypocrisy
 economicly

10 generousity
 beggarly
 keenest
 seafaring
 bronchial

Test 6

1 allotment
 electoral
 patern *pattern*
 statistics
 elevate

2 tryed
 suspicious
 influential
 conscience
 miniature

3 divine
 corridor *per*
 apiece
 battery
 choosing

4 parish
 tremendus
 isolate
 suitable
 similarly

5 happenning
 category
 precede
 unnecessary
 arrangement

6 adjournment
 preference
 heroine
 challenge *knowledge*
 acknowlege

7 orchestral
 beseiged *i e*
 perpetual
 connotation
 cordially

8 chronic
 sympathy
 laboratory
 disipline *weird*
 weird *ei*

9 subscription
 anonymous
 definately
 familiar
 embarrass

10 specify
 studying
 confusion
 performence *ance*
 noticeable
 noticable

Test 7

1 refuel
   ascend
   economical
   completly
   innocent

2 microscope
   finanical
   nylon
   postponement
   ordeal

3 authority
   vagueness
   captain
   locallity
   noticeable

4 proprietor
   adjasent
   partial
   assess
   tariff

5 truely
   management
   responsible
   capacity
   hymn

6 luxury
   intensely
   wierd
   demolish
   galaxy

7 indispensable
   collegiate
   analysis
   athletic
   acceptance

8 vandalism
   transistor
   vetoes
   journal
   arrangement

9 suffrage
   superstitious
   mistreatment
   consonant
   curency

10 falsify
    homecoming
    expediant
    helicopter
    treasurer

Chapter 4 The Reading Comprehension Test (Questions 41-60)

THE IMPORTANCE OF READING

Consider how important reading is. If you read well, you will be able to continue your education throughout life solely by reading. You will be able to succeed in college. (If you cannot read well, you may have to drop out.) You will probably advance more rapidly in your chosen employment, business, or profession. You will be better informed and, therefore, more intelligent as a citizen. You will be able to enjoy the leisure reading of good books. Your friends will find you a more interesting person. In a very real sense, your future success and happiness require that you be able to read well.

As you might expect, the Comprehensive Examination in English attaches major importance to reading. It tests reading in two ways:

1. Every question on the examination is, in a way, a reading test, since you must be able to understand what each question calls for before you can answer it successfully.

2. The examination includes a separate reading comprehension test (questions 41–60) worth twenty points.

THE TEST PASSAGES

The passages you will encounter in the reading comprehension test are likely to contain subtleties, or hints, that you may not fully understand in your first reading. Also, you will probably be questioned about these subtleties; you may be asked to indicate what the passage *implies*, or what the author *suggests*, or what the reader may *infer*. To answer such questions, you will have to reread the entire passage, or parts of it, with maximum attention.

A READING COMPREHENSION PASSAGE OFTEN REQUIRES SEVERAL READINGS TO BE FULLY UNDERSTOOD.

THE PROPER APPROACH

In seeking the right answers, be guided only by what is printed in the passage. Rigidly exclude from your mind any previous information you may have about the topic in the passage. Suppose, for example, you are confronted with a selection about stamp collecting. Suppose, further, that you have been a stamp collector for years and have read books and articles on this subject. Beware! Do not allow any outside information to influence you in answering questions about the passage.

BE GUIDED ONLY BY THE TEXT OF THE PASSAGE YOU ARE READING.

TYPICAL READING COMPREHENSION TEST

To help you in your preparation for the reading comprehension test, we have added two features in reprinting the typical test below:

1. We have numbered every sentence in each passage to facilitate reference.

2. We have fully discussed and answered the questions asked about each passage before going on to the next passage.

Directions (41–60): Below each of the following passages, there are one or more incomplete statements or questions about the passage. For each, select the word or expression that best completes the statement or answers the question *in accordance with the meaning of the passage,* and write its *number* in the space provided on the separate answer sheet.   [20]

The correct answers have been inserted in brackets at the end of each question. Carefully observe the reasoning involved in arriving at the answers.

Passage A

(1) Every night she listened to her father going around the house, locking the doors and windows. (2) She listened: the back door closed, she could hear the catch of the kitchen window click, and the restless pad of his feet going back to try the front door. (3) It wasn't only the outside doors he locked: he locked the empty rooms, the bathroom, the lavatory. (4) He was locking something out, but obviously it was something capable of penetrating his first defenses. (5) He raised his second line all the way up to bed.

(6) In fifteen years, she thought unhappily, the house will be his; he had paid twenty-five pounds down and the rest he was paying month by month as rent.   (7) "Of course," he was in the habit of saying, "I've improved the property."   (8) "Yes," he repeated, "I've improved the property," looking around for a nail to drive in, a weed to be uprooted.   (9) It was more than a sense of property, it was a sense of honesty.   (10) Some people who bought their homes through the society let them go to rack and ruin and then cleared out.

(11) She stood with her ear against the wall, a small, dark, furious, immature figure.   (12) There was no more to be heard from the other room; but in her inner ear she still heard the chorus of a property owner, the tap-tap of a hammer, the scrape of a spade, the whistle of radiator steam, a key turning, a bolt pushed home, the little trivial sounds of men building barricades.   (13) She stood planning. . . .

QUESTION 41

Apparently the father is concerned that
1 his daughter respect him
2 he provide for his daughter's future
3 he feel secure
4 he avoid his neighbors
5 his daughter love him

$$\left[\, 3 \,\right]$$

ANSWER EXPLAINED

The first three sentences, by describing how the father locked the doors, windows, empty rooms, and even the bathroom and lavatory, indicate that 3 is the correct answer.

WRONG CHOICES

There is no evidence in the passage to support answers 1, 2, 4, or 5.

QUESTION 42

In this passage, the father is shown to be
1 unkind to his daughter   4 friendly to his neighbors
2 suspicious of home improvements   5 confident of others' good will
3 methodical in his actions

$$\left[\, 3 \,\right]$$

ANSWER EXPLAINED

The father's routine of systematically locking up every night (sentences 1-3) and "looking around for a nail to drive in, a weed to be uprooted" (sentence 8) prove that 3 is the answer.

WRONG CHOICES

1. Though the girl is unhappy, the passage offers no direct evidence that her father is *unkind* to her.
2. Sentences 7 and 8 indicate that the father approves of home improvements.
4 and 5. The elaborate system of defenses with which the father surrounds himself (sentences 1-5) suggests that he is neither friendly to his neighbors nor confident of the good will of others.

QUESTION 43

In this passage, the girl's attitude is one of
1 grateful acceptance   4 studied indifference
2 great resentment   5 vague dislike
3 mild distaste

[2]

ANSWER EXPLAINED

The passage states (sentence 11) that the girl is "furious" over her father's activities. The tone of sentence 12, particularly, shows that she strongly disapproves of his preoccupation with the property and his barricade-building. The suggestion in sentence 13 that she is planning some countermove is further evidence of her great resentment.

WRONG CHOICES

1, 3, 4, and 5 cannot be correct, in light of the evidence in sentences 11-13.

QUESTION 44

This passage *as a whole* conveys a feeling of
1 heartlessness   4 greed
2 envy   5 tenseness
3 peace

[5]

ANSWER EXPLAINED

There is a feeling of increasing tenseness with each sentence in the opening paragraph, as the father constructs elaborate defenses against some vague, unmentioned entity, and the daughter listens with obvious disapproval. The conflict between father and daughter suggested in sentences 6–8 of the second paragraph adds to the tenseness. In the final paragraph, the tension reaches a climax with the daughter's fierce resentment and the implication that she is about to strike back.

WRONG CHOICES

The passage offers no proof that either 1, 2, 3, or 4 is the right answer.

QUESTION 45

The last sentence of this passage conveys a feeling of

1 simple faith
2 great unconcern
3 joyous anticipation

4 vague foreboding
5 constructive criticism

ANSWER EXPLAINED

The last sentence is vague; it does not reveal what the girl is planning. Also, it contains a note of foreboding; in view of what we have just been told in sentences 11 and 12, it is likely that the girl's plan, whatever it turns out to be, will unleash her deep resentment against her father.

WRONG CHOICES

There is no support in the passage for answers 1, 2, 3, or 5.

QUESTION 46

In reality, which did *not* happen?

1 The girl apparently eavesdropped on her father.
2 The father punished the girl.
3 Some property owners let their homes deteriorate.
4 The father bought the house on the installment plan.
5 The father built his defenses carefully.

[2]

ANSWER EXPLAINED

The passage fails to show that the father punished the girl.

WRONG CHOICES

1. When one eavesdrops, he listens secretly. The fact that the girl not only listened (sentences 1 and 2) to her father's activities, but listened "with her ear against the wall" (sentence 11), shows that she apparently did eavesdrop on her father.
3. Sentence 10 shows that some property owners did, in fact, let their homes deteriorate.
4. Sentence 6 proves that the father did buy his house on the installment plan.
5. The first paragraph, particularly sentences 3–5, shows that the father did, in fact, build his defenses carefully.

Passage B

(1) If you have ever passed an hour wandering through an antique shop (not looking for anything exactly, but simply looking), you must have noticed how your taste gradually grows numb, and then—if you stay—becomes perverted. (2) You begin to conjure up charm in those hideous pictures of plump girls fondling pigeons, you develop a psychopathic desire for spinning wheels and cobblers' benches, you are apt to pay out good money for a bronze statuette of Otto von Bismarck, with a metal hand inside a metal frock coat and metal pouches under his metallic eyes. (3) As soon as you take the things home, you realize that they are revolting. (4) And yet they have a sort of horrible authority; you don't like them; you know how awful they are; but it is a tremendous effort to drop them in the garbage, where they belong. (5) The nineteenth century produced an appalling amount of junky art like this, and sometimes I imagine that clandestine underground factories are continuing to pour it out like illicit drugs. (6) There is a name for such stuff in the trade, a word apparently of Russian origin, "kitsch": it means vulgar showoff, and it is applied to anything that took a lot of trouble to make and is quite hideous.

QUESTION 47

The phrase that best expresses the ideas of this passage is
1 the fascination of kitsch
2 looking for 20th-century antiques
3 how to buy a bronze statuette

4 the illicit drugs

5 hidden charms in 19th-century art

$$[\diagup]$$

ANSWER EXPLAINED

The phrase that best expresses the ideas of this passage must be the one that is supported by more evidence than any of the four remaining phrases. Phrase 1, "the fascination of kitsch," is supported by every sentence in the passage. (See pages 105–107 for a demonstration of how to select "the phrase that best expresses the ideas" of a passage.)

WRONG CHOICES

2 is not discussed. The customer, according to sentence 1, is "not looking for anything exactly." Besides, the antiques in this passage, according to sentences 2 and 5, represent the *nineteenth* century.

3 is one of the details mentioned in sentence 2, but it is too limited in scope to express the ideas of the passage as a whole.

4 appears only in a simile ("like illicit drugs") in sentence 5, where the main topic is kitsch. The passage is obviously not about drugs.

5 is incorrect because, as the passage abundantly makes clear in sentences 2–6, kitsch is not genuine art. Whatever charm it possesses is not *hidden*, but rather *conjured up* (sentence 2) in the mind of the customer when his judgment is perverted (sentence 1) by his remaining in the shop too long.

QUESTION 48

Which sentence most strongly suggests the buyer's feeling of surprise?

(1) 1   (2) 2   (3) 3   (4) 4   (5) 6

$$[\mathcal{3}]$$

ANSWER EXPLAINED

Surprise involves the sudden, the unexpected, and the astonishing. In sentence 3 the buyer suddenly comes into the unexpected and astonishing realization that he has purchased kitsch, not art.

WRONG CHOICES

Sentences 1, 2, and 4 describe feelings that develop gradually and do not have the suddenness of surprise.

Sentence 6 merely explains the origin and meaning of the term "kitsch." It does not involve surprise.

QUESTION 49

The buyer of these antiques eventually regards them with

1 mixed feelings
2 complete fondness
3 vague indifference
4 unquestioning faith
5 tremendous reverence

[✓]

ANSWER EXPLAINED

Sentence 6 indicates that the buyer does not like the antiques he has bought, yet he cannot, as sentence 4 indicates, drop them in the garbage. He has *mixed feelings* about them.

WRONG CHOICES

2, 3, 4, and 5 are disproved by the evidence in sentence 6.

QUESTION 50

According to the passage, which is true of the atmosphere of an antique shop?

1 It makes the truly beautiful seem commonplace.
2 It leads the customer to lose his ability to discriminate.
3 It is designed to trap the unwary buyer.
4 It is designed to promote the sale of shoddy goods.
5 It focuses attention on the art of the nineteenth century.

[2]

ANSWER EXPLAINED

The customer's sense of values becomes "perverted" (sentence 1) if he stays in the antique shop, and he begins to "conjure up" (imagine) charm in "hideous" art (sentence 2) which really has no charm at all. To sum up, the atmosphere of the antique shop leads him to lose his ability to discriminate between true art and kitsch.

WRONG CHOICES

1 is not discussed. On the contrary, the passage shows how the perverted judgment of the customer turns the truly commonplace into the beautiful (sentence 2).

3 is incorrect because, as sentences 1 and 2 show, it is the customer who traps himself.

4 is wrong for the same reason. The passage indicates not that the shop is promoting the sale of shoddy goods, but that the buyer himself is apt to choose these goods (sentence 2).

5 is wrong for two reasons. First, as sentence 2 shows, the buyer himself focuses his attention on what appeals to him. Secondly, the passage deals with the "junky art" rather than the art of the nineteenth century.

QUESTION 51

Which statement can best be made about the structure of the passage?
1 Sentence 1 is not essential to the passage.
2 Sentence 2 supports sentence 1.
3 Sentence 4 explains sentence 2.
4 Sentence 5 contradicts sentence 4.
5 Sentence 6 is not related to sentence 5.

ANSWER EXPLAINED

Sentence 2 supports sentence 1 by showing the mistakes the customer makes when his judgment becomes perverted and he loses his ability to discriminate.

WRONG CHOICES

Sentence 1 is essential. It is the topic sentence. Without it, we could not readily know where we are or what the passage is about.

Sentence 4, to be exact, does not *explain* sentence 2, but *describes the things taken home* in sentence 3.

Sentence 5 does not contradict sentence 4, but explains how the kitsch discussed in sentence 4 came into being.

Sentence 6 is closely related to sentence 5; it explains the name for the "junky art" discussed in sentence 5.

QUESTION 52

The author's chief purpose in writing this passage seems to be to
1 warn people against buying cheap antiques
2 describe a weakness of shoppers for antiques
3 define the word "kitsch"
4 criticize present-day art
5 persuade people to develop higher sales resistance

ANSWER EXPLAINED

The author has devoted the major part of the passage (sentences 1, 2, the first half of 3, and all of 4) to describing a weakness of shoppers for antiques.

WRONG CHOICES

1 is wrong because it states that the antiques discussed are cheap. The passage does not bear that out. On the contrary, sentence 2 discusses antiques for which the shopper is "apt to pay out good money."

3. The author defines "kitsch" only in sentence 6. In the rest of the passage, he describes a weakness of antique shoppers.

4. Nowhere in the passage does the author criticize present-day art.

5 is too general. The author's purpose is not to persuade people to develop sales resistance. This would mean that he wants them to resist buying anything and everything. His purpose is to persuade them to resist buying one thing in particular—junky art.

Passage C

With Apples

The last leaves are down, and the iron
Trunks, solitary, say they can stand there
Seven cold months without perceptible
Change.   But the green ground changes
5   Daily, so that Hallaway's old horses,
The brown one, the black one,
Nibble at next to nothing where the hoarfrost
Of hours ago gave way before the yellow and still blowing,
Blowing—some of them purple—leaves.
10   These move, head down, but listen:
Someone may be coming, even now, in the bright wind,
With apples.   I am coming.
Four pockets full, and extras on the hip.
Hi, there, Handsome Jerry!
15   Don't you know me, Slobbery Mack?

QUESTION 53

The phrase that best expresses the ideas of this poem is

1 iron trunks
2 green ground
3 welcome visitor
4 blowing leaves
5 secret rendezvous

[ɜ]

ANSWER EXPLAINED

The phrase that best expresses the ideas of this poem must be the one that is supported by more evidence than any of the four remaining phrases. Phrase 3, "welcome visitor," is supported by every line of the poem, as well as its title. The visitor, coming "with apples," is welcome because, as lines 1–9 show, there is very little growing for the horses to graze on. Therefore, as they nibble on "next to nothing," they listen for the coming of the visitor (lines 10–15) who is most welcome since he brings the horses a good supply of apples.

WRONG CHOICES

1, "iron trunks," is mentioned only in lines 1–4, and it is not the subject of this poem.

2, "green ground," though mentioned in line 4, is fast disappearing with the onset of winter. It cannot be the subject of this poem.

4, "blowing leaves," is just a descriptive detail in lines 8 and 9.

5, "secret rendezvous," is incorrect because the rendezvous (meeting) of the visitor with the horses is not secret. It takes place in the open.

QUESTION 54

We may most safely conclude from the passage that the narrator

1 is very rich
2 has always coveted the horses
3 has many friends
4 knows the horses
5 is visiting Hallaway

ANSWER EXPLAINED

From the fact that the narrator addresses the horses by their names, *Handsome Jerry* and *Slobbery Mack*, in lines 14 and 15, we may safely conclude that he knows them.

WRONG CHOICES

1, 2, 3, and 5 must be regarded as wrong conclusions because there is no specific evidence in the poem to support any of them.

QUESTION 55

The phrase "iron trunks" refers specifically to
1 the fence posts
2 the strength of nature
3 Hallaway's horses
4 the horse barns
5 the trees

ANSWER EXPLAINED

The opening words of the poem, "The last leaves are down," prove that the phrase "iron trunks," which follows, refers to the trees.

WRONG CHOICES

1, 2, 3, and 4 are incorrect choices because of the evidence in line 1.

QUESTION 56

The area in which Hallaway's horses are found most probably has been
1 recently plowed
2 thoroughly grazed
3 converted to new crops
4 hit by drought
5 abandoned for years

ANSWER EXPLAINED

To *graze* is to "feed on growing grass." Lines 4–8 show that with the approach of winter there is "next to nothing" for the horses to nibble at. Line 10 shows the horses continuing in the position of grazing, moving "head down." Together, these lines suggest that the horses have consumed practically everything still growing and that the area is thoroughly grazed.

WRONG CHOICES

1 and 3 are incorrect because they entail man-made changes. The passage shows in lines 1–5 that the changes in the area are being gradually produced by nature.

4 is wrong. The changes to the area are the result of a change in season rather than drought.

5 is not supported by any reference at all.

QUESTION 57

From the passage we can most safely conclude that the horses
1 are housed in a cold stable
2 have been put out to pasture
3 are lost in the leafy woods
4 have been abandoned
5 are trying to escape

$$[2]$$

ANSWER EXPLAINED

The references to nibbling in line 7 and to moving head down in line 10 permit us to conclude that the horses have been put out to pasture (graze).

WRONG CHOICES

1. The passage offers no clue as to where the horses are housed.
3 and 5. The horses are not lost or trying to escape. They are grazing in an apparently familiar area
4. Since they are referred to as "Hallaway's old horses" (line 5), they apparently have not been abandoned.

QUESTION 58

In line 10, "These" refers to the
1 old horses
2 blowing leaves
3 cold months
4 passing hours
5 passers-by

$$[1]$$

ANSWER EXPLAINED

"These" refers to the old horses, as shown by line 10: "These move, head down..." The antecedent of "These" is "Hallaway's old horses" in line 5. The head-down movement is characteristic of grazing horses.

WRONG CHOICES

Neither 2, 3, nor 4 can "move head down." 5 is wrong because there is no mention of passers-by.

QUESTION 59

In line 11, "Someone" is most probably

1 Hallaway
2 a casual passer-by
3 a sympathetic person

4 a stranger
5 Handsome Jerry

$$\left[\,3\,\right]$$

ANSWER EXPLAINED

The "Someone" in line 11 is probably a sympathetic person because he is coming "With apples . . . Four pockets full, and extras on the hip" (lines 12 and 13) for the hungry horses.

WRONG CHOICES

1. There is no mention of Hallaway except as the owner of the horses (line 5). The one who is coming, described as "Someone" (line 11) and "I" (line 12), is clearly the narrator, not Hallaway.

2. The "Someone" is no casual (chance) passer-by, but a person acquainted with the plight of the horses who is making a planned trip with relief supplies of apples.

4. The fact that the "Someone" addresses the horses by their names (lines 14 and 15) shows he is no stranger.

5. Handsome Jerry, being one of the horses, would not be "coming . . . with apples" (lines 11–12).

QUESTION 60

From this poem we gain the *least* information about

1 Hallaway's horses
2 the weather
3 the leaves

4 Hallaway
5 the land

$$\left[\,4\,\right]$$

ANSWER EXPLAINED

About Hallaway the passage tells nothing, except that he owns the horses (line 5).

WRONG CHOICES

1. Hallaway's horses are the main topic of lines 5–15.

2. Information about the weather appears in lines 1–9 and in line 11.

3. The leaves are described in line 1 and again in lines 8 and 9.

5. The land is described in lines 1, 4–5, and 7–8.

SELECTING THE PHRASE THAT BEST EXPRESSES THE IDEAS OF A PASSAGE

One of the commonest reading comprehension questions is that which asks you to select the phrase that best expresses the ideas of a passage. For the correct answer, you must read the passage through more than once —several readings are often necessary—to follow the thought, sentence by sentence.

You will have little trouble choosing the correct phrase if you remember this principle: THE PHRASE THAT BEST EXPRESSES THE IDEAS OF A PASSAGE IS THE ONE THAT IS SUPPORTED BY MORE EVIDENCE FROM THE PASSAGE THAN ANY OF THE OTHER SUGGESTED PHRASES.

What you have to do, then, is to *measure* the amount of support in the passage for each of the five suggested phrases. To help you do this, use a practical approach that has proved very successful; we call it the "yardstick" method.

USING THE "YARDSTICK" METHOD

To show you how to use this measuring device, let us apply it to Question 47 of Passage B (reprinted below) from our Typical Reading Comprehension Test, pages 96–97.

Passage B

(1) If you have ever passed an hour wandering through an antique shop (not looking for anything exactly, but simply looking), you must have noticed how your taste gradually grows numb, and then—if you stay—becomes perverted. (2) You begin to conjure up charm in those hideous pictures of plump girls fondling pigeons, you develop a psychopathic desire for spinning wheels and cobblers' benches, you are apt to pay out good money for a bronze statuette of Otto von Bismarck, with a metal hand inside a metal frock coat and metal pouches under his metallic eyes. (3) As soon as you take the things home, you realize that they are revolting. (4) And yet they have a sort of horrible authority; you don't like them; you know how awful they are; but it is a tremendous effort to drop them in the garbage, where they belong. (5) The nineteenth century produced an appalling amount of junky art like this, and sometimes I imagine that clandestine underground factories are continuing to pour it out like illicit drugs. (6) There is a name for such stuff in the trade, a word apparently of Russian origin, "kitsch": it means vulgar showoff, and it is applied to anything that took a lot of trouble to make and is quite hideous.

QUESTION 47

The phrase that best expresses the ideas of this passage is

1 the fascination of kitsch
2 looking for 20th-century antiques
3 how to buy a bronze statuette
4 the illicit drugs
5 hidden charms in 19th-century art

PASSAGE B ANALYZED

(1) If you have ever passed an hour wandering through an antique shop (not looking for anything exactly, but simply looking), you must have noticed how your taste gradually grows numb, and then—if you stay—becomes perverted.

Tells how shopper's artistic taste is perverted; supports phrase 1. Not phrase 2, since the shopper is not looking for anything exactly.

(2) You begin to conjure up charm in those hideous pictures of plump girls fondling pigeons, you develop a psychopathic desire for spinning wheels and cobblers' benches, you are apt to pay out good money for a bronze statuette of Otto von Bismarck, with a metal hand inside a metal frock coat and metal pouches under his metallic eyes.

Shows shopper's fascination with phony art called "kitsch" later in the passage; supports phrase 1. Also, possibly, phrase 3 because it shows how shopper may buy a particular bronze statuette. Not phrase 5 because the charms are not hidden but imagined by the shopper.

(3) As soon as you take the things home, you realize that they are revolting.

Proves shopper was fascinated by junk; supports phrase 1.

(4) And yet they have a sort of terrible authority; you don't like them; you know how awful they are; but it is a tremendous effort to drop them in the garbage, where they belong.

Shows shopper under spell of the trash he has bought; supports phrase 1. Not phrase 5 because it is about garbage, not art.

(5) The nineteenth century produced an appalling amount of junky art like this, and sometimes I imagine that clandestine underground factories are continuing to pour it out like illicit drugs.

Implies such junky art has fascination, since so much of it was produced; supports phrase 1. Not phrase 5 because junky art is not art.

(6) There is a name for such stuff in the trade, a word apparently of Russian origin, "kitsch": it means vulgar showoff, and it is applied to anything that took a lot of trouble to make and is quite hideous.

Describes origin of the term "kitsch," and the vulgar fascination of the stuff it is applied to; supports phrase 1.

ANSWER

The above analysis shows that the amount of support for each of the phrases is as follows:

1 (the fascination of kitsch) .... 17 lines

2 (looking for 20th-century antiques) .... 0 lines

3 (how to buy a bronze statuette) .... 2 lines

4 (the illicit drugs) .... 0 lines

5 (hidden charms in 19th-century art) .... 0 lines

Phrase 1, obviously, best expresses the ideas of this passage because it is supported by more lines from the passage than any of the other four phrases.

VERIFYING THE ANSWER: "DOUBLE CHECKS"

As with all problems, you should verify your choice for the best phrase by applying as many "double checks" as possible. Here are a few suggestions:

a. Check the thought of the topic and concluding sentences with the thought of the selected phrase.

Example: In the passage just analyzed, the topic sentence shows how one's artistic taste becomes perverted as he wanders through an antique shop. The closing sentence deals with the origin of the term "kitsch" and the vulgar fascination of such stuff. Both of these key sentences support phrase 1 (the fascination of kitsch).

b. Check to see that the selected phrase is not too broad for the passage.

c. Check to see that the selected phrase is not too narrow for the passage.

d. Use the process of elimination. Don't settle for your selected answer until you have carefully considered and eliminated every alternate answer.

MORE TEST PASSAGES ANALYZED

Below are detailed model answers for some additional test passages. You will find questions of the types just discussed, plus a few other types.

Passage D

(1) American women have been maneuvered back into the kitchen. (2) The evidence is unmistakable: a flurry of specialized cookbooks, a kaleidoscope of luscious food pages in magazines, and, even in the most ordinary kitchen, mingled odors of garlic, sesame and coriander.

(3) The situation is more insidious than it appears. (4) In many communities homemade mayonnaise has more feminine prestige than mink, and the zealous housewife can lose face finally and terribly by leaving the eel out of the bouillabaisse. (5) Cooking has become roughly competitive.

(6) Perversely, this is happening in an era when kitchens are entering the pushbutton stage; foods are premixed, prebreaded, prefried—everything but predigested, and the meat-tenderizer people are working on *that* goal.

(7) One rather pat sociological explanation is that the direct expenditure of money on food is no longer impressive. (8) Time is now the valued commodity, and frequently the modern cook lavishes hours and effort, rather than vulgar old money, in order to hold up her head.

*QUESTION

The title below that best expresses the ideas of this passage is:

1 The importance of foreign foods   4 Precooked foods
2 New savings through cooking   5 The new interest in cooking
3 Time versus money

$$\boxed{5}$$

ANSWER EXPLAINED

Every sentence in the passage deals with title 5 (The new interest in cooking).

WRONG CHOICES

1 and 2 are not discussed in the passage.

3 is discussed in sentence 8, *but only in relation to the new interest in cooking.*

4 is suggested only in sentence 6.

---

* To find a *"title* that best expresses the ideas" of a passage, use exactly the same method we have used to find a *"phrase* that best expresses the thought" of a passage.

QUESTION

The author implies that American women have gone back to the kitchen as a result of (1) their desire to please their husbands (2) the new conveniences for cooking (3) their study of sociology (4) their desire to keep up with their neighbors (5) their interest in spices

$$[\cancel{4}]$$

ANSWER EXPLAINED

The following statements support 4 as the correct answer:
(S4) "mayonnaise has more feminine *prestige* than mink" and "the zealous housewife can *lose face*"
(S5) "Cooking has become roughly *competitive.*"
(S8) "the modern cook lavishes hours and effort, rather than vulgar old money, in order to *hold up her head*"

WRONG CHOICES

1 and 3 are not discussed in the passage.
2—"Perversely" in S6 tells us that American women have gone back to the kitchen *in spite of* (not as a result of) the new conveniences for cooking.
5—S2 tells us that American women are using spices—not that they have returned to the kitchen because of their interest in them.

QUESTION

The tone of the passage indicates that the attitude of the author toward his subject is one of (1) amusement (2) indifference (3) reverence (4) severe criticism (5) outspoken defense

$$[\checkmark]$$

ANSWER EXPLAINED

The author's use of words clearly indicates that he is having fun with his subject.
(S1) By "maneuvered back," he jokingly discusses the return of American women to the kitchen as if it were a military setback.
(S4) His comparison of two such widely different things as "mayonnaise" and "mink" is obviously comic. So, too, is "the zealous housewife can lose face finally and terribly by leaving the eel out of the bouillabaisse."

(S6) He pokes fun at modern food processing: "foods are premixed, prebreaded, prefried—everything but predigested, and the meat-tenderizer people are working on *that* goal."

(S8) "vulgar old money" is further proof that the attitude of the author toward his subject is one of amusement.

WRONG CHOICES

2, 3, 4, and 5 are not supported by the passage.

QUESTION

The author of this passage makes the point that in many communities (1) people are spending too little money on food   (2) "pushbutton" kitchens are undesirable   (3) people are using meat tenderizers for purposes other than that for which they were intended   (4) mink coats are no longer such an important measure of social prestige   (5) the modern cook values her time too much to spend needless hours in the kitchen

ANSWER EXPLAINED

The following statement in S4 supports 4 as the correct answer: "In many communities homemade mayonnaise has more feminine prestige than mink."

WRONG CHOICES

1, 2, 3, and 5 are not stated in the passage.

Passage E

(1) Nevertheless, there is such a voluble hue and cry about the abysmal state of culture in the United States by well-meaning, sincere critics that I would like to present some evidence to the contrary.   (2) One is tempted to remind these critics that no country has ever achieved the complete integration of *haute culture* into the warp and woof of its everyday life. (3) In the wishful memories of those who moon over the passed glories of Shakespeare's England, it is seldom called to mind that bearbaiting was far more popular than any of Master Shakespeare's presentations.   (4) Who cares to remember that the same Rome that found a Juvenal proclaiming *mens sana in corpore sano* could also watch an Emperor Trajan celebrate his victory over Decebalus of Dacia in 106 A.D. with no fewer than 5,000 pairs of gladiators matched to the death?   (5) And this in the name of amusement!

QUESTION

The title that best expresses the ideas of this passage is:
1 The hue and cry of the critics
2 Reflections on culture
3 Dangers in contemporary criticism
4 The world's amusements
5 Everyday life

$$[2]$$

ANSWER EXPLAINED

Every sentence in the passage contains a *reflection on culture.*

S1 refers to a reflection on culture in the United States with which the author disagrees.

S2 is the author's reflection on culture in general in past history.

S3 is his reflection on the culture of England in Shakespeare's time.

S4 and S5 are his reflection on the culture of Rome in Juvenal's time.

WRONG CHOICES

1, 3, 4, and 5 are too general and fail to "cover" enough of the passage.

1 does not say what the "hue and cry" is about. It is very vague.

3 —The passage deals with the specific topic of culture—not with the general area of contemporary criticism. S1 points out an error (not a danger) in contemporary criticism.

4 —We cannot, on the basis of the two amusements discussed (bear-baiting in S3 and gladiatorial combats in S4), say that this passage deals with the entire world's amusements.

5 is too general. The passage deals specifically with *reflections on culture* of everyday life.

QUESTION

The paragraph preceding this passage most probably discussed (1) the increased interest of Americans in public affairs (2) the popularity of Shakespeare during his lifetime (3) the interest of Americans in the arts (4) the duties of a literary critic (5) Juvenal's contributions to poetry

$$[3]$$

ANSWER EXPLAINED

The introductory word "Nevertheless" (S1) tells us that the preceding paragraph most probably discussed a topic which is the opposite of "the abysmal state of culture in the United States" (S1). Of the five choices offered, the only "opposite" one is 3 (*the interest of Americans in the arts*).

WRONG CHOICES

1, 2, 4, and 5 are all wrong answers because they are not "opposites" of "the abysmal state of culture in the United States."

QUESTION

According to the passage, those who criticize the level of culture in America are (1) amusing (2) outspoken (3) unappreciated (4) sarcastic (5) popular

[2]

ANSWER EXPLAINED

In S1, *voluble* (meaning "characterized by ease and smoothness of utterance") and *hue and cry* (meaning "shouts of protest") prove that those who criticize the level of culture in America are *outspoken*, choice 2.

WRONG CHOICES

1, 3, 4, and 5 are not supported by the passage.

QUESTION

The author's attitude toward culture is essentially (1) despairing (2) realistic (3) distorted (4) uncritical (5) childish

[2]

ANSWER EXPLAINED

Unlike the critics (S1), the author feels that no nation can be completely cultured. He proves this by showing how, in the past, highly cultured people like Shakespeare and Juvenal lived with deplorably uncultured contemporaries (S3 and S4). The author's attitude, based on the lessons of history, is therefore *realistic*, answer 2.

WRONG CHOICES

1, 3, 4, and 5 are not supported by the passage.

QUESTION

One can conclude from the passage that   (1) the masses instinctively recognize artistic achievement   (2) the popularity of culture depends on economic factors   (3) human nature has not changed too much over the years   (4) "a sound mind in a sound body" ought to be America's educational goal   (5) Americans do not appreciate intelligence

$$[3]$$

ANSWER EXPLAINED

Some human beings in the past were so depraved as to be able to enjoy bearbaiting (S3) and gladiatorial fights to the death (S4). Some humans today lack culture, too, as hinted by "the abysmal state of culture in the United States" (S1). From these circumstances one can conclude that *human nature has not changed too much over the years,* choice 3.

WRONG CHOICES

1, 2, 4, and 5 are not supported by the passage.

Passage F

(1) There is controversy and misunderstanding about the proper functions of juvenile courts and their probation departments.   (2) There are cries that the whole process produces delinquents rather than rehabilitates them. (3) There are speeches by the score about "getting tough" with the kids. (4) Another large group thinks we should be more understanding and gentle with delinquents.   (5) This distrust of the services offered can be attributed in large part to the confusion in the use of these services throughout the country.

(6) On the one hand, the juvenile courts are tied to the criminal court system, with an obligation to decide guilt and innocence for offenses specifically stated and formally charged.   (7) On the other, they have the obligation to provide treatment, supervision and guidance to youngsters in trouble, without respect to the crimes of which they are accused.   (8) These two conflicting assignments must be carried out—quite properly— in an informal, private way, which will not stigmatize a youngster during his formative years.

(9) And, as the courts' preoccupation with the latter task has increased, the former (that of dispensing justice) has retreated, with the result that grave injustices are bound to occur.

QUESTION

The title below that best expresses the ideas of this passage is:

1 Grave injustices
2 A problem for today's teenagers
3 Rehabilitating youthful criminals
4 Fitting the punishment to the crime
5 Justice for juvenile offenders

$$[5]$$

ANSWER EXPLAINED

Every sentence in the passage deals with some aspect of 5.

WRONG CHOICES

1 is too general. An improvement would be "Grave injustices against juvenile offenders," but even this more specific title can be supported only by S2 and the end of S9.

2 —The passage deals with a problem for society as a whole—not just for today's teenagers. Besides, the passage does not deal in general with teenagers, but more specifically with: delinquents (S2 and S4), youngsters formally charged with crimes (S6), youngsters in trouble (S7), etc.

3 is only one of the main topics in the passage. Another important one is judging the guilt or innocence of accused youngsters. A title like 5, which combines both of these topics, would be much better.

4 is too general. An improvement would be "Fitting the punishment to the crime for juvenile offenders." But this more specific title would still not "cover" the topic of rehabilitation, which gets major attention in the passage (S2, 7, 8, and 9).

QUESTION

The author contends that public distrust of juvenile courts is primarily the result of (1) resentment on the part of those convicted by them (2) the dual function of these courts   (3) lack of a sufficient number of probation officers   (4) injustices done by the courts   (5) the cost of keeping up the courts

$$[2]$$

ANSWER EXPLAINED

In S5 the author states: "This distrust of the services offered (by the juvenile courts) can be attributed in large part (primarily) to the confusion in the use of these services. . . ." In S6, 7, and 8, he indicates that the confusion is the result of *"two* (dual) conflicting assignments" (functions) of these courts: "to decide guilt and innocence" (S6), and "to provide treatment, supervision and guidance" (S7). The evidence in S5–8 clearly establishes 2 as the correct answer.

WRONG CHOICES

The passage does not indicate that public distrust of the juvenile courts is primarily the result of 1, 3, 4, or 5.

QUESTION

The passage suggests that the author   (1) is familiar with the problem   (2) is impatient with justice   (3) sides with those who favor leniency for juvenile offenders   (4) regards all offenses as equally important   (5) favors maximum sentences at all times

$$[\checkmark]$$

ANSWER EXPLAINED

S2, 3, and 4 indicate that the author is acquainted with three points of view in the controversy over the proper functioning of the juvenile courts. S5, 6, 7, and 8 show that he knows the reasons for the misunderstanding and distrust of the courts; they also show that he knows how the courts should function. S9 implies that he has studied the juvenile courts over a period of time. The passage as a whole, therefore, strongly suggests that the author *is familiar with the problem,* answer 1.

WRONG CHOICES

2, 3, 4, and 5 are not supported by the passage.

QUESTION

The tone of this passage is   (1) highly emotional   (2) highly personal   (3) optimistic   (4) calm   (5) sarcastic

$$[\checkmark]$$

ANSWER EXPLAINED

The author believes neither in "getting tough" (S3) nor in being "more understanding and gentle with delinquents" (S4). He neither attacks nor distrusts the courts; he tries to understand them. Instead of finding fault, he is more interested in arriving at a solution of the problem, as S8 shows. The tone of this passage may therefore properly be described as 4, *calm.*

1 may describe the attitude of those who hold the beliefs expressed in S2 and S3. It certainly does not describe the author's attitude, nor the tone of the passage as a whole.

2 —Nowhere in the passage does the author use *I, me, my, myself,* etc., or say anything of a personal nature.

3 —The passage does not indicate that a solution to the problem will surely be found or that it will be easy.

5 is not supported by the passage.

Passage G

(1) The economic struggle in America continues; but it seems apparent that the struggle is no longer between the giant segments of our society, but within them. (2) Battles for power and control are being fought within some of the large corporations, enlivened by wars in which the big prizes are stockholders' votes or proxies. (3) Similarly, struggles for power are taking place within the large labor organizations. (4) In each case public opinion seems to be playing an increasingly important part, judging by the dramatic efforts being made to inform the people about the partisan positions. (5) And so long as the battleground involves public favor, moderation seems neither implausible nor unnatural.

QUESTION

The title below that best expresses the ideas of this passage is:
1 The people in power
2 A compromise in disputes between labor and capital
3 The importance of votes and proxies
4 Public influence in internal industrial conflicts
5 The need for moderation in economic disputes

ANSWER EXPLAINED

S1–3 describe "internal industrial conflicts." S4 and S5 tell of "public influence" in these conflicts.

1 and 2 are not discussed in the passage.

3 deals with a very small part of the passage—the end of S2.

5 —The passage mentions "moderation" (S5) but says nothing about the *need* for it.

QUESTION

According to this passage, the economic struggle in America is currently (1) between government and industry (2) between capital and labor (3) within both capital and labor (4) between large and small corporations (5) among stockholders and workers

$$[3]$$

ANSWER EXPLAINED

S2 discusses struggles within capital. S3 discusses struggles within labor.

WRONG CHOICES

1, 2, 4, and 5 are not discussed.

QUESTION

As used in this passage, the word "partisan" (line 9) means (1) revolutionary (2) important (3) unfavorable (4) unusual (5) opposing

$$[5]$$

ANSWER EXPLAINED

Even if you do not know the meaning of "partisan," the passage compels you to choose *opposing*. The words "economic struggle" (S1), "Battles for power and control" (S2), and "struggles for power" (S3) imply that opposing sides are present. S4 indicates that each opposing side is informing the public of its position in an effort to win public support. "Partisan" positions must therefore mean 5, *opposing* positions.

WRONG CHOICES

1, 2, 3, and 4 are not supported by the passage, and they are not synonyms for "partisan."

FORMER REGENTS READING COMPREHENSION TESTS

Directions (41–60): Below each of the following passages, there are one or more incomplete statements or questions about the passage. For each, select the word or expression that best completes the statement or answers the question *in accordance with the meaning of the passage,* and write its *number* in the space provided on the separate answer sheet.   [20]

TEST 1

Passage A

On June 17, 1744, the commissioners from Maryland and Virginia nego-
tiated a treaty with the Indians of the Six Nations at Lancaster, Pennsylvania. The Indians were invited to send boys to William and Mary College.
In a letter the next day they declined the offer as follows:

We know that you highly esteem the kind of learning taught in those
Colleges, and that the Maintenance of our young Men, while with you,
would be very expensive to you. We are convinced that you mean to do us
Good by your Proposal; and we thank you heartily. But you, who are wise,
must know that different Nations have different Conceptions of things, and
you will therefore not take it amiss if our Ideas of this kind of Education
happen not to be the same as yours. We have had some Experience of it.
Several of our young People were formerly brought up at the Colleges of
the Northern Provinces: they were instructed in all your Sciences; but, when
they came back to us, they were bad Runners, ignorant of every means of
living in the woods . . . neither fit for Hunters, Warriors, nor Counselors,
they were totally good for nothing.

We are, however, not the less oblig'd by your kind Offer, tho' we decline
accepting it; and, to show our grateful Sense of it, if the Gentlemen of
Virginia will send us a Dozen of their Sons, we will take Care of their Education, instruct them in all we know, and make Men of them.

41. Which phrase best expresses the main idea of this passage?   (1) implications of the treaty of 1744   (2) a review of the Colleges of the
Northern Provinces   (3) the values of the Indians of the Six Nations
(4) the importance of the commissioners of Maryland and Virginia
(5) the significance of William and Mary College
42. The Indians' chief purpose in writing the letter seems to be to   (1)
politely refuse a friendly gesture   (2) express their opinions on
equality   (3) please the intended reader   (4) describe Indian
customs   (5) ask for money to start a new school
43. The Indians who are responsible for the letter would probably agree
that they   (1) have no right to deny Indian boys the opportunity
for schooling   (2) are being insulted by the offer of the commissioners   (3) know more about the various branches of science than
the commissioners do   (4) have a better way of educating young
men than the commissioners do   (5) should not offer to educate the
sons of the Gentlemen of Virginia
44. According to this passage, the Indians' idea of education differs from
that of the Gentlemen of Virginia in that the Indians   (1) also be-

lieve in educating young women   (2) have different goals   (3) teach different branches of science   (4) include different aspects of nature   (5) speak a different language
45. The tone of the letter as a whole is best described as   (1) angry   (2) demanding   (3) joyous   (4) inquiring   (5) courteous

Passage B

We should also know that "greed" has little to do with the environmental crisis. The two main causes are population pressures, especially the pressures of large metropolitan populations, and the desire—a highly commendable one—to bring a decent living at the lowest possible cost to the largest possible number of people.

The environmental crisis is the result of success—success in cutting down the mortality of infants (which has given us the population explosion), success in raising farm output sufficiently to prevent mass famine (which has given us contamination by pesticides and chemical fertilizers), success in getting people out of the noisome tenements of the 19th-century city and into the greenery and privacy of the single-family home in the suburbs (which has given us urban sprawl and traffic jams). The environmental crisis, in other words, is largely the result of doing too much of the right sort of thing.

To overcome the problems that success always creates, one must build on it. But where to start? Cleaning up the environment requires determined, sustained effort with clear targets and deadlines. It requires, above all, concentration of effort. Up to now we have tried to do a little bit of everything—and tried to do it in the headlines—when what we ought to do first is draw up a list of priorities.

46. This passage assumes the desirability of   (1) using atomic energy to conserve fuel   (2) living in comfortable family lifestyles   (3) settling disputes peacefully   (4) combating cancer and heart disease with energetic research   (5) having greater government involvement in people's daily lives
47. According to this passage, one early step in any effort to improve the environment would be to   (1) return to the exclusive use of natural fertilizers   (2) put a high tax on profiteering industries   (3) ban the use of automobiles in and around cities   (4) study successful efforts in other countries   (5) set up a timetable for corrective actions
48. The passage indicates that the conditions that led to overcrowded roads also brought about   (1) more attractive living conditions for many people   (2) a healthier younger generation   (3) greater occupational opportunities   (4) the population explosion   (5) greater concentration of population pressures

49. The author criticizes those concerned with the environment for (1) attacking the establishment   (2) trying to limit population growth (3) opposing farm price supports   (4) trying to do everything through headlines   (5) proposing that people leave metropolitan centers

50. One support for the author's claim that success has contributed to environmental problems is that   (1) pesticides have been used to reduce infant mortality   (2) doing too much of the right thing has helped only certain people   (3) in escaping from crowded cities, people have caused urban sprawl   (4) greed has caused technological advances (5) fertilizers have helped farmers to earn higher incomes

51. According to this passage, one error environmentalists have made is to   (1) plan too complicated strategies   (2) forget that poorer crops may cause starvation   (3) overlook the welfare of the majority   (4) reduce farm output   (5) wage the battle on too many fronts at the same time

52. It could logically be assumed that the author of this passage would support legislation to   (1) ban the use of all pesticides   (2) prevent the use of automobiles in the cities   (3) build additional conventional power plants immediately   (4) organize an agency to coordinate efforts to cope with environmental problems   (5) restrict the press coverage of protests led by environmental groups

53. According to this passage, the effort to improve the environment will require   (1) a number of years to complete   (2) a lowering of the living standards of most people   (3) the elimination of motor traffic in cities   (4) many sacrifices on the part of the well-to-do (5) some censorship of news coverage of the topic

Passage C

Black Music Man

As a Masai warrior
With his Burning Spear
Blessed by the Gods
The epitome of man
5 BLACK MUSIC MAN
In smoke-filled cafes
The sound of your golden horn calls
to me
You blow, sad, sorrowful, and blue
10 But cannot know
That my throat pains

As sound bursts forth
Your mournful prose you offer to me
Yet, you cannot feel
15 My heart as it dies
You cry
But do not see
That tears fall from my eyes
You think that all is lost
20 You rip away your soul
And fling it naked to the world
And I stand bleeding
But you do not look
Then you stop
25 (when the soul is torn away the body lives no more)
You walk the streets
Cold, quiet, alone
Never once do you turn
Never once do you know
30 That behind you I walk
And in my arms
I carry your soul

54. The speaker in this poem is most likely   (1) a relative of the musician
(2) a person with a strong feeling for the musician   (3) an observer
of culture and society   (4) an unconcerned customer of the cafe
(5) an unemployed musician
55. The reaction the speaker has to the musician's music is one of
(1) pain   (2) fear   (3) hope   (4) joy   (5) hatred
56. The Masai warrior is to the Black Music Man as the weapon is to
(1) blood   (2) an omen   (3) the sun   (4) an instrument
(5) a religious symbol
57. The reaction of the music man to the speaker is one of   (1) concern   (2) love   (3) contentment   (4) dissatisfaction   (5)
indifference
58. In line 13, "mournful prose" refers to   (1) employment   (2) finances
(3) lyrics   (4) conversation   (5) emotion
59. Lines 28-32 suggest that, at the end of the poem, the speaker's mood is
one of   (1) disgust   (2) success   (3) frustration   (4) superiority   (5) bliss
60. The last line suggests that the speaker   (1) has been accepted by the
music man   (2) is carrying the music man's instrument   (3) is no
longer concerned about the music man   (4) still loves and respects
the music man   (5) steals the music man's soul or love

TEST 2

Passage A

Water is necessary to us, but a waterfall is not. Where it is to be found, it is something extra, a beautiful ornament. We need daylight and to that extent it is utilitarian, but moonlight we do not need. When it comes, it serves no necessity. It transforms. It falls upon the banks
5 and the grass, separating one long blade from another; turning a drift of brown, frosted leaves from a single heap to innumerable flashing fragments; or glimmering lengthways along wet twigs as though light itself were ductile. Its long beams pour, white and sharp, between the trunks of trees, their clarity fading as they recede into the powdery,
10 misty distance of beech woods at night. In moonlight, two acres of coarse bent grass, undulant and ankle deep, tumbled and rough as a horse's mane, appear like a bay of waves, all shadowy troughs and hollows. The growth is so thick and matted that even the wind does not move it, but it is the moonlight that seems to confer stillness upon it.
15 We do not take moonlight for granted. It is like snow, or like the dew on a July morning. It does not reveal but changes what it covers. And its low intensity—so much lower than that of daylight—makes us conscious that it is something added to the down, to give it, for only a little time, a singular and marvelous quality that we should admire while we
20 can, for soon it will be gone again.

41. The feeling established in the passage is one of   (1) suspense
    (2) liveliness   (3) admiration   (4) joy
42. In lines 6-7, the use of the words "innumerable flashing fragments" pro-
    vides a   (1) calm and tranquil description of the beams   (2)
    lively vision of a pile of moonlit leaves   (3) precise picture of
    meadow grass   (4) detailed image of the wet twigs in moonlight
43. Which statement best explains lines 9-10, "their clarity fading as they
    recede into the powdery, misty distance of beech woods . . ."?   (1)
    The moon is rising too high in the sky.   (2) The clouds are passing
    over and hiding the moon.   (3) The undergrowth causes the beams
    to disappear.   (4) The distance erases the sharpness of each beam.
44. As used in line 12, the words "like a bay of waves" describe the   (1)
    grass   (2) horse's mane   (3) water   (4) moonbeams
45. Which statement best expresses the main idea of this passage?   (1)
    Many things are useful and therefore beautiful.   (2) Water and light
    are necessary to life.   (3) One can discover a foreign world after
    dark.   (4) The beauty of moonlight should be appreciated.
46. Which statement best rephrases the author's description "a singular
    and marvelous quality that we should admire while we can" (lines 19-

20)?   (1) Moonlight is beautiful and shortlived.   (2) Night provides the Earth with a marvelous quality.   (3) Daylight reveals beauty far better than moonlight does.   (4) Dew changes the appearance of whatever it covers.

47. Which idea appears first in the passage? (1) Moonlight transforms. (2) Moonlight confers stillness.   (3) Moonlight is unnecessary. (4) Moonlight has a singular quality.

Passage B

The bonsai tree
in the attractive pot
could have grown eighty feet tall
on the side of a mountain
5 till split by lightning.
But a gardener
carefully pruned it.
It is nine inches high.
Every day as he
10 whittles back the branches
the gardener croons,
It is your nature
to be small and cozy,
domestic and weak;
15 how lucky, little tree,
to have a pot to grow in.
With living creatures
one must begin very early
to dwarf their growth:
20 the bound feet,
the crippled brain,
the hair in curlers,
the hands you
love to touch.

48. Judging from the poem, which would the poet prize most highly? (1) cheerfulness (2) honesty   (3) faithfulness   (4) individuality
49. In which line does the poet change the subject of the poem?   (1) "Every day as he" (line 9)   (2) "It is your nature" (line 12)   (3) "how lucky, little tree" (line 15)   (4) "With living creatures" (line 17)
50. In relation to the overall meaning of the poem, lines 15 and 16 are meant to be   (1) cynical   (2) ironic   (3) humorous   (4) predictable

51. Lines 12-14, "It is your nature to be small and cozy, domestic and weak" apply to the bonsai tree, and through implication in lines 20-24 to (1) women   (2) the gardener   (3) dwarfs   (4) all trees
52. Which statement about the bonsai tree is made in the poem?   (1) It is frightened by the gardener.   (2) It was split by lightning. (3) It grows in an attractive pot.   (4) It has a crippled brain.
53. In lines 17-24, the poet most probably means that   (1) young people need more direct guidance   (2) society limits the development of females through early training   (3) living creatures need to be pruned and whittled back   (4) growing up in the world is like being planted in an attractive pot

Passage C

We might as well accept it as a fact that our present mode of living, with its intricate technical aspects, requires a correspondingly intricate organization. It would be foolish to talk of turning this clock back or slowing its pendulum to the tempo of Walden Pond. Corporations and
5 labor unions have conferred great benefits upon their employees and members as well as upon the general public. But if a power becomes too concentrated in a corporation or a union and its members are coerced into submission, or if either assumes and selfishly exploits a monopolistic position regardless of the public interest, the public safeguards of
10 individual freedom are weakened. Tyranny is tyranny, no matter who practices it; corruption is corruption. If citizens get used to these things and condone them in their private affairs, they school themselves to accept and condone them in public affairs.

But it is not so much these more flagrant (and less frequent) trans-
15 gressions as it is the everyday organizational way of life that threatens individual freedom. For the obvious transgressions there are obvious remedies at law. But what shall we say about the endless sterile conferences held in substitution for individual inventiveness; the public opinion polls whose vogue threatens even our moral and aesthetic
20 values with the pernicious doctrine that the customer is always right; the unctuous public relations counsels that rob us of both our courage and our convictions? This continuous, daily deferral of opinion and judgment to someone else becomes a habit. The undeveloped negative remains a negative. It conjures a nightmare picture of a whole nation
25 of yes-men, of hitchhikers and eavesdroppers, tiptoeing backwards offstage with their fingers to their lips—this, the nation whose prophets once cried "Trust thyself!"

54. As used in line 8, the word "either" refers to   (1) tyranny or corruption   (2) a corporation or a union   (3) the public interest or a power   (4) turning the clock back or slowing the pendulum

55. Which does the author regard as unchangeable?   (1) the complexity of modern life   (2) public interest   (3) the integrity of our traditions   (4) the deterioration of public morality
56. As used in line 16, the word "transgressions" most nearly means   (1) institutions   (2) criminals   (3) crimes   (4) freedoms
57. The author suggests that in people's everyday lives, they should   (1) join worthwhile organizations   (2) treat their rivals with contempt   (3) improve their knowledge of world affairs   (4) respect their own views
58. As used in line 24, the word "conjures" most nearly means   (1) contradicts   (2) judges   (3) presents   (4) questions
59. The last two sentences of the passage suggest that people   (1) value their right to disagree   (2) are becoming conformists   (3) are overwhelmed by helpful opinions   (4) resent the actions of those who disagree with them
60. The author's main purpose in writing this passage seems to be to   (1) arouse the public to action   (2) praise a previous way of life   (3) show the function of law in modern society   (4) explain the intricacies of modern life

TEST 3

Passage A

When a new musical runs into trouble on the road you can generally predict what it's going to look like in town. The "book" will nearly have vanished. Musical comedy "books" are everybody's trouble, and the first thing to do with the dialogue when it shows signs of making the customers wish they'd stayed home to read is to dump it. A narrative can always be reduced to a few simple statements of passion, with chords from the orchestra pit throbbing beneath them to supply what language has left out, and once the statements have been made the orchestra can take over altogether. Now four new songs are rushed in for the star. Because the star will get laryngitis no matter how many songs he or she has, four more won't make matters much worse. And wherever a certain slackness continues to be felt, the choreographer can be called upon to stage one more relay race. The show shall have music wherever it goes, and dancing will make it go faster. The results, by the way, may be good or bad depending upon the natural character of the entertainment; a show that means to be no more than a lively pastime may very well profit from the radical, realistic surgery.

41. Most frequently the problem which a new musical faces is the   (1) financial backing   (2) demands of unions   (3) star   (4) "book"   (5) uncooperativeness of personnel

42. According to the passage, which factor forces the changes in a musical? (1) a whim of the producer   (2) the temperamental behavior of the star   (3) the reaction of tryout audiences   (4) the brilliant work of the choreographer   (5) the poor music
43. In the passage, those who make the changes in a musical are shown to be   (1) inexperienced   (2) resourceful   (3) lazy   (4) trusting   (5) patriotic
44. According to the passage, which factor, in the final analysis, largely determines whether a show will succeed?   (1) its basic appeal   (2) its star   (3) its financial backing   (4) its reception by the critics   (5) the combination of the star and the orchestra
45. The passage as a whole suggests that making changes in a musical is (1) unnecessary   (2) hectic   (3) unpopular   (4) unexpected (5) useless
46. From the passage we can most safely conclude that   (1) good shows are produced by luck   (2) the number of songs is the prime factor in the successful show   (3) most good musical shows undergo no changes   (4) inventiveness plays a major role in the successful musical   (5) songs are extremely important to the star
47. From the passage we can most safely conclude that a musical   (1) may be an uncertain enterprise   (2) is an integral part of our culture (3) has a small audience   (4) is dependent upon the critics for survival   (5) usually is carelessly produced

Passage B

I have known the inexorable sadness of pencils,
Neat in their boxes, dolor of pad and paper-weight,
All the misery of manila folders and mucilage,
Desolation in immaculate public places.
5 Lonely reception room, lavatory, switchboard,
The unalterable pathos of basin and pitcher,
Ritual of multigraph, paper-clip, comma,
Endless duplication of lives and objects.
And I have seen dust from the walls of institutions,
10 Finer than flour, alive, more dangerous than silica,
Sift, almost invisible, through long afternoons of tedium,
Dropping a fine film on nails and delicate eyebrows,
Glazing the pale hair, the duplicate gray standard faces.

48. The phrase that best expresses the main idea of this poem is   (1) the public place   (2) keeping up appearances   (3) why employers are miserable   (4) the look of sameness   (5) the danger of silica

49. In the poem, the dust is compared to   (1) nails and eyebrows (2) flour and silica   (3) hair and faces   (4) walls and afternoons (5) lives and objects
50. "Duplicate" in line 13 has the meaning of   (1) uniformity   (2) change   (3) authority   (4) grief   (5) foolishness
51. The poet chooses as a reflection of modern life the world of   (1) the dead   (2) the office   (3) the movie   (4) the stationery supplier (5) the dust

Passage C

There was a stumbling rush for the cover of fortification proper; and there the last possible line of defense was established instinctively and in a moment. Officers and men dropped on their knees behind the low bank of earth, and continued an irregular deliberate fire, each discharg-
5   ing his piece as fast as he could load and aim. The garrison was not sufficient to form a continuous rank along even this single front, and on such portions of the works as were protected by the ditch, the soldiers were scattered almost as sparsely as sentinels. Nothing saved the place from being carried by an assault except the fact that the assailants were
10 unprovided with scaling ladders. The adventurous fellows who had flanked the palisade rushed to the gate, and gave entrance to a torrent of tall, lank men in butternut or dirty gray clothing, their bronzed faces flushed with the excitement of supposed victory, and their yells of exultation drowning for a minute the sharp outcries of the wounded, and
15 the rattle of the musketry. But the human billow was met by such a fatal discharge that it could not come over the rampart. The foremost dead fell across it, and the mass reeled backward. Unfortunately for the attack, the exterior slope was full of small knolls and gullies, besides being cumbered with rude shanties, of four or five feet in height made
20 of bits of board, and shelter tents, which had served as the quarters of the garrison. Behind these covers, scores if not hundreds sought refuge and could not be induced to leave them for a second charge.

52. Which statement is true of the final defense line?   (1) It was organized by the officers.   (2) It was abandoned by the cowardly.   (3) It was guarded by sentinels.   (4) It was discharged by the officers. (5) It was arranged without command.
53. Which was a handicap of the defenders?   (1) improper communications   (2) the ditch   (3) no protection whatsoever   (4) too few men   (5) a continuous rank
54. The reader can infer from this passage that   (1) there are many guards in the garrison   (2) sentinels fight alongside regular soldiers

(3) sentinels are placed widely apart   (4) sentinels are usually officers   (5) guards and sentinels form a continuous rank

55. The men who were attacking the garrison lacked   (1) sufficient food   (2) adequate medical supplies   (3) a battle plan   (4) shelter tents   (5) special equipment

56. Which statement is most probably true of the men who flanked the palisade?   (1) They were warmly dressed.   (2) They followed up an initial advantage.   (3) They were supported by the sentinels.   (4) They were scattered widely in the attack.   (5) They drowned in the ditches.

57. In line 15, the "human billow" means the   (1) wounded   (2) guards   (3) attacking force   (4) brave defenders   (5) rattle of musketry

58. The attackers were most hindered in their attack by   (1) the terrain   (2) their wounded   (3) lack of ammunition   (4) their presupposed victory   (5) their cowardly leaders

59. Many of the attackers   (1) surrendered to the garrison   (2) were hampered by inferior training   (3) refused to make another assault   (4) were overwhelmed by superior numbers   (5) were scattered sparsely around the fortification

60. Which lines tell the turning point of the battle?   (1) 1 through 5   (2) 5 through 8   (3) 10 through 15   (4) 15 through 17   (5) 17 through 21

TEST 4

Passage A

Next to his towering masterpiece, *Moby Dick*, *Billy Budd* is Melville's greatest work. It has the tone of a last testament, and the manuscript was neatly tied up by his wife, Elizabeth, and kept in a trunk for some thirty years. It was not until 1924 that it was first published. Slowly it has become recognized as the remarkable work it is. *Billy Budd* has been dramatized for Broadway, done on TV, made into an opera, and reached a highly satisfying form in Ustinov's movie.

Scholars disagree, somewhat violently, about what Melville was trying to say. He did make it pretty clear that he was recounting a duel between Good and Evil.

Several times he remarked that Billy Budd is as innocent and ignorant as Adam before the fall. His enemy is like Satan in Milton's *Paradise Lost*.

When Billy Budd destroys the letter, and is sentenced to be hanged according to the letter of the law, controversy exists as to whether the Captain is simply a mortal man preserving order, or a Jehovah-like figure, dispensing cruel justice.

Melville, it is claimed, cleverly took pains to hide his heretical feelings. *Billy Budd* is written as if told by a pious, God-loving man.

Ironically, Melville's iconoclasm has largely misfired, for the story today is accepted as either one of simple suspense or a reverent parable of God, Satan, and Adam. Meanwhile the scholars are still arguing, and *Billy Budd* remains like a porcupine, thorny, with interesting ambiguities.

41. The phrase that best expresses the ideas of this passage is   (1) a controversial work   (2) the dramatization of *Billy Budd*   (3) life's ambiguities   (4) the Captain's revenge   (5) the King's justice
42. Regarding *Billy Budd,* critics seem to disagree about the book's   (1) plot   (2) theme   (3) mood   (4) setting   (5) introduction
43. As used in this passage, the word "recounting" (line 9) most nearly means   (1) adding up   (2) adding again   (3) figuring   (4) telling   (5) complaining about
44. The passage suggests that the character Billy Budd was   (1) Satanic   (2) ambiguous   (3) naive   (4) brutal   (5) vain
45. The author's purpose in writing this passage seems to be to   (1) point out aspects of *Billy Budd*   (2) show that *Billy Budd* is well written   (3) defend Melville against his critics   (4) defend Melville's iconoclasm   (5) describe Melville's growth as a literary artist
46. The passage indicates that the Captain   (1) disobeyed the law   (2) treated his crew very badly   (3) disliked Billy intensely   (4) was incapable of action   (5) was responsible for discipline
47. Certain lines in this passage suggest that Melville was   (1) Jehovah-like   (2) childishly naive   (3) very scholarly   (4) rather shrewd   (5) immune to pain

Passage B

The propensity of Americans to join is not new. It goes back to the ladies' reading clubs and other cultural groups which spread on the moving frontier, and which were the forerunners of parent-teacher associations and the civic and forum groups of today. The jungle of voluntary associations was already dense enough for De Tocqueville to note that "in no country in the world has the principle of association been more unsparingly applied to a multitude of different objects than in America." The permissiveness of the State, the openness of the society, the newness of the surroundings, the need for interweaving people from diverse ethnic groups—or conversely, their huddling together inside the ethnic tent until they could be assimilated—all these shaping forces were present from the start. What came later was the breaking up of the rural and small-town life of America and the massing in impersonal cities, bringing a dislocation that strengthened the impulse to join like-minded people.

48. The phrase that best expresses the ideas of this passage is   (1) the ancestor of the PTA   (2) Americans as joiners   (3) the growth of organizations in cities   (4) the end of the small town   (5) associations in rural America

49. De Tocqueville apparently believed that Americans   (1) improved themselves by joining clubs   (2) overcame many difficulties as pioneers   (3) used the principle of association freely   (4) valued friendships greatly   (5) were greedy for many riches

50. De Tocqueville pointed out that the associations he observed were   (1) illegal   (2) permissive   (3) varied   (4) dense   (5) large

51. According to the passage, which statement can best be made about the desire to join?   (1) It was fostered by laws.   (2) It probably fulfilled a need.   (3) It resulted in less assimilation than ever.   (4) It was basically an autocratic, not a democratic, phenomenon.   (5) It caused the breakup of rural and small-town life.

52. The author's chief purpose in writing this passage seems to be to   (1) encourage people to join clubs   (2) discredit De Tocqueville's viewpoint   (3) defend people's right to join clubs   (4) explain the basis for certain groups in America   (5) indicate why ethnic groups have increased

53. One can conclude from the passage that   (1) the ethnic tent proved to be too large   (2) Americans were used to a "closed" society   (3) joining has had uniformly good results   (4) the State has tended to restrict the joining movement   (5) the desire to join has persisted among Americans

Passage C

With notes and preface and the rest
And every kind of teacher's aid
To harry schoolboys into learning
The unpremeditated verse,
Written because the heart was hot
With quite a different kind of burning.
And that is the revenge of time,
And that, they say, the workman's pay.

It may be so, I wouldn't know.
I wrote it poor, in love, and young,
In indigestion and despair
And exaltation of the mind,
Not for the blind to lead the blind;
I have no quarrel with the wise,

No quarrel with the pedagogue,
And yet I wrote for none of these.

And yet these are the words, in print,
And should an obdurate old man
Remember half a dozen lines
Stuck in his mind like thistle seed,
Or if, perhaps, some idle boy
Should sometimes read a page or so
In the deep summer, to his girl,
And drop the book half finished there,
Since kissing was a better joy,
Well, I shall have been paid enough.
I'll have been paid enough indeed.

54. Lines 1 through 4 strongly imply that   (1) schoolboys are required to study the poet's verse intensively   (2) unpremeditated verse has a great appeal for schoolboys   (3) a poet should provide his readers with explanatory notes   (4) memorizing poetry requires little effort   (5) the poet's verse is unpopular with teachers

55. The writer apparently does *not* approve of   (1) workman's pay   (2) the way poetry often is taught   (3) unpremeditated verse   (4) inspiration   (5) time's passing

56. The poem being discussed was written because the poet   (1) desired recognition   (2) wished to avenge himself on teachers   (3) needed to give expression to his feelings   (4) hoped to impress people with his wisdom   (5) felt that he had a message for both the young and the old

57. The poem to which the writer is referring was written when he was   (1) in college   (2) recovering from a serious illness   (3) teaching schoolboys   (4) helping the blind   (5) young and poor

58. According to the writer, one good reason for a reader's leaving the book of poems half read is that   (1) the book contains ideas that are no longer valid   (2) the book was written before the poet had perfected his style   (3) actual experiences may be more rewarding than reading   (4) poetry is boring for most people   (5) only a half dozen lines are worth remembering

59. We may most safely conclude that the poet is no longer   (1) young   (2) ill   (3) in love   (4) warmhearted   (5) exalted in mind

60. The poet considers that time had its revenge (line 7) in that his poem   (1) earned him only a day laborer's pay   (2) has become a subject for formal study   (3) offended the wise   (4) is remembered only in part   (5) has little appeal for young lovers

TEST 5

Passage A

One evening we heard the distant cry of wild geese. That was our signal for departure. We made a last round of the deadfalls, sprung each one that was set, and the next day made up two bundles of the peltries that we were to take with us. There were in all sixty-one marten, ten fisher, seventeen mink, five wolverine, one mountain-lion, eight lynx, and two otter skins. Fortunately, there was little weight in all that number, and we bound them so compactly that there was little bulk. A quantity of moose meat, cut into thin sheets and dried, made up the rest of our pack. Nor did we forget the fire drill, and a small, hard piece of birch wood that had been seasoning by the fire all the winter for a drill base.

The goatskin sleeping bag was too heavy to take along; it would have added much to our comfort, of course, but there was now no night cold enough to be very disagreeable so long as we could have fire, and of that we were assured. However, Pitamakan did not intend that the bag should be wasted; almost the last thing that he did was to make an offering of it to the sun. Lashing the bundle in a tree, he prayed that we might survive all perils by the way, and soon reach the lodges of our people.

At sundown we ate our last meal in the lodge and enjoyed for the last time its cheerful shelter. Somehow, as we sat by the fire, we did not feel like talking. To go away and leave the little home to the elements and the prowlers of the night was like parting forever from some near and dear friend.

41. One can conclude from the passage that the area described in it   (1) possessed varieties of game   (2) was in the custody of the Indians   (3) had been stripped of most of its game   (4) was not popular with hunters   (5) was inhabited by many rare animals
42. The first paragraph suggests that the men trapped   (1) for certain game only   (2) in the summer only   (3) on a wide scale   (4) in violation of the law   (5) in great haste
43. In their preparations for departure, the men are shown to be   (1) thorough   (2) brave   (3) loud   (4) discomfited   (5) carefree
44. The feeling that the men had at the prospect of leaving the lodge was one of   (1) hope   (2) despair   (3) disgust   (4) cheerfulness   (5) regret
45. The passage implies that the camp was   (1) an overnight stopping place   (2) a shelter of long duration   (3) a haven from a sudden storm   (4) an Indian outpost   (5) a vacation resort
46. From the selection, it can be inferred that "the distant cry of wild geese" (line 1) tells the men that   (1) spring is coming   (2) the winter will be a severe one   (3) dangerous animals are in the area   (4)

the geese have been frightened by hunters   (5) a storm is on the way

47. Pitamakan lashed the sleeping bag in the tree when he found that the (1) tree needed protection from fire   (2) sleeping bag was not needed on the return journey   (3) men wanted the sleeping bag kept safe for the next trip   (4) men wanted to give thanks to the gods for a successful hunt   (5) sleeping bag was worn out and soiled

48. As used in the passage, the phrase "drill base" (line 10) most probably means   (1) peltry   (2) lodge   (3) stretcher for curing hides (4) kindling device   (5) dried moose meat

49. The "elements" referred to in the last sentence are   (1) the Indians (2) wild animals   (3) other campers   (4) friends of the men (5) weather conditions

Passage B

I am an amateur, a man who does a thing because he loves doing it. The amateur's lot is not an easy one in a country run by antiamateurs: condescending experts, arrogant specialists, and slick perfectionists. They call us dabblers and dilettantes because we can't do a thing well.

They are wrong. The truth is, we are so crazy about doing a thing that we don't mind doing it badly. What makes us really suspect to all trueblood, regular nonamateurs is that we practioo a particular pursuit without any hope of financial reward. We don't want to improve our standard of living. We want to improve our lives.

Time was when gifted dabblers pioneered new thought and stimulated discovery. Think of Leonardo da Vinci, amateur physicist and amateur builder. Goethe, dilettante mathematician and statesman. Voltaire, Humboldt, Thoreau, Edison, Ford—fellow amateurs with brilliant ideas, men of universal rather than specialized thinking. But today universality is unpopular, individualism is dangerous, nonconformism is suspect. The amateur, a man of catholic tastes, an individualist and nonconformist, must not be taken seriously. Experts tell you everything right down the line—how to live, how to be adjusted, what to eat, where to go. If you don't happen to be an expert of sorts, you're a "dope"—an amateur.

50. The phrase that best expresses the ideas of the passage is   (1) Working without pay   (2) The century of the expert   (3) Contributions of gifted dabblers   (4) In praise of amateurs   (5) The expert's superiority over the amateur

51. A characteristic of the amateur is that he   (1) is limited in talent (2) enjoys his ordered life   (3) distrusts other amateurs   (4) has great enthusiasm   (5) gets easily discouraged

52. The author implies that men such as Voltaire, Thoreau, and Edison were (1) maladjusted   (2) condescending   (3) curious   (4) arrogant (5) professional

53. According to the passage, today amateurism   (1) thrives in cities (2) has little competition from nonamateurs   (3) is based upon the prevailing standard of living   (4) is based upon science   (5) is greatly criticized

54. According to the passage, the view that an amateur must *not* be taken seriously is held by the   (1) specialist   (2) individualist   (3) nonconformist   (4) amateur   (5) pioneer

55. In the third paragraph, the main idea is developed by means of   (1) cause and effect   (2) contrast   (3) reasons   (4) definitions (5) incidents

56. From the passage, one could most safely conclude that the author sees danger in   (1) nonconformism   (2) uniform thinking   (3) imperfection   (4) taking the amateur seriously   (5) lower standards of living

Passage C

They called him Trotty from his pace. He could have walked faster perhaps; most likely, but rob him of his trot, and Toby would have taken to his bed and died. It bespattered him with mud in dirty weather; it cost him a world of trouble; he could have walked with infinitely greater ease; but that was one reason for his clinging to it so tenaciously. A weak, small, spare old man, he was a very Hercules, this Toby, in his good intentions. He loved to earn his money. He delighted to believe—Toby was very poor, and couldn't well afford to part with a delight—that he was worth his salt. With a shilling or an eighteenpenny message or small parcel in hand, his courage, always high, rose higher. As he trotted on, he would call out to fast Postmen ahead of him, to get out of the way; devoutly believing that in the natural course of things he must inevitably overtake and run them down; and he had perfect faith—not often tested—in his being able to carry anything that man could lift.

57. The phrase that best expresses the ideas of this passage is   (1) Walking versus trotting   (2) An unusual mode of travel   (3) A wellmeaning man   (4) Why Toby failed   (5) How nicknames are determined

58. Toby is described as being   (1) timid   (2) troublesome   (3) optimistic   (4) miserly   (5) loyal

59. Toby is shown to possess   (1) greediness   (2) cleanliness   (3) openmindedness   (4) self-respect   (5) kindliness

60. Toby preferred to trot because trotting was   (1) easier than walking (2) faster than walking   (3) more unusual than walking   (4) more fun than walking   (5) more indicative of his intentions than walking

Chapter 5 The Correct Usage Test
(Questions 61-65)

NOTE: Questions 61–65 may deal with either correct usage or related areas of English. This chapter will review correct usage. The next, Chapter 6, will discuss the related areas of English.

WHAT IS CORRECT USAGE?

To answer this question, we must realize that there are several levels of usage. Examples:

NONSTANDARD:	"Dey ain't done nothin'."
INFORMAL:	"They've done nothing."
FORMAL.	"They have done nothing."

The correct level of usage is the one that is appropriate for the occasion. Suppose you are writing dialogue in a play or story in which some of the characters have not been influenced by schooling. To represent their speech, you will use *nonstandard* English.

For ordinary conversation and friendly letters, you will use *informal* English.

But for reports, term papers, minutes, letters of application, business letters, speeches, lectures—in short, for formal writing and speaking—you will use *formal* English.

Both *informal* and *formal* English are considered *standard usage*. This chapter aims to improve your command of *standard usage*.

Don't be misled by the fact that the correct usage test (questions 61–65) is worth only five points. Your skill in usage will be rated also in Part II in your literature essay (twenty points) and in Part III in your composition (thirty points). For these reasons, you should pay very careful attention to the review of correct usage in the following pages.

TYPICAL CORRECT USAGE TEST

Try this typical correct usage test. Then compare your answers with the correct ones at the end of the test.

Directions (61–65): Each of the following contains an underlined word or expression which may or may not be correct. Below each are four ways of writing the underlined word or expression. Decide which way is correct and write its *number* in the space provided on the answer sheet. [5]

61. The chairman of the board, with ten of the <u>directors, was</u> elected for another term.

    1 Correct as is   3 directors were
    2 directors, were   4 directors was

62. <u>While walking along the road,</u> a car nearly struck me.

    1 Correct as is
    2 Walking along the road,
    3 While I was walking along the road,
    4 When walking along the road,

63. "I believe," the man <u>said, "That</u> you are wrong."

    1 Correct as is   3 said; "That
    2 said, "that   4 said; "that

64. There were all sorts of games for us to <u>play: tennis,</u> soccer, baseball, and golf.

    1 Correct as is   3 play, tennis,
    2 play; tennis,   4 play tennis,

65. <u>There have been many an argument about it's</u> proper usage.

    1 Correct as is
    2 There have been many an argument about its
    3 There has been many an argument about it's
    4 There has been many an argument about its

    Answers: 61 (1)   62 (3)   63 (2)   64 (1)   65 (4)

ANALYSIS OF THE TYPICAL CORRECT USAGE TEST

61. ANSWER

    The chairman of the board, with ten of the <u>directors, was</u> elected for another term.

ANSWER EXPLAINED

a. The interrupting expression *with ten of the directors* must be set off from the rest of the sentence not only by a comma before *with,* but also by a comma after *directors.*

b. The singular subject *chairman* requires the singular verb *was.* The interrupting expression *with ten of the directors* does not affect agreement between the subject (*chairman*) and verb (*was*).

62. ANSWER

While I was walking along the road, a car nearly struck me.

ANSWER EXPLAINED

Because *While I was walking along the road* has the pronoun *I,* it tells who did the walking. The other choices do not; they are dangling constructions.

63. ANSWER

"I believe," the man said, "that you are wrong."

ANSWER EXPLAINED

a. Since the direct quotation is divided into two parts—"*I believe*" and "*that you are wrong*"—it must be set off from the rest of the sentence not only by a comma after *believe,* but also by a comma after *said.*

b. In the second half of a divided quotation ("*that you are wrong*"), the opening word (*that*) must not be capitalized, unless it begins a new sentence. In the above, *that* does not begin a new sentence.

64. ANSWER

There were all sorts of games for us to play: tennis, soccer, baseball, and golf.

ANSWER EXPLAINED

The correct punctuation mark for introducing a series is the colon [:].

65. ANSWER

There has been many an argument about its proper usage.

ANSWER EXPLAINED

a. A noun preceded by *many a (an)* is singular; therefore, the noun *argument* is singular. Since it is the subject of the sentence, it requires the singular verb *has been.*

Note that all of the following expressions are singular: *many a* boy, *any* gift, *each* article, *every* title, etc.

b. The word *its* is a pronoun meaning "of it." On the other hand, *it's* is a contraction meaning "it is." From the context of the above sentence, it is clear that the pronoun *its* is required.

A REVIEW OF CORRECT USAGE

The rest of this chapter will develop your skill in the various areas of the correct usage test. They are as follows:

1. PRONOUNS

WHAT IS A PRONOUN?

A pronoun is a word that stands for a noun. The word *it* in the following sentence is a pronoun:

Food is essential because *it* provides energy.

You can tell *it* is a pronoun because it stands for the noun *food.*

WHY ARE PRONOUNS TROUBLESOME?

Pronouns often trouble us because they have different forms for different uses. Notice that the following pronouns have one form as a subject, another as an object, and a third as a possessive:

AS SUBJECT (*Nominative Case*)	AS OBJECT (*Objective Case*)	AS POSSESSIVE (*Possessive Case*)
I	me	my, mine
you	you	your, yours
he	him	his
she	her	her, hers
it	it	its
we	us	our, ours
they	them	their, theirs
who	whom	whose
whoever	whomever	whosever

Let us review the rules for using pronouns and at the same time analyze questions about pronouns adapted from former Regents examinations. Note that the correct answer is italicized.

Rule 1: A pronoun used as a subject takes the nominative case.

1. I know of no other person in the club who is as kindhearted as (*she*, her).

ANSWER EXPLAINED

she is subject of the understood verb *is*. ("I know of no other person in the club who is as kindhearted as she *is*.")

HINT

Mentally supply the understood verb. It will help you choose the correct pronoun.

2. (*Who*, Whom) do you believe is the most capable?

ANSWER EXPLAINED

Who is subject of the verb *is*.

HINT

Ignore interrupting expressions like *do you believe* (*do you suppose, think, say,* etc.). They do not affect the case of *who* and *whom.*

3. He voted against (*whoever,* whomever) favored that proposal.

ANSWER EXPLAINED

whoever is subject of the verb *favored.*

HINT

Don't choose *whomever* in the belief that it is the object of the preposition *against.* It isn't. The object of *against* is the entire clause *whoever favored that proposal.*

Exception to Rule 1: A pronoun used as the subject of an infinitive takes the objective case.

(The infinitive is the form of the verb preceded by *to*: *to be, to tell, to read,* etc.)

4. Father expects Fred and (I, *me*) to pass.

ANSWER EXPLAINED

me (together with *Fred*) is the subject of the infinitive *to pass*—not the object of *expects.* The entire phrase *Fred and me to pass* is the object of *expects.*

HINT

In an instance like this, construct two sentences. Then combine them for the correct answer.

Sentence 1: Father expects Fred to pass.
Sentence 2: Father expects *me* (not *I*) to pass.

Answer: Father expects Fred and *me* to pass.

Rule 2: A pronoun used as a predicate nominative takes the nominative case.

[A noun or pronoun after some form of *to be* (*is, was, might have been,* etc.) is called a predicate nominative.]

5. It was (*we*, us) girls who swept the gym floor after the dance.

ANSWER EXPLAINED

we is a predicate nominative after the verb *was*.

HINT

Remember that the verb *to be*, in all of its forms, is the same as an equals sign (=). Whatever case comes before it (practically always nominative case) must also follow it:

It	was	we.
(nominative)	=	(nominative)

Rule 3: **A pronoun used as direct object of a verb, object of an infinitive, object of a preposition, or indirect object takes the objective case.**

6. "(Who, *Whom*) can you send to help us?" inquired Aunt May.

ANSWER EXPLAINED

Whom is direct object of the verb *can send*.

HINT

With a *who-whom* question, change the word order: You can send *whom* to help us? Obviously, *you* is subject and *whom* is object of *can send*.

7. The lawyer promised to notify my mother and (I, *me*) of his plans for a new trial.

ANSWER EXPLAINED

me (together with *mother*) is object of the infinitive *to notify*.

HINT

In a case like this, construct two sentences. Then combine them for the correct answer.

Sentence 1: The lawyer promised to notify my mother.
Sentence 2: The lawyer promised to notify *me* (not *I*).

Answer: The lawyer promised to notify my mother and *me* of his plans for a new trial.

8. It is always a pleasure for (we, *us*) boys to visit a firehouse.

ANSWER EXPLAINED

us is object of the preposition *for*.

HINT

When a pronoun is combined with a noun (*we boys, we girls,* etc.), temporarily omit the noun.

Noun omitted: It is always a pleasure for *us* (not *we*) to visit a firehouse.

Noun added: It is always a pleasure for *us boys* to visit a firehouse.

9. All the pupils except George and (she, *her*) plan to order the book.

ANSWER EXPLAINED

her (together with *George*) is object of the preposition *except*. (*Except* is a preposition, as are *to, by, of, for, with, between,* etc. Prepositions are followed by the objective case.)

HINT

In a case like this, construct two sentences. Then combine them for the correct answer.

Sentence 1: All the pupils except George plan to order the book.
Sentence 2: All the pupils except *her* (not *she*) plan to order the book.

Answer: All the pupils except George and *her* plan to order the book.

10. Grandfather gave my sister and (I, *me*) a year's subscription to a magazine.

ANSWER EXPLAINED

me (together with *my sister*) is the indirect object of the verb *gave*. (An indirect object tells *to* or *for* whom something is done.)

HINT

In a case like this, construct two sentences. Then combine them for the correct answer.

Sentence 1: Grandfather gave my sister a year's subscription.
Sentence 2: Grandfather gave *me* (not *I*) a year's subscription.

Answer: Grandfather gave my sister and *me* a year's subscription.

You can tell that a word is an indirect object if you can temporarily insert *to* or *for* before it without changing the meaning:

Grandfather gave (*to*) my *sister* (indirect object) and (*to*) *me* (indirect object) a year's *subscription* (direct object).
Grandmother baked (*for*) *us* (indirect object) a *cake* (direct object).

Rule 4: A pronoun used in apposition with a noun is in the same case as that noun.

11. Two contestants, Martha and (*she,* her), were disqualified by the judges.

ANSWER EXPLAINED

The pronoun must be in the nominative case (*she*) because it is in apposition with the noun *contestants,* which is in the nominative case.

HINT

contestants is in the nominative case because it is the subject of *were disqualified.*

12. The judges disqualified two contestants, Martha and (she, *her*).

ANSWER EXPLAINED

The pronoun must be in the objective case (*her*) because it is in apposition with the noun *contestants,* which is in the objective case.

HINT

contestants is now in the objective case because it is the object of *disqualified.*

Rule 5: A pronoun that expresses ownership is in the possessive case.

13. The girl refused to admit that the note was (her's, *hers*).

ANSWER EXPLAINED

hers is the correct spelling of the possessive case, which is needed here to express ownership (*belonging to her*).

HINT

Pronouns that express ownership (*yours, his, hers, its, ours,* etc.) never require an apostrophe.

14. He became an authority on the theater and (*its*, it's) great personalities.

ANSWER EXPLAINED

its is the correct spelling of the possessive case, which is needed here to express ownership (*belonging to it*).

HINT

Don't confuse possessive pronouns with contractions.

POSSESSIVE PRONOUNS		CONTRACTIONS	
its	(belonging to it)	*it's*	(it is)
your	(belonging to you)	*you're*	(you are)
their	(belonging to them)	*they're*	(they are)
whose	(belonging to whom)	*who's*	(who is)

15. Father disapproves of (me, *my*) staying up late before examinations.

ANSWER EXPLAINED

my (possessive case) is required by the meaning.

HINT

Of what does Father disapprove? *Me?* Certainly not. He disapproves of *my* (*belonging to me*) *staying up late.*

Exercise on pronouns. Write the correct choice, and state the reason for your choice.

1. I wonder whether that scheme of (yours, your's) will work.
2. (It's, It's) paw injured, the animal limped down the road.
3. In the first row of the orchestra sat Robert and (he, him).
4. Did you know that Frank knows his Latin better than (she, her)?
5. Are you willing to allow (we, us) boys to form a cooking class?
6. There was a serious difference of opinion between her and (me, I).
7. (Us, We) two boys have been very close friends for a long time.
8. The committee consisted of John, Henry, Tom, and (I, me).
9. The audience gave our opponents and (we, us) a rousing ovation.
10. It was (they, them) who objected to the decision.
11. Tom knew he would have to start action before there was a chance of (them, their) planning an attack.
12. Divide the responsibilities between Jane and (her, she).

13. This is John (who, whom), I am sure, will be glad to serve you.
14. Few student officers have served as conscientiously as (she, her).
15. (Whom, Who) shall we invite to the Arista installation?
16. Father would not permit Tom and (I, me) to go swimming today.
17. Please let her and (I, me) do it.
18. The money found on the stairs proved to be neither John's nor (our's, ours).
19. (Who, Whom) do you think will be designated "most likely to succeed"?
20. I don't know what I would do if I were (him, he).
21. "(It's, Its) victory for them or (I, me)," he shouts.
22. Father criticized (me, my) playing the radio when I do my homework.
23. (We, Us) upperclassmen always have a greater share of responsibility.
24. When the dance was held, all came except (she, her).
25. Is this term paper (your's, yours) or Helen's?
26. We have room in the car for only two boys, you and (he, him).
27. Gerald and (he, him) are always dependable in emergencies.
28. Mary and John wish to go because (their, they're, there) eager to visit the museum.
29. John was the only one of the boys (who, whom), as you know, was not eligible.
30. I shall ask my father to let Louis and (he, him) come with us to the beach.
31. When that program is over, the children know (it's, its) time for bed.
32. Between you and (I, me) there have never been any serious misunderstandings.
33. Such a comment about anyone (who, whom) we know to be thoughtful is unfair.
34. The co-captains, Nick and (he, him), will sit on the platform.
35. It was (they, them) who first suggested that I should apply for membership.
36. He is the boy (who's, whose) poster was chosen.
37. I have always been able to read a map better than (she, her).
38. It must have been (they, them) who purchased the class gift.
39. Call on (whoever, whomever) raises his hand, provided he has not yet spoken.
40. The house looked (its, it's) age.
41. Why were Jane and (him, he) permitted to go?
42. It would not be safe for you or (me, I) to travel through the jungle.
43. Father does not approve of (you, your) studying so late.
44. That is the man (who, whom), I believe, was the driver of the car.
45. The girls stated that the dresses were (theirs, their's).
46. This is the story of a girl (who's, whose) father was a doctor.

47. I am as good in trigonometry as (she, her).
48. I find that an essential item for (we, us) beginners is missing.
49. I am certain that these books are not (our's, ours).
50. If you will describe (it's, its) color, perhaps we can find it.

2. IRREGULAR VERBS

HOW TO RECOGNIZE A VERB

You can in most cases tell that a word is a verb if you can add *s, ing,* and *ed* to its basic form.

The word *play* in "We *play* games" is a verb. Proof: *plays, playing, played.*

Similarly, *smile* in "Please *smile*" is a verb. Proof: *smiles, smiling, smiled.*

IRREGULAR VERBS

Some verbs cannot add *ed,* but they are verbs nevertheless. The word *bring* in "*Bring* your lunch" is a verb. Proof: *brings, bringing, brought* (not "bringed").

Verbs that cannot add *ed* are irregular verbs. Many questions on past usage tests have dealt with irregular verbs. You must know the principal parts of common irregular verbs if you are to speak and write good English.

PRINCIPAL PARTS

The principal parts of a verb are:

1. The present tense: *break*
2. The past tense: *broke*
3. The past participle: *broken* (This principal part comes after a helping verb, such as *is, are, was, were, has been, would have been, might have been,* etc.)

One of the most common verb errors is the use of the past tense instead of the past participle, as in this actual Regents question:

When I first saw the car, its steering wheel was broke.

To correct this sentence, you must change *broke* (past tense) to *broken* (past participle). Obviously you should know your principal parts. The following list is well worth reviewing:

PRINCIPAL PARTS OF IRREGULAR AND TROUBLESOME VERBS

PRESENT TENSE	PAST TENSE	PAST PARTICIPLE
arise	arose	arisen
bear	bore	borne, or born
beat	beat	beaten
become	became	become
begin	began	begun
bend	bent	bent
bite	bit	bitten
blow	blew	blown
break	broke	broken
bring	brought	brought
burst	burst	burst
catch	caught	caught
choose	chose	chosen
come	came	come
creep	crept	crept
dig	dug	dug
dive	dived, or dove	dived
do	did	done
draw	drew	drawn
drink	drank	drunk
drive	drove	driven
eat	ate	eaten
fall	fell	fallen
fight	fought	fought
flee	fled	fled
fly	flew	flown
forget	forgot	forgotten
forgive	forgave	forgiven
freeze	froze	frozen
get	got	got, or gotten
give	gave	given
go	went	gone
grow	grew	grown
hang (suspend a thing)	hung	hung
hang (execute a person)	hanged	hanged

PRESENT TENSE	PAST TENSE	PAST PARTICIPLE
hide	hid	hidden
hold	held	held
hurt	hurt	hurt
kneel	knelt	knelt
know	knew	known
lay (put down)	laid	laid
lead	led	led
lend	lent	lent
lie (be in a horizontal position)	lay	lain
lie (tell a lie)	lied	lied
lose	lost	lost
mistake	mistook	mistaken
pay	paid	paid
prove	proved	proved, or proven
rid	rid	rid
ride	rode	ridden
ring	rang	rung
rise	rose	risen
run	ran	run
say	said	said
see	saw	seen
set	set	set
sew	sewed	sewed, or sewn
shake	shook	shaken
show	showed	showed, or shown
shrink	shrank	shrunk
sing	sang	sung
sink	sank	sunk
sit	sat	sat
slay	slew	slain
slide	slid	slid
speak	spoke	spoken
spend	spent	spent
spring	sprang	sprung
steal	stole	stolen
strike	struck	struck
swear	swore	sworn
sweep	swept	swept
swim	swam	swum
take	took	taken

PRESENT TENSE	PAST TENSE	PAST PARTICIPLE
teach	taught	taught
tear	tore	torn
throw	threw	thrown
wake	waked, or woke	waked, or woken
wear	wore	worn
weep	wept	wept
wind	wound	wound
wring	wrung	wrung
write	wrote	written

TYPICAL QUESTIONS ON IRREGULAR VERBS

Rule: After a helping verb, use the past participle (third principal part), rather than the past tense (second principal part).

1. If you had been more patient, you might not have (tore, *torn*) it.

ANSWER EXPLAINED

The helping verb *might* **have** requires the third principal part (tear, tore, *torn*).

HINT

Review the list of principal parts.

2. There were fewer candidates than we had been (*led*, lead) to expect.

ANSWER EXPLAINED

The helping verb *had been* requires the third principal part (lead, led, *led*).

HINT

Don't confuse *led* with an altogether different word that happens to sound the same—*lead* (a metal).

Exercise on irregular and troublesome verbs. Write the correct choice, and state the reason for your choice.

1. I could not do the assignment because the pages were (tore, torn) from my book.
2. Last night the stranger (lead, led) us down the mountain.
3. After George had (ran, run) the mile, he was breathless.

4. In all the confusion, nobody took the trouble to find out who had (rung, rang) the bell.
5. I can assure you that he has always (spoke, spoken) well of you.
6. When was the last time your picture was (took, taken)?
7. After she had (sang, sung) the national anthem, the game started.
8. I had (rode, ridden) over the same course many times before.
9. Your sweater has (laid, lain) on the floor for a week.
10. Mary, aren't you (suppose, supposed) to take part in the play?
11. Jack no sooner (laid, lay) down than he fell asleep.
12. My dog has never (bit, bitten) anyone, except when provoked.
13. How can you be so sure that he (did, done) it?
14. We were not allowed to skate on the pond until the ice had (froze, frozen) to a depth of ten inches.
15. Richard concluded that his pen must have (fell, fallen) from his pocket as he was running for the bus.
16. How much have food costs (raised, risen) during the past year?
17. When he (began, begun) to give us advice, we stopped listening.
18. Mary was so thirsty that she (drank, drunk) two glasses of water.
19. My cousin framed the photographs and (hung, hanged) them on the wall of his den.
20. They are (use, used) to living very quiet lives.

3. VERBS OFTEN CONFUSED

Does air pollution *affect* (or *effect*) our health? Did the dog *lie* (or *lay*) asleep at your feet?

Because pairs of verbs like *affect—effect* and *lie—lay* are so commonly confused, they are often the subject of Regents questions.

Review the following verb pairs, giving special attention to those that you may not yet have mastered.

1. to *accept:* to receive, agree to
   He *accepted* my apology.

   to *except:* to leave out
   Food purchases were *excepted* from the sales tax.

2. to *affect:* to influence
   His dog's death *affected* him deeply.

   to *effect:* to bring about
   The enemy *effected* a quick retreat.

3. to *borrow:* to take with the expressed intention of returning
   May I *borrow* your pen?

   to *lend:* to give with the expressed intention of getting back
   I shall gladly *lend* you my pen.

4. to *bring:* to carry toward the speaker
   Bring the newspaper when you return from shopping.
   to *take:* to carry from the speaker
   Take these shirts to the laundry.

5. *can:* a helping verb expressing ability
   Can you (Are you able to) swim across the pool?
   may: a helping verb expressing permission or possibility
   May I (not *Can* I) have another chance?
   It *may* rain tomorrow.

6. to *learn:* to receive knowledge
   I *learned* safe driving from Dad.
   to *teach:* to impart knowledge
   Dad *taught* me safe driving.

7. to *leave:* to depart, let remain
   When you *leave*, please shut the door.
   Leave the key under the mat.
   to *let:* to permit, allow
   Let (not *Leave*) them do their work without interruption.

8. to *lie:* to be in a horizontal position
   Present: The dog *lies* (*is lying*) on the ground.
   Future: The dog *will lie* on the ground.
   Past: The dog *lay* on the ground.
   Perfect Tenses: The dog *has lain* (*had lain, will have lain*) on the ground.
   to *lay:* to put down
   Present: The player *lays* (*is laying*) his cards on the table.
   Future: The player *will lay* his cards on the table.
   Past: The player *laid* his cards on the table.
   Perfect Tenses: The player *has laid* (*had laid, will have laid*) his cards on the table.

9. to *precede:* to go before in rank or time
   Evening *precedes* night.
   to *proceed:* to move forward, advance
   Proceed to the main entrance.

10. to *raise:* to lift, elevate
    How can I *raise* my marks?
    to *rise:* to go up, get up
    Will the cost of living *rise?*
    To ask a question, please *rise* and face the class.

TYPICAL QUESTIONS ON VERBS OFTEN CONFUSED

1. Overnight the river had (raised, *risen*) another foot.

ANSWER EXPLAINED

The meaning of the sentence requires *risen,* which is the third principal part of *to rise,* meaning "to go up"; *raised* is the third principal part of another verb, *to raise,* meaning "to lift."

HINT

Review "Verbs Often Confused."

2. Where have you (lain, *laid*) the book I was reading?

ANSWER EXPLAINED

The meaning of the sentence requires *laid,* the third principal part of *to lay,* meaning "to put down"; *lain* is the third principal part of another verb, *to lie,* meaning "to be in a horizontal position."

Exercise on verbs often confused. Write the correct choice and state the reason for your choice:

1. Have you ever tried to (learn, teach) a boy to tie knots?
2. Although he had (accepted, excepted) a deposit on the new automobile, he refused to deliver it for the agreed price.
3. May I (borrow, lend) your French dictionary over the weekend?
4. I had (lain, laid) awake all night, worrying about the final test.
5. The cost of living is (raising, rising) again.
6. (Bring, Take) these books to the library, as they will soon be overdue.
7. Where did you (lay, lie) the magazine I was reading?
8. When operas are performed on radio or television, they (effect, affect) the listener in that after hearing them he wants to buy recordings of the music.
9. My father didn't (leave, let) me go to the last dance because I had failed two subjects.
10. Weekly dances have become a popularly (accepted, excepted) feature of the summer schedule.
11. (Can, May) I have another helping of ice cream?
12. If anyone wants the book, tell him that it (lays, lies) on the table.
13. The news of his narrow escape (affected, effected) her visibly.
14. In these ways we are (preceding, proceeding) toward the goal of an educated and informed public.
15. At first, passengers were forbidden to enter the lifeboats, women and children (accepted, excepted).

16. Please (bring, take) this suit to the dry cleaner.
17. If you won't (let, leave) her solve the problem by herself, she will never learn.
18. With the new advances in medicine, doctors have been able to (affect, effect) some remarkable recoveries.
19. I could not recall where I had (lain, laid) my glasses.
20. When the fire alarm sounds, (precede, proceed) calmly to the nearest exit.

4. TENSES OF VERBS

A *tense* is the *time* of a verb action. Verbs have six tenses, each expressing a different time.

PRESENT TENSE:	he *answers*
PAST TENSE:	he *answered*
FUTURE TENSE:	he *will answer*
PERFECT TENSE:	he *has answered*
PAST PERFECT TENSE:	he *had answered*
FUTURE PERFECT TENSE:	he *will have answered*

TYPICAL QUESTIONS ON TENSES OF VERBS

Let us review some important rules for using tenses and at the same time analyze some questions about tenses adapted from former Regents examinations.

Rule 1: Do not shift unnecessarily from one tense to another.

1. Whenever I asked him to explain, he (says, *said*), "Later, not now."

ANSWER EXPLAINED

said (past tense) is required because the sentence begins in the past tense (*asked*).

HINT

says (present tense) would be correct only if the sentence were to begin in the present tense (*ask*): Whenever I *ask* him to explain, he *says*, "Later, not now."

Exception to Rule 1: Use the present tense to express a universal truth (something that is true regardless of time).

2. He said that health (was, *is*) better than riches.

ANSWER EXPLAINED

is (present tense) is required to express a universal truth.

HINT

It has been, is, and always will be true that "health *is* better than riches."

Rule 2: In describing two past actions in the same sentence, use the past perfect tense for the earlier action.

3. In the bus I realized that I (took, *had taken*) my brother's notebook by mistake.

ANSWER EXPLAINED

had taken (past perfect tense) is needed to describe an action earlier than that of *realized* (past tense).

HINT

To form the past perfect tense, use *had* plus the past participle.

Rule 3: After *if*, do not use the helping verb *would have;* use *had*.

4. If he (would have, *had*) studied harder, he would have received a passing grade.

ANSWER EXPLAINED

had (not *would have*) is required after *if*.

HINT

would have may be used in a main clause (he *would have* received a passing grade) but never in an *if* clause, which is a dependent clause.

Rule 4: Use the present infinitive to express action not completed at the time of the preceding verb.

Verbs have a present infinitive (*to do, to tell*, etc.) and a past infinitive (*to have done, to have told*, etc.).

5. We intended (*to go,* to have gone) before Tuesday.

ANSWER EXPLAINED

to go (the present infinitive) is required because the action of "going" had not yet happened at the time of the preceding verb *intended*.

HINT

Ask yourself: At the time of the preceding verb (*intended*), had the "going" already taken place? Obviously not. Therefore, use *to go*, the present infinitive.

Note the correct use of the past infinitive: I am sorry *to have scolded* you yesterday. The past infinitive *to have scolded* is required because the action of "scolding" had already happened at the time of the preceding verb *am*.

Exercise on tenses. Write the correct choice, and state the reason for your choice.

1. Magellan's voyage proved that the world (was, is) round.
2. If you (would have, had) called me earlier, I would unquestionably have gone with you.
3. Suddenly he yelled "George!" and (dashes, dashed) up the stairs.
4. The doctor suspected that I (sprained, had sprained) my ankle.
5. From that experience I learned that a friend in need (is, was) a friend indeed.
6. If he (had, would have) drunk more milk, his health would have been better.
7. At the box office I realized that I (forgot, had forgotten) to bring my wallet.
8. Our teacher explained that the Grand Canyon (was, is) in Arizona.
9. I am sorry to (cause, have caused) so much trouble yesterday.
10. She could not recall the title of any one-act play that she (read, had read) in previous terms.
11. Mother would gladly have set an extra place for dinner if she (had, would have) known you were coming.
12. Aren't you sorry to (be, have been) so discourteous when she phoned?
13. If it (had not, would not have) rained, the mishap would never have occurred.
14. Does Phil plan to (finish, have finished) the essay before he rides down to the beach?
15. If more nations (had, would have) fought against tyranny, the course of history would have been different.
16. As soon as Mother learned of my plan, she (begins, began) to worry.
17. I would have taken Latin if it (had, would have) been offered.
18. Mr. Lopez was reputed to (be, have been) an outstanding athlete in his youth.
19. You're expected to (graduate, have graduated) next June.
20. Jim is ashamed to (be, have been) so rude to your guests last Saturday.

5. ACTIVE AND PASSIVE VERBS

ACTIVE VERBS

A verb is *active* when its subject is the doer of the action.

Frank *answered* the question.

The verb *answered* is active because its subject, *Frank,* is the doer: he did the answering.

PASSIVE VERBS

A verb is *passive* when the action is done to its subject.

The question *was answered* by Frank.

The verb *was answered* is passive because it describes an action done to its subject, *question.* The doer of the action, Frank, is now the object of the preposition *by.*

FURTHER EXAMPLES OF ACTIVE AND PASSIVE VERBS

ACTIVE: Storms *damage* crops.
PASSIVE: Crops *are damaged* by storms.

ACTIVE: Marie *will make* the sandwiches.
PASSIVE: The sandwiches *will be made* by Marie.

ACTIVE: The audience *applauded* the speaker.
PASSIVE: The speaker *was applauded* by the audience.

FORMING PASSIVE VERBS

To form the passive, add some form of *to be* (*is, was, will be, has been,* etc.) to the past participle (third principal part) of a verb. Examples:

is broken   *was collected*   *are being kept*
has been told   *had been sent*   *were introduced*

USING ACTIVE VERBS

In general, *use active verbs*. They will allow you to express yourself clearly, naturally, and briefly. Compare these sentences:

PASSIVE: Our business was minded by us.   (6 words)
ACTIVE: We minded our business.   (4 words)

Note that the sentence with the active verb is clearer, more natural, and briefer.

Active verbs are much more common in English than passive verbs. Except for a few special situations, like those noted below, *use active verbs*.

USING PASSIVE VERBS

Among the situations when the passive may be used effectively are the following:

1. When you wish not to mention the doer.

   A word *has been misspelled.*

2. When necessary to avoid vagueness.

   Furniture *is manufactured* in Grand Rapids.

   (Instead of "They *manufacture* furniture in Grand Rapids," where the subject *They* is vague.)

3. When the doer is not known.

   The store *was robbed.*

4. When the result of the action is more important than the doer.

   The driver *was arrested* for speeding.

TYPICAL QUESTION ON ACTIVE AND PASSIVE VERBS

QUESTION:

Below, the same idea is expressed in four different ways. Select the way that is best and write its *number* on your separate answer sheet.

1 It was decided by the team that the post-season game would be played by them.
2 Having been decided, the team will play the post-season game.
3 The team decided that they would play the post-season game.
4 The team having decided, the post-season game would be played by them.

ANSWER: (3)

ANSWER EXPLAINED:

Sentence 3 is clearer and more direct than any of the other choices because it uses active verbs—"The team *decided* . . . they *would play.*"

WRONG CHOICES:

Sentence 1 is less effective because it uses passive verbs—"It *was decided* . . . the post-season game *would be played* by them."

Sentence 4 is poor because it, too, uses a passive verb—"the post-season game *would be played* by them."

Sentence 2 is spoiled by the dangling construction "Having been decided," which is vague because it cannot be attached to anything in the rest of the sentence. (See page 178 for a fuller discussion of dangling constructions.)

Exercise on active and passive verbs. Rewrite the sentence with an active or passive verb, if necessary. If the sentence is correct, write "Correct."

1. An agreement with Dad was entered into by my brothers and me.
2. Eight kittens were had by our cat.
3. They grow oranges in Florida and California.
4. The players wore their old uniforms.
5. Another look at my examination paper was taken by Miss Benson.
6. A terrible mistake has been made.
7. In high school, knowledge is gained and plans for the future are formulated by the students.
8. The implications of what he had heard were considered by the judge.
9. They sell hot dogs and soda at the ball game.
10. I hope that a good time will be had by you.

6. TROUBLESOME WORD PAIRS

Several word pairs sound so alike, or nearly alike, that one is often mistaken for the other. Let us learn to distinguish between them by examining some questions adapted from former Regents examinations.

TYPICAL QUESTIONS ON TROUBLESOME WORD PAIRS

advise, advice

1. In schools, teachers (*advise,* advice) their students to listen to or to view certain programs.

ANSWER EXPLAINED

The verb *advise* is required by the sentence.

OTHER WORD

advice is used only as a noun. (The teacher gave us good *advice.*)

altogether, all together

2. I am not (*altogether,* all together) in agreement with the author's point of view.

ANSWER EXPLAINED

altogether, meaning "completely," is required by the sentence.

OTHER WORD

all together, written as two words, means "all at one time." (We recited the pledge of allegiance *all together.*)

effect, affect

3. We expect the (affects, *effects*) of the trip will be beneficial.

ANSWER EXPLAINED

effects, meaning "results," is required by the sentence.

OTHER WORD

affect is used mostly as a verb meaning "to influence." (Alcohol *affects* the brain.)

have, of

4. If people had helped Burns, instead of talking about him, he might (of, *have*) become a greater poet.

ANSWER EXPLAINED

have, a verb, is required by the sentence.

OTHER WORD

of is a preposition. (The rest *of* us protested.)

its, it's

5. When that program is over, the children know (its, *it's*) time for bed.

ANSWER EXPLAINED

it's (contraction for "it is") is required by the sentence.

OTHER WORD

its means "belonging to it." (The dog injured *its* leg.)

lead, led

6. The general (lead, *led*) his troops into battle.

ANSWER EXPLAINED

led, the past tense of *to lead*, is required by the sentence.

OTHER WORD

lead, as a noun, is a metal. (These boots are as heavy as *lead*.)

loose, lose

7. How did you (loose, *lose*) your wallet?

ANSWER EXPLAINED

lose, a verb meaning "part with accidentally," is required by the sentence.

OTHER WORD

loose is an adjective meaning "free, not fastened." (Who turned the dog *loose?*)

passed, past

8. We (*passed*, past) the bus stop.

ANSWER EXPLAINED

passed, the past tense of "to pass," a verb meaning "to go by," is required by the sentence.

OTHER WORD

past may be
a. an adjective. (He presided at *past* meetings.)
b. a noun. (Forget the *past*.)
c. a preposition. (We went *past* the bus stop.)

personal, personnel

9. All the (personal, *personnel*) involved, even the lowest paid "extra," are glad when the picture is finished.

ANSWER EXPLAINED

personnel, a noun meaning "employees," is required by the context.

OTHER WORD

personal is an adjective meaning "private." (Every student will be assigned a *personal* locker.)

principal, principle

10. The teacher explained the (principal, *principle*) of refrigeration.

ANSWER EXPLAINED

principle, meaning "underlying rule" or "general truth," is required by the sentence. Notice that the last two letters of princip*le* and ru*le* are the same.

OTHER WORD

principal, as a noun, means "main teacher." (Next year our school will have a new *principal*.)
principal, as an adjective, means "main." (Broadway is our city's *principal* street.)

quiet, quite

11. When the teacher spoke, the room became (quite, *quiet*).

ANSWER EXPLAINED

quiet, meaning "silent," is required by the sentence.

OTHER WORD

quite means "completely." (By bedtime the children were *quite* exhausted.)

respectfully, respectively

12. The blue, red, and yellow sweaters belong to Jean, Marie, and Alice (respectfully, *respectively*).

ANSWER EXPLAINED

respectively, meaning "in the order stated," is required by the sentence.

OTHER WORD

> *respectfully* means "with proper respect." (As the principal rose to speak, the audience applauded *respectfully*.)

than, then

13. Try to find one that is shorter (*than,* then) this one.

ANSWER EXPLAINED

> *than,* a conjunction used in comparisons, is required by the sentence.

OTHER WORD

> *then* means "at that time." (He was *then* a lad of twelve.)

their, they're, there

14. The enemy fled in many directions, leaving (*their,* they're, there) weapons on the battlefield.

ANSWER EXPLAINED

> *their* (*belonging to them*) is required to show ownership.

OTHER WORDS

> *they're* is a contraction for "they are." (*They're* altogether right.)
> *there* means "in that place." (Have you ever been *there*?)

to, too, two

15. He felt that he had paid (to, *too,* two) high a price for one mistake.

ANSWER EXPLAINED

> *too,* meaning "excessively," is required by the sentence. (Sometimes *too* means "also": Donald is ill and his brother *too*.)

OTHER WORDS

> *to* is a preposition. (Give it *to* me.)
> *two* is a number. (One and one are *two*.)

who's, whose

16. (Who's, *Whose*) money is on this desk?

ANSWER EXPLAINED

> *Whose* (*belonging to whom*) is required to show ownership.

OTHER WORD

Who's is a contraction for "Who is." (*Who's* there?)

your, you're

17. Do not hand in the report until (your, *you're*) certain that it is complete.

ANSWER EXPLAINED

you're, a contraction for "you are," is required by the sentence.

OTHER WORD

your means "belonging to you." (What is your principal worry?)

Exercise on troublesome word pairs. Write the correct choice and state the reason for your choice.

1. John and Mary wish to go because (their, there, they're) eager to visit the museum.
2. Is that (your, you're) jacket on the floor?
3. Have you successfully (passed, past) all your final examinations?
4. The article describes the (principal, principle) (affects, effects) of the new drug.
5. (Who's, Whose) at the door?
6. In the violent storm, the boat broke (loose, lose) from its moorings.
7. We did not realize that the boys' father had forbidden them to keep (there, their, they're) puppy.
8. We want to go to the movies (to, too, two).
9. In the (passed, past) we have always held our commencement exercises in the evening.
10. He is taller (then, than) his brother.
11. He is the boy (who's, whose) poster was chosen for the contest.
12. I was advised to review the (principals, principles) of correct usage.
13. Howard, Richard, and Henry scored ninety, eighty, and seventy-five (respectfully, respectively).
14. She was (quite, quiet) breathless from running upstairs.
15. Macbeth was afraid he would (loose, lose) his crown to one of Banquo's descendants.
16. There were fewer candidates (then, than) we had been (led, lead) to expect.
17. Your interpretation of the results of the test is (all together, altogether) inaccurate.
18. Did you see that truck speed (passed, past) the red light?
19. How will the new tax (affect, effect) your business?

20. The (principle, principal) cause of failure is excessive absence.
21. The reward must (of, have) pleased them very much.
22. The pages in my old dictionary are (loose, lose) and dog-eared.
23. The horse lifted (its, it's) head and snorted.
24. My English teacher gave me ample opportunity to make up for (passed, past) mistakes.
25. You have been (led, lead) astray by your own carelessness.
26. (You're, Your) coming to visit me in the hospital cheered me up.
27. (Who's, Whose) car is that?
28. Doing a task promptly is better (than, then) worrying about it.
29. It's (your, you're) turn to drive now, if you're ready.
30. The alumni have announced that (their, there, they're) sending a representative to our graduation.
31. You should (of, have) been in the assembly yesterday.
32. (Who's, Whose) going to make the arrangements for the dance?
33. What is the (affect, effect) of sunlight on plants?
34. (It's, Its) advisable to apply to at least three colleges early in your senior year.
35. (They're, There, Their) altogether overjoyed with the results.
36. Let them try to do it (there, their, they're) own way.
37. Tell me (who's, whose) on third base; I don't recognize him.
38. On his doctor's (advice, advise) he resumed a full program of physical activities.
39. The dog wagged (its, it's) tail and barked happily.
40. The merchant promised to refund my money if I were not (all together, altogether) satisfied.

7. AGREEMENT

Should you say that a quantity of strawberries *costs,* or *cost,* a dollar? Should you ask everyone to open *his,* or *their,* book?

The first question involves agreement between subject and verb; the second between a pronoun and its antecedent. To help you answer such questions, let us review some of the principles of agreement and analyze typical examination questions dealing with agreement.

TYPICAL QUESTIONS ON AGREEMENT

Rule 1: A singular subject requires a singular verb. A plural subject requires a plural verb.

1. Too many commas in a passage often (*cause,* causes) confusion in the reader's mind.

ANSWER EXPLAINED

The plural subject *commas* requires the plural verb *cause*.

HINT

causes is singular—don't be misled by the final *s*.
Notice how we conjugate a verb in the present tense:

SINGULAR	PLURAL
I cause	we cause
you cause	you cause
he (she, it) causes	they cause

2. There ('s, *are*) several ways to solve that problem.

ANSWER EXPLAINED

The plural subject *ways* requires the plural verb *are*.

HINT

When an expression such as *There is* (*There are*), *Here is* (*Here are*), or *It is* begins a sentence, look for the real subject to appear later in the sentence. In the sentence above, for example, the real subject is not *There* but *ways*.

3. A box of materials (*is*, are) in the cabinet.

ANSWER EXPLAINED

The singular subject *box* requires the singular verb *is*.

HINT

Disregard *of*- phrases that come between subject and verb (example: *of materials* in the sentence above). They do not affect agreement.

4. The leader of the flock, as well as most of his followers, (*has*, have) jumped the fence.

ANSWER EXPLAINED

The singular subject *leader* requires the singular helping verb *has*.

HINT

Interrupting expressions beginning with *as well as, together with, in addition to, rather than*, etc., do not affect agreement between subject and verb.

Rule 2: Subjects that are singular in meaning but plural in form (*news, economics, measles,* etc.) require a singular verb.

5. Mathematics (*is,* are) extremely important in today's world.

ANSWER EXPLAINED

The singular subject *Mathematics* requires the singular verb *is.*

ADDITIONAL EXAMPLE

The United States *has* (not *have*) many beautiful national parks.

Rule 3: Singular subjects connected by *or, nor, either ... or,* or *neither ... nor* require a singular verb.

6. Either the witness or the defendant (*is,* are) lying.

ANSWER EXPLAINED

The singular subjects *witness* and *defendant* are connected by *either ... or* and require the singular verb *is.*

ADDITIONAL EXAMPLE

Neither the sergeant nor the corporal *was* (not *were*) off duty.

Rule 4: A compound subject connected by *and* requires a plural verb.

7. The arrival and departure (was, *were*) on schedule.

ANSWER EXPLAINED

The compound subject *arrival and departure* requires the plural verb *were.*

ADDITIONAL EXAMPLE

His study and preparation for the test *were* (not *was*) thorough.

Exception to Rule 4: A compound subject regarded as a single entity requires a singular verb.

8. Spaghetti and meatballs (*is,* are) a popular dish.

ANSWER EXPLAINED

Spaghetti and meatballs, regarded as a single entity, requires the singular verb *is.*

ADDITIONAL EXAMPLE

The long and short of the matter *is* (not *are*) that we won the game.

Rule 5: If a subject consists of two or more nouns or pronouns connected by *or* or *nor*, the verb agrees with the nearer noun or pronoun.

9. Neither my cousins nor Marie (*is*, are) leaving for the summer.

ANSWER EXPLAINED

The verb *is* agrees in number with the nearer noun *Marie*.

ALSO CORRECT

"Neither Marie nor my cousins *are* (not *is*) leaving for the summer." In this case the verb *are* agrees in number with the nearer noun *cousins*.

10. Either she or you (is, *are*) to blame.

ANSWER EXPLAINED

The verb *are* agrees in person with the nearer pronoun *you*.

ALSO CORRECT

"Either you or she *is* to blame." In this case the verb *is* agrees in person with the nearer pronoun *she*.

Rule 6: Make a pronoun agree with its antecedent.

(An antecedent is the previous word to which a pronoun refers.)

11. If anyone has any doubt about the value of this tour, refer (*him*, them) to me.

ANSWER EXPLAINED

The singular antecedent *anyone* requires the singular pronoun *him*.

HINT

Remember that the following words are singular: *anyone, everyone, someone, no one, one, each, each one, either, neither, anybody, everybody, nobody, somebody, every* (person, etc.), *many a* (person, etc.).

12. *Hamlet* is the greatest of all the plays that (has, *have*) ever been written.

ANSWER EXPLAINED

The plural subject *that* requires the plural helping verb *have*. We know *that* is plural because its antecedent is *plays*.

HINT

To determine whether *that, which,* or *who* is singular or plural, look at the antecedent.

13. He is one of those persons (which, *who*) deserve great credit for perseverance.

ANSWER EXPLAINED

The antecedent *persons* requires the pronoun *who; which* cannot refer to people.

HINT

Use *who* to refer to people, *which* to refer to things, and *that* to refer to people or things.

Exercise on agreement. Write the correct choice, and state the reason for your choice.

1. The general, with all his soldiers, (was, were) captured.
2. Both the body and the mind (need, needs) exercise.
3. Each of the papers (are, is) filed for future reference.
4. There ('s, are) several reasons for that boy's popularity.
5. The new movie has a number of actors (which, who) have been famous on Broadway.
6. A sight to inspire fear (are, is) wild animals on the loose.
7. How much (has, have) food costs risen?
8. Jackson is one of the few sophomores who (has, have) ever made the varsity team.
9. Charles' presence in his aunts' household resulted in many changes that (was, were) not to their liking.
10. I found that one of the toys (was, were) broken.
11. There, crouching in the grass, (was, were) four enemies.
12. There (was, were) a dog and a cat in the chair.
13. Calisthenics (is, are) a part of Bob's morning routine.
14. The books they read (show, shows) their taste in literature.
15. He (don't, doesn't) speak very well on formal occasions.
16. Children's health (is, are) a serious concern of all parents.
17. Each of the girls (observe, observes) all the restrictions.
18. Neither he nor we (was, were) fully aware of the serious nature of your illness.

19. The number of foursomes on the course today (was, were) very small.
20. Macbeth himself, rather than the witches, (was, were) responsible for his downfall.
21. Everybody (was, were) asked to remain seated.
22. There, Alice, (is, are) some of my classmates.
23. Burns is one of the poets (which, that) we studied last term.
24. Corned beef and cabbage (is, are) on tonight's menu.
25. The present series of discussions on current events (was, were) started in January.
26. One of the girls lost (their, her) books as a result of the confusion.
27. (Are, Is) each of the pies the same size?
28. An important ingredient of high school life (is, are) intramural athletics.
29. Either your mother or your father (is, are) supposed to sign the report card.
30. (Doesn't, Don't) either of you girls want this?
31. The dog together with its puppies (has, have) come into the parlor again.
32. He is one of the juniors who (was, were) nominated for the G.O. presidency.
33. Each of the men did (his, their) duty with exemplary courage.
34. Interesting news (is, are) what sells our paper.
35. John was the only one of the boys who, as you know, (was, were) not eligible.
36. If anyone wants the book, tell (him, them) that it is in my desk.
37. A bushel of peaches (cost, costs) five dollars.
38. Many a person had to earn (his, their) way through college.
39. The combination of the three colors (give, gives) a pleasing effect.
40. Your approach and delivery (is, are) faulty and need improvement.
41. Being both observant and curious about things (promote, promotes) learning.
42. A box of cigars (was, were) found on the porch, unopened.
43. Radio and television programs, along with other media of communication, (helps, help) us to appreciate the arts and to keep informed.
44. A magazine and a book (was, were) lying in disorder on the floor.
45. Neither of you (seem, seems) to be paying the slightest attention.
46. When operas are performed on radio or television, they affect the listener in that after hearing them (he wants, they want) to buy recordings of the music.
47. Will everyone please open (their, his) book to the preface.
48. The captain as well as six of his men (was, were) wounded in the skirmish.

49. The students' ingenuity (was, were) particularly challenged by the third question on the physics test.
50. Such a rapid succession of unfortunate events (is, are) enough to discourage anybody.

8. ADJECTIVES AND ADVERBS

WHAT IS AN ADJECTIVE?

An *adjective* is a word that modifies a noun or a pronoun.

    Buy a *new* hat.   (adjective *new* modifies noun *hat*)
    I am *tired*.   (adjective *tired* modifies pronoun *I*)

WHAT IS AN ADVERB?

An *adverb* is a word that modifies a verb, an adjective, or another adverb.

    Did she speak *clearly?*   (adverb *clearly* modifies verb *did speak*)
    I am *extremely* tired.   (adverb *extremely* modifies adjective *tired*)
    She spoke *very* clearly.   (adverb *very* modifies adverb *clearly*)

Review the following rules. They will help you to make proper use of adjectives and adverbs and to answer examination questions.

TYPICAL QUESTIONS ON ADJECTIVES AND ADVERBS

Rule 1: Use an adverb to modify a verb.

1. Mathematics problems must be done (accurate, *accurately*).

ANSWER EXPLAINED

We need the adverb *accurately* to modify the verb *must be done*.

HINT

An adverb answers such questions about a verb as *How? To what extent? Where?* or *When?* To tell *how* the "problems must be done," we need the adverb *accurately* (not the adjective *accurate*).

An adjective describes a noun or pronoun. In "accurate clock," the adjective *accurate* describes the noun *clock*. In *"It is accurate,"* the adjective *accurate* describes the pronoun *It*.

Rule 2: Use an adverb to modify an adjective.

2. Violet had an (unbelievable, *unbelievably*) large capacity for food.

ANSWER EXPLAINED

The adverb *unbelievably* is needed to modify the adjective *large*.

HINT

Note that *unbelievably* tells "how" large Violet's capacity for food is.

Rule 3: Use an adjective after a linking verb.

[A linking verb is a verb that "links" or connects the subject with a modifier. The following are linking verbs: *be* (*is, am, was, were,* etc.), *seem, appear, look, feel, smell, sound, taste, become, grow, remain, stay, turn.*]

3. Food prepared in this manner tastes more (*delicious,* deliciously).

ANSWER EXPLAINED

The adjective *delicious* is required after the linking verb *tastes*.

HINT

Study these further examples of the same rule:
The flowers smell *sweet.*   (not *sweetly*)
This sounds *strange.*   (not *strangely*)
The food looks *good.*   (not *well*)

Rule 4: Use the comparative degree (the -er or more form) for comparing two persons or things; use the superlative degree (the -est or most form) for comparing more than two.

Adjectives and adverbs have three degrees, as follows:

POSITIVE	COMPARATIVE	SUPERLATIVE
(adj.) wide	wider	widest
(adv.) widely	more widely	most widely
(adj.) faithful	more faithful	most faithful
(adv.) faithfully	more faithfully	most faithfully

Good and *bad* have irregular forms:

(adj.)	good	better	best
(adv.)	well	better	best
(adj.)	bad	worse	worst
(adv.)	badly	worse	worst

4. It was the (worse, *worst*) storm that the inhabitants of the island could remember.

ANSWER EXPLAINED

The superlative *worst* is needed because the sentence compares more than two storms.

HINT

The comparative *worse* can be used when only two persons or things are compared, as in the following:
This storm was *worse* than the last one.

Rule 5: Use the adjective *other* when you compare a person (or thing) with the rest of his (or its) group.

5. Peter is younger than any of (the, *the other*) boys.

ANSWER EXPLAINED

other must be included because the sentence compares Peter with the rest of his group (*boys*). Peter is a boy too.

HINT

Note that *other* is not required in the following:
Pauline is younger than any of the boys. Pauline is not a member of the group *boys*.

Exercise on adjectives and adverbs. Write the correct choice, and state the reason for your choice.

1. I wish he would take his work more (serious, seriously).
2. At the picnic, the young children behaved very (good, well).
3. The food looks (delicious, deliciously) and is quite reasonable.
4. Our old television set works just as (good, well) as our new one.
5. Did you notice how (beautiful, beautifully) the sky looked?

6. The birds' morning song sounded (sweet, sweetly) to our ears.
7. A person who works as (efficient, efficiently) as John deserves high praise.
8. The butter tastes (rancidly, rancid).
9. Da Vinci was more brilliant than (any, any other) person in his century.
10. Yes, my brother can do this work as (good, well) as I.
11. How (strange, strangely) the noise sounded in the quiet, abandoned house!
12. I am (real, really) sorry to have disturbed you, Mr. Jones.
13. Clara's piano playing seems no (worse, worst) than yours.
14. You are not likely to encounter another pupil who studies as (diligent, diligently) as Anne.
15. He has always done his work (well, good) and cheerfully.
16. This material feels so (soft, softly) that it reminds me of fur.
17. He was voted the most (handsome, handsomely) dressed boy in the senior class.
18. He (sure, surely) appeared glad to see me receive the award.
19. Notice how (rapid, rapidly) that chemical solution dissolves the salt.
20. Sam should have received a trophy too, for he played just as (good, well).
21. I felt (bad, badly) when Mother scolded me about my failing history.
22. He could throw a fast ball and field a bunt as (good, well) as any pitcher I have ever seen.
23. If you try a slice, you'll see how (delicious, deliciously) the melon tastes.
24. When Paul first joined the team, he was no better than any of (the, the other) players.
25. That oriental music sounded (strange, strangely) to my ears.
26. Our car has always run (good, well) on that kind of gasoline.
27. Herman Melville is one of the (real, really) distinguished authors in American literature.
28. Your conduct during this period has been the (worse, worst) in the class.
29. Our teacher (sure, surely) knows how to recite a poem to the class.
30. Florence listened (attentively, attentive) to the music.
31. The sun made us feel (warm, warmly) and glad to be alive.
32. You must admit, Dorothy, that you behaved very (rude, rudely).
33. Nothing smells as (tempting, temptingly) as Mother's homemade pie.
34. Ben was brighter than (any, any other) pupil in his class.
35. No other character behaved more (faithful, faithfully) than Diggory Venn.
36. Be sure that the list is copied (accurately, accurate).
37. To the terrified wedding guest, the ancient mariner looked very (strange, strangely).

38. Jack does not swim so (good, well) as Fred.
39. Please turn down the radio; it is altogether too (loud, loudly).
40. He works more (diligently, diligent) now that he has become vice president of the company.

9. DOUBLE NEGATIVES

"I *didn't* do *nothing*" is nonstandard English because it uses two negatives: (1) the *n't* in *didn't*, and (2) *nothing*.

To make the sentence acceptable as standard English, we must remove one of the negatives:

> I did *nothing*.   (*n't* removed)
> I *didn't* do anything.   (*nothing* removed)

RECOGNIZABLE NEGATIVES

We can easily recognize these negatives:

no	*nobody*	*nowhere*
not	*no one*	*never*
n't	*nothing*	*neither*

HARD-TO-RECOGNIZE NEGATIVES

The following five words, too, are negatives, and unless we realize this we are likely to make the double-negative error:

> *barely, hardly, scarcely, only,* and *but* (when it means "only," as in "I had *but* one dollar.")

TYPICAL QUESTIONS ON DOUBLE NEGATIVES

Rule: Use only one negative word to express a negative idea.

1. He (*has,* hasn't) hardly a friend.

ANSWER EXPLAINED

has is correct because the sentence already has one negative (*hardly*).

2. You haven't (no one, *anyone*) to blame but yourself for your low grades.

ANSWER EXPLAINED

Since *haven't* is a negative word, do not use *no one*, which is also a negative expression. Use *anyone*.

3. Although he searched all over for the glue, he couldn't find (*any*, none).

ANSWER EXPLAINED

Since *couldn't* is a negative word, do not use *none*, which is also a negative expression. Use *any*.

4. Henry is short; he (*is*, isn't) barely able to reach the first shelf.

ANSWER EXPLAINED

is is correct because the sentence already has one negative (*barely*).

5. I saw Jane and Frances at the party, but I didn't get a chance to speak to (*either*, neither) one all evening.

ANSWER EXPLAINED

Since *didn't* is a negative word, do not use *neither*, which is also a negative expression. Use *either*.

Exercise on double negatives. Write the correct choice, and state the reason for your choice.

1. I (could, couldn't) hardly believe that he would desert the cause.
2. With their best player disqualified, Lincoln High (can, can't) barely hope to tie us in Saturday's game.
3. Johnson has scarcely (an, no) equal as a quarterback.
4. Jody (had, hadn't) no reason to doubt his father's judgment.
5. After paying our senior dues, we didn't have (anything, nothing) left in our savings account.
6. They stayed home and didn't go (nowhere, anywhere) all summer.
7. Jack looked everywhere for earthworms, but he didn't see (none, any).
8. Her older brother scarcely (ever, never) works harder than necessary.
9. Where are Joe and Alec? I haven't seen (either, neither) one all week.
10. The term (had, hadn't) hardly begun when we got our first full-period test.
11. When we got to the dance, there wasn't (anybody, nobody) there yet from our club.
12. If you haven't (anything, nothing) better to do, why not join us at the beach?

13. There (is, isn't) barely an hour left before the train leaves.
14. Margaret's illness hadn't (nothing, anything) to do with this problem.
15. Our high-jump star had hardly (a, no) rival during the whole season.
16. How can you plan to go bowling if you (have, haven't) but two days to study?
17. I looked at all the passengers on the train but I didn't recognize (no one, anyone).
18. Alice gets the highest grades, yet she scarcely (ever, never) studies.
19. When my grandfather arrived in this country, he (had, hadn't) only ten dollars in his pocket.
20. I don't know why the dean questioned me because I didn't have (nothing, anything) to do with it.

10. PARALLEL STRUCTURE

To express yourself clearly and effectively, put ideas of the same rank into the same (parallel) grammatical structure.

> DON'T SAY: TV is good for *news* (noun), *movies* (noun), and *to watch sports* (infinitive phrase).
>
> SAY: TV is good for *news* (noun), *movies* (noun), and *sports* (noun).

Because *news* and *movies* are nouns, the sentence requires a third noun, *sports* (rather than the infinitive phrase *to watch sports*), to achieve parallel structure.

TYPICAL QUESTIONS ON PARALLEL STRUCTURE

Rule: Put ideas of the same rank into the same grammatical structure.

1. Mailing a letter a few days early is better than (to run, *running*) the risk of its arriving late.

ANSWER EXPLAINED

The verbal noun *running* is required for parallel structure with the verbal noun *mailing*.

HINT

If the sentence had begun with the infinitive *to mail*, the correct answer would have been the infinitive *to run:* "*To mail* a letter a few days early is better than *to run* the risk of its arriving late."

2. You should select foods that are nourishing and (*tasty*, taste good).

ANSWER EXPLAINED

The predicate adjective *tasty* is required for parallel structure with the predicate adjective *nourishing*.

3. Brian doesn't know whether he should watch TV or (to go, *go*) to the movies.

ANSWER EXPLAINED

The verb *go*, rather than the infinitive *to go*, is required for parallel structure with the verb *watch*.

4. Cotton is comfortable and (one can wash it, *washable*).

ANSWER EXPLAINED

The adjective *washable* is needed for parallel structure with the adjective *comfortable*.

5. To do the job at hand takes more character than (planning, *to plan*) heroic deeds.

ANSWER EXPLAINED

The infinitive *to plan* is required for parallel structure with the infinitive *to do*.

Exercise on parallel structure. Write the correct choice, and state the reason for your choice.

1. I expected him to be angry and (that he would scold, to scold) her.
2. The modern automobile has the advantages of strength and (being speedy, speed, moving swiftly).
3. To do a task promptly is better than (worrying, to worry) about doing it.
4. He likes dancing, skating, and (to go swimming, swimming).
5. Nylon dresses wash easily, drip dry readily, and (you can wear them a long time, wear durably).
6. He appeared tired and (disappointed, a disappointed man).
7. As a freshman George was unruly, inattentive, and (had no patience, impatient).
8. Mr. Smith promised me a good position and (to pay me a fair salary, a fair salary).
9. Last-minute studying is not so effective as (keeping up, to keep up) with the daily assignments.

10. My ambition is to be a doctor and (specializing, to specialize) in surgery.
11. Our neighbor is helpful, friendly, and (he talks a great deal, talkative).
12. To be completely outclassed is not so annoying as (losing, to lose) by one point.
13. We plan to go to college to study, to prepare for a career, and (for the purpose of making, to make) new friends.
14. The pioneers were industrious, ambitious, and (courageous, they had a great deal of courage).
15. A calculating machine offers the benefits of speed and (you can get accurate results, accuracy).
16. In the summer we enjoy picnicking, outdoor camping, and (to go sightseeing, sightseeing).
17. Paperback books are handy, inexpensive, and (you can get them anywhere, easily available).
18. She couldn't decide whether she should repeat the subject or (to drop, drop) it entirely.
19. To climb the mountain is much more fun than (to go, going) up by the scenic railway.
20. Henderson, the president of the class and (who is also captain of the team, captain of the team), will lead the rally.

11. DANGLING CONSTRUCTIONS

WHAT IS A DANGLING CONSTRUCTION?

Coming up the stairs, the clock struck twelve.

The phrase *Coming up the stairs* has nothing to modify and is therefore *dangling.* It would appear to modify *clock,* but it obviously doesn't, for clocks can't climb stairs.

Coming up the stairs is a dangling construction because it cannot be attached to any word in the sentence.

CORRECTING A DANGLING CONSTRUCTION

The way to correct the error is to provide a noun or pronoun to which the dangling construction can be attached. Examples:

1. Coming up the stairs, *he* heard the clock strike twelve.
2. As *he* was coming up the stairs, the clock struck twelve.

Note that in both previous examples we stopped the construction from dangling by providing the pronoun *he*.

TYPICAL QUESTIONS ON DANGLING CONSTRUCTIONS

Rule: Be sure to include the noun or pronoun to which a phrase or a clause refers. Otherwise, you will have a *dangling construction*.

1. (After preparing, After having prepared, *After I had prepared*) all day for Jane's visit, my desire to see her increased.

ANSWER EXPLAINED

Because *After I had prepared* has the pronoun *I*, it tells who did the preparing. The other choices do not; they are dangling constructions.

2. While driving along the highway, (a fatal head-on collision was seen, *we saw a fatal head-on collision*).

ANSWER EXPLAINED

The italicized clause is correct because it includes the pronoun *we*, telling who saw the collision.

3. Although (tired, *they were tired*) of climbing, it was cheering to see their goal just ahead.

ANSWER EXPLAINED

The pronoun *they*, in the clause *they were tired*, tells who was tired.

4. While (at, *he was at*) lunch, the soup bowl slid onto his lap.

ANSWER EXPLAINED

The pronoun *he*, in the phrase *he was at*, identifies the person at lunch. The other phrase would suggest that the soup bowl was at lunch.

5. To succeed in life, (hard work can't be escaped, *you can't escape hard work*).

ANSWER EXPLAINED

The pronoun *you*, in the clause *you can't escape hard work*, tells who is *to succeed in life*.

Exercise on dangling constructions. Some of the following sentences are correct, but most are incorrect. Rewrite the incorrect sentences.

1. All the next week, while driving back and forth to work, the scene remained vivid in my mind.
2. Knowing little about algebra, it was difficult to solve the equation.
3. The tomb of an Egyptian pharaoh commanded attention coming into the museum.
4. As she hurried down the stairs, her shoe fell off.
5. While passing a large boulder, a sudden noise made me jump.
6. While shopping in the supermarket, their parking lights remained on.
7. Humbled by the loss of prestige, his plans changed.
8. After failing the examination, the teacher advised them to study regularly.
9. Sailing up the harbor, the Statue of Liberty was seen.
10. The five-o'clock whistle blew as we came down the avenue.

12. MISPLACED MODIFIERS

Through carelessness we sometimes place a phrase, clause, or word too far from the word, or words, it modifies. As a result, the sentence fails to convey our exact meaning and may produce a kind of amusement that we did not intend.

TYPICAL CASES OF MISPLACED MODIFIERS

MISPLACED PHRASE: Francis caught sight of the train passing *through the kitchen door.*
    Obviously the train did not pass through the kitchen door. The phrase *through the kitchen door* modifies *caught sight of* and should be placed nearer to it, rather than next to *passing.*

ERROR CORRECTED: *Through the kitchen door* Francis caught sight of the train passing.

MISPLACED CLAUSE: They brought a puppy for my sister *that they call Rex.*
    The clause *that they call Rex* modifies *puppy,* not *sister.*

ERROR CORRECTED: They brought a puppy *that they call Rex* for my sister.

MISPLACED WORD: To get to the beach we *nearly* traveled six miles.
    The word *nearly* modifies *six.*

ERROR CORRECTED: To get to the beach we traveled *nearly* six miles.

Exercise on misplaced modifiers. If a modifier has been misplaced, rewrite the sentence to correct the error.

1. We came upon a police station rounding the corner.
2. The plant was given to us by a friend that was supposed to flower in the spring.
3. A qualified physician can only prescribe medicine.
4. Occurring in April, we were surprised by the event.
5. Through the corner of my eye, I saw a squirrel approaching.
6. Reserve a room for the gentleman with a bath.
7. I caught a glimpse of the old piano walking down the hall.
8. Joe found a letter in his mailbox that doesn't belong to him.
9. My brother nearly earned five dollars by cutting our neighbors' lawns yesterday.
10. Coming up the hill we saw the moon rising.
11. Her mother is the woman talking to the policeman in the red dress.
12. He discovered a bird's nest trimming the hedges.
13. Brenda put the books on the bed that she borrowed from the library.
14. We made a profit of almost ten dollars.
15. Karen bought a coat in the department store with a detachable hood.

13. SUPERFLUOUS WORDS

Always revise your writing to remove superfluous (unnecessary) words, such as those in italics:

Doesn't she have a beautiful smile *on her face?*
On my next birthday I will be seventeen *years old.*
We rowed to a small island *surrounded by water* and pitched our tent.

TYPICAL QUESTIONS ON SUPERFLUOUS WORDS

Rule: Omit words that add unnecessary details or repeat ideas already expressed.

1. This is a club with which I wouldn't want to be (*associated,* associated with).

ANSWER EXPLAINED

> *associated* ends the sentence correctly. The preposition *with* appears earlier in the clause and should not be repeated.

HINT

> Do not begin and end a clause with the same preposition.

2. He refused (to accept my invitation, *my invitation*) to our club party.

ANSWER EXPLAINED

    to accept adds nothing to the meaning of the sentence.

3. Your answer is correct; please (*repeat it*, repeat it again) for the class.

ANSWER EXPLAINED

    again is unnecessary. If the student repeated his answer *again*, he would be giving it for the *third* time.

4. Are you telling me the (*truth*, real truth)?

ANSWER EXPLAINED

    real adds nothing to the meaning of *truth* and should be eliminated.

Exercise on removing superfluous words. Rewrite the following sentences, omitting the unnecessary words:

1. A boy of about nine years old opened the door.
2. Dennis, where will the game be held at?
3. A heavy dew lay on the surface of the grass.
4. On his head he wore a hunting cap.
5. She feels better, now that the operation is over with.
6. Karen found the old hair styles of bygone days amusing.
7. My new car is heavier in weight than yours.
8. They didn't know to whom to give the supplies to.
9. We can't make a decision until we know the true facts.
10. The headline at the top of the main article says: "Fire Out of Control."
11. After each stanza, repeat the chorus again.
12. Take this prescription over to the nearest pharmacy.
13. Tell me for whom you are now working for.
14. Most department stores run special sales in the month of January.
15. Only one of their starting players was shorter in height than our men.
16. My brother Tim slept throughout the entire performance.
17. I cannot remember where I met him at.
18. We received a letter from Ruth written on her personal stationery.
19. In my opinion, I think you are wrong.
20. He thought that, if he apologized, that he would be excused.
21. The end result was that I was given a new test.
22. Fresh fruit and vegetables are more expensive in price now.
23. The secretary declined to accept my offer to type the report.
24. Richard, why are you so upset for?
25. Parents prefer small children to play indoors when it rains outside.

14. SOME EXPRESSIONS TO AVOID

Below are some common expressions—most of them nonstandard—that you should learn to avoid.

1. AVOID: He wants that TV set *irregardless* of cost.
   SAY: He wants that TV set *regardless* of cost.

2. AVOID: What kind (sort, type) of *a book* are you reading?
   SAY: What kind (sort, type) of *book* are you reading?

3. AVOID: She *graduated* high school last year.
   SAY: She *graduated from* high school last year.

4. AVOID: *Being that* I'm older, I'll go first.
   SAY: *Since* I'm older, I'll go first.

5. AVOID: He (She, It) *don't* appear to be old.
   SAY: He (She, It) *doesn't* appear to be old.

6. AVOID: Credit is *when you trust somebody*.
   SAY: Credit is *trust*.

7. AVOID: I was *sure* happy to meet her.
   SAY: I was *surely* happy to meet her.

8. AVOID: He dances *good*.
   SAY: He dances *well*.

9. AVOID: We *had ought* to go in now.
   SAY: We *ought* to go in now.

10. AVOID: My *father, he* says I'm lazy.
    SAY: My *father* says I'm lazy.

11. AVOID: *This here* book was just published.
    SAY: *This* book was just published.

12. AVOID: He will help *hisself* if they will help *theirselves*.
    SAY: He will help *himself* if they will help *themselves*.

13. AVOID: *In "Sea-Fever"* it tells about the lure of the sea.
    SAY: *"Sea-Fever"* tells about the lure of the sea.

14. AVOID: Try *and* do better.
    SAY: Try *to* do better.

15. AVOID: The reason is *because* I was sick.
    SAY: The reason is *that* I was sick.

16. AVOID: *Like* I told you, he moved to Seattle.
    SAY: *As* I told you, he moved to Seattle.

17. AVOID: *Me and my friend* went to the circus.
    SAY: *My friend and I* went to the circus.

18. AVOID: *Most* always April is cool there.
    SAY: *Almost* always April is cool there.

19. AVOID: Please get *off of* the platform.
    SAY: Please get *off* the platform.

20. AVOID: That was a *real* good movie.
    SAY: That was a *really* good movie.

21. AVOID: Would you hand me *them* tools?
    SAY: Would you hand me *those* tools?

22. AVOID: His project is different *than* mine.
    SAY: His project is different *from* mine.

23. AVOID: *That there* boy is my cousin.
    SAY: *That* boy is my cousin.

24. AVOID: Eleanor seems *kind (sort) of* tired.
    SAY: Eleanor seems *rather* tired.

25. AVOID: I read in the newspapers *where* the coach resigned.
    SAY: I read in the newspaper *that* the coach resigned.

TYPICAL QUESTIONS ON EXPRESSIONS TO AVOID

1. (Irregardless, *Regardless*) of what you believe, your answer is correct.

ANSWER EXPLAINED

Regardless is standard English. *Irregardless* is nonstandard.
Regardless means "without regard." *Irregardless* is poor because it says "without" twice: (1) in the prefix *ir-* (meaning *not*), and (2) in the suffix *-less.*

2. Will you please tell me what (*kind of,* kind of a) book you would like to read.

ANSWER EXPLAINED

The article *a* in "kind of *a* book" is useless. Say "kind of book."
Similarly, say *sort of,* instead of *sort of a.*

Exercise on expressions to avoid. Some of the following sentences are correct, but most are incorrect. Rewrite the incorrect sentences.

1. Being that he was the best qualified person, he received the appointment.
2. You had ought to return this book before it becomes overdue.
3. Music, for example, most always has listening and viewing audiences numbering in the hundreds of thousands.
4. What kind of ending does *Moby Dick* have?
5. When will your brother graduate law school?
6. The reason for my refusal is that you're undependable.
7. He hurriedly took the luggage off of the bus rack.
8. Would you please lend me them notes for tonight?
9. What type of a jacket are you interested in?
10. My teacher, he said we should memorize that table.
11. Give me that there book lying on the desk.
12. All of us were kind of upset when we heard the news.
13. Most everyone there wore a campaign button.
14. Try and call me up before ten-thirty.
15. We always get a friendly welcome in that there place.
16. I'm going to the party irregardless of what you say.
17. Being that he broke the watch, he should pay for the repairs.
18. They went to bed early, as little children should.
19. It don't make the slightest difference to us.
20. Bliss is when you are perfectly happy.
21. They did it theirselves in less than an hour.
22. In *The Return of the Native,* it tells about a beautiful girl named Eustacia.
23. Me and my brother have always attended the same schools.
24. Can you recommend a really good short story?
25. The second problem was hardly different than the first.
26. Henry took all the old magazines off the shelf.
27. Mr. Adams recites Shakespearean soliloquies very good.
28. This here apparatus is certainly quite complicated.
29. Most always we have a dance before the final examinations.
30. Did you read in the sports column where the Rovers are getting a new manager?
31. The reason is because we were unavoidably delayed in leaving the house.
32. The club members prepared the stage setting all by theirselves.
33. I checked all my answers, like my teacher had suggested.
34. After the first marking period, Helen resolved that she would try to do better.
35. My uncle, he says that fishing is the most relaxing sport.

15. PUNCTUATION

If you know the rules of correct punctuation, you will be both a better writer and a better reader. In your writing you will be unlikely to commit such blunders as "After eating grandmother washed the dishes." When you encounter a colon [:] in your reading, you will immediately sense the author's next move: he will either present a series or explain more fully an idea he has just stated. To improve your punctuation skill, review the rules and do the exercises on the following pages.

REVIEW OF PUNCTUATION RULES

1. USE THE PERIOD [.]

a. After a statement.
Our school has a new physics laboratory.

b. After a command.
Put your pens down.

c. After most abbreviations.
Mr.   etc.   p.m.   op. cit.

Use *only one period* after an abbreviation that ends a sentence.
The sports editor is William A. Harris, Jr.

WITH CLOSING QUOTATION MARKS: The period is inside.
Mother said, "Dinner is ready."

2. USE THE QUESTION MARK [?] after a question.

When will you hand in your report?
"Where are you going?" asked Dad.

EXCEPTION: After a request phrased as a question for the sake of politeness, you may use a period.
Will you please detach the stub and return it with your payment.

WITH CLOSING QUOTATION MARKS: The question mark is inside if it belongs to the quotation only.
Mr. Rossi asked, "Who would like to volunteer?"
The question mark is outside if it belongs to the sentence as a whole.
Do you know who wrote "The Death of the Hired Man"?

3. USE THE EXCLAMATION POINT [!] after an exclamation.

What a fine throw Sam made!
"Look out!" someone shouted.

WITH CLOSING QUOTATION MARKS: The exclamation point is inside if it belongs to the quotation only.
She exclaimed, "What a delightful surprise!"
The exclamation point is outside if it belongs to the sentence as a whole.
How thrilling it was to hear the band play "Stars and Stripes Forever"!

Exercise 1. Rewrite each sentence, inserting omitted periods, question marks, and exclamation points.

1. Suddenly someone screamed, "Help me"
2. Have you read "Annabel Lee" she asked
3. Place hands on shoulders
4. Susan asked, "Is Tom coming"
5. *Punctual* means "on time"
6. What a beautiful day
7. Didn't George Gershwin write *Rhapsody in Blue*
8. The official replied, "No comment"
9. Fasten your seat belts
10. Asked to apologize, she screamed, "Never"

4. USE THE COMMA [,]

a. To set off words of direct address (words that tell to whom a remark is addressed).
Mr. Jones, that is the reason for my absence. (one comma)
That is the reason for my absence, *Mr. Jones.* (one comma)
That, *Mr. Jones,* is the reason for my absence. (Use two commas to set off a word or expression that neither begins nor ends a sentence.)

b. To set off words in apposition (words that give additional information about the preceding or following word or expression).
A light sleeper, my father is the first to awake. (one comma)
The first to awake is my father, *a light sleeper.* (one comma)
My father, *a light sleeper,* is the first to awake. (two commas)

CAUTION: Use no commas when the appositive is so closely associated with the word it modifies that the two are pronounced as one expression, with no pause between them.

Do you know my friend *Jack?*
Alexander *the Great* died of a fever.
Some consider the number *thirteen* unlucky.
Have you read the play *Julius Caesar?*

c. To set off a direct quotation.

The chairman said, *"The meeting is adjourned."*
"The meeting is adjourned," said the chairman.
"The meeting," said the chairman, *"is adjourned."* (Use two commas to set off a divided quotation.)

d. To set off an interrupting, or parenthetic, expression.

My sister, *Heaven help her,* has three finals on Friday.
These prices, *we are well aware,* are the lowest in town.

e. After such words as *yes, no, ah, oh, well,* etc., at the beginning of a sentence.

Oh, I'm sorry to hear it.

f. Before the conjunction (*and, but, or, for*) in a compound sentence.

Geraldine was the first to leave the examination room, *and* I followed about five minutes later.

NOTE: The comma is unnecessary in a short compound sentence:
Sarah washed the dishes and I dried them.

EXCEPTION: Use the comma before the conjunction *for* to prevent misreading.
Dad stopped the car, *for* Emma was ill.

g. After each item in a series, except the last.

The fruit bowl contained *peaches, pears, nectarines, plums, grapes,* and *bananas.* (The comma before *and* may be omitted.)

h. To set off a contrasting expression.

The girls did most of the work, *not the boys.*
The girls, *not the boys,* did most of the work.

i. After an introductory prepositional phrase.

Along the route from the airport to City Hall, the hero was wildly acclaimed.

NOTE: The comma may be omitted if the phrase is short:
Along the route the hero was wildly acclaimed.

j. After an introductory subordinate clause.

> *When I brought home a report card with three A's,* Dad was surprised.

k. After an introductory participial phrase.

> *Frightened by our approach,* the burglar fled.

l. To set off a nonessential clause (a clause that *can be omitted* without making the sentence illogical or changing its basic meaning).

> Franklin D. Roosevelt, *who was elected President four times,* was an avid stamp collector.

> CAUTION: Do not set off an essential clause (a clause that *cannot be omitted*).

> Franklin D. Roosevelt is the only American *who was elected President four times.* (Note that if we omit the clause "who... times" we are left with the illogical sentence "Franklin D. Roosevelt is the only American." This proves the clause "who... times" is *essential;* therefore, *no comma before "who."*)

m. To set off a nonessential participial phrase.

> The patient, *weakened by loss of blood,* lapsed into unconsciousness.

> CAUTION: Do not set off an essential participial phrase.

> People *weakened by loss of blood* need transfusions. (no commas)

n. After the salutation in a friendly letter.

> Dear Joe,   Dear Agnes,   Dear Dad,

o. After the complimentary close in a friendly or business letter.

> Your friend,   Sincerely yours,   Yours truly,

p. Between the day of the month and the year.

> December 7, 1941   October 12, 1492

q. Before the state in an address.

> Fort Lauderdale, Florida 33310   St. Louis, Missouri 63166

r. To set off such expressions as *however, moreover, furthermore, nevertheless, on the other hand, incidentally, of course, for example,* etc.

> The results, nevertheless, were quite satisfactory.

WITH CLOSING QUOTATION MARKS: The comma is inside.

> "Remember to revise your paper," Mr. Brown concluded.

Exercise 2. Rewrite each sentence, adding the necessary punctuation.

1. All students who have not presented parent consent notes will be excluded from the trip
2. No I have never been there
3. Have you ever considered Mr Jones began how exciting it is to operate a computer
4. Jackson High is the only school that beat us last year but we expect to beat them this year
5. At the start of our hike up the mountain everybody was in a good mood
6. For these reasons my fellow students I ask you to vote for me
7. The first orbital flight was made on April 12 1961
8. Anthony Gallo the captain of the track team is in my chemistry class
9. The results I am happy to say took us completely by surprise.
10. Don't you agree that the parents not the children should be held responsible
11. Students failing in the first quarter may attend a special help class after school
12. Encouraged by her success in Spanish Marian is now planning to begin French
13. My shopping list included aluminum foil cereal milk sugar and potatoes
14. We left Chicago at midnight hoping for better weather by morning
15. It is not possible however that the judge will suspend the sentence
16. He was eager to work for Mrs Bailey had praised his attitude
17. As I entered my friend George exclaimed Look who's here
18. Beverly Edwards our class representative will make a brief report
19. When did Ivan the Terrible reign
20. Every home destroyed in the storm is being rebuilt

5. USE THE SEMICOLON [;]

a. To separate items in a series when the items contain commas.
> The following officers were elected: *Marvin Bloch, president; Eleanor Swenson, vice president;* and *Mildred White, secretary.*

b. Between main clauses that contain commas.
> Sydney Carton, the hero, worships Lucie Manette; and he eventually sacrifices his life to save Charles Darnay, Lucie's husband.

c. Between main clauses when the conjunction (*and, but, for, or*) has been left out.
> We have made many suggestions to your committee; not a single one has been accepted.

d. Between main clauses connected by *however, moreover, nevertheless, for example, consequently,* etc.

It was really a comfortable seat; *consequently,* she felt no inclination to move.

WITH CLOSING QUOTATION MARKS: The semicolon is outside.

Edna St. Vincent Millay was only nineteen when she wrote "Renascence"; nevertheless, it is an outstanding poem.

6. USE THE COLON [:]

a. After the word *following* and similar expressions that introduce a list or series.

The dinner menu offered a choice of the *following:* broiled chicken, roast beef, liver and bacon, or baked mackerel.

b. Before a long quotation, especially a formal one.

Article VIII of the Constitution states: "Excessive bail shall not be required, nor excessive fines imposed, nor cruel and unusual punishments inflicted."

c. Before a part of a sentence that merely restates, explains, or gives an example of what has just been stated.

Our firm has a fixed policy: we will not be undersold.

A Shakespearean sonnet consists of four parts: three quatrains and a couplet.

d. After the salutation of a business letter.

Dear Sir: Gentlemen: Dear Mr. O'Brien:

WITH CLOSING QUOTATION MARKS: The colon is outside.

There are three characters in "The Death of the Hired Man": Mary, Warren, and Silas.

7. USE THE DASH [—]

a. To show a sudden change in thought.

We have a democratic student government—*of course, we don't make all the rules*—that gives us a voice in school affairs.

b. Before a summary of what has just been stated in the sentence.

Staying on the team, graduating, going to college—*everything depended on my getting better marks.*

8. USE PARENTHESES ( )

   a. To enclose information added to the sentence to guide the reader.
The decline in exports in the past two years has been considerable *(see graph on p. 291).*

   b. To enclose numbers or letters used to list items in a sentence.
A book owned by a library is usually represented in the card catalog by (1) a title card, (2) an author card, and (3) a subject card.

9. USE BRACKETS [ ] to enclose a comment that interrupts a direct quotation.

   She said, "I helped Tom occasionally with his Latin [*in fact, she saved him from failing*] when he had Mrs. Brown."

10. USE QUOTATION MARKS [" "]

   a. To set off titles of short works: poems, essays, short stories, one-act plays, songs, magazine articles, etc.
"The Rime of the Ancient Mariner" (poem)
"On Doors" (essay)
"The Gift of the Magi" (short story)
"The Star-Spangled Banner" (song)

   NOTE: In handwritten or typewritten matter, underline titles of full-length works (novels, biographies, full-length plays, anthologies, nonfiction books, etc.) and titles of newspapers, magazines, operas, and motion pictures.
<u>Macbeth</u> (full-length play)
<u>Modern American and British Poetry</u> (anthology)
<u>Giants in the Earth</u> (novel)
<u>Newsweek</u> (magazine)

   b. To set off a definition. (The word or expression being defined should be underlined.)
The expression <u>to aggravate</u> means "to make worse."

   c. To set off a direct quotation (a speaker's exact words).
The principal said, *"We have been informed that our cafeteria will be renovated."* (Capitalize the first word of a direct quotation: use *We,* not *we.*)
"We have been informed that our cafeteria will be renovated," the principal said.

"*We have been informed,*" the principal said, "*that our cafeteria will be renovated.*" (Two sets of quotation marks are needed when a direct quotation is divided.)

CAUTION: Do not use quotation marks with an indirect quotation.

The principal said that we had been informed that our cafeteria would be renovated. (no quotation marks)

NOTE: To set off a quotation within a direct quotation, use single quotation marks.

"Please explain," the prosecutor asked, "what you mean by '*I don't remember exactly.*'"

Exercise 3. Rewrite each of the following sentences, correcting the errors in punctuation.

1. Four words may be unfamiliar to you in "The Man With the Hoe:" stolid, seraphim, Pleiades, and immedicable.
2. "If we don't hurry, said Marcia, we will miss our bus."
3. Give dollars, quarters, dimes, pennies anything you can spare.
4. One of Poe's finest short stories is *The Tell-Tale Heart.*
5. The expression *a baker's dozen* means "thirteen".
6. Your outline should provide for three parts; an introduction, a body, and a conclusion.
7. Miss Burke stated "Wednesday is absolutely [she stressed this word] the last day for handing in reports".
8. The manager is very busy: nevertheless, he will try to help you.
9. To qualify you must be a senior have at least an 85% average, and present recommendations from three teachers.
10. The assembly leader then announced, "Let us all rise to sing America and our school song."

TYPICAL QUESTIONS ON PUNCTUATION

Each of the following sentences contains an underlined expression. Below each sentence are four suggested answers. The correct answer has been inserted at the end of the question.

1. In his locker we found the <u>following;</u> an old textbook, a banner, and an overcoat.

   1. Correct as is
   2. following:
   3. following.
   4. following,

[2]

ANSWER EXPLAINED

A colon [:] is needed after *following* to introduce the series "an old textbook, a banner, and an overcoat." (Rule involved: 6*a*, page 191.)

2. That, my friend is not the correct answer.

   1. Correct as is   3. , my friend,
   2. my friend,   4. my friend

ANSWER EXPLAINED

The words *my friend* are in direct address and must be set off from the rest of the sentence by two commas. (Rule involved: 4*a*, page 187.)

3. Every man, who breaks the law, should be punished.

   1. Correct as is
   2. man who breaks the law; should
   3. man who breaks the law should
   4. man, who breaks the law should

ANSWER EXPLAINED

The clause *who breaks the law* is essential to the sentence and must not be set off by any punctuation. If we temporarily remove this clause, we are left with the illogical statement "Every man should be punished." This proves that the clause *who breaks the law* is essential to the sentence. Essential clauses must not be set off by any punctuation from the rest of the sentence. (Rule involved: 4*l*, page 189.)

4. Have you read "The Murders in the Rue Morgue?"

   1. Correct as is
   2. The Murders in the Rue Morgue?
   3. The Murders in the Rue Morgue.
   4. "The Murders in the Rue Morgue"?

ANSWER EXPLAINED

The work mentioned in this sentence is a short story and should be enclosed by quotation marks. The question mark should follow the quotation marks, for it belongs to the sentence as a whole. (Rules involved: 10*a*, page 192, and 2, page 186.)

REVIEW EXERCISE ON PUNCTUATION

Each of the following sentences contains an underlined expression. Below each sentence are four suggested answers. Decide which answer is correct. Be prepared to give the reasons for your choice.

(1) "Will you come too" she pleaded?

    1. Correct as is   3. too?" she pleaded.
    2. too,?" she pleaded.   4. too," she pleaded?

(2) Vegetable prices are much cheaper now; for example string beans are nineteen cents.

    1. Correct as is   3. now, for example,
    2. now: for example,   4. now; for example,

(3) The three main characters are Johnny Hobart, a teenager, his mother a widow, and the local druggist.

    1. Correct as is
    2. teenager; his mother, a widow; and
    3. teenager; his mother a widow; and
    4. teenager, his mother, a widow and

(4) Please fellows don't drop the ball.

    1. Correct as is   3. Please fellows;
    2. Please, fellows   4. Please, fellows,

(5) "Our next short story," Miss Pine announced, "Will be "Haircut" by Ring Lardner."

    1. Correct as is   3. will be "Haircut"
    2. "will be "Haircut"   4. "will be 'Haircut'

(6) All the students, whose reports were not handed in, failed.

    1. Correct as is
    2. students who's reports were not handed in failed.
    3. students, who's reports were not handed in, failed.
    4. students whose reports were not handed in failed.

(7) We saw three Shakespearean plays on television: "Macbeth," "Hamlet," and "Richard III."

    1. Correct as is
    2. television: "Macbeth," "Hamlet," and "Richard III".
    3. television: Macbeth, Hamlet, and Richard III.
    4. television; Macbeth, Hamlet, and Richard III.

(8) Russ, the first pitcher, had poor control; but Artie, his successor, was even wilder.

1. Correct as is
2. control, but Artie,
3. control; but Artie
4. control: but Artie,

(9) You may not like spinach, however, it's good for you.

1. Correct as is
2. spinach; however, its
3. spinach, however, its
4. spinach; however, it's

(10) "Before starting to write your composition plan what you are going to say," Miss Wright advised.

1. Correct as is
2. composition plan what you are going to say",
3. composition, plan what you are going to say,"
4. composition, plan what you are going to say",

(11) Oh its a long, sad tale.

1. Correct as is
2. Oh, its
3. Oh, its'
4. Oh, it's

(12) The contest winners are as follows; Mary, first; Agnes, second; and John, third.

1. Correct as is
2. follows: Mary, first; Agnes, second; and John, third.
3. follows: Mary, first, Agnes, second, and John, third.
4. follows; Mary first; Agnes second; and John third.

(13) "When you come to the stop sign", Dad repeated, "make a full stop."

1. Correct as is
2. sign" Dad repeated,
3. sign," Dad repeated
4. sign," Dad repeated,

(14) My friends warned me, "Mrs. Ott doesn't like students, who chew gum in class."

1. Correct as is
2. students who chew gum in class".
3. students who chew gum in class."
4. students, who chew gum in class".

(15) I have always liked "Sea-Fever"; in fact, I know the first stanza by heart.

1. Correct as is
2. "Sea-Fever;" in fact,
3. Sea-Fever; in fact,
4. "Sea-Fever"; In fact,

(16) Bill suggested, "Lets not wait, for the lines are too long."

    1. Correct as is   3. "Let's not wait, for
    2. "Lets not wait for   4. "Let's not wait for

(17) Every motorist, who is caught speeding, should lose his license.

    1. Correct as is
    2. motorist who is caught speeding should
    3. motorist who is caught speeding; should
    4. motorist, who is caught speeding should

(18) Your answer, not her's, caused all the excitement.

    1. Correct as is   3. not hers,
    2. not hers   4. not her's

(19) Mabel asked, "To which colleges has Joan applied."

    1. Correct as is   3. applied".
    2. applied"?   4. applied?"

(20) Have you read the poem by Robert Frost entitled "Mending Wall?"

    1. Correct as is   3. Mending Wall?
    2. "Mending Wall"?   4. Mending Wall?

16. CAPITALIZATION

Review your capitalization rules. They are essential for good writing technique.

Should you write *the Reader's Digest* or *The Reader's Digest?* Which is correct—*my Uncle John* or *my uncle John?* Are the names of the seasons capitalized (*spring* or *Spring*)? Is it *Seventy-second Street* or *Seventy-Second Street?*

The answers to these and other capitalization problems appear in the next few pages. Study the examples. Then do the exercises.

REVIEW OF CAPITALIZATION RULES

1. CAPITALIZE the opening word:

    a. Of a sentence.

        It is a pleasure to go hiking in spring.

    b. Of a direct quotation.

        The officer explained, "If you go two blocks north, you will see the main entrance."

DO NOT CAPITALIZE the opening word of the second half of a divided quotation, unless it begins a new sentence.

"If you go two blocks north," the officer explained, "you (*no capital*) will see the main entrance."

"Go two blocks north," the officer explained. "There (*a capital is used to begin the new sentence*) you will see the main entrance."

c. Of a line of poetry.

"Tomorrow, and tomorrow, and tomorrow
Creeps in this petty pace from day to day."
—*William Shakespeare*

DO NOT CAPITALIZE the opening word of a line if the poet himself did not do so.

"The fog comes
on (*no capital*) little cat feet."
—*Carl Sandburg*

d. Of the salutation in a letter. In addition, capitalize a *noun* or a *title* in the salutation.

Dear Pat,   My dear Mr. Blum:
Dear Uncle Mike,   Dear Sirs:

e. Of the complimentary close of a letter. (Capitalize the opening word only.)

Your friend,   Sincerely yours,
Your best pal,   Very truly yours,
Your former pupil,   Yours very truly,

f. Of each item in an outline. (Note these items from an outline on "How I Learned to Drive":)

   I. Driver-training course

      A. In the classroom

      B. Behind the wheel

   II. Practice in the family car

2. CAPITALIZE proper nouns (names of particular persons, places, things, etc.) and proper adjectives (adjectives formed from proper nouns).

   A *common noun* refers to no particular person, place, or thing and is not capitalized. Examples: man, country, building.

   A *proper noun* refers to a particular person, place, or thing and is always capitalized. Examples: Shakespeare (a particular man), Mexico (a particular country), Empire State Building (a particular building).

An adjective derived from a proper noun is also capitalized. Examples: a Shakespearean play, a Mexican village.

Learn to CAPITALIZE the proper nouns and proper adjectives in these important categories:

a. Names of persons.

> John Hancock, Marian Anderson, William Faulkner

b. Names of geographical places.

> Europe, Pacific Ocean, United States, Ohio River, Mt. Washington, Atlantic City, Main Street, Yellowstone National Park

> DO NOT CAPITALIZE the second part of a hyphenated number: Example: Forty-second Street.

c. Names of sections of countries (especially of the United States) and their people.

> New England, the South, the West, Northerner

> DO NOT CAPITALIZE *north, south, east,* and *west* when used to indicate direction.

> Go one mile south and then turn east.

d. Names of buildings, museums, churches, trains, ships, etc.

> Municipal Building, Seattle Art Museum, Church of the Holy Family, Ambassador Hotel, Brighton Beach Express, S.S. *Constitution*

e. Names of institutions and organizations.

> Sewanhaka High School, American Automobile Association, General Motors Corporation, Boy Scouts of America

f. Names of governmental subdivisions.

> House of Representatives, Department of Agriculture, Bureau of Motor Vehicles, Boulder Police Department

g. Names of days, months, and holidays.

> Monday, December, Labor Day

> DO NOT CAPITALIZE the seasons: spring, summer, autumn (fall), winter.

h. Names of historical events, eras, and documents.

> Battle of the Coral Sea, the Renaissance, the Declaration of Independence

i. Names of languages.

   English, French, Russian, Spanish, Hebrew

j. Names of nationalities.

   American, Japanese, Egyptian, Israeli

k. Names of races.

   Caucasian, Negro, Mongolian

l. Names of religions.

   Christian, Roman Catholic, Protestant, Jewish, Mohammedan, Hindu

m. References to the Supreme Being.

   God, the Creator, the Almighty, the Lord, Heaven, Jehovah, Jesus Christ, Savior, His name

   "I will fear no evil: for Thou art with me."
   —Twenty-third Psalm

   DO NOT CAPITALIZE references to pagan divinities—only their names.

   Zeus was the chief of the ancient Greek gods, and Jupiter was his Roman counterpart.

n. Titles preceding persons' names.

   Mr. Lombardi, Dr. Berg, Professor Holmes, General Lee, President Lincoln, Uncle Jack, Cousin Ruth

   DO NOT CAPITALIZE titles used alone, except for very high government officials.

   The doctor came.
   Who is the president of your club?
   At the airport, the President was greeted by the Mayor and several city councilmen.

o. Titles of parents and relatives not preceded by a possessive word (e.g., my, your, Frank's, etc.).

   I saw Father with Uncle George.
   I saw my father with my uncle.

   EXCEPTION: If a name follows the title, capitalize the title, even when preceded by a possessive word.

   My Uncle George plays golf.

p. Titles of books, plays, articles, poems, short stories, etc.

DO NOT CAPITALIZE the following unless they stand first in the title: (1) the articles (*a, an, the*); (2) conjunctions (*and, or,* etc.); (3) short prepositions (*to, of, for,* etc.).
The Old Man and the Sea, An Enemy of the People, "**A Night at an Inn,**" "**To a Mouse**"

q. Titles of newspapers and magazines.

DO NOT CAPITALIZE the word *the* before the title of a newspaper or magazine, unless it begins a sentence.
I read the *New York Times, Newsweek,* and the *Saturday Review.*

r. Titles of courses.
This term I am taking **English** 8, **Economics** 1, **Math** 12, **Physics** 2, and **French** 6.

DO NOT CAPITALIZE school subjects, except languages.
This term I am taking **English**, economics, math, physics, and **French.**

s. Titles of holy writings and their subdivisions.
the **B**ible, the **O**ld **T**estament, the **N**ew **T**estament, the **B**ook of **R**uth, the **G**ospel of **St. M**atthew

t. Brand names (but not the product).
Electrolux vacuum cleaner, **F**ord sedan, **S**unkist orange

3. CAPITALIZE the words *I* and *O*.
Jane and **I** hope you will come.
Hail to thee, **O** Caesar!

DO NOT CAPITALIZE the word *oh,* except at the beginning of a sentence.
"Destroyer and preserver; hear, **o**h, hear!"
—*Percy Bysshe Shelley*

4. CAPITALIZE personifications (ideas or abstract objects treated as persons).
"**O** Liberty! Liberty! what crimes are committed in thy name!"
—*Madame Roland*

TYPICAL QUESTION ON CAPITALIZATION

The sentence below contains an underlined expression. Below the sentence are four suggested answers. The correct answer is printed at the end of the question.

QUESTION

After I had finished <u>High School, I went on to college</u>.

1. Correct as is
2. High School having been finished,
3. After finishing High School,
4. After I had finished high school,

$$[4]$$

ANSWER EXPLAINED

Since they do not refer to a particular high school, the words *high school* should not be capitalized.

RULE INVOLVED

A common noun (a noun referring to no particular person, place, or thing) is not capitalized. (See 2, page 198.)

REVIEW EXERCISES ON CAPITALIZATION

A. Each of the following sentences contains an underlined expression. Below each sentence are four suggested answers. Decide which answer is correct. Be prepared to explain the reasons for your answers.

(1) I showed my <u>father your copy of the</u> *Reader's Digest*.

1. Correct as is
2. Father your copy of the
3. father your copy of *The*
4. Father your copy of *The*

(2) At what time did <u>the President summon his Doctor</u> to the White House?

1. Correct as is
2. The President summon his Doctor
3. the president summon his doctor
4. the President summon his doctor

(3) "<u>My Cousin Arthur,</u>" he said, "has just left for Annapolis."

1. Correct as is
2. cousin Arthur," he said, "has
3. cousin Arthur," he said, "Has
4. Cousin Arthur," he said, "Has

(4) Is there a crosstown bus on Thirty-Fourth Street?
 1. Correct as is
 2. Thirty-Fourth street?
 3. Thirty-fourth Street?
 4. thirty-fourth street?

(5) The letter concluded with the words "Yours very truly, Salvatore De Vito."
 1. Correct as is
 2. "Yours Very Truly,
 3. "yours very truly,
 4. "yours very Truly,

(6) Mr. Berson teaches us economics and American History.
 1. Correct as is
 2. Economics and American History.
 3. economics and American history.
 4. economics and american history.

(7) "Until three years ago," explained Bob, "My family lived in the South."
 1. Correct as is
 2. "my family lived in the south."
 3. "my family lived in the South."
 4. "My family lived in the south."

(8) Before coming here, she had attended High School in the city of Denver.
 1. Correct as is
 2. high school in the city
 3. High School in the City
 4. high school in the City

(9) You can see wonderful botanical displays in Prospect Park in the Spring.
 1. Correct as is
 2. park in the spring.
 3. park in the Spring.
 4. Park in the spring.

(10) I earned my best marks in chemistry 2 and Spanish 4.
 1. Correct as is
 2. Chemistry 2 and Spanish 4.
 3. chemistry 2 and spanish 4.
 4. Chemistry 2 and spanish 4.

(11) "There are several fine national parks in the west," said Uncle Ben.
 1. Correct as is
 2. west," said uncle Ben.
 3. West," said uncle Ben.
 4. West," said Uncle Ben.

(12) Didn't you know that Grandfather and Aunt Isabel were coming for dinner?
 1. Correct as is
 2. grandfather and Aunt Isabel
 3. Grandfather and aunt Isabel
 4. grandfather and aunt Isabel

(13) We shall read *The Call of the Wild* in our Literature class this spring.
1. Correct as is
2. The *Call of the Wild* in our literature class this Spring.
3. *The Call of the Wild* in our literature class this spring.
4. *The Call Of The Wild* in our literature class this spring.

(14) "My speech teacher is a Westerner," said Emily, "he was raised in California."
1. Correct as is
2. Westerner," said Emily, "He
3. westerner," said Emily. "He
4. Westerner," said Emily. "He

(15) The turning point in the Civil War was the Battle of Gettysburg.
1. Correct as is   3. war was the battle
2. War was the Battle   4. War was The Battle

(16) At Friday's assembly, Janet read the Twenty-Third Psalm from the Bible.
1. Correct as is
2. the Twenty-third Psalm from the Bible.
3. The Twenty-Third Psalm from The Bible.
4. the Twenty-third Psalm from The Bible.

(17) "A tree that looks at God all day,
   And lifts Her leafy arms to pray."
1. Correct as is   3. and lifts Her
2. and lifts her   4. And lifts her

(18) Dad bought Mother a Norge refrigerator last summer.
1. Correct as is
2. mother a Norge Refrigerator last summer.
3. Mother a Norge refrigerator last Summer.
4. mother a Norge Refrigerator last Summer.

(19) Shall we learn about the middle ages in European History I?
1. Correct as is
2. Middle Ages in European history I?
3. Middle Ages in European History I?
4. middle ages in european history I?

(20) "Dear old Pete," began the letter from my Cousin Harvey, "You'll probably be surprised to get this letter."
1. Correct as is
2. "Dear Old Pete," began the letter from my cousin
3. "Dear old Pete," began the letter from my cousin
4. "Dear Old Pete," began the letter from my Cousin

B. Rewrite each of the following sentences, correcting all errors in capitalization:

1. Drive east about a mile and a half to the Sixty-Ninth Road exit.
2. In Junior High School I had excellent teachers in English, French, and Art.
3. "When you telephone mother," said Dad, "Tell her when you expect to be home."
4. The Lieutenant was asked to describe his experiences in The Korean War.
5. Tell us, o mathematical genius, how you solved the second Physics problem.
6. I expect to specialize in American Literature at College next Fall.
7. My aunt Rose works in The Central Public Library at Mackinaw Avenue and Thirty-Seventh Street.
8. Wordsworth's Poem "Daffodils" ends as follows:
   "And then my heart with pleasure fills,
   and dances with the daffodils."
9. As we traveled through the South last March, we saw many Spring shrubs already in bloom.
10. "In Chicago," advises the travel book, "Be sure to visit the museum of Science and Industry and The Oriental Institute."

Chapter 6   The Related Areas Test
(Questions 61-65)

NOTE: Questions 61–65 may deal with either correct usage or related areas of English. The last chapter discussed correct usage. This chapter will deal with related areas of English.

Past questions in the related areas test have dealt with a variety of topics, including words and language, library and research skills, parliamentary procedure, the newspaper, magazines, propaganda techniques, letter-writing skills, and abbreviations.

SAMPLE RELATED AREAS TEST

Try the following examination. Then compare your answers with the answers and explanations at the end of the examination.

Directions (61–65): For each question in this group, select the best answer and write its *number* in the appropriate space on the separate answer sheet.   [5]

61. In the following entry from *Readers' Guide to Periodical Literature*, what does "My '77" mean?

> Savagery on the Playing Field, H. Adams. il
> Smithsonian 91:161–65, My '77

  1 the date the article was written
  2 the date the article was copyrighted
  3 the date of the magazine in which the article appears
  4 the date of the *Readers' Guide* supplement

62. In the library book call number $\dfrac{943.086}{S}$, what does the "S" under the line stand for?

  1 the author's last name
  2 a certain section of the library
  3 the Dewey Decimal System
  4 the seventh edition

63. In which magazine are condensations of popular magazine articles printed?

   1 *Harper's*   3 *Newsweek*
   2 *Atlantic Monthly*   4 *Reader's Digest*

64. Which reference book should be consulted *first* to locate the latest information on peanut production in Georgia?

   1 *The New York Times Index*
   2 *World Almanac*
   3 *Columbia-Lippincott Gazetteer of the World*
   4 Rand McNally *World Atlas*

65. Which magazine would most likely carry a discussion of recent classical recordings?

   1 *Saturday Review*   3 *Fortune*
   2 *People*   4 *Family Circle*

ANSWERS AND EXPLANATIONS

61. ANSWER: (3) the date of the magazine in which the article appears

   ANSWER EXPLAINED: The last item in an entry in *Readers' Guide to Periodical Literature* is the date of the magazine in which the article appears. Here, "My '77" indicates that the issue of the *Smithsonian* in which the article "Savagery on the Playing Field," by H. Adams, can be found is *May 1977*.

62. ANSWER: (1) the author's last name

   ANSWER EXPLAINED: In the call number $\dfrac{943.086}{S}$, *943.086* stands for the subject of the book, and S for the first letter of the author's last name. A call number for a book on a card in the card catalog tells where you may find the book on the library shelves.

63. ANSWER: (4) *Reader's Digest*

   ANSWER EXPLAINED: *Reader's Digest* prints condensations (abridgements) of articles that appeared originally in other popular magazines.

64. ANSWER: (1) *The New York Times Index*

   ANSWER EXPLAINED: Normally, for the latest information of a statistical nature, an almanac should be consulted first. As a follow-up, *The New*

York Times Index should be consulted, too, to see whether there have been more recent developments. However, the *1979 World Almanac* reports the number of bushels of peanuts produced in the United States *as a whole* for the year 1977. *It does not break this production figure down by states.* The *1978 World Almanac*, similarly, reports peanut production for the United States as a whole for the year 1976.

(Note, however, that the *1978 Statistical Abstract,* another almanac, does report the millions of pounds of peanuts produced in Georgia in 1977.)

The *1978 New York Times Index,* under PEANUTS, summarizes eight articles dealing with peanut production in Georgia, particularly with the Georgia peanut business owned by President Carter's family.

65. ANSWER: (1) *Saturday Review*

ANSWER EXPLAINED: The *Saturday Review*'s music columnist Irving Kolodin discusses composers, conductors, musicians, opera singers and, occasionally, recent classical recordings.

ADDITIONAL SAMPLE RELATED AREAS QUESTIONS

How would you have answered the following questions? Compare your answers with the answers and explanations on pages 210–211.

1. A group leader, in a good discussion, should
   1 let the "discussion hog'" talk himself out
   2 ignore disruptive action by group members
   3 remain generally neutral in the matter discussed
   4 make certain that every person in the group speaks at least twice

2. In a play, a person's "role" refers chiefly to his
   1 particular part   3 costume and dress
   2 first appearance on stage   4 final exit

3. Which word is the most abstract in meaning?
   1 sand   3 stone
   2 silver   4 stupidity

4. Which communicates its meaning most directly and exactly?
   1 a lyric poem   3 a group of words
   2 a traffic light   4 a musical composition

5. A condensation of a bestseller would most probably appear in
   1 *Reader's Handbook*
   2 *Readers' Guide to Periodical Literature*
   3 *Reader's Digest*
   4 *Books for You*

6. Which statement about a word is true?
   1 Its function may change from sentence to sentence.
   2 It has more denotations than connotations.
   3 It has the same part of speech regardless of the sentence in which it appears.
   4 Its origin has a great effect upon its use in a sentence.

7. The quotation below appears in Lewis Carroll's "Jabberwocky."

   > And, as in *uffish* thought he stood,
   >   The Jabberwock, with eyes of flame,
   > Came whiffling through the *tulgey* wood...

   Which indicates to the reader that the italicized words are adjectives?
   1 the word endings and word order
   2 the word beginnings and word order
   3 the lack of capital letters
   4 the use of the comparative form

8. In a telephone directory, the entries in the Yellow Pages section usually are arranged first alphabetically by names of
   1 manufacturing brands   3 products and services
   2 merchants and business firms   4 communities

9. Which sentence has more than one meaning?
   1 He gave dog biscuits to her.
   2 He gave her biscuits to the dog.
   3 He gave biscuits to her dog.
   4 He gave her dog biscuits.

10. Which person is primarily responsible for interpreting a film script and seeing that the finished film tells the story as he sees it?
    1 the photographer   3 the director
    2 the producer   4 the script writer

11. In a book of nonfiction, to find a reference to a certain topic one should first consult the book's
    1 table of contents   3 appendix
    2 index   4 frontispiece

12. The *New York Times Magazine* regularly contains
    1 book reviews   3 informational articles
    2 columns of poetry   4 film listings

ANSWERS AND EXPLANATIONS

1. ANSWER: (3) remain generally neutral in the matter discussed

   ANSWER EXPLAINED: Good parliamentary practice, which enables a discussion to proceed democratically and efficiently, requires the discussion leader to be impartial. He may not take sides, though he should offer the group any information he has that may help it arrive at a decision. He may not even cast a vote, except to break a tie.

2. ANSWER: (1) particular part

   ANSWER EXPLAINED: A person's "role" in a play is the particular part to which he has been assigned.

3. ANSWER: (4) stupidity

   ANSWER EXPLAINED: sand, silver, and stone exist in the physical world —they can be seen and touched; they are *concrete* words. But stupidity has no physical existence; it is an *abstract* word.

4. ANSWER: (2) a traffic light

   ANSWER EXPLAINED: A traffic light communicates its message at sight directly and exactly. Red means "stop"; green "go." No other interpretations are possible. This is not the case with the other choices.

5. ANSWER: (3) *Reader's Digest*

   ANSWER EXPLAINED: Each issue of the *Reader's Digest,* a monthly magazine, carries a book condensation as a regular feature.

6. ANSWER: (1) Its function may change from sentence to sentence.

   ANSWER EXPLAINED: Note, for example, how the word *substitute* changes in function in the following sentences:

   1. A *substitute* takes the place of a regular.
      (*substitute* is a noun used as a subject)
   2. A *substitute* batter is called a "pinch hitter."
      (*substitute* is an adjective modifying *batter*)
   3. Managers often *substitute* one player for another.
      (*substitute* is a verb)

7. ANSWER: (1) the word endings and word order

ANSWER EXPLAINED: *-ish*, in *uffish*, and *-y*, in *tulgey*, are adjectival suffixes, as we can easily tell them from adjectives like *foolish, childish, boyish, girlish*, and *snowy, foggy, misty, sleepy*. Also, the usual position for an adjective is immediately before the noun it modifies. Examining the word order, we find *uffish* immediately before the noun *thought*, and *tulgey* in the same position before the noun *wood*.

8. ANSWER: (3) products and services

ANSWER EXPLAINED: The Yellow Pages are arranged alphabetically by products and services: *Accordions, Acting Instruction, Building Materials, Carpet and Rug Cleaners*, etc. Under each of these entries, listed alphabetically, are the names, together with addresses and telephone numbers, of the merchants and business firms selling the product or providing the service.

9. ANSWER: (4) He gave her dog biscuits.

ANSWER EXPLAINED: As it appears in print, sentence 4 can have two meanings. The first is that he gave dog biscuits (regarding these two words as a compound noun) *to her;* the second (regarding *dog* as an independent noun) is that he gave biscuits *to the dog*. If sentence 4 were spoken, we would be able to tell the speaker's exact meaning from his pronunciation of the last two words.

10. ANSWER: (3) the director

ANSWER EXPLAINED: The director gives instructions to the actors in accordance with his interpretation of the film script, so that the finished film will be faithful to that interpretation.

11. ANSWER: (2) index

ANSWER EXPLAINED: The *index,* located at the very end of the book, is a complete alphabetical listing of the topics dealt with in the book, including page numbers. The fastest way to find information in a book is to consult the index.

12. ANSWER: (3) informational articles

ANSWER EXPLAINED: The *New York Times Magazine,* included in the Sunday edition of the *New York Times,* provides informational articles on local, national, and international developments.

The remainder of this chapter is designed to improve your competence in the following related areas of English:

1. WORDS AND LANGUAGE

Concrete and Abstract Words

Words stand for things, persons, places, and ideas. Words are symbols.

Concrete words stand for things that can be seen, touched, heard, smelled, or tasted: *snapshot, fur, thunder, perfume, apple,* etc.

Abstract words stand for ideas or feelings—things that do not exist physically: *ambition, inflation, loyalty, injustice, fear,* etc.

General and Specific Words

A *general word* is one that stands for any of a number of things belonging to the same *genus,* or category. For example, *fish* is a general word: it can describe any member of the fish category, such as cod, flounder, bluefish, trout, salmon, etc.

A *specific word* stands for only one thing: *cod, flounder, salmon,* etc. To say that you ate baked salmon is to be more specific than to say that you ate baked fish. For clarity and exactness, use specific words.

Denotation and Connotation

The *denotation* of a word is its dictionary meaning. For example, both a *house* and a *home* have the denotation of a "dwelling."

The *connotation* of a word is the meaning suggested by that word in addition to its dictionary meaning. Unlike *house, home* carries with it the associated meaning (connotation) of comfort, security, and privacy. Because of its connotation, *home* is much richer in meaning.

Letters and Sounds

There are twenty-six letters in the English alphabet, but there are many more sounds in our language. To represent sounds, we use a *phonetic alphabet*, which has a separate symbol for each distinguishable sound. The letter *a* alone has several sounds. Here are just four of them, each represented in brackets by a phonetic symbol: mat [a]; day [ā]; father [ä]; and sofa [ə].

Language and Change

The English language is constantly changing and growing. It borrows words from foreign languages. It gives new meanings to existing words. It forms compounds from words already in the language.

a. Anglo-Saxon Contributions

About a fourth of our vocabulary comes from the language of the Angles and Saxons, Germanic tribes who invaded Britain about 450 A.D. Despite the vast numbers of foreign words incorporated into English over the years, the basic words of English today are Anglo-Saxon. They include the articles *a, an, the;* the words for numbers; the verb *to be;* the prepositions *at, by, from, in, out, with,* etc.; the conjunctions *and, but, as, when,* etc.; many commonly used verbs, such as *to go, to sleep, to eat,* and *to fight;* many commonly used nouns, such as *father, mother, land, house,* and *water;* and most pronouns, including *I, you, he, she, it, we, who, which,* and *that.*

b. Borrowings From Other Languages

In 1066, the French-speaking Normans conquered England, and for the next two centuries French was England's official language. During this period, a considerable number of French words combined with the Anglo-Saxon-derived language of the common people to form what eventually became today's English. Note that since French is almost entirely derived from Latin, the bulk of the French words that came into English at this time were ultimately of Latin origin. It is no wonder then that English often has two or more words for the same idea. For example, for the Anglo-Saxon noun *home,* we have the Latin-derived synonyms *domicile* and *residence.* English has a rich abundance of synonyms.

During the Renaissance (1500–1650), more borrowing occurred as numerous words were absorbed into English directly from Latin and Ancient Greek. These languages, particularly the latter, to this day continue to supply English with words for new scientific and technical concepts: *supersonic, astronaut, cybernetics,* etc.

English continues to borrow from modern languages, too, especially

French, whenever it discovers a word that can be useful. Here are some sample loanwords: *encore* (French); *fiasco* (Italian); *siesta* (Spanish); *sauerkraut* (German); *sputnik* (Russian); *karate* (Japanese).

Changes in Meaning

The meanings of words change with the times. *Quick,* in the time of Elizabeth I, meant "living" ("The *quick* and the dead"), a meaning now lost. *Meat,* once a general word meaning "food" of any kind (as in *sweetmeat,* meaning "candy"), now is a specific word for "animal tissue used as food."

Sometimes new meanings are given to existing words. A "dove," besides denoting a particular bird, now also means "a conciliatory person," or "one who advocates peace," while a "hawk" has acquired the added meaning of "a belligerent person," or "one who advocates war."

Compounds

English creates many words by compounding existing words: *feedback, mainstream, passerby, drive-in, blast-off,* etc. Also, it forms new words by using combining elements (roots, prefixes, and suffixes) from Greek, Latin, and Anglo-Saxon. Examples:

> Greek -ITIS (inflammation of):
> *appendicitis, laryngitis, tonsillitis*
> Latin SEMI- (half):
> *semiannual, semidetached, semiskilled*
> Anglo-Saxon UN- (not):
> *unabridged, unbiased, uncertain*

Blends

Occasionally a word is created by the blending of two independent words, as in *smog* (smoke + fog) and *motel* (motor + hotel).

Slang

Slang consists of very informal and recently coined expressions that are usually more vivid, playful, and emphatic than the corresponding terms in Standard English. Sometimes slang may be the most effective way of expressing an idea, as, for example, when we describe someone as *uptight,* instead of "tense," "jittery," or "nervous." Most slang expressions are short-lived. Hardly anyone nowadays would recognize *skedaddle*—Civil War slang for "leave in a hurry." However, a few like *O.K., girlfriend,* and *boy-*

friend, are eventually adopted into Standard English, especially for informal usage.

Colloquial English

Colloquial means "conversational." It describes usage appropriate for ordinary speech and informal writing, but not for formal situations. Some colloquialisms are *lots of* (instead of *many*), *math* (for *mathematics*), and "*Who* did you meet?" (instead of "*Whom* did you meet?").

Gobbledygook

Gobbledygook is a term for writing characterized by the excessive and often unnecessary use of big words, especially abstract words, so that the reader is annoyed and confused. The following gobbledygook could have been stated in simple English as "If the pain returns, continue with the medicine as prescribed":

Immediately subsequent to the observation of any symptom indicative of a recurrence of the discomfort, it is imperative that you resume taking the medication as originally prescribed by your physician.

EXERCISE ON WORDS AND LANGUAGE

Write the *number* of the choice that correctly completes the statement or answers the question.

1. Which word is the *least* specific in meaning?   (1) acre   (2) democracy   (3) photograph   (4) ship
2. Which in the following list is *most* specific?   (1) woman   (2) humanitarian   (3) nurse   (4) Clara Barton
3. The connotation of a word is its   (1) literal meaning   (2) associated meaning   (3) pronunciation   (4) spelling.
4. Which statement about word meanings is true?   (1) The number of meanings for a word is fixed by those compiling a dictionary.   (2) The meanings of a word may change with the times.   (3) Most words have at least three meanings.   (4) Word meanings do not vary in different sections of the United States.
5. Which word is most specific?   (1) cosmetic   (2) luxury   (3) lipstick   (4) makeup
6. Which sentence contains a colloquial expression?   (1) Justice will ultimately triumph.   (2) The decision of the lower court is hereby overruled.   (3) There were lots of people at the game.   (4) Your presence is requested at the wedding.

7. Which word is the most general in meaning? (1) trumpet (2) horse (3) electronics (4) education

8. Which word has the largest number of meanings? (1) foot (2) mile (3) triangle (4) hypotenuse

9. Which word connotes the most extreme reaction? (1) spectator (2) fanatic (3) adherent (4) fan

10. The most abstract word in the following list is (1) knife (2) culture (3) pillar (4) typewriter.

11. An important fact about the English language is that it (1) undergoes change (2) has relatively few synonyms (3) is based primarily upon writing, not speech (4) has borrowed from very few languages.

12. Which expression produces a positive reaction in most people? (1) red, white, and blue (2) under duress (3) unwritten law (4) irrelevant and immaterial

13. Which statement about words is true? (1) They are symbols for things. (2) They exist on only one level. (3) They are our only form of communication. (4) They are more important than what they stand for.

14. Which is the most specific term? (1) Warren (2) student (3) boy (4) human

15. Which method is *not* used to add new words to the English language? (1) borrowing from foreign languages (2) giving new meanings to existing words (3) forming compounds from existing words (4) formal introduction by the American Academy of Arts and Sciences

16. The alphabet of sounds that aids a speaker in the pronunciation of unfamiliar words is referred to as (1) semantic (2) linguistic (3) phonetic (4) syllabic.

17. Which statement about slang is true? (1) In most situations, it is the preferable way to express an idea. (2) It does not convey any meaning to an intelligent audience. (3) It is sometimes the most effective way of expressing an idea. (4) It is not acceptable in writing a friendly letter.

18. Which word usually has an unfavorable connotation? (1) communication (2) table (3) assistant (4) henchman

19. "Gobbledygook" is a name given to words which (1) originated in slang (2) are not used by cultured persons (3) are characterized by unintelligibility (4) are used to give explicit directions.

20. Which was an effect of the Norman Conquest upon the English language? (1) more borrowing from the Celtic tongue (2) the addition of many foreign words (3) major changes in the nature of its grammatical construction (4) the introduction of Latin in the secondary schools

2. LIBRARY AND RESEARCH SKILLS

Practically everything that our civilization has achieved is recorded in our libraries. Unless you become familiar with library and research tools, you cannot have ready access to this vast store of information and recreation. Past Regents questions indicate that you are expected to be acquainted with the following:

(One important tool, the *Readers' Guide to Periodical Literature,* will be discussed in the section on *Magazines* on pages 247–248.)

A. THE PARTS OF A BOOK

To locate and make wise use of the information in a book, you should know these parts of a book and their functions:

Title page—the page at the very beginning of the book that officially states (1) the complete title, (2) the author's full name, (3) the publisher's name, (4) the place of publication, and (5) occasionally, the publisher's date of actual printing (not to be confused with copyright date).

Copyright page—the reverse side of the title page. It contains the all-important *copyright date,* which is a clue to the up-to-dateness of the material in the book.

Preface (also known as *introduction* or *foreword*)—a statement of the author's purpose.

Table of contents—an outline of the subjects treated in the book. It lists chapter titles in the order in which they appear, telling on which page each chapter begins. By glancing at the table of contents you can obtain an overview of the material in a book.

List of maps or illustrations—a summary of the maps or illustrations and their page locations.

Footnote—an explanatory note at the bottom (foot) of a page.

Bibliography—a list of (1) the books consulted by the author, or (2) books containing further information on the subject under discussion. A bibliography may appear at the end of the book or the end of each chapter. An *annotated* bibliography provides *annotations* (brief notes of explanation) after each book listed.

Appendix—a section added at the end of the book to supplement the main text. An appendix may include notes, tables, lists, etc.

Glossary—an alphabetical list of unfamiliar terms used in the book, together with their definitions.

Index—an alphabetical list (at the very end of the book) of the topics dealt with in the book. It gives the exact pages on which each topic is discussed. The fastest way to locate information in a book is to consult its index.

B. THE CARD CATALOG

A library's *card catalog* is the index of all the books owned by that library. It consists of small cards filed alphabetically in a cabinet of drawers. For each book the library owns you will normally find three cards in the card catalog: (1) an *author card*, (2) a *title card*, and (3) a *subject card*. The first is useful for locating a book when you know only its *author's name;* the second, when you know only its *title;* the third, when you know only the *subject* of the book. Following are three cards for the same book:

1. Author card (so called because the *author's name* is on the first line). Sometimes the author may be an institution, as the Smithsonian Institution, or a Government department, as the U.S. Department of Agriculture.

Author cards are filed by the author's last name. For James Fenimore Cooper, look under *C.*

944.025
T   Tuchman, Barbara Wertheim.
                 A distant mirror; the calamitous
            14th century.
                 New York, Knopf, 1978.
                 677 p., illus., ports.
                 Includes bibliographical references.

Author Card Explained

UPPER LEFT-HAND CORNER: the *call number* $\left(\begin{smallmatrix}944.025\\T\end{smallmatrix}\right)$ is made up of the class number for the subject of the book (944.025) and the initial of the author's last name (T). The call number indicates where you may find the book on the shelves.

FIRST LINE: the *author's full name* (Tuchman, Barbara Wertheim)

SECOND-FIFTH LINES:

the *title* and *subtitle* (A distant mirror; the calamitous 14th century)
the *place of publication* (New York)
the *publisher* (Knopf)
the *copyright date* (1978)
the *number of pages* (677)
an indication that the book has *illustrations* (illus.)
    and *portraits* (ports.)
an indication that the book offers *bibliographical information*
    (Includes bibliographical references)

2. Title card (so called because the *title* is on the first line).

944.025	A distant mirror.
T	Tuchman, Barbara Wertheim.
	A distant mirror; the calamitous
	14th century.
	New York, Knopf, 1978.
	677 p., illus., ports.
	Includes bibliographical references.

The, A, and *An* before a title are disregarded in filing. For the title card for *The Last of the Mohicans,* look under *L,* not *T.*

3. Subject card (so called because the *subject* of the book is on the first line in black capitals or red letters).

> ### FRANCE—HISTORY—14TH CENTURY
>
> **944.025**
> **T**   **Tuchman, Barbara Wertheim.**
>   A distant mirror; the calamitous
>   14th century.
>   New York, Knopf, 1978.
>   677 p., illus., ports.
>   Includes bibliographical references.

Sometimes the subject of a book may be a person, as in a biography.

Cross-reference cards are cards containing the words "See" or "See also." They tell you under what other subject headings to look for the information you are seeking. Examples:

> MISSILES, BALLISTIC
>
> See
>
> GUIDED MISSILES

> CYBERNETICS
>
> See also
>
> AUTOMATIC CONTROL; CALCULATING MA-
> CHINES;   COMMUNICATION;   ELECTRONIC
> CALCULATING   MACHINES;   ELECTRONICS;
> INFORMATION THEORY

C. CALL NUMBERS: THE DEWEY DECIMAL SYSTEM

The *call number* is the number by which you look for a book on the shelves. Examples:

583	821	574.973
M	K	T

The call number appears on the back binding of a book and also on each of the cards for that book in the card catalog. The lower part of a call number is the initial of the author's last name. The upper part, known as the *class number,* identifies the subject of the book.

The widely used *Dewey Decimal System* groups books by subject into ten large classes. Each class has numerous subdivisions. Below are the ten classes plus a typical subdivision in each class:

CLASS	TYPICAL SUBDIVISION
000-099 General Works	030 Encyclopedias
100-199 Philosophy	150 Psychology
200-299 Religion	220 The Bible
300-399 Social Sciences	330 Economics
400-499 Languages	423 English Dictionaries
500-599 Science	570 Biology
600-699 Useful Arts	641 Cook Books
700-799 Fine Arts	770 Photography
800-899 Literature	822.3 Shakespeare
900-999 History	973 United States History

Full-length biography and autobiography are commonly assigned the letter *B* instead of a class number. They are shelved alphabetically by the last name of the *subject,* i.e., the person written about. (A *biography* is a book about a person's life written by another person; an *autobiography* is a book about a person's life written by the person himself.)

Collective biography (any book containing several short biographies) is grouped under 920.

Fiction (novels and short stories) written in English has no call number. It is shelved alphabetically by the author's last name.

D. THE VERTICAL FILE

The *vertical file* is a cabinet of large drawers containing pamphlets, bulletins, and leaflets from educational, scientific, and industrial organizations; government publications; and important newspaper articles and pictures.

These materials are usually filed alphabetically by subject. When you are doing research on a current topic, the vertical file is one resource you must not overlook. Another is the *Readers' Guide,* the key to information in magazine articles (see pages 247–248).

E. THE DICTIONARY

An *abridged* dictionary is a shortened dictionary. Though condensed from an *unabridged* (complete) work, it is adequate for normal reference purposes. Examples:

> ABRIDGED: *Webster's New Students Dictionary*
> UNABRIDGED: *Webster's Third New International Dictionary*

You should be able to understand everything that the dictionary says about a word. Much of this information is conveyed with the aid of symbols and abbreviations fully explained in the introduction of the dictionary.

What follows is a dictionary paragraph for the word *alleviate.** Arrows have been added to focus attention on seven important items. On a sheet of paper, jot down all the information you can extract from each of these items. Then compare with the full explanation below the paragraph.

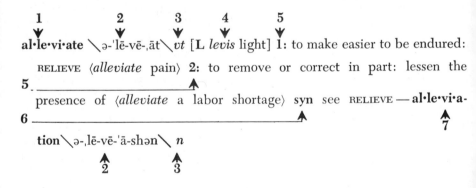

1. The word being defined, known as the **main entry** or **vocabulary entry,** tells us:

   a. How to spell *alleviate.*
   b. How to hyphenate *alleviate* at the end of a line. We may use a hyphen wherever there is a **centered period:** after *al-, alle-,* or *allevi-.*

2. The **pronunciation,** set off by **slant lines,** respells the word in phonetic symbols explained in key words at the foot of the dictionary page. This respelling tells us:

   a. that *alleviate* has four syllables, as shown by the **hyphens** used to separate them.

   b. that the first syllable [ə] is pronounced like the *a* or *u* in *abut*; the ē in the second syllable ['lē] and the ē in the third [vē] sound like the *e* in *equal*; and the ā in the fourth syllable [‚āt] is equivalent to the *a* in *bake*.

   Note: Pay attention to **diacritical marks,** as, for example, the ‾ above vowels. From the key words at the bottom of the dictionary page, you can tell that vowels so marked (ē, ā) have a different sound from the same vowels unmarked (e, a), or having some other diacritical mark (ä).

   c. that the second syllable ['lē] gets the main stress, as shown by the **high vertical stress mark** ['] preceding it; and the fourth syllable [‚āt] receives a secondary, or lighter stress, indicated by the **low vertical stress mark** [‚].

   Notice that *alleviation,* which has five syllables, has its main stress on the fourth ['ā] and a secondary stress on the second [‚lē].

3. The **part of speech,** abbreviated in italics, tells us how the word is used: *vt* shows that *alleviate* is used as a *transitive verb* (a verb that takes a direct object).

   n shows that *alleviation* is used as a *noun.*

4. The **derivation,** enclosed in **brackets,** gives information about the source of the word and its original, or literal, meaning. Thus we learn that *alleviate* comes from the Latin (L) *levis,* meaning "light."

5. The **definitions** tell us the meanings of the main entry. You should find out the order in which your dictionary lists definitions. For this information consult the preface. *Webster's New Students Dictionary* lists definitions in historical order.

   Of the two definitions, number 1 (to make easier to be endured: RELIEVE) is the earlier. Number 2 (to remove or correct in part: lessen the presence of) developed later.

   The fact that RELIEVE is in capital letters means that it is a **synonym** of *alleviate.* It is also a **cross-reference,** suggesting that you should look up the main entry *relieve* for additional information about *alleviate.*

   The definitions are enriched by verbal illustrations in **angle brackets,** e.g., ⟨*alleviate* pain⟩ and ⟨*alleviate* a labor shortage⟩. These show us how to use *alleviate* in specific contexts.

6. The **abbreviation** *syn* followed by the **cross-reference** "see RELIEVE" tells us that a detailed explanation of the synonyms for *alleviate* appears under the main entry for *relieve.* There we can learn exactly how the synonyms *alleviate* and *relieve* are similar and different.

7. The **run-on entry** (*alleviation*) is a word derived from the main entry, as shown by the **dash** that precedes it. *Alleviation* has not been defined because we can tell its meaning from the definition of *alleviate.*

Archaic, obsolete, and colloquial

These designations are frequently attached to definitions. *Archaic,* abbreviated *arch.,* means that the definition is no longer used except in a special phrase. For example, in "the quick and the dead," *quick* means "living." This meaning, though, is archaic.

Obsolete, abbreviated *obs.,* means "no longer used." In Shakespeare's time, *to owe* meant "to own or possess," but this meaning is now obsolete.

Colloquial, abbreviated *colloq.,* means "correct for everyday informal writing or conversation, but not for formal occasions." For example, *dad* is colloquial for *father.*

F. OTHER REFERENCE WORKS

General Encyclopedias

Encyclopedia Americana
Encyclopaedia Britannica
Collier's Encyclopedia
World Book Encyclopedia

When using a general encyclopedia, you will save time if you use the *index volume* first. This will let you see all the references in that encyclopedia to your topic. For leads to additional information, see the *bibliographies* at the end of encyclopedia articles.

One-Volume Encyclopedias

Columbia Encyclopedia
Lincoln Library of Essential Information

Encyclopedia Supplements

Americana Annual
Britannica Book of the Year

Collier's Year Book
World Book Year Book

Encyclopedia publishers supply their subscribers with up-to-date information by issuing an *annual supplement* or *yearbook* that sums up the events and discoveries of the preceding year.

Almanacs and Yearbooks

Consult an almanac or yearbook for statistical information about a specific year. Since the contents are not arranged alphabetically, consult the *index* first.

World Almanac and Book of Facts (News summaries, world facts, major events in medicine and science, Academy Award films, sports champions, etc. Index at the beginning of the book.)

Information Please Almanac (News chronology, map section, books, television, opera, etc.)

Statistical Abstract of the United States (Summary of statistics on the social, political, and economic organization of the United States.)

Statesman's Year-Book (Population, exports, constitutions, government officials, etc., of countries of the world.)

Biographical Reference Works

FOR NOTABLE CONTEMPORARY PERSONS:

Who's Who (Prominent living persons, mainly British.)

Who's Who in America (Prominent living Americans.)

Current Biography (Prominent persons of many countries. Portraits. Published monthly and in annual cumulated volumes.)

Twentieth Century Authors (Informal treatment. Portraits.)

Official Congressional Directory (Sketches of important government officials in Washington, D.C.)

FOR NOTABLE PERSONS OF THE PAST:

Dictionary of National Biography (Prominent British persons no longer living.)

Dictionary of American Biography (Prominent Americans no longer living.)

Webster's Biographical Dictionary (Prominent persons of all countries, including some living persons.)

Unabridged Dictionaries

Funk and Wagnalls New Comprehensive International Dictionary
Oxford English Dictionary
Random House Dictionary of the English Language
Webster's Third New International Dictionary of the English Language

Indexes

ESSAYS AND MISCELLANEOUS ARTICLES:

Essay and General Literature Index

MAGAZINE ARTICLES: CURRENT

(The term *magazine articles* includes reviews of books, motion pictures, plays, and recordings published in magazines.)

Readers' Guide to Periodical Literature (See pages 247–248.)
Magazine Index

MAGAZINE ARTICLES: 1802–1907

Poole's Index to Periodical Literature

NEWSPAPER ARTICLES PUBLISHED IN THE "NEW YORK TIMES":

New York Times Index

PLAYS:

Logasa and Ver Nooy—*Index to One-Act Plays*
West, Peake, and Fidell—*Play Index*

POEMS:

Granger's Index to Poetry

SCIENCE AND TECHNOLOGY ARTICLES:

Applied Science and Technology Index

SHORT STORIES:

Cook, Munro et al.—*Short Story Index*

Reference Works for a Particular Subject

ART:

McGraw-Hill—*Encyclopedia of World Art*

CONGRESS—DAILY PROCEEDINGS IN BOTH HOUSES:

Congressional Record

ENGLISH—USAGE, SYNONYMS, ANTONYMS:

Craigie—*Dictionary of American English on Historical Principles*
Evans and Evans—*Dictionary of Contemporary American Usage*
Fowler—*Dictionary of Modern English Usage*
Nicholson—*Dictionary of American-English Usage*
Roget's International Thesaurus (A *thesaurus* is a dictionary of synonyms and antonyms.)
Webster's Dictionary of Synonyms

ETIQUETTE:

Emily Post—*Etiquette*
Amy Vanderbilt—*New Complete Book of Etiquette*

GEOGRAPHY:

Goode's World Atlas (An *atlas* is a book of maps.)
Rand McNally Cosmopolitan World Atlas
Webster's Geographical Dictionary
Columbia Lippincott Gazetteer of the World (A *gazetteer* is a dictionary of geographical names.)

LITERATURE:

ANTHOLOGIES OF POETRY

An *anthology* is a collection of selections from the works of many authors.

Oxford Book of American Verse
Oxford Book of English Verse
Stevenson—*Home Book of Modern Verse*
Stevenson—*Home Book of Verse, American and English*
Untermeyer—*Modern American and British Poetry*

DRAMA

Reader's Encyclopedia of World Drama
McGraw-Hill Encyclopedia of World Drama

HANDBOOKS OF LITERATURE

Benét—*Reader's Encyclopedia*
Brewer—*Reader's Handbook of Famous Names in Fiction*
Hart—*Oxford Companion to American Literature*
Harvey—*Oxford Companion to English Literature*
Herzberg—*Reader's Encyclopedia of American Literature*
New Century Handbook of English Literature

HISTORY OF LITERATURE

Boas and Hahn—*Social Backgrounds of English Literature*
Cambridge History of American Literature
Cambridge History of English Literature
Oxford History of English Literature
Spiller and others—*Literary History of the United States*

PLOT SUMMARIES

Keller—*Reader's Digest of Books*
Magill—*Masterplots*

MUSIC:

Grove's Dictionary of Music and Musicians

MYTHOLOGY:

Brewer's Dictionary of Phrase and Fable
Bulfinch's Mythology
Frazer—*The Golden Bough*

PARLIAMENTARY PROCEDURE:

Robert's Rules of Order
Sturgis—*Standard Code of Parliamentary Procedure*
Wines and Card—*Come to Order!*

QUOTATIONS:

Bartlett's Familiar Quotations
Hoyt's New Cyclopedia of Practical Quotations
Oxford Dictionary of Quotations
Stevenson's Home Book of Quotations

REVIEWS OF IMPORTANT BOOKS (1905–PRESENT):

Book Review Digest

SCIENCE AND TECHNOLOGY:

McGraw-Hill Encyclopedia of Science and Technology
Van Nostrand's Scientific Encyclopedia

EXERCISES ON LIBRARY AND RESEARCH SKILLS

A. Excluding title page, copyright date, and list of illustrations, name *five* important parts of the contents usually found in nonfiction books, and explain the use of *each*.

B. State briefly and clearly the nature of the information given by the *five* underlined items in the following main entry from a dictionary:

*el·i·gi·ble \'el-i-jə-bəl\ adj [L *eligere* to choose]: qualified to be chosen

⟨*eligible* to be president⟩ : ENTITLED ⟨*eligible* to retire⟩—el·i·gi·bil·i·ty

\,el-i-jə-'bil-ət-e'\ *n*—eligible *n*—el·i·gi·bly \'el-i-jə-blē\ *adv*

C. Explain *each* of the following items with reference to the card below, reproduced from the card catalog: (*a*) NATURAL HISTORY—U.S.   (*b*) T   (*c*) 1899–   (*d*) Wandering through winter   (*e*) 1965.

NATURAL HISTORY—U.S.

574.973 **Teale, Edwin Way, 1899–**
T   Wandering through winter; a naturalist's record of a 20,000-mile journey through the North American winter. With photos. by the author. New York, Dodd, Mead, 1965.

D. Identify a reference work associated with *each* of the following names:

Bartlett

Roget

Granger

Fowler

Grove

Goode

Van Nostrand

Emily Post

Robert

Benét

E. Write the letter of the word or expression that best completes the statement or answers the question.

1. To find a list of important positions held by the current Chief Justice of the United States Supreme Court, one should first consult (*a*) *Webster's Biographical Dictionary* (*b*) *Dictionary of American Biography* (*c*) *Who's Who in America* (*d*) *The World Almanac.*

2. The vertical file in a library is most often used to hold (*a*) pamphlets or clippings (*b*) card-catalog cards (*c*) book reviews (*d*) reference book cards.

3. To locate the book *A Man Called Peter,* one should look in the card catalog under (*a*) A (*b*) Man (*c*) Peter (*d*) Called.

4. An article in an encyclopedia is often followed immediately by (*a*) a list of unfamiliar terms used in the article (*b*) a biography of the author (*c*) the date of writing of the article (*d*) a bibliography.

5. *Roget's International Thesaurus* contains (*a*) synonyms and antonyms (*b*) miscellaneous facts (*c*) pictures of world-famous personalities (*d*) digests of book reviews.

6. One main purpose of a bibliography is to (*a*) refer the reader to additional sources (*b*) describe the author's background (*c*) explain special terms used in the book (*d*) include additional material, such as statistics, tables, etc.

7. A word which a dictionary labels "obs." is a word which (*a*) is no longer used (*b*) is used only in speech (*c*) has two acceptable pronunciations (*d*) has more than one meaning.

8. To obtain an overview of the material in a book, one should first consult the (*a*) preface (*b*) table of contents (*c*) glossary (*d*) index.

9. Which reference contains the most complete information on the Amazon River? (*a*) *Information Please Almanac* (*b*) *Webster's Third New International Dictionary* (*c*) *Encyclopedia Americana* (*d*) *Goode's World Atlas.*

10. For detailed current information about a subject, one should consult (*a*) the card catalog (*b*) the vertical file (*c*) an atlas (*d*) an abridged dictionary.

11. As applied to a word, the term *colloquial* means that the word is (*a*) new   (*b*) no longer in use   (*c*) used only in writing   (*d*) appropriate for informal writing and ordinary speech.

12. Part of an entry in the *Readers' Guide to Periodical Literature* reads "720:46-7." The "46-7" refers to   (*a*) the pages on which the article appears   (*b*) the number of words in the article   (*c*) the author's code number   (*d*) the volume number of the magazine.

13. The index in the *World Almanac* is unusual in that it   (*a*) is printed and distributed separately   (*b*) may be removed for independent use   (*c*) is located in the front of the book   (*d*) is not alphabetized.

14. Which one of the following is published monthly as well as annually? (*a*) *Congressional Record*   (*b*) *World Almanac*   (*c*) *Information Please Almanac*   (*d*) *Current Biography*.

15. Which library aid should be consulted first to find the address of a famous living American author?   (*a*) *Dictionary of American Biography*   (*b*) *Who's Who in America*   (*c*) *Readers' Guide to Periodical Literature*   (*d*) the card catalog.

16. In writing a term paper on the subject "Strikes," one source to consult for the most recent information would be   (*a*) *Lincoln Library of Essential Information*   (*b*) *New York Times Index*   (*c*) *Current Biography*   (*d*) *Reader's Encyclopedia*.

17. In the library call number $\frac{020}{S23}$, the S indicates the   (*a*) subject of the book   (*b*) first letter of the title   (*c*) first letter of the author's last name   (*d*) identification letter of the bookshelf.

18. A summary of the most important news events of the past year can be found in   (*a*) *Statesman's Year-Book*   (*b*) *Lincoln Library*   (*c*) *World Almanac*   (*d*) *Columbia Encyclopedia*.

19. *Roget's International Thesaurus* serves the same general purpose as (*a*) *Who's Who*   (*b*) *Information Please Almanac*   (*c*) *Columbia-Lippincott Gazetteer of the World*   (*d*) *Webster's Dictionary of Synonyms*.

20. Which one of the following is *not* usually found on the title page of a book?   (*a*) place of publication   (*b*) author   (*c*) date of printing of that copy of the book   (*d*) copyright date.

3. PARLIAMENTARY PROCEDURE

WHAT IS "PARLIAMENTARY PROCEDURE"?

Parliamentary procedure is a set of rules that enables a group to function efficiently and democratically. Certain democratic principles are at the heart of parliamentary procedure. Among these are: (1) the will of the majority must prevail; (2) the rights of the minority must be safeguarded; (3) all members must have equal rights and responsibilities; and (4) free and full discussion must be allowed. Parliamentary procedure is widely used by clubs, organizations, and legislative bodies.

REVIEWING PARLIAMENTARY PROCEDURE

Past Regents questions on parliamentary procedure indicate that you are expected to be familiar with the following:

A. PROCEDURE FOR ORGANIZING A CLUB

Suppose you decide, after conferring with a few interested individuals, that it would be a good idea to form a debating club. To make sure that you are going about it in the right way, you will want to consult an authoritative book on parliamentary procedure, such as *Robert's Rules of Order.* Here are the basic steps required to complete the organization of a club:

BEFORE THE FIRST MEETING

1. You and your associates announce the time, place, and object of the meeting.

AT THE FIRST, OR ORGANIZATIONAL, MEETING

2. The assembly (those who have come) elects a temporary chairman.
3. The assembly elects a temporary secretary.
4. The temporary chairman states the object of the meeting: to organize the club.
5. The assembly adopts a resolution formally organizing the club.
6. The temporary chairman, on a motion of the assembly, appoints a committee to draft a constitution and bylaws. (The bylaws are not a part of the constitution; they deal with secondary matters, such as dues, time of meetings, etc.).

7. The temporary chairman, on a motion of the assembly, adjourns (closes) the meeting.

AT THE SECOND MEETING

8. The committee reports the constitution and the bylaws.
9. The assembly discusses the constitution and the bylaws, making necessary amendments. If a majority votes in favor, the constitution and the bylaws are adopted. At this time all who wish to become members sign the constitution.
10. The members elect the permanent officers.

B. ORDER OF BUSINESS IN CONDUCTING MEETINGS

Now that your club has been established, it can proceed to hold regular meetings. Parliamentary procedure requires meetings to be conducted in the following order, known as the *order of business:*

1. Call to order.
2. Reading, correction, and adoption of the minutes.
3. Officers' reports and reports of standing (permanent) committees.
4. Reports of special committees.
5. Old business (also called unfinished business).
6. New business.
7. Program for the day (a guest speaker, a debate, etc.).
8. Adjournment.

Note: If the members wish to take up an item of business out of its parliamentary order, they must adopt a motion to *suspend the rules,* which requires a two-thirds vote.

C. DUTIES OF OFFICERS

The *president,* or *chairman* (referred to as "the chair")
Calls the meeting to order.
Announces the business before the organization.
Recognizes speakers entitled to the floor.
States the question when a vote is to be taken.
Announces the results of voting.
Makes appointments to committees.
Conducts elections.
Determines points of order.
Adjourns the meeting.
Represents the organization in its outside relationships.

The president is an *ex officio* member of certain committees, which means that he is a member of these committees because of the office he holds. He may not vote on a motion except in cases where his vote would change the result; for example, to break a tie vote.

The *secretary*

Records the minutes.
Reads the minutes of the previous meeting.
Calls the roll when necessary.
Repeats the exact wording of a motion.
Keeps the official copy of the constitution and bylaws.
Conducts correspondence.

The *treasurer*

Keeps the financial records.
Collects dues.
Deposits funds.
Makes authorized payments.
Makes a periodic treasurer's report.

The *parliamentarian* is appointed by the president to advise him on matters of parliamentary procedure.

The *sergeant-at-arms* maintains order and rounds up absent members (for example, in Congress) when less than a quorum is present.

D. PROCEDURE FOR PASSING A MOTION

1. You say "Mr. Chairman" to indicate that you wish to have the floor.
2. When the chairman recognizes you, begin your motion with "I move that." Example: "I move that our club hold a dance on May 20."
3. Your motion is seconded by another member who, without waiting to be recognized, says, "I second the motion." If not seconded, your motion cannot be placed before the group.
4. The chairman states the motion and calls for discussion: "It has been moved and seconded that our club hold a dance on May 20. Is there any discussion?"
5. Members who wish to do so may speak for or against your motion when the chairman recognizes them. No other motion may be proposed while your motion is on the floor.
6. When there is no further discussion, the chairman states the question and conducts the voting: "The motion before the house is that our club hold a dance on May 20. All in favor say *Aye.* Those opposed say *No.*"
7. If a majority votes *Aye,* the chairman announces, "The motion is carried." Otherwise he says, "The motion is defeated."

E. PARLIAMENTARY MOTIONS

The following commonly used motions have been arranged in order of rank from 1 (highest rank) to 13 (lowest rank):

1. *To fix the time of the next meeting* (not debatable).

2. *To adjourn* (not debatable).

3. *To take a recess* (not debatable).

4. *To raise a question of privilege*—as when a member wishes to reply to an attack on his character, or to request that the heating, lighting, or ventilation be adjusted, etc. (no seconding required and not debatable).

5. *To call for the orders of the day*—to insist that the group return to the agenda of the meeting (no seconding required and not debatable).

6. *To lay on the table*—to put aside a pending motion so that the group may take up more pressing business (not debatable).

7. *To move the previous question* (or *to call for the question*)—to stop debate and to take an immediate vote on the question before the group (two-thirds vote required and not debatable).

8. *To limit or extend debate* (two-thirds vote required and not debatable).

9. *To postpone a question to a certain time* (debatable).

10. *To refer a question to a committee*—as when a motion requires extensive rewording or more careful investigation (debatable).

11. *To amend*—to change the wording of a pending motion (debatable). Suppose it has been moved and seconded that the club hold a party during the month of May, and you wish to recommend an exact date. Therefore, when recognized, you say, "I move the motion be amended to read 'May 20,' instead of 'during the month of May.'" Note: An amendment to a motion must be voted on *before* the motion itself.

12. *To postpone indefinitely* (debatable).

13. *Main motion*—a motion to bring up any topic for consideration by the group (debatable). Note: It is the motion of lowest rank.

Whenever more than one motion is on the floor, the one of highest rank must be taken up at once; motions ranking below it are declared out of order.

PROBLEM: Suppose that a *main motion* (rank #13) is on the floor: "Resolved that our club accept the invitation of the Forum

Club to participate in a joint debate next September 20." Suppose further that there has been a lengthy discussion of this motion, and you have therefore *moved the previous question* (rank #7). What happens?

ANSWER: Further discussion on the *main motion* (rank #13) is out of order. The *previous question* (rank #7) takes precedence. This motion, if seconded and adopted by a two-thirds vote, has the effect of shutting off further discussion on the main motion and putting it to an immediate vote.

F. COMMON PARLIAMENTARY TERMS

Ad hoc committee. A special committee appointed to deal with a specific situation only. As soon as it completes its assignment, an *ad hoc committee* goes out of existence. Do not confuse with *standing* (permanent) *committee.*

Adjournment. Closing of a meeting.

Agenda. List of the items of business to be taken up at a meeting.

Bylaws. Rules of secondary importance governing dues, the time and place of meetings, methods of voting, etc. The more important rules are stated in the constitution.

Division of the house. A rising vote. Also known as a standing vote. When a member questions the outcome of a voice (*viva voce*) vote, he may call for a division of the house. This requires first the affirmative and then the negative to stand and be counted.

Ex officio. "Because of one's office." The bylaws usually state that the president shall be an ex officio member of certain committees.

Majority vote. A vote of more than half of the votes cast. If 100 votes are cast, 51 or more constitute a *majority.*

Plurality vote. A larger vote than that received by any other, but less than a majority. If, out of 100 votes cast, A receives 40, B 35, and C 25, A is said to have a *plurality.*

Point of information. When a member desires information about a matter on the floor, he may interrupt (without waiting to be recognized) by stating, "Mr. Chairman, I rise to a point of information."

Point of order. When a member notices a violation of parliamentary procedure, or feels that his rights are being infringed upon, he may interrupt (without waiting to be recognized) by stating, "Mr. Chairman, I rise to a point of order."

Quorum. The minimum number of members that must be present before a meeting can legally be held. The number constituting a quorum is usually stated in the constitution.

Roll call. A vote taken by calling the roll. As a member's name is called, he rises and declares his vote. The secretary records each vote and gives the tally to the chairman, who announces the results.

Seconding. Endorsement of a motion by a member other than its maker.

   Note: *No seconding* is required for the following:

      questions of privilege
      nominations
      points of information
      points of order
      calls for division of the house
      calls for orders of the day

Standing committee. A permanent committee (not to be confused with an *ad hoc, or special, committee* appointed, as the need arises, for a special purpose).

Suspend the rules. When the group wants to take an action in conflict with its rules (consider an item not on the agenda, vote on a motion without debate, etc.), it must adopt a motion to suspend the rules. This requires a two-thirds vote.

Table. Put off discussion of a motion. Same as *to lay on the table* (see page 235).

Teller. A member appointed by the chairman to distribute the ballots, collect the ballots, and count the votes.

EXERCISES ON PARLIAMENTARY PROCEDURE

A. A small group of high school students, talking informally, agree that an athletic association with membership open to all students in the school is desirable. Beginning at this point, give in order *five* distinct steps *required by parliamentary procedure* to complete the organization of such an association.

B. State briefly, but clearly and in correct order, the procedure that should be followed, according to the rules of parliamentary practice, in beginning, conducting, and closing the business of a regular meeting of a club or school organization. (Your answer may be in outline form and should include at least *five* major steps.)

C. Complete correctly, in accordance with parliamentary practice, each of the *five* statements below, by choosing from among the following expressions the one that best applies: [Use no expression twice.]

amend	limit debate	amend the amendment
adjourn	take a recess	rise to a point of order
nominate	lay on the table	

1. Of the motions listed above, highest privilege is given to the motion to
2. It requires a two-thirds vote to
3. A correct procedure for interrupting one who has the floor is to
4. No seconding statement is required to
5. A proposal is defeated indirectly by a vote to

D. Write the *number* of the word or phrase that correctly completes the statement or answers the question.

1. In the order of business of a club meeting, which one of the following precedes the others?   (1) the treasurer's report   (2) new business   (3) reports of standing committees   (4) the secretary's report.
2. A motion that has as its purpose to change the wording of a previous motion is a motion to   (1) limit debate   (2) amend   (3) move the previous question   (4) withdraw the motion.
3. The number of persons who must be present before business can be conducted is called a   (1) quorum   (2) majority   (3) plurality   (4) division.
4. If there has been a violation of parliamentary procedure, a member may   (1) rise to a point of order   (2) propose an amendment   (3) call for the previous question   (4) move to table the motion.
5. A member who calls for the orders of the day wishes to   (1) present a resolution   (2) hear the secretary's report   (3) return the group to the agenda of the meeting   (4) hear a report by the committee.
6. The person responsible for stating the question when a vote is to be taken by the group is the   (1) secretary   (2) sergeant-at-arms   (3) parliamentarian   (4) chairman.
7. If a motion requires extensive rewording, the usual procedure is to   (1) refer it to a committee   (2) table it indefinitely   (3) reconsider it   (4) debate it indefinitely.
8. An authoritative book on parliamentary procedure is   (1) *The Statesman's Year-Book*   (2) *It's More Fun When You Know the Rules*   (3) *This Way, Please*   (4) *Robert's Rules of Order*.
9. A motion to suspend the rules usually requires, to pass,   (1) a two-

thirds affirmative vote   (2) a majority vote   (3) a roll call   (4) a division of the house.

10. After several persons have spoken on a motion, a member may   (1) call for a division of the house   (2) call for the question   (3) make a new motion   (4) move to reconsider the question.

11. In most organizations, when a meeting is held, which step precedes the others listed?   (1) secretary's report   (2) old business   (3) new business   (4) treasurer's report.

12. In a meeting, it is *not* necessary to wait for recognition by the chair in (1) making a nomination   (2) rising to a point of order   (3) moving that debate be limited   (4) moving that a motion be tabled.

13. An organizational meeting called to consider whether it might be desirable to form a French club requires   (1) no elected officers   (2) a sergeant-at-arms   (3) a temporary president and a temporary secretary   (4) a permanent president and a permanent secretary.

14. In good parliamentary practice, one should make a motion to "refer to a committee" when there is   (1) an insufficient number of persons present   (2) considerable opposition to a motion   (3) insufficient information available on the topic   (4) little opposition to a motion.

15. In good parliamentary practice, if a member feels that his rights are being violated, he may   (1) request an adjournment   (2) appeal to the sergeant-at-arms   (3) rise to a point of order   (4) call for a division of the house.

16. Which method of voting would be most accurate for a chairman of a meeting to use if he believed the results of the voting would be close? (1) voice vote   (2) standing vote   (3) show of hands   (4) general consent.

17. In parliamentary procedure, a motion to "lay on the table" means to (1) set aside   (2) filibuster   (3) arrange for a roll call   (4) bring up for discussion.

18. In a club meeting, member A moves that the club purchase an outboard motor. Member B immediately gets recognition from the chairman and says, "I move that we purchase a small yacht." At this point the chairman should   (1) ask A to withdraw his motion   (2) ask B to second A's motion   (3) rule A's motion out of order   (4) rule B's motion out of order.

19. The bylaws for an organization are   (1) the most important part of the constitution   (2) amendments to the constitution   (3) rules not in the constitution   (4) unwritten rules.

20. In a club meeting, a motion has been made and seconded that the club hold a dance during the month of January. Member A wishes to make the date definite. How should member A word his motion?   (1) I move to limit debate on this motion.   (2) I move that we have this

dance on January 14.   (3) I move that we vote whether to have it on January 14 or on January 30.   (4) I move that the motion be amended to read "January 14" rather than "during the month of January."

4. THE NEWSPAPER

READING A NEWSPAPER INTELLIGENTLY

One of the lifelong habits you are expected to develop in high school is reading a good daily newspaper intelligently. This means being able quickly to locate the important news of the day, editorials, special columns, sports news, reviews (of books, movies, television programs), letters to the editor, weather reports, and other newspaper features. It means being able to get a maximum of news in a minimum of time. Above all, it means being able to distinguish fact from opinion. Intelligent reading of a good daily newspaper will enrich your social, cultural, and business life and help you to make the decisions required of an American citizen.

REVIEWING THE NEWSPAPER

Past Regents questions on the newspaper show that you are expected to be familiar with the following:

A. Structure of a News Story

A news story is so written as to give the busy reader a maximum of news in a minimum of time. First comes the *headline,* a compressed summary consisting of one or more lines of large, heavy type:

Californian Trying
To Cross Atlantic
In a Tiny Aircraft

Then there is the *lead* (rhymes with *feed*), or opening paragraph. The lead sums up the main facts of the news story by answering most, if not all, of these questions: who? what? how? why? where? when? Notice how the following lead has done this:

> GLASGOW, Scotland, May 13 (AP)—Miroslav Slovak, a California airline pilot, took off from Glasgow today in an attempt to fly the Atlantic in what he asserts is the smallest aircraft ever to attempt the crossing.

QUESTION	ANSWER
Who?	Miroslav Slovak, a California airline pilot
What?	took off
Where?	Glasgow, Scotland
When?	today
Why?	in an attempt to fly the Atlantic
How?	in what he asserts is the smallest aircraft ever to attempt the crossing

Following the lead come the *details*. As the news story continues, the details diminish in importance.

Even if he has little time, a reader can keep abreast of the news by reading only the headlines and leads on the front page.

B. Arrangement of the Front Page

The front page is reserved for the important news of the day. By custom, the most important news story appears in the extreme right-hand column. The second most important story is in the extreme left-hand column. Between these two columns, on the upper half of the page, are the articles next in importance. To increase the amount of space for important news on page 1, newspapers usually continue page 1 stories on the inside pages.

C. Principles of Accurate Reporting

Good journalism requires the writer of a news story to give an impartial, objective, factual account of events, rigidly excluding his own feelings and opinions. The bad practice of injecting opinions into a news story is known as *editorializing*, or *slanting the news*.

EDITORIALIZING: Our baseball team, the best in the league, lost its first game yesterday because of an unfair decision at the plate in the ninth inning.

BETTER REPORTING: The previously undefeated Memorial High School baseball team lost its first game yesterday after a close decision at the plate in the ninth inning.

Every year, *Pulitzer Prizes* are awarded to newspapers, reporters, editors, cartoonists, and photographers for outstanding achievement in journalism.

D. Expression of Opinion

Newspapers may properly express opinions through editorials, columns, and cartoons.

An editorial is an essay. It expresses the views of those who control the newspaper. Editorials are intended to enlighten readers and influence their views. Usually an editorial begins by referring to the facts of a current news item. It then analyzes and interprets these facts, ending with the editorial writer's "point," or conclusion.

A column, too, is an essay that appears as a regular feature and is usually signed. In it, the columnist is expected to express his views, either on familiar subjects or on a particular specialty—politics, sports, a new book or movie, a TV program, a play, etc. Even though the column often appears on the same page as the editorials, the columnist's views are not necessarily those of the newspaper.

Cartoons, especially political cartoons, are another way by which newspapers may interpret the news and influence the thinking of readers. In their drawings cartoonists use the technique of exaggeration to attack what they consider follies and abuses.

The letters-to-the-editor department provides an opportunity for readers to express their opinions. A good newspaper will print letters representing a fair sampling of reader opinion, but will not publish anonymous letters.

Some newspapers exercise a further influence on public opinion by their ownership of radio stations or TV channels.

E. News Service Agencies

No newspaper can send its own reporters to all news fronts. For news of nonlocal events, most newspapers must rely upon reports by news service agencies, also known as *wire services*. Three such agencies are AP (Associated Press), UPI (United Press International), and Reuters.

F. Newspaper Syndicates

Newspaper syndicates help newspapers reduce the cost of expensive features. Organizations like King Features Syndicate, Field Enterprises, Inc., and Universal Press Syndicate purchase columns on a variety of subjects, as well as comic strips, dress patterns, puzzles, etc., for simultaneous publication in subscribing newspapers.

G. Common Newspaper Terms

A *beat* is (1) a reporter's regular route of news sources, or (2) the publishing of a news story ahead of rival newspapers (known also as a *scoop*).

A *by-line* is the line at the head of an article telling by whom it was written. Example: By Eileen Shanahan.

A *caption* is (1) a title or explanatory note accompanying a picture, or (2) the headline of an item in a newspaper.

A *classified ad* is one of a group of advertisements arranged according to subject, usually appearing under specific headings (Help Wanted, Apartments Wanted, etc.) in a definite section of a newspaper.

Copy is manuscript prepared for publication.

A *dateline* is a line at the beginning of a news story giving the source and date of the story. Example: Beirut, Lebanon, Feb. 23.

A *display ad* is an ad that "shows off" a product by choice and arrangement of words, type, illustrations, and photographs. It is usually composed by an advertising agency.

Editorializing is the bad practice of slanting the news by injecting opinions into a news story.

A *feature story*. See *human-interest story*.

A *galley* or *galley proof* is an impression (a copy) of the first setting of type. It is used for (1) proofreading, and (2) makeup into pages.

A *headline* is a line (or lines) of large type at the top (head) of an article, summarizing its contents. A *banner headline* is a headline in large type running across the entire front page of a newspaper.

A *human-interest story* is a story differing from the typical news story in appealing primarily to the emotions of the reader. Examples: a story on the daily rounds of a veterinarian at the zoo, the closing of a famous business establishment, etc. Also known as a *feature story.*

A *lead* (rhymes with *feed*) is the first sentence of a news story. It gives a summary of the story by answering most of these questions: who? what? how? why? when? where?

The *magazine section* is a supplement, usually included on Sunday, containing articles of general interest.

Makeup is the general arrangement of headlines, stories, and pictures on a newspaper page.

The *masthead* is the statement of the newspaper's title and ownership. It appears on the editorial page.

The *morgue* is the reference library in a newspaper office. It keeps on file information about important personalities in the news.

A *news service agency* (also known as a *wire service*) is an organization that supplies subscribing newspapers with reports of nonlocal events. Examples: United Press International (UPI), Associated Press (AP), and Reuters.

An *obituary* is a notice of death, often with a brief account of the person's life.

A *scoop.* See item (2) under *beat.*

A *syndicate* is an association that purchases columns, comic strips, dress patterns, etc., for simultaneous publication in member newspapers.

A *tabloid* is a newspaper having half the ordinary size newspaper page, numerous pictures, and compressed news stories.

A *want ad* is a short classified advertisement, usually found in the last pages of an issue, stating that something is wanted. Example: Sales Help Wanted.

A *wire service.* See *news service agency.*

EXERCISE ON THE NEWSPAPER

Write the number of the word or expression that best completes the statement or answers the question.

1. "Slanting" a news story means   (1) featuring human interest aspects
   (2) revealing the writer's feelings indirectly   (3) cutting down a
   story to fit a column space   (4) identifying the source of the story.
2. In addition to editorials, the editorial pages of such newspapers as the
   New York Times frequently contain   (1) stock market reports   (2)
   synopses of novels   (3) crossword puzzles   (4) letters to the editor.
3. A function of a newspaper syndicate is to (1) collect foreign news
   (2) provide opportunities for inexperienced writers   (3) sell columns
   to member newspapers   (4) regulate a group of newspapers.
4. Which is a national news service?   (1) AT & T   (2) HNS   (3)
   AP   (4) NNS.
5. Which item in a newspaper contains an example of editorializing?
   (1) The American political system is the most democratic in the world.
   (2) For today, milder weather is predicted here.   (3) The County
   Fair will admit children under twelve at half price.   (4) The Cubs
   defeated the Dodgers, 11-10.
0. An award for outstanding achievement in journalism is the   (1) Pea-
   body Award   (2) Pulitzer Prize   (3) Emmy Award   (4) Nobel
   Prize.
7. Upon which technique do most political cartoons rely for their effect?
   (1) understatement   (2) objectivity   (3) alliteration   (4) exaggeration.
8. In a news story, which phrase would most strengthen the reader's belief
   in the report?   (1) A reliable police court source indicated . . .   (2)
   Judging from the reports of the police, it is believed . . .   (3) According to Chief of Police Adams . . .   (4) In the opinion of the
   observers . . .
9. One reason that the lead of a news story in a newspaper summarizes the
   essential information is to   (1) aid the hurried reader   (2) reduce
   the length of subsequent paragraphs   (3) save work for the reporter
   (4) encourage the reading of advertisements.
10. Most serious newspaper cartoonists are nearest in point of view to
    (1) comic strip artists   (2) drama critics   (3) editorial writers
    (4) "roving reporters."
11. The first paragraph in a news story   (1) gives a detailed account of
    the event that occurred   (2) gives a summarized statement of the
    event   (3) seeks to entertain the reader   (4) receives little attention
    from most readers.
12. A *beat* is   (1) a kind of teletype   (2) an explanatory note in a news

story (3) a reporter's regular route of news sources (4) a file of old news stories.

13. In a Sunday newspaper, articles of general interest are included in the (1) magazine section (2) book review section (3) monthly news summary (4) financial section.

14. The point of view of the publishers of our best newspapers is usually set forth (1) on the first pages of an issue (2) on the editorial page (3) in the financial section (4) in feature stories.

15. Most daily newspapers obtain news of nonlocal events by relying upon (1) "tips" telephoned in by long distance (2) local reporters (3) the newspaper "grapevine" (4) reports by news service agencies.

16. From the standpoint of high-grade journalism, the most important factor in a news story is its (1) location in the paper (2) length (3) headline (4) impartial reporting.

17. The *masthead* of a newspaper is (1) a summary of the day's news (2) a heading over a picture (3) the statement of the newspaper's title and ownership (4) the chief editorial of each issue.

18. The most important purpose of political cartoons is to (1) make readers laugh (2) help readers keep up-to-date (3) meet reader demand for "escape" reading (4) influence readers' views.

19. The *dateline* of a news story indicates the date that (1) the story was written or filed (2) the event happened (3) the story was sent out by the news service (4) the story was due on the editor's desk.

20. Newspaper want ads are usually found (1) in the last pages of an issue (2) throughout an issue (3) at the foot of each page (4) at the end of the first section.

21. Newspapers increase the amount of space for important news on the front page by (1) using double headlines (2) continuing stories on inside pages (3) placing all local news on inside pages (4) printing action pictures of the news.

22. Some newspapers influence public opinion by their ownership of (1) radio stations (2) book manufacturing companies (3) motion picture studios (4) varied public utilities.

23. It is a function of the newspaper columnist to (1) assign pages for advertisements (2) divide the news into columns (3) write the headlines for the front page (4) express his personal opinions.

24. The Associated Press and the United Press International distribute stories to (1) movie critics (2) member papers (3) syndicates (4) book companies.

25. Which of the following statements about the newspaper is *not* true? (1) The chief source of income for most newspapers is advertising. (2) The Associated Press is a news service agency. (3) A headline helps to "slant" the news. (4) The size of a newspaper's circulation proves its worth.

5. MAGAZINES

WHY MAGAZINES ARE IMPORTANT

Magazines are a popular source of entertainment and information. They provide us with recreational reading through fiction, nonfiction, poetry, cartoons, and pictures. Through articles and essays they help us to interpret national and world developments and to understand our cultural heritage. They instruct us in the art of daily living. Magazines are an important source of information and new ideas. On many topics we can find more up-to-date information in magazines than in books.

Since there are thousands of magazines, the problem of locating information in them might appear complicated. To help us, however, we have the valuable research tool known as the *Readers' Guide to Periodical Literature.*

WHAT YOU ARE EXPECTED TO KNOW
ABOUT MAGAZINES

Past Regents questions in this area indicate that you should be acquainted with the *Readers' Guide to Periodical Literature,* as well as with several magazines of general interest.

READERS' GUIDE TO PERIODICAL LITERATURE

The *Readers' Guide* is a directory to articles in about 160 leading magazines. It is published twice monthly from September through June, and monthly in July and August. When looking for information in magazines, first consult the *Readers' Guide.* You will find the entries are for the most part arranged alphabetically by (*a*) subject, and (*b*) author.

a. **Sample Entry by Subject**

MOUNTAINEERING

> **Ten women challenge earth's tenth highest mountain: triumph and tragedy on Annapurna. A. Blum. il por maps Nat Geog 155:294-311 Mr '79**

For an interpretation of the above entry, turn to the next page.

LINE 1:

MOUNTAINEERING—the subject of the article

LINES 2 AND 3:

Ten women challenge earth's tenth highest mountain;
triumph and tragedy on Annapurna—the complete title
of the article, including the subtitle

LINE 4:

A. Blum—the author's name
il por maps—the article is accompanied by illustrations,
portraits, and maps
Nat Geog—*National Geographic* (the name of the magazine)
155:—the volume number of the issue
294–311—the pages on which the article appears

LINE 5:

Mr 79—March 1979 (the date of this issue)

b. **Sample Entry by Author**

BLUM, Arlene

**Triumph and tragedy on Annapurna. il por maps
Nat Geog 155: 294-311 Mr '79**

SOME MAGAZINES OF GENERAL INTEREST

Below are thumbnail descriptions of several magazines that you might
wish to consult for pleasure or information. Acquaint yourself with four or
five that you do not already know by leafing through their current issues
on your next visit to the library.

The Atlantic, published monthly, offers reports and comment on current
issues from correspondents at home and abroad, informal essays, book
reviews, and original fiction and poetry. Among the contributors are
some of our most distinguished living writers.

Changing Times, published monthly, is intended to help the family manage
its finances. The articles offer buying hints, attempt to forecast living costs
and employment trends, suggest economical vacations, and in general
concern themselves with the welfare of consumers.

Ebony, published monthly, deals with the current problems and achievements of black people in the United States. An *Ebony* department,
"Speaking of People," consists of biographical sketches and photographs
of black men and women coming to the top in their professions.

Field and Stream, published monthly, deals mainly with hunting and fishing. Several "how-to-do-it" and "where-to-go" articles offer detailed information for the pursuit of these sports. Included, too, are articles underscoring the need to conserve our forest and wildlife resources.

Fortune, issued fortnightly (every fourteen days), reports developments in leading corporations, presents sketches of key business figures, and advises on business problems. Typical departments are "Business Roundup" and "Personal Investing."

Good Housekeeping, a monthly, offers a novel and short stories, plus articles about celebrities, family life, sewing, decorating, fashion, beauty, and diet.

Harper's, published monthly, presents articles by outstanding writers on general topics, politics, and public issues. It also contains short stories, poetry, reviews of books, and a department of editorial comment entitled "The Easy Chair."

Ladies' Home Journal, published monthly, presents articles on family living, home management, food, beauty, fashion, and decorating. Some of the articles deal with the personal lives of celebrities. Also offered are short stories and book condensations.

Life, published monthly, contains articles richly supported by photography on current national and international topics. A page is devoted to letters from readers.

Mademoiselle, published monthly, is intended mainly for the college girl. It offers hints on fashion, beauty, and shopping; articles on travel, colleges, and careers; and some short stories and poems.

McCall's, published monthly, is intended for the American woman and her family. It contains articles on fashions, food, child-rearing, decorating, health, and beauty, plus short stories, and excerpts from recent books.

The National Geographic is published monthly for members of the National Geographic Society, sponsor of dozens of scientific expeditions. The articles, maps, and abundant color photographs provide reliable facts about places, peoples, customs, animal and plant life, and undersea phenomena.

National Wildlife, published six times a year for members of the National Wildlife Federation, contains articles, illustrated by excellent color photography, on plant life, wildlife, and ecology.

Natural History, the Journal of the American Museum of Natural History, is published ten times a year. It offers articles, supported by excellent color photographs and illustrations, on nature, anthropology, and ecology.

Newsweek, published weekly, reports the news in about twenty categories, such as "National Affairs," "International," "Business," "Television," "Music," "Books," and "Sports."

The New York Times Magazine, published weekly as a section of the Sunday *New York Times,* contains informational articles on contemporary matters, plus articles on food, fashion, and gardening, a page of puzzles, and letters to the editor.

The New Yorker, published weekly, presents "Goings On About Town," a guide to cultural events and entertainment in New York City. The magazine gently satirizes contemporary life through its cartoons. Also offered are short stories, poems, and reviews of books, movies, plays, and TV programs.

People, published weekly, except for two issues combined in one at year-end, focuses on the personal lives of people in the news in politics, the economy, sports, and the arts. It provides a checklist of the week's recommended TV shows, books, records, and films.

Popular Mechanics, published monthly, contains dozens of short articles on automobiles and bikes; house and yard; shop and crafts; electronics, radio, and TV; science and engineering; etc. They offer practical suggestions, clearly presented with the aid of pictures and diagrams.

Popular Science, published monthly, is very similar in content, as can be seen from the headings under which it organizes its articles: "Cars and Driving," "Home and Yard," "New Products and Inventions," "Electronics," "New Technology," "Space and Aviation," etc.

Reader's Digest, issued monthly, condenses articles from other magazines. It also contains uncut articles written to order for the *Reader's Digest.* The articles generally present an optimistic picture of our nation or of human nature. They deal with health, science, or current problems, or discuss entertaining, little-known facts on various subjects. Each issue contains a book condensation, and a department of reader-contributed anecdotes entitled "Life in These United States." Two additional features are "Toward More Picturesque Speech" (a collection of puns) and "It Pays to Enrich Your Word Power" (a vocabulary exercise).

Redbook, incorporating *American Home,* is a monthly offering a novel, short stories, and articles on beauty, child care, home equipment and furnishings, food and nutrition, and fashion and needle crafts.

The Saturday Evening Post, published monthly, except for bimonthly issues for January-February, May-June, and July-August, offers new fiction and articles on current topics, plus book reviews, editorials, and travel and food departments.

The Saturday Review, published biweekly, except monthly in August and September, divides its material into *Issues* (articles on contemporary matters), and *Pleasures* (articles on theater, movies, photography, books, dance, and music).

Scientific American, published monthly, offers articles by outstanding scientists on the newest developments in the different sciences. Departments include "Science and the Citizen," "Mathematical Games," and "The Amateur Scientist."

Seventeen, a monthly magazine for the teen-age girl, offers short informational picture articles under such headings as "Fashion," "Food," "Beauty," and "Young Living." There are some short stories too.

Time, "the weekly newsmagazine," reports the news in story form under about twenty sections: "Nation," "World," "Economy and Business," "Environment," "Sport," "Television," "Medicine," etc. *Time* reviews current movies, plays, and books.

Travel-Holiday, a monthly subtitled "The Magazine that roams the globe," offers articles on places worth visiting in the U.S.A. and abroad.

U.S. News and World Report, published monthly, is "devoted entirely to national and international affairs." Its "Worldgram" is a telegram-style newsletter "from the capitals of the world." An editorial appears on the last page.

EXERCISE ON MAGAZINES

1. Study the following entry from the *Readers' Guide to Periodical Literature.* Then answer questions *a–e* below.

    SPACE vehicles
      Coming: the space shuttle. J. C. Fletcher.
      il Sat Eve Post 245:68-71 My '73

    Explain fully:
    a. SPACE vehicles   *c.* il   *e.* 68–71 My '73
    b. J. C. Fletcher   *d.* Sat Eve Post 245

2. A South American wants to learn more about the United States and our way of life through subscribing to five of our magazines. List *five* good magazines that represent varied interests of American life and, in a sentence or two for *each,* give specific reasons for your choice.

3. Of the following magazines, choose *five* and indicate in one or two sentences for *each* its special values to the reader. (Where alternates are given, choose only one.)

Newsweek (or *Time,* or *U.S. News and World Report*)
The National Geographic Magazine (or *Scientific American*)
The Atlantic (or *Harper's*)
Seventeen (or *Mademoiselle*)
Popular Science (or *Popular Mechanics*)
Ebony

4. Name the magazine that regularly features the following:
   a. "It Pays to Enrich Your Word Power"   d. "The Easy Chair"
   b. "The Amateur Scientist"   e. "Business Roundup"
   c. "Speaking of People"

5. Each of the following statements concerns magazines. Write the *number* of the expression that best completes the statement.
   a. Magazine articles are indexed in   (1) *The Reader's Handbook* (2) Ayer's *Index to Newspapers and Periodicals*   (3) the card catalog   (4) *Readers' Guide to Periodical Literature.*
   b. "Life in These United States" appears in   (1) *Time*   (2) *Harper's*   (3) *The Reader's Digest*   (4) *Life.*
   c. A magazine that regularly features articles on business enterprise is (1) *Fortune*   (2) *Scholastic*   (3) *Variety*   (4) *Popular Science.*
   d. Which magazine regularly contains short stories or poetry?   (1) *Time*   (2) *Popular Mechanics*   (3) *Sports Illustrated*   (4) *Harper's.*
   e. Informal essays regularly appear in   (1) *The Atlantic*   (2) *Time*   (3) *Popular Mechanics*   (4) *Natural History.*
   f. Book reviews regularly appear in   (1) *Harper's*   (2) *Encyclopedia Americana*   (3) *Popular Science*   (4) *The Reader's Digest.*
   g. *The New York Times Magazine* regularly contains   (1) book reviews   (2) columns of poetry   (3) informational articles (4) film listings.

6. PROPAGANDA TECHNIQUES

WHAT IS PROPAGANDA?

Propaganda is the expression of ideas, opinions, arguments, or allegations with the deliberate intent of helping or hurting a person, group, or cause. Propaganda can be good or bad, depending on its purpose. If used to prevent fires or improve highway safety, propaganda is clearly good. If employed to encourage poor health habits or excite race hatred, it is clearly bad. Regardless of whether the intention is good or bad, propaganda always attempts to get us to make decisions or take actions *without using reason.*

WHY MUST WE BE ABLE TO RECOGNIZE PROPAGANDA?

Today's mass media of communication, including television, radio, newspapers, and magazines, have made it possible for propaganda to be spread on a vaster scale than ever before. This means that we must be specially alert in deciding what causes to support, whom to vote for, and what products to buy. Both as consumers and as citizens, we must learn to recognize propaganda, so that we may discount it and make our decisions on the *basis of reason.*

REVIEWING PROPAGANDA TECHNIQUES

Past Regents questions show that you are expected to be able to recognize the principal propaganda techniques. They are as follows:

The Testimonial Technique

> EXAMPLE: "For more pep, try brand X cereal. I have some for breakfast every day."
> Signed: Jerry B., professional athlete

The *testimonial* is a statement by a celebrity, endorsing a product or a service. Such endorsements are very common on billboards, and in newspaper, magazine, and television advertising. Celebrities who recommend a breakfast cereal may be respected for achievement in their own fields, but they are not experts in nutrition. If, however, a qualified nutritionist were to present evidence on the merits of this cereal, we should then examine that evidence seriously.

Testimonials are used in politics, too. A candidate for a minor post usually reprints endorsements from well-known officeholders in his party. As voters, we must rely on facts rather than testimonials, since the latter are often given automatically, as a matter of party loyalty.

The Transfer Technique

> EXAMPLE: Candidate Y, running for re-election, includes in her campaign literature a picture of herself with the dome of the U.S. Capitol in the background.

Transfer is used to make a person, group, or cause popular by associating them with popular ideas or institutions. The dome of the U.S. Capitol, for example, evokes feelings of loyalty and respect. By associating herself with that dome, Candidate Y hopes that we will unthinkingly "transfer" to her some of those very same feelings. Or she may have herself photographed with the American flag, another way to achieve "transfer."

The Name-Calling Technique

> EXAMPLES: "We shall punish the *imperialist aggressors*" (nation A's name for the troops of its foe, nation B).
>
> "The *communist infiltrators* (nation B's name for the force of its enemy, nation A) were repelled with heavy losses."

Name-calling is the use of bias words or defamatory labels to describe someone or something that the name-callers want us to reject. They use names that arouse fear and hate to make us condemn without examining the facts. When we encounter any of the following designations, supported by little or no proof, we should suspect name-calling: red, communist, pinko, fascist, reactionary, racist, imperialist, appeaser, infiltrator, aggressor, extremist, radical, alien, do-gooder, bureaucrat, beatnik, fanatic, etc.

The Glittering Generalities Technique

> EXAMPLE: "Our party stands for *justice, truth, freedom,* and *democracy.* A vote for us is a vote for *progress, fair play, decency,* and *good government.*"

Glittering generalities is a technique for promoting someone or something by association with high-sounding words or phrases. Practically everyone reacts favorably to such attractive ("glittering") ideals as truth, honor, liberty, justice, freedom, progress, patriotism, the American way, etc. They are typical of the prestige words in which propagandists clothe any person, group, or cause that they want us to accept uncritically. Lofty associations for which no specific proof is offered should be dismissed as "glittering generalities."

The Bandwagon Technique

> EXAMPLE: "Just about everyone who comes to town stays at the wonderful new Hotel X."

The *bandwagon* technique fools those who, like sheep, thoughtlessly follow the herd. When advertisers or propagandists state, with little or no proof, that everyone is flocking to their product, service, or cause, they are using the bandwagon technique. They hope that we, too, will "hop on the bandwagon," that is, do what they allege everyone else is doing.

The Card-Stacking Technique

> EXAMPLE: Following a truce, one side reports that it has been bombed and that several of its civilians have been killed. It does not report that it provoked the attack by bombing the other side first.

The *card-stacking* technique creates a false impression by withholding significant information. By presenting only those facts that make one side look good and the other bad, the propagandist tries to mislead the public.

The Plain-Folks Technique

> EXAMPLE: In a campaign swing through her district, a candidate for reelection, accompanied by photographers and reporters, buys a hamburger at a sandwich stand, shakes hands with passersby, and kisses a baby.

When candidates want to convey the impression that they are just like the great majority of people, they use the *plain-folks* technique. This calls for them to do such "folksy" things as work at chores in old clothes, ride a bicycle, go fishing, show affection for babies, eat a frankfurter or a piece of pizza, etc., especially before news and television cameras. Many voters, unfortunately, are swayed by the plain-folks technique to the point of overlooking what is most important—the candidate's record.

The Snob-Appeal Technique

> EXAMPLE: "The man of distinction wears Nobility hose."

The *snob-appeal* technique, the opposite of the *plain folks* technique, is based on the theory that many people like to consider themselves superior. Propagandists who use *snob appeal* identify their products or services with qualities that would appeal to a snob (a person convinced of his or her superiority). These qualities include the high cost or rarity of the product, or its association (as in the example above) with an elite.

EXERCISE ON PROPAGANDA TECHNIQUES

Below are ten examples of propaganda. Analyze each one and state what propaganda technique it illustrates.

1. "Movie star Maria Bella says that she keeps her skin smooth and glowing by frequent use of our product. If you use this preparation, your skin will glow as Miss Bella's does."
2. A candidate, accompanied by reporters, appears at a local playground and briefly joins in a game with a group of neighborhood youths.
3. "Buy a brand-new Whizzer bike like the ones all your friends have."
4. A campaign photograph shows a nominee with the American flag and portraits of Washington and Lincoln in the background.
5. "Thirty-five personal endorsements from statesmen, judges, and educators prove the value of our publication."

6. A rug clearance sale advertises "hundreds" of rugs at $99–$299, but neglects to state that only two of the rugs are priced at $99.

7. A magazine article on a legislator running for a second term shows her at work altering a dress for her oldest daughter.

8. A campaign orator exhorts the audience to vote only for members of his party in order to turn out the "bureaucrats, do-gooders, and pinkos."

9. A newspaper ad reads as follows: "Rare offering! Elegant North Shore ranch in executive estate section. Asking $72,500."

10. A political candidate is introduced as "that great humanitarian and defender of justice."

7. LETTER WRITING SKILLS

In your English courses you have practiced writing various types of letters that people frequently have occasion to write: the letter of application, the letter of complaint, the letter to a sick friend, etc. Several past Regents examinations have included questions about the structure, punctuation, and content of such letters.

The following review aims to improve your ability to write business and friendly letters.

A. BUSINESS LETTERS

THE LETTER OF COMPLAINT

On the next page is a letter of complaint, a typical business letter. Let us examine it as a model of business letter form.

Margins

By attention to margins, you can give your letter the neat, balanced appearance of a well-framed picture. Center your letter horizontally by making your right-hand and left-hand margins the same size, as in the model. Balance it vertically by making the blank spaces above and below the letter approximately equal.

Parts of a Business Letter

1. Heading

Line 1: 3499 Bell Boulevard
Line 2: Bayside, New York   11364
Line 3: January 3, 1980

Lines 1 and 2 are for your address. Line 3 is for the date of writing.

3499 Bell Boulevard
Bayside, New York 11364
January 3, 1980

Martin Products, Inc.
6800 Railroad Avenue
Charlotte, North Carolina 28202

Gentlemen:

When I unpacked the parts of my Model #14 Walnut Record Cabinet delivered today, I noticed a trim screw was missing. According to the instructions for assembling the cabinet, I am supposed to fasten the handles to the doors with four small trim screws. However, there were only three in the carton. Please send the missing trim screw as quickly as possible so that I may finish assembling the cabinet.

Yours truly,

Mona Pace

Mona Pace

Required punctuation—

Line 2: a comma between city (or town) and state
Line 3: a comma between day and year

Often, the appearance of a letter is spoiled at the very outset by careless placement of the heading. To avoid this, first determine the longest line of your heading (line 2). Write that line so that it ends flush with the right-hand margin you plan to maintain for the rest of the letter. Then begin the other lines of the heading flush with the beginning of the longest line.

Be accurate. Remember that your correspondent will refer to the heading to address a reply to you. Be sure to include your ZIP code number.

If you use stationery with a printed letterhead, omit lines 1 and 2. Make line 3 (the date) the first line of your letter.

2.   *Inside Address.*   The inside address, below and to the left of the heading, is exactly the same as the envelope address. Examples:

To a firm or organization:
Martin Products, Inc.
6800 Railroad Avenue
Charlotte, North Carolina   28202

To a specific person in a firm or institution:
Mr. James C. Park, President
Martin Products, Inc.
6800 Railroad Avenue
Charlotte, North Carolina   28202

To a government official:
Superintendent of Documents
U.S. Government Printing Office
Washington, D. C.   20402

Required punctuation.   The last line of the inside address: a comma between city (or town) and state. In addition, a comma is often required in the first line. Examples:

Before *Inc.* or *Incorporated:*
Martin Products, Inc.

After a person's name, if a title follows:
Mr. James C. Park, President

Make the inside address flush with the left-hand margin you plan to maintain for the rest of the letter.

3.   *Salutation.*   The salutation, directly below the inside address, is determined by the addressee (the first line of the inside address). Following are some common salutations and the addressees for whom they are appropriate.

Gentlemen:	(*Martin Products, Inc., College Entrance Examination Board,* etc.)
Ladies:	(*League of Women Voters*)

Dear Mr. Park: (*Mr. James C. Park*)
Dear Mrs. Blake: (*Mrs. Eileen M. Blake*)
Dear Ms. Gallo: (*Ms. Roberta Gallo*)
Dear Dr. Herman: (*Dr. Chester W. Herman*)

Dear Sir: (government officials; also all addressees desig-
Dear Madam: nated only by title, without mention of their
                               names: *Superintendent of Documents, Service
                               Manager, Supervising Nurse*, etc.)

Required punctuation.   A colon [:] follows the salutation.

4. Body.   The body follows the salutation. Every line of the body is flush with the previously established right and left margins, except that the beginning of each paragraph is indented.

The body should be as brief as possible without being unclear or impolite. In the following body, the writer could have expressed her understandable anger and frustration. But she checked these feelings, realizing that the best way to get satisfaction is to let the facts speak for themselves. This she has done in a tactful paragraph of four sentences:

When I unpacked the parts of my Model #14 Walnut Record Cab inet delivered today, I noticed a trim screw was missing. According to the instructions for assembling the cabinet, I am supposed to fasten the handles to the doors with four small trim screws. However, there were only three in the carton. Please send the missing trim screw as quickly as possible so that I may finish assembling the cabinet.

Analysis: The first sentence clearly states the complaint in specific language: *Model #14 Walnut Record Cabinet; trim screw.* The next two sentences add supplementary details. The last sentence tactfully and politely asks for remedial action.

5. Closing.   The closing, just below the body, should begin flush with the heading. Only the first word should be capitalized. The following are common business-letter closings:

Yours truly,   Yours sincerely,
Very truly yours,   Sincerely yours,

Required punctuation. A comma follows the closing.

6. Signature.   The signature, next after the closing, should begin flush with the closing. *Miss, Mrs.*, or *Ms.* may be enclosed in parentheses before a woman's signature, but other titles (*Mr., Dr.*, etc.) are not permitted:

Mona Pace *or* (Ms.) Mona Pace *or* (Miss) Mona Pace
James C. Park NOT *Mr.* James C. Park
Roberta Gallo *or* (Mrs.) Roberta Gallo

If you type your letter, leave a three-line space between the closing and your typewritten name. Then write your signature in that space.

Yours truly,

Mona Pace

Mona Pace

The Envelope

The envelope requires: (1) your name and address (known together as the *return address*) in the upper left-hand corner, and (2) the name and address of the person or organization to whom you are sending the letter (addressee), centered slightly below the middle of the envelope.

Mona Pace
3499 Bell Boulevard
Bayside, New York   11364

Martin Products, Inc.

6800 Railroad Avenue

Charlotte, North Carolina   28202

Note that: (1) the last two lines of the return address are an exact replica of the first two lines of the heading of the letter (page 257), and (2) the name and address of the addressee are an exact replica of the inside address of the letter.

Exercise 1.   Write any *one* of the following business letters. Be brief, clear, and courteous.

1. Today you lost two 50¢ coins in a defective machine at the Acme Washomat in your local shopping center. Write to Executive Office, Acme

Washomats, Inc., 12 Main Street (you supply the rest of the address), asking for a refund.

2. Write to Merit Film Processors, Inc., of 2202 University Boulevard, Boulder, Colorado 80302. When you received your vacation film, you noticed two pictures were missing. Nothing seems to be wrong with the negatives for these pictures. State that you are enclosing the two negatives, and request that the pictures be sent to you.

3. Write to a local public official (for example, the Mayor) suggesting a needed improvement (for example, the installation of a traffic light at a dangerous intersection).

4. Write to the Superintendent of Documents, U.S. Government Printing Office, Washington, D.C. 20402, requesting a copy of Home and Garden Bulletin No. 64 entitled *Subterranean Termites, Their Prevention and Control in Buildings*. State that you are enclosing a check for $1.00.

5. Write to the Book-of-the-Month Club, Inc., Camp Hill, Pennsylvania 17012, stating that you are considering joining the club and would appreciate receiving details about membership.

Complete the envelope for the letter you have written.

THE LETTER OF APPLICATION

Another typical business letter, the letter of application, is one that you will write at some time or another to apply for a position that you may have heard about or seen advertised. Before responding to such an advertisement, analyze it to determine what it calls for, so that you may plan your answer accordingly.

Consider the following advertisement:

HIGH SCHOOL STUDENT, 16+.
Summer work as museum guide. Meet and greet public. Must be well-spoken. References required. $150 week. Apply in handwriting. Box 672, *Times*.

Advertisement Analyzed

The advertisement calls for three qualifications:

(1) You must be over 16. (If not, or if you will not shortly be 16, do not apply for this position.)

(2) You must be "well-spoken," i.e., able to express yourself fluently. (You should be able to offer some evidence of this, tactfully.)

(3) You must be able to provide references as to your character and ability. (Do not mention a person's name as a reference unless you have that person's permission.)

In addition, though it does not directly say so, the advertisement suggests that certain other qualifications are desirable:

(1) a favorable attitude toward museums

(2) the ability to welcome people courteously

(3) the ability to express yourself in correct, legible written English (since a handwritten letter is requested)

Let us now examine one student's letter of application for the above position.

---

298 Ocean Avenue
Brooklyn, New York   11225
May 6, 1980

Box 672, *Times*
229 West 43 Street
New York, N.Y.   10036

Dear Sir:

I should greatly appreciate your considering me as an applicant for the summer position of museum guide advertised in today's *Times*.

I am sixteen and a half years old and have had experience and training that I believe may be helpful to a museum guide. At West End High School, where I am completing the junior year, I have been on the Usher Squad for two years. I have three certificates of commendation from the principal for courteous and efficient service as an usher at assemblies, plays, concerts, games, and graduation exercises. As to my speaking experience, I represent my homeroom class in the Student Council. Besides speaking on the floor of the Council, I make oral reports to my classmates each Monday morning about what the Council is doing. I should like to add that I regularly visit our local museums, especially to see the art collections.

The following members of the West End High School faculty have kindly consented to furnish additional information about my character, scholarship, and service:

Dr. Stuart C. Olsen, Principal
Mrs. Grace M. Panaroni, Teacher of English
Mr. Aaron Uhl, Faculty Adviser of the Usher Squad

The school is at 900 Bailey Boulevard, Brooklyn, New York 11226.

My telephone number is 553-4662. I shall be very happy to appear for an interview at your convenience.

Very truly yours,
Regina Wesson

Reply Analyzed

Strengths

PLANNING: Regina's letter is well organized.

Paragraph 1 briefly, clearly, and politely states the purpose of the letter.
Paragraph 2 indicates that Regina meets all of the stated and implied qualifications, except for the references.
Paragraph 3 offers the names of three references and their addresses.
Paragraph 4 concludes the letter with a polite request for an interview.

TACT: If Regina were to claim to be *well-spoken,* she might give the impression of being conceited. Instead, she tactfully offers evidence (Student Council activity, classroom reports) that *suggests* she is well-spoken.

Other evidences of Regina's tact are her mention of the commendation certificates (they suggest she is courteous and efficient) and the inclusion of her telephone number (it makes an interview that much more likely).

Weakness

REFERENCES: All of Regina's references are school people. At least one of them should be a non-school person. Regina can strengthen her application by omitting the name of Mr. Aaron Uhl, a repetitive reference. (He serves mainly to corroborate what the principal has testified to, by his certificates.) As a replacement, she should try to offer the name and address of a neighbor, community business person, or family adviser.

Exercise 2. Answer *a* or *b*.

a. Compose a letter of application for *one* of the positions advertised below.

TRAINEE. Act as title clerk for new car dealer, doing paper work dealing with sale of cars. Some knwl typing, abil to keep records. Must be neat worker. Start July 7. Exc oppty to learn auto retailing. Apply by letter, Mrs. C. Loeb, Automart, Inc., 8360 Queens Blvd., Kew Gardens, N.Y. 11415

COUNSELORS, 17+, dedicated. Fine co-ed day camp. June 29 to Aug 21. 5-day week. Openings in archery, arts and crafts, dramatics, golf, music, swimming, tennis. Some experience with children desirable. J. R. Begg, Director, P.O. Box 590, Hicksville, New York 11802

JUNE H.S. GRADS. $140 wk. Willing to start at bottom July 1 and work your way up with a company that pays for performance? Fire ins firm will start you in the mailroom, review your salary in September & eventually move you into an administrative training program. Advancement, benefits, cafeteria, opportunity to continue education, and chance for a lifetime insurance career. Walsh Insurance Agency, Box 4411, Rochester, New York 14602.

PART-TIME CLERK. General office routine. Very little typing. Write, stating age, experience, salary desired, days & hours available. Personnel Dept., 12 James Center, Newburgh, New York 12550.

---

b.   From a local newspaper, select a help-wanted advertisement and reply to it in a letter of application. Attach the advertisement, or a copy of it, to the completed letter.

Complete the envelope for your letter of application.

B. FRIENDLY LETTERS

The friendly letter, as the name implies, is for correspondence with friends, family, and other relatives. It is conversational in tone. To the degree warranted by your relationship with the addressee, it permits the use of informal English. Its layout, too, is more flexible than that of the business letter. You may use either the block or the indented style.

BLOCK STYLE   **INDENTED STYLE**

Parts of a Friendly Letter

1. Heading

> 9 Raleigh Place
> Hawthorne, New York   10532
> July 21, 1980

Variations:

(1) If the person you are writing to is well acquainted with your address, omit lines 1 and 2. Make the date the first line of your letter.

(2) Do the same if using stationery imprinted with your address.

(3) If you prefer, use the indented style:

> 9 Raleigh Place
> Hawthorne, New York   10532
> July 21, 1980

Required punctuation. Same as in business letter:

Line 2: a comma between city (or town) and state
Line 3: a comma between day and year

Caution: The style you choose for the heading determines the layout of the rest of the letter and the envelope. See block and indented styles shown on the preceding page.

2. Salutation. Here are typical salutations:

Dear Bob,	Dear Mother,	Dear Uncle,
Dear Anne,	Dear Mom and Dad,	Dear Uncle Al,

Required punctuation. A comma follows the salutation.

3. Body.
Maintain a friendly tone throughout the body of the letter, and especially in your remarks at the beginning and the end. Use the language you would normally use if you were conversing with the friend.

4. Closing.
The form of the closing depends on your relationship with the recipient. Here are some typical closings:

Sincerely,	Affectionately,	Your nephew,
Cordially,	Love,	Sincerely yours,

Begin the closing flush with the top line of your heading. If it consists of more than one word, capitalize only the first word.

Required punctuation. A comma follows the closing.

5. *Signature.* Write your first name.

BLOCK STYLE: Sincerely,   INDENTED STYLE: Sincerely,
                Alice   Alice

Let us now examine a typical friendly letter.

---

9 Raleigh Place
Hawthorne, New York   10532
July 21, 1980

Dear Bob,

How have you been enjoying your vacation? Our Florida trip was a big flop.

On the way down we had fair but very hot weather all the way to North Carolina. Then it began to rain. About this time, at gas stations and restaurants, we kept running into people returning from Florida who told us it had rained there every day of their stay. But we kept going, hoping by the time we got there the rains would be over.

Well, it rained most of the time as we drove through South Carolina and Georgia, and it poured in Florida for the nine days we were there. We drove in the rains down the Atlantic coast of Florida and up the Gulf coast, sometimes over roads that were several inches under water. The natives told us it's been the wettest season ever. Dad let me take the wheel some of the time. Mom didn't drive at all. Visibility was often very poor, but luckily our air conditioner kept the windshield from fogging up. Not until we approached Virginia, on the return home, did the rains let up. It was a harrowing trip.

Right now we're home, recovering from our "vacation." You would grin if you could see our supply of unused suntan lotion, swim gear, and color film. If you ever get a hankering to go South for a vacation, take a tip from me: don't go in the monsoon season.

Cordially,
Frank

Analysis

TONE: Frank has maintained a friendly tone through two principal means:

   (1) *By showing he is thinking of Bob.* This is apparent particularly in the opening sentence, and also in the last two sentences.

   (2) *By using informal, conversational English.* Below are some of the informal expressions Frank has used. Think how different the tone of the letter would have been, had Frank substituted the formal English equivalents.

INFORMAL	FORMAL
flop	failure
running into people	encountering people
poured	rained heavily
it's been	it has been
Dad	My father
Mom	My mother
take the wheel	drive
fogging up	becoming clouded
hankering	strong desire

PLANNING: Frank has organized his letter mainly by the method of chronological order:

   Paragraph 1 introduces the topic ("Our Florida Trip").
   Paragraph 2 discusses the early part of the trip.
   Paragraph 3 deals with the later stages.
   Paragraph 4 takes up the final chronological part, the homecoming.

Exercise 3. Answer *a, b,* or *c* in a letter of at least three paragraphs.

a. Imagine that you have just received a friendly letter from a summer friend, or a close friend who has moved, or a brother or sister at college. Reply to that letter.

b. A classmate is in the hospital, recovering from an automobile accident. Write a letter expressing your sympathy and informing the classmate of something interesting or amusing that has occurred in his or her absence.

c. You have just returned from an enjoyable weekend at a friend's home. Write a letter to your friend's mother, thanking her for her hospitality. (This is known as a "bread-and-butter" letter.)

Complete the envelope for your friendly letter.

REVIEW EXERCISE ON BUSINESS AND FRIENDLY LETTERS

Write the letter of the expression that best completes the statement or answers the question.

1. In a letter of application for a position as clerk, which is the most appropriate statement of experience?

   a. Last winter I worked as a clerk.
   b. During January and February 1972, I worked as a clerk for the *ABC* Publishing Company, 110 Adams Street, Corona, New York 11368.
   c. I once worked for the *ABC* Publishing Company, but I was laid off through no fault of my own.
   d. I have done some work as a clerk.

2. Which is an acceptable salutation for a business letter?

   a. Dear Gentlemen: *c.* Dear sir:
   b. Dear Sir: *d.* Gentleman:

3. Which is an inappropriate closing for a friendly letter?

   a. Sincerely yours,   *c.* Yours truly,
   b. Love,   *d.* Sincerely,

4. Which is correct as the last line of an address?

   a. Dearborn, Michigan 48121.   *c.* Dearborn, Michigan. 48121
   b. Dearborn, Michigan, 48121   *d.* Dearborn, Michigan 48121

5. In a letter of application, which is the most effective close of the letter?

   a. It should be easy for you to see, then, why I am ideally suited for the position. My telephone number is 8-7191.
   b. I can come for an interview at any time, except on Thursdays, when I play volleyball. My telephone number is 8-7191.
   c. I can come for an interview at your convenience, and my telephone number is 8-7191.
   d. May I come for an interview at your convenience? My telephone number is 8-7191.

6. Which is *not* a true statement about the inside address?

   a. It follows the salutation.
   b. It is not part of a friendly letter.
   c. It is the same as the envelope address.
   d. It is part of a business letter.

7. Which of the following written signatures is inappropriate in a business letter?

   a. Mr. James C. Brown   *c.* William Santora
   b. (Miss) Barbara Frankel   *d.* (Mrs.) Lillian N. Thomas

8. Which of the following should not be offered as a reference in a letter of application?

   a. a teacher   *c.* a relative
   b. a club adviser   *d.* a former employer

9. In both business and friendly letters, there is no punctuation

   a. after the salutation.
   b. between city and state in the heading.
   c. after the signature.
   d. after the closing.

10. In a letter of complaint, which would be the most effective opening sentence?

   a. The merchandise I sent you for repair has not yet been returned to me.
   b. How much longer do I have to wait for you to return my wristwatch?
   c. I have not yet received the L-10 Crescent wristwatch that I mailed to you for repair on November 9.
   d. If you can't show consideration for your customers, you don't deserve to be in business.

8. ABBREVIATIONS

As you read newspapers, magazines, and books, and refer to the dictionary and other reference works, you are bound to come across abbreviations like *e.g.*, *cf.*, and *NASA*. This section will review the meanings of these and similar common abbreviations. Questions about the meaning of such abbreviations have appeared on past Regents examinations.

PERIODS IN ABBREVIATIONS

1. Use periods with most abbreviations.

2. Don't use periods with abbreviations for alphabetical agencies of our government, and certain business establishments and international organizations, *especially if the abbreviation is regularly used*

in place of the name. Examples: FBI, IBM, RCA, NATO, UNESCO, etc.

3. Don't use a period in an abbreviation containing an apostrophe. For example, *secy.* is an acceptable abbreviation for *secretary;* so is *sec'y* —but *sec'y.* is not.

ABBREVIATIONS OF DICTIONARY AND REFERENCE TERMS

adj. adjective
adv. adverb
anon. anonymous
ant. antonym
bibliog. bibliography
cap. capital
cf. compare
circ., ca., c. about, approximately
colloq. colloquial
conj. conjunction
cont., contd. continued
contr. contraction
ed. edited, edition, editor
e.g. for example
esp. especially
et al. and others
et seq. and the following
fem. feminine
ff. and what follows
ibid. in the same place
id. the same
i.e. that is
interj. interjection

lit. literally
loc. cit. in the place cited
masc. masculine
n. noun, neuter
N.B., n.b. note well
obs. obsolete
op. cit. in the work cited
p. page
pl. plural
pop. population
pp. pages
prep. preposition
pron. pronoun, pronunciation
pseud. pseudonym
q.v. which see
sing. singular
supp. supplement
syn. synonym
v. verb
v.i. verb intransitive
vol. volume
v.t. verb transitive

ABBREVIATIONS OF MEASUREMENT, QUANTITY, ETC.

amt. amount
bbl. barrel(s)
bu. bushel(s)
C. Celsius
cc. cubic centimeter(s)
cm. centimeter(s)
cu. cubic
cwt. hundredweight

doz. dozen
ea. each
F. Fahrenheit
ft. foot, feet
gal. gallon(s)
ht. height
in. inch(es)
kc. kilocycle(s)

kt. carat(s)
lat. latitude
lb. pound(s)
l.c. lower case
log. logarithm
long. longitude
M thousand
max. maximum
min. minimum
mm. millimeter(s)
m.p.h., mph miles per hour

no. number
nos. numbers
nt. wt. net weight
oz. ounce(s)
pt. pint(s)
qt. quart(s)
r.p.m., rpm revolutions per minute
sq. square
wt. weight
yd. yard(s)

ABBREVIATIONS OF BUSINESS TERMS

acct. account, accountant
assn. association
bal. balance
B/L bill of lading
Co. Company
C.O.D., COD cash on delivery
Corp. Corporation
enc., encl. enclosure
f.o.b., F.O.B. free on board
Inc. Incorporated
incl. inclusive, inclosure

Ltd. Limited
mdse. merchandise
mfg. manufacturing
mgr. manager
mtg. mortgage
pat. patent, patented
payt. payment
pd. paid
pkg. package
secy. secretary

ABBREVIATIONS OF TITLES, DEGREES, ETC.

B.A. Bachelor of Arts
B.S. Bachelor of Science
Col. Colonel
C.P.A. Certified Public Accountant
D.A. District Attorney
D.D. Doctor of Divinity
D.D.S. Doctor of Dental Surgery
Gen. General
Gov. Governor
Hon. Honorable
Jr. Junior
Lt. Lieutenant
M.A., A.M. Master of Arts
Maj. Major

M.D. Doctor of Medicine
Messrs. plural of Mr.
Mlle. Mademoiselle
Mme. Madame
M.S. Master of Science
Pfc. Private First Class
Ph.D. Doctor of Philosophy
Pvt. Private
Rev. Reverend
R.N. Registered Nurse
Sgt. Sergeant
Sr. Senior
St. Saint
Supt. Superintendent

ABBREVIATIONS OF AGENCIES, ORGANIZATIONS, ETC.

ABC American Broadcasting Company

AFL-CIO American Federation of Labor and Congress of Industrial Organizations

AP Associated Press

BBC British Broadcasting Corporation

CBS Columbia Broadcasting System

CIA Central Intelligence Agency

FBI Federal Bureau of Investigation

FCC Federal Communications Commission

FDA Food and Drug Administration

FHA Federal Housing Administration

IBM International Business Machines

ICC Interstate Commerce Commission

NASA National Aeronautics and Space Administration

NATO North Atlantic Treaty Organization

NBC National Broadcasting Company

NLRB National Labor Relations Board

PTA Parent-Teacher Association

RCA Radio Corporation of America

ROTC Reserve Officers' Training Corps

SALT Strategic Arms Limitation Talks

SEC Securities and Exchange Commission

TVA Tennessee Valley Authority

UNESCO United Nations Educational, Scientific, and Cultural Organization

UPI United Press International

OTHER COMMON ABBREVIATIONS

A.D. in the year of our Lord

a.m., A.M. before noon

AM amplitude modulation

asst. assistant

atty. attorney

A.W.O.L. absent without official leave

B.C. before Christ

cat. catalog

chm. chairman

C.O. Commanding Officer

c/o care of

Dem. Democrat

dept. department

do. ditto (the same)

DST, D.S.T. Daylight Saving Time

etc. et cetera (and so forth)

ex lib. from the books (of)

FM frequency modulation

govt. government

H.M.S. His (Her) Majesty's Service (or Ship)

H.Q. headquarters

hr. hour(s)

ICBM intercontinental ballistic missile

I.Q. intelligence quotient

min. minute(s)

misc. miscellaneous

mo. month
ms. manuscript
opp. opposite
pfd. preferred
p.m., P.M. after noon
pro tem. for the time being
P.S. postscript
Rep. Republican
    (or Representative)
RFD Rural Free Delivery
R.I.P. May he (she) rest in peace
R.S.V.P. Please reply

S.R.O. standing room only
SST supersonic transport
S.S. steamship
TV television
UK, U.K. United Kingdom
UN, U.N. United Nations
USSR, U.S.S.R. Union of Soviet
    Socialist Republics
VIP very important person
viz. namely
vs. versus (against)
yr. year

EXERCISES ON ABBREVIATIONS

A. Explain the abbreviations in each expression below.

1. London, December 27 (AP)
2. 212° F.
3. George Eliot, pseud.
4. op. cit., p. 182 ff.
5. Author: C. T. Jones et al.

6. ibid., p. 192 et seq.
7. 11 A.M., D.S.T.
8. Peter Hall, B.A., M.A.
9. e.g., fares, lunches, etc.
10. Sarah Quinn, Chairman pro tem.

B. Give the meaning of each of the following abbreviations commonly used in the dictionary:

1. syn.	6. obs.	11. pron.	16. ant.
2. adj.	7. v.i.	12. fem.	17. adv.
3. viz.	8. n.	13. id.	18. interj.
4. esp.	9. i.e.	14. v.	19. cf.
5. pl.	10. masc.	15. pp.	20. v.t.

C. Give the common meaning of each of the following abbreviations:

1. vs.	11. atty.	21. enc.
2. vol.	12. FM	22. anon.
3. e.g.	13. no.	23. D.S.T.
4. C.O.D.	14. N.B.	24. ICBM
5. lit.	15. colloq.	25. mm.
6. Hon.	16. Pvt.	26. B.C.
7. acct.	17. A.D.	27. M
8. R.S.V.P.	18. UPI	28. m.p.h.
9. r.p.m.	19. cc.	29. prep.
10. VIP	20. UN	30. U.S.S.R.

PART II OF THE EXAMINATION

Chapter 7   The Literature Test (Questions A and B)

PURPOSE OF THE LITERATURE TEST

The purpose of this twenty-credit test is to evaluate how well you have understood and appreciated literature that you have read as a secondary-school student. This includes:

1. the works you have read in class in the principal literary types—novels, short stories, plays, biographies, books of true experience, essays, poetry—and

2. the personal supplementary reading you have done in these literary types.

At this point you should skim through the "Guide to Good Literature," which describes about 600 literary works beginning on page 343. The brief annotations in the guide will help you recall works that you have already studied, and they will also suggest worthwhile and enjoyable titles for your future reading.

CHOICES OFFERED IN THE LITERATURE TEST

The literature test requires you to answer *one* of two questions: *A* or *B*. Each is worth twenty credits.

In answering *A* or *B*, you will be confronted with a question about literary works. Usually one of these questions (either *A* or *B*) asks you to discuss four short works. The other asks you to discuss two full-length works.

TYPICAL DISCUSSION-TYPE LITERATURE TEST: QUESTIONS A AND B

A. A reader may be satisfied with the ending of a story because it seems to be the natural result of the events in the story. On the other hand, the reader may be dissatisfied because the ending does not seem logical or believable in view of what has happened in the story or because it leaves questions unanswered in his mind. From the short stories and narrative poems you have read, choose a total of any *four,* and in *each* case show by definite references that you found the ending satisfying or unsatisfying for one of the reasons mentioned. Give titles and authors.

B. People make adjustments with varying degrees of success to certain factors in their environment. These factors may be their physical surroundings, other people, or the customs and traditions of the society in which they live. From the novels and full-length plays you have read, choose a total of any *two* books. In *each* case show by definite references to what extent a person in the book was successful in adjusting to one or more of the above factors. Give titles and authors.

Later in this chapter you will find eight pupil answers to question *A* and seven to question *B*. About half of these answers have been analyzed (for strengths and weaknesses) and rated. You will be asked (and helped) to analyze and rate the rest.

THE RATING OF QUESTIONS A AND B

To learn what is expected in your answer to *A* or *B*, study these instructions to teachers on the rating of such answers:

"Judge literature answers primarily on content, but expect adequate technique of composition.

"In general, require that a pupil in his answer (1) meet the requirements of the question, (2) show familiarity with the piece of literature he is discussing, (3) demonstrate his power to judge and to generalize with clearness and forcefulness of expression, (4) use specific references in support of statements made, and (5) show adequate technique of composition."

The previous excerpt is from *Suggestions on the Rating of Regents Examination Papers in English,* New York State Education Department.

PENALTY FOR PLOT SUMMARIES

Some pupils, either because they fail to understand the question or do not take the trouble to do so, make the mistake of retelling the whole plot. If you do this, the maximum credit you can receive for your answer is half the number of points allotted to the question.

IMPORTANCE OF DEFINITE REFERENCES

No answer to a question about a literary work is worth much unless supported by *definite references* (also known as *specific references*). Some examples of definite references are the names of characters, their actions and ideas, incidents, the setting, a brief quotation, etc.

Question: What would you do if, in discussing a work that you have read, you find yourself momentarily unable to recall the exact name of a character?

Answer: Identify the character by *briefly* describing who he is or what he does. For example, if you have forgotten that *Gawaine* is the main character of Heywood Broun's essay "The Fifty-First Dragon," refer to him as *a young student who has been failing all his subjects in knight school.*

HELPS FOR ANALYZING QUESTIONS A AND B

You should not begin your answer to *A* or *B* unless you have carefully read and analyzed the question and found out what it requires you to do. A good procedure is to hold a "silent conversation" with yourself, in which you ask yourself these four guiding questions:

1. What does question *A* (or *B*) ask me to do?

2. How many works must I discuss, and of what literary types (novels, full-length plays, poems, etc.) must they be?

3. What are the titles and authors of two works (or four, if the question so specifies) suitable for answering the question?

4. What definite references (specific incidents, characters, ideas) can I remember that will help me to do what the question asks me to do? (Jot these down.)

Memorize the four guiding questions so that you will be able to write them on a sheet of scrap at the examination. They will help you to analyze the literature question (*A* or *B*) that you choose to write about.

SOME TERMS USED IN DISCUSSING LITERATURE

Prose is the language we ordinarily speak and write.

Verse is the rhythmical, measured language of poetry.

Fiction is prose writing consisting of made-up stories about imaginary or real people and events. Novels and short stories are *fiction*.

Nonfiction is prose writing that is not a novel or a short story. Nonfiction deals with real people and events. Biographies and histories are examples of *nonfiction*. For convenience, however, librarians classify all literature except novels and short stories as *nonfiction*. Therefore, you will find plays and poetry on the *nonfiction* shelves even though plays and much poetry are not nonfictional in character.

LITERARY TYPES

1. The Novel—a full-length work of prose fiction that involves several characters in a series of incidents, or plot. Examples: Edith Wharton's *Ethan Frome,* Thomas Hardy's *The Return of the Native.*

Caution: Fictionalized biographies are classified as *novels.* Example: Irving Stone's *Love Is Eternal,* a fictionalized portrayal of Mrs. Abraham Lincoln, is a novel.

2. The Short Story—a short work of prose fiction, more concentrated than the novel, with fewer characters and only one main incident. Examples: Edgar Allan Poe's "The Cask of Amontillado," Maureen Daly's "Sixteen."

3. The Full-Length Play—a work written for stage performance and divided into acts, the plot unfolding through the conversations and actions of the characters. It may be in prose or in verse. Examples:

PROSE DRAMA: Lorraine Hansberry's *A Raisin in the Sun*
VERSE DRAMA: William Shakespeare's *As You Like It*

4. The One-Act Play—a short prose drama, more concentrated than the full-length play because it consists of only one act. Examples: Susan Glaspell's "Trifles," John M. Synge's "Riders to the Sea."

5. The Biography—a prose nonfiction work about a person's life written by another person. When a person writes a work about his own life, we call it an *autobiography*. Examples:

> FULL-LENGTH BIOGRAPHY: James Boswell's *Life of Samuel Johnson,* Eve Curie's *Madame Curie*
>
> FULL-LENGTH AUTOBIOGRAPHY: Lincoln Steffens' *The Autobiography of Lincoln Steffens,* Helen Keller's *The Story of My Life*
>
> COLLECTIONS OF SHORT BIOGRAPHIES: Paul de Kruif's *Microbe Hunters,* John F. Kennedy's *Profiles in Courage*

(Reminder: Fictionalized biographies are considered *novels,* not biographies.)

6. Books of True Experience (Travel, History, Current Events, Art, Science, etc.)—These prose nonfiction works present factual information. Examples: Thor Heyerdahl's *Kon-Tiki,* Barbara W. Tuchman's *A Distant Mirror.*

7. The Essay—a short prose nonfiction work in which an author discusses from his personal point of view a topic that interests him, no matter how serious or trivial it may be. Examples: William Faulkner's "Nobel Prize Acceptance Speech," Jan Struther's "One of the Best."

8. The Poem—a literary composition in verse. Each line of a poem usually has a fixed number of syllables. Poetry compresses more thought, feeling, and beauty into its carefully chosen words than any other type of literature. Two principal kinds of poetry are:

a. The *narrative poem,* a poem that tells a story. Example: Robert Frost's "The Death of the Hired Man."

b. The *lyric poem,* a poem that expresses personal emotion. Example: Christina Rossetti's "My Heart Is Like a Singing Bird."

ANALYZING A QUESTION ABOUT FOUR SHORT WORKS

Let us show you how to analyze a question about four short works. For this reason, we reprint question A from page 276.

A. A reader may be satisfied with the ending of a story because it seems to be the natural result of the events in the story. On the other hand, the reader may be dissatisfied because the ending does not seem logical or believable in view of what has happened in the story or because it leaves questions unanswered in his mind. From the short stories and narrative poems you have read, choose a total of any *four,* and in *each* case show by definite references that you found the ending satisfying or unsatisfying for one of the reasons mentioned. Give titles and authors.

GUIDING QUESTION 1. **What does the question ask you to do?**

ANSWER. You have to show why each of four endings was either "satisfying or unsatisfying" to you, but you must be careful to discuss only the kinds of endings specified in the question. There are three kinds:

1. An ending that is satisfying "because it seems to be the natural result of events in the story."

2. An ending that is unsatisfying because it "does not seem logical or believable in view of what has happened in the story."

3. An ending that is unsatisfying "because it leaves questions unanswered in your mind."

You may *not* discuss endings that are satisfying or unsatisfying for a reason other than the three given above.

GUIDING QUESTION 2. **How many works must you discuss, and of what literary types must they be?**

ANSWER. You may discuss any four works from the category "short stories and narrative poems."

    QUESTION: What is a narrative poem?
    ANSWER: It is a poem that tells a story.

GUIDING QUESTION 3. **What are the titles and authors of four works suitable for answering the question?**

ANSWER

"The Gift of the Magi" by O. Henry (short story)
"The Tell-Tale Heart" by Edgar Allan Poe (short story)
"The Highwayman" by Alfred Noyes (narrative poem)
"Richard Cory" by Edwin Arlington Robinson (narrative poem)

GUIDING QUESTION 4. **What definite references (specific incidents, characters, ideas) can you remember that will help you to do what the question asks you to do?**

ANSWER

First Work: "The Gift of the Magi"

Story ends as Della and Jim exchange Christmas gifts. Della had sold her long hair to buy Jim a watch chain, but he had sold his watch to buy a set of combs for her beautiful hair. Ending is nevertheless satisfying, as it is the natural result of the love they have for each other.

QUESTION: Suppose I can't remember the exact names of the characters. Should I use another short story?

ANSWER: The exact names are not important as long as you identify the characters properly. For example, instead of "Della and Jim," you may write "a young wife and her husband."

Second Work: "The Tell-Tale Heart"

Murderer buries victim under floorboards. Detectives arrive. Murderer confesses when he can no longer endure ticking of victim's watch, which he thinks is the dead man's heart—still beating. Ending is satisfying because it is natural result of murderer's bad conscience.

Third Work: "The Highwayman"

Bess, landlord's daughter, shoots herself so that the shot may warn highwayman of trap set for him. When he hears of her death, highwayman deliberately rides into Redcoats' gunfire. Ending is satisfying because highwayman, naturally, did not care to live after his sweetheart's death.

Fourth Work: "Richard Cory"

Richard Cory seemed to have everything—money, good looks, clothes, jewelry. One day he went home and put a bullet through his head. Ending is unsatisfying because it leaves unanswered the question of why he committed suicide.

ANALYZING PUPIL ANSWERS

One way to improve your ability to write answers to discussion-type literature questions is to study the weaknesses and strengths of answers by other pupils. The following four pupil essays are answers to question A. Notice that the sentences have been numbered. This will enable you to locate quickly the weaknesses and strengths discussed in the evaluation.

Pupil A

(1) The main character in "The Highwayman," a narrative poem by Alfred Noyes, risked his life many times to see his beloved Bess. (2) Bess gave her life so that he would not be captured by the British. (3) A stable-hand, also in love with Bess, informed the Redcoats that the highwayman was coming on this particular night.

(4) As the soldiers lay in waiting, with Bess bound so as not to give a warning, the hoofbeats of the highwayman's horse were heard approaching. (5) Bess managed somehow to grab hold of a rifle. (6) The shot that killed her warned the highwayman of the impending danger. (7) He could not stay away very long, however, and as he returned to find out what had happened, he was shot and killed.

(8) This ending, though sad, is satisfying because it seems natural. (9) Since these two characters loved each other so much, it is evident that neither would have been happy living if the other were dead.

EVALUATION: PUPIL A

1. *Content:* The choice of "The Highwayman" is excellent, as it is a narrative poem with an ending that fits the requirements of the question. The generalizations in S8 and 9 are clearly superior and richly supported by the definite references in the previous sentences.

2. *Composition Technique:* Pupil A's writing is on the whole excellent, except for his somewhat faulty organization. We get the impression that Pupil A is disregarding the question and merely retelling the plot, until we get to S8. The thought of S8 should have been stated at the beginning of the answer.

   Rating: 4½ (out of 5) or 90%

Pupil B

(1) A story that I liked was "Disertation about Roast Pig" by Lamb. (2) He tells how a Chinese boy, Bobo, discovered roast pig long ago. (3) By accident when his house burned down with a young pig in it. (4) The roast pig was so delicious that people use to burn down houses with pigs in them. (5) Until they learned you don't have to burn up a house to roast a pig. (6) I enjoyed the ending because it was very funny.

EVALUATION: PUPIL B

1. *Content:* Since Pupil B made an incorrect choice ("A Dissertation Upon Roast Pig" is neither a short story nor a narrative poem, but an essay), the maximum credit he may receive for this part of his answer is 2½ (out of 5) or 50%. Furthermore, his answer fails to meet the requirements of the question. He states that he is satisfied with the ending "because it was very funny," whereas he is supposed to show that it was satisfying "because it seems to be the natural result of the events in the story." Pupil B does show familiarity with the work he discusses.

2. *Composition Technique:* Pupil B stated the title incorrectly and omitted an "s" in his spelling of "Dissertation." In S4 "use" should be "used." There are two sentence fragments: S3 and 5.

   S3 should be joined to S2 as follows: He tells how a Chinese boy, Bobo, discovered roast pig long ago by accident, when his house burned down with a young pig in it.

   S5 should be joined to S4: The roast pig was so delicious that people used to burn down houses with pigs in them, until they learned you don't have to burn up a house to roast a pig.

   (For additional help in correcting sentence fragments, see pages 411–412.)

   Rating: 1½ (out of 5) or 30%

Pupil C

(1) In the short story, "The Gift of the Magi" by O. Henry, I was satisfied with the ending. (2) Della and her husband did not have much money. (3) It was Christmas and Della decided to sell her most prized possession, her beautiful long hair, to buy her husband a present. (4) With the money she bought an expensive chain for her husband's watch. (5) But as fate would have it, Jim had sold his watch to buy Della some beautiful ivory combs for her long hair. (6) Even though it was sad when they gave each other the presents, I think it was perfectly natural for them to make such sacrifices for each other. (7) It only brought them more love and happiness.

EVALUATION: PUPIL C

1. *Content:* The short story Pupil C chose meets the requirements of the question excellently. Her statement in S6 shows that she has the ability to generalize intelligently. The definite references in S2, 3, 4, and 5 present the necessary supporting details briefly and effectively.

2. *Composition Technique:* Very good.

Rating: 5 (out of 5) or 100%

Pupil D

(1) In the poem "Richard Cory" I found the ending dissatisfying because it does not seem logical. (2) I do not believe a man with all the money Richard Cory had would kill himself just because he had no friends. (3) Richard Cory could have made many friend from the people in the town but he thought he was to good for them. (4) This is where the poem loses logic, if he wanted friends bad enought he would have gotten many from the town, but he kills him self instead.

EVALUATION: PUPIL D

1. *Content:* Pupil D is to be commended for his choice of "Richard Cory" and for his statement in S1 about the ending. However, he goes too far in declaring that Richard Cory killed himself "because he had no friends (S2)" and "thought he was to(o) good" for the townspeople (S3). The author (Edwin A. Robinson, whom the pupil did not name) does not make these statements. He leaves the reasons for Richard Cory's suicide to our imagination. Pupil D's statements in S2 and S3 are his own (they are plausible), and he should have labeled them as his own by stating, "*I think* that Richard Cory killed himself because . . ."

2. *Composition Technique:* In S4 "bad" should be "badly" and "kills" should be "killed."

There is a serious error in the structure of S4, which is a long run-on sentence. It should be rewritten as three separate sentences: "This is where the poem loses logic. If he wanted friends badly enough, he would have gotten many from the town. But he killed himself instead."

(For help in correcting run-on sentences, see page 411.) Note also the spelling errors:

SENTENCE	ERROR	CORRECT SPELLING
3	"friend"	friends
3	"to"	too
4	"enought"	enough
4	"him self"	himself

Rating: 3 (out of 5) or 60%

Exercise. See how well you can evaluate the following four students' answers. Before rating an answer, carefully consider its main strengths and weaknesses with the help of the evaluation aids below. (The teachers who graded these answers rated them 60%, 70%, 90%, and 100%. Can you tell which is which?)

Pupil E

(1) I found the ending of "Richard Cory" by E. A. Robinson both natural and satisfying. (2) For me it left no unanswered questions. (3) It confirmed a belief that I, and perhaps many others, have held for quite a while: it is impossible to know the workings of a person's mind simply from his outward appearance.

(4) Richard Cory was the man everyone else hoped to be. (5) While the poorer men and women worked constantly just so they might eat, Richard Cory had everything without lifting a finger. (6) His looks were admired; his possessions coveted.

(7) Yet no one really knew Richard Cory. (8) If someone had, perhaps he could have told us why he went home one night and put a bullet through his head.

EVALUATION AIDS: PUPIL E

1. Compare E's answer with D's. Who impresses you as having a better understanding of "Richard Cory"? Why?

2. What admirable generalization does E make in S3? With what definite references does E support it?

3. Find a sentence in paragraph 2 that conveys meaning effectively with a minimum of words. Find another in paragraph 3.

Rating: 60%, 70%, 90%, or 100%?

Pupil F

(1) The Gift of the Magi by O. Henry also had a natural ending. (2) In this household there were two things that were cherished. (3) The wifes long beautiful hair and her husbands gold watch.

(4) In order to buy each other a Christmas present each sold his most cherished possession. (5) There was much love between these two that it was only natural that they do what they did for one another.

EVALUATION AIDS: PUPIL F

1. Pupils F and C both discussed O. Henry's "The Gift of the Magi." Whose answer meets the requirements of the question better? Why?

2. Which "sentence" is really a sentence fragment? Find two additional errors in that sentence. Find an error in S1.

Rating: 60%, 70%, 90%, or 100%?

Pupil G

(1) Poe's short story, "The Tell-Tale Heart," expresses once again the moral that "crime does not pay." (2) Somehow the lawbreaker is always found out. (3) The events of the story, which included the murderer's strange fear of his victim's one eye, the dismembering of the victim's body, and the supposed beating of the victim's heart, led to the natural result of being found out. (4) As the detectives were questioning him, the murderer's guilty conscience showed itself when he imagined he heard the continued beating of his victim's heart from under the floor-boards, louder and louder. (5) The murderer's natural nervousness led me to believe that he would be found out. (6) The ending was very satisfying since I believe criminals should not go unpunished.

EVALUATION AIDS: PUPIL G

1. Compare G's S1 with C's. Which meets the requirements of the question better? Why? In what sentence does G really begin to answer the question? Why?

2. To make S3 clearer, what word or words should be inserted before "being found out"?

3. How do the words "supposed" (S3) and "imagined" (S4) prove that G has understood the story well?

Rating: 60%, 70%, 90%, or 100%?

Pupil H

(1) In the poem "The Highwayman" by Alfred Noyes the reader could easily be dissatisfied because there was so much love between the Highwayman and the landlords daughter. (2) Because of their love each one died. (3) The daughter trying to save her lover and he because she was gone.

EVALUATION AIDS: PUPIL H

1. Before rating H's answer, reread A's, as it too deals with "The Highwayman." Why are H's supporting references inferior to A's?

2. Why might H's S1 puzzle a reader who is not familiar with the poem?

3. What is wrong with S3? Suggest a way of eliminating the error.

4. Find an error in S1 that appears also in S3 of F's answer.

Rating: 60%, 70%, 90%, or 100%?

ANALYZING A QUESTION ABOUT TWO FULL-LENGTH WORKS

Let us now analyze a question about two full-length works. For this purpose, we reprint question *B* from page 276:

B. People make adjustments with varying degrees of success to certain factors in their environment. These factors may be their physical surroundings, other people, or the customs and traditions of the society in which they live. From the novels and full-length plays you have read, choose a total of any *two* books. In *each* case show by definite references to what extent a person in the book was successful in adjusting to one or more of the above factors. Give titles and authors.

Here is how to analyze the above question by using the suggested "four guiding questions":

GUIDING QUESTION 1. **What does the question ask you to do?**

ANSWER. You have to show how successful two persons were in adjusting to their environment. Each person must be taken from a different book.

Here are some related questions that may occur to you. In each case you can arrive at the answer by carefully reading the test question.

QUESTION: What does "environment" mean?

ANSWER: The question defines it as the "physical surroundings, other people, or the customs and traditions of the society in which they (the persons you are to write about) live."

QUESTION: Is it necessary to write about all three of these environmental factors?

ANSWER: Obviously not, for the question asks you to discuss "one or more of the above factors" for "each case."

QUESTION: Is it permissible to write about a person who was *not* successful in adjusting?

ANSWER: Of course. The question asks you to show "to what extent" each person was successful in adjusting to his or her environment. This permits you to discuss characters who succeeded in adjusting, as well as those who failed.

QUESTION: If I write about adjustment to "physical surroundings" for person 1, will any deduction be made if I write about adjustment to "physical surroundings" for person 2 also?

ANSWER: None whatsoever. The wording of the question clearly allows you to write about the same environmental factor for each character, if you wish.

GUIDING QUESTION 2. **How many works must you discuss, and of what literary types must they be?**

ANSWER. You may discuss any two works from the category "novels and full-length plays." This means you may write about: (*a*) two novels, or (*b*) two full-length plays, or (*c*) one novel and one full-length play.

Caution: If, through carelessness, you should write about a character from a literary type not permitted by the test question (for example, a one-act play or a biography), you would immediately lose half credit for that part of the answer.

GUIDING QUESTION 3. **What are the titles and authors of two works suitable for answering the question?**

ANSWER. O. E. Rölvaag's *Giants in the Earth* (a novel) and Eugene O'Neill's *Beyond the Horizon* (a full-length play).

QUESTION: Suppose I don't remember too much about *Beyond the Horizon.* On the other hand, I am very familiar with a novel that I feel is excellently suited for answering the question, *The Return of the Native,* but I can't remember the author's name. Which work should I write about— *Beyond the Horizon* or *The Return of the Native?*

ANSWER: Write about *The Return of the Native,* since you are better acquainted with it. The most you may lose for omitting the author's name (Thomas Hardy) is a half point or a point.

GUIDING QUESTION 4. **What definite references (specific incidents, characters, ideas) can you remember that will help you to do what the question asks you to do?**

ANSWER

FIRST WORK: *Giants in the Earth*

Per Hansa made a very good adjustment to his physical surroundings, as proved by his:

—building a comfortable house and barn under one roof
—planting crops
—whitewashing the sod walls
—introducing landscaping
—learning to love the vast prairie

and to other people, too, as proved by his:

— winning the Indians' friendship by healing their chief
— carrying on a profitable trade with neighboring settlements, the Indians, and the Irish
— persuading the Solum boys to stay in the community and become schoolteachers

SECOND WORK: *The Return of the Native*

Eustacia Vye made a poor adjustment to her physical surroundings (Egdon Heath) as proved by her:

— regarding Egdon as a prison
— inability to appreciate Egdon's beauties
— yearning to go to Paris

and to other people, as proved by her:

— keeping aloof from Egdon's residents
— quarrels with Wildeve
— feud with Mrs. Yeobright
— failure to adjust to her husband's way of life

ANALYZING PUPIL ANSWERS

Here is a detailed analysis of four pupil answers to the question we have just analyzed, question *B:*

Pupil I

(1) In the novel *Giants in the Earth* by O. E. Rölvaag, Beret, Per Hansa's wife, did not adjust too well to the Dakota plains. (2) Brought up in decent surroundings in Norway, Beret found it depressing to live in a sod hut with the earth for a floor and a barn and animals under the same roof. (3) The vast, treeless prairie frightened her. (4) She imagined it was an ominous demon closing in on her with its long tentacles. (5) This, she felt, was God's punishment for her sins. (6) She had broken her parents' hearts by marrying the reckless Per Hansa against their wishes and emigrating to America.

(7) Gradually Beret became depressed almost to the point of losing her mind. (8) Instead of encouraging her husband or appreciating everything he did to make life pleasanter for her, she brooded and said little. (9) When he was gone for supplies, she would cover up the windows with pieces of material to keep out the prairie. (10) She was short-tempered

with the children and beat them for almost no reason. (11) During the locust plague Per Hansa found her and the two youngest children shut up in a large wooden chest, where Beret had sought to hide from an evil demon. (12) Because of his wife's strange behavior, Per Hansa was in constant fear that she might harm herself or the little ones.

(13) With the aid of a kind minister who visited the settlement, Beret was finally able to tolerate her physical surroundings. (14) However, she became so stubbornly pious and virtuous that she drove her husband to his death by sending him on an impossible mission to get a minister for a dying neighbor.

EVALUATION: PUPIL I

1. *Content:* Pupil I is to be commended for selecting Beret as one of the two characters to be discussed. His generalizations about Beret in S1, 7, and 13 show a fine insight into her character and are very well supported by definite references. His understanding of the novel is clearly superior.

2. *Composition Technique:* Excellent.

Rating: 10 (out of 10) or 100%

Pupil J

(1) People make adjustments with varying degrees of success to certain factors in their environment. (2) These factors may be their physical surroundings, other people, or the customs and traditions of the society in which they live. (3) In *Giants in the Earth* by O. Rölvaag, Beret found it almost too difficult to adjust herself to her new environment.

(4) All Beret's life had been spent in the mountains of Norway surrounded by trees, lakes and streams. (5) The change from this environment to one of flat prairie and open country was a drastic one. (6) Her terrible fear of the western part of the United States, where she felt no one could hide, caused her slowly to lose control of her senses. (7) She spoke very little and was constantly seeing monsterous figures in the sky. (8) Her husband, Per Hansa, once came back at night and found her locked in the hope chest, where she had tried to escape from the evils of the surrounding country. (9) Later on she began talking to her dead mother and insisting that she was being called away.

(10) The only success she was able to obtain in adjusting to her new life came at the end of the novel. (11) Here she became completely enveloped

within herself and confided only in God, to whom she had intrusted all her faith.

EVALUATION: PUPIL J

1. *Content:* By his statements about Beret in S3, 5, and 10, adequately supported by specific references, Pupil J has proved that he is well acquainted with the novel and knows how to make intelligent judgments about it.

2. *Composition Technique:* Pupil J's ability to write is commendable but not perfect. S1 and 2 should have been omitted altogether, as they merely repeat the first two sentences of the question; S3 by itself can serve as an adequate introduction for Pupil J's essay. S7 contains a misspelling—"monsterous," instead of "monstrous." Aside from these minor faults, Pupil J shows good ability to organize his ideas in correct, clear, and forceful sentences.

Rating: 9 (out of 10) or 90%

Pupil K

(1) People make adjustments with varying degrees of success to certain factors in their environment. (2) These factors may be their physical surroundings, other people, or the customs and traditions of the society in which they live. (3) In *Giants in the Earth* by Rölvaak, a character who was able to adjust to his physical surroundings was Per Hansa. (4) He was among the many settlers who came to the West to start a new life. (5) Per Hansa's surroundings was one in which contained many miles of prairie and open grasslands. (6) From every direction of the small settlement all that one could see was the many miles of wilderness. (7) It wasn't easy for Per Hansa to adjust himself to this kind of environment. (8) During the long cold winters he would try to keep himself busy and occupied at all times. (9) He thought of ways of improving his home to make it feel and look more comfortable for himself and his family. (10) During the winters the people had no choice but to stay in their houses because of the heavy snowstorms that lasted sometimes for a week or more. (11) Per Hansa helped create a school for the people. (12) In the summer months he also tried new methods of farming and building. (13) The people listened to many of his ideas, which many times proved effective. (14) Per Hansa was not only able to adjust to this wilderness and barren way of life, but he also tried to help the others overcome the effects of the environment.

EVALUATION: PUPIL K

1. *Content:* Pupil K's choice of Per Hansa, it must be conceded, is a very good one for answering the question. However, he makes several general statements that he fails to support with definite references. For example, he writes in S13 that "the people listened to many of his (Per Hansa's) ideas, which many times proved effective," but he neglects to mention any of these ideas or times. Again, in S12, Pupil K states that Per Hansa "tried new methods of farming and building," but he does not explain a single one of these methods. Pupil K makes no untrue statement about the novel. It is nevertheless clear that his ability to generalize about the novel is inferior to that of Pupil I or Pupil J, and his supporting references are comparatively few and weak.

2. *Composition Technique:* Though Pupil K knows how to write grammatically complete sentences, many of them are not too effective because of such faults as the following:
    a. *Repetition:* "*many* settlers (S4)," "*many miles* of prairie (S5)," "*many miles* of wilderness (S6)," "*many* of his ideas, which *many* times proved effective (S13)."
       As in the case of Pupil J, Pupil K receives no credit at all for S1 and S2, since they are verbatim repetitions of part of the question.
    b. *Lack of agreement:* In S5, "Per Hansa's surroundings was one" should be revised to "Per Hansa's environment was one."
    c. *Awkward expressions:* The word "in" in S5 should be removed. Likewise, omitting "feel and look" in S9 will improve that sentence.
    d. *Spelling:* Except for the misspelling of the author's name in S3, Pupil K's spelling is excellent.

Rating: 7½ (out of 10) or 75%

Pupil L

(1) People make adjustments with varying degrees of success to certain factors in their environment. (2) Roovalg points out in Giants in the Earth one character that adjusted himself with degrees of success to certain factors in their environment. (3) This character is Per Hansa.

(4) Per Hansa, his wife Beret, and a group of other people started out for the West. (5) They wanted to start a new settlement. (6) It was hard to

adjust themselves to this kind of life. (7) Beret didn't want to come out West, but she went anyway because she loved her husband. (8) Per Hansa had to build there new house and plant crops so they can eat. (9) It took them along time to get started and before you knew it most of it was done. (10) Per Hansa had to take alot from his wife Beret. (11) She never wanted to go out there and she kept on nagging Per. (12) Per Hansa kept on telling her not to worry everything would turn out okay. (13) The reason why she was worrying so much is that she was expecting a baby. (14) There were no doctors there and she was afraid of having a baby without a doctor. (15) One night Indians came, everyone in the settlement was afraid. (16) Per Hansa was too but he went to them. (17) There chief was badly injurged, he was ready to die. (18) Per Hansa helped him get well. (19) When the Indians left, they gave Per Hansa a pony for saving there chief.

(20) Per Hansa had to get adjusted to that kind of life if he wanted to stay there. (21) He also had to get adjusted to his wife.

EVALUATION: PUPIL L

1. *Content:* Pupil L indicates in his first paragraph that he is going to discuss how Per Hansa adjusted to his environment. Unfortunately, he hardly discusses this; instead he devotes the bulk of his essay to retelling the plot. Pupil L obviously knows many of the facts about the novel, but he does not give evidence of being able to select and organize the specific facts necessary for a good answer. The weak and uncertain language of S20 and 21 suggests that Pupil L is not too confident about his understanding of Per Hansa or of the question he was supposed to answer.

2. *Composition Technique:* Pupil L is seriously deficient in composition skills. There is an error in agreement in S2: "their" should be changed to "his." Also, the title in S2 should have been underlined. S10 and S12 contain slangy expressions that should be avoided in formal writing (*"had to take alot* from his wife," and "okay"). There is a tense error in S8 ("can" should be "would be able to") and another in S11 ("wanted" should be "had wanted").

   In addition, Pupil L has three run-on sentences: S12, 15, and 17. These sentences should be corrected as follows:

   S12: Per Hansa kept on telling her not to worry because everything would turn out all right.

   S15: One night Indians came. Everyone in the settlement was afraid.

   S17: Their chief was badly injured. He was ready to die.

There are numerous spelling errors:

SENTENCE	ERROR	CORRECT SPELLING
2	"Roovalg"	**Rölvaag**
8, 17, 19	"there"	**their**
9	"along"	**a long**
10	"alot"	**a lot**
17	"injurged"	**injured**

Rating: 5½ (out of 10) or 55%

Exercise. Test yourself by rating the following three pupil answers to the question just discussed. They are all based on a novel often studied in high school: Thomas Hardy's *The Return of the Native.* Evaluation aids have been provided after each answer to guide you to some of the strengths and weaknesses and to help you arrive at a sound rating. (The teachers who marked these essays rated one 100%, another 80%, and the third 60%. Which is which?)

Pupil M

(1) People make adjustments with varying degrees of success to certain factors in their environment. (2) One of these factors may be their physical surroundings. (3) In *Return of the Native,* a novel by Thomas Hardy, Eustacia was unsuccessful in adjusting to her environment. (4) Unlike Beret in *Giants in the Earth,* Eustasia couldn't adjust because she didn't want to. (5) She thought herself above the others on the heath and all she wanted was escape. (6) She was a beautiful and intelligent woman and could have had ·a good life on the heath if she had tried. (7) Instead of that she attempted to escape but failed each time. (8)Her first attempt to escape occurred when she married Clym. (9) She though he would take her away from the heath. (10) This attempt failed and soon she became desperate. (11) In her second attempt, she tried to kill herself but was stopped by a servant. (12) In Wildeve, she saw another means of escape. (13) Eustasia and Wildeve tried to run away. (14) Finally she would be rid of this horrible place. (15) In her efforts, she ended everything by falling and drowning. (16) Because of her unwillingness to adjust to her environment, she lost her life.

EVALUATION AIDS: PUPIL M

1. Would M's answer be weakened or improved if S1 and 2 were omitted? Why?

2. How many definite references does M offer in support of his statement in S7?

3. In which sentence is the heroine's name spelled correctly, S3 or 4? Find a spelling error in S9 and another in S13.

Rating: 100%, 80%, or 60%?

Pupil N

(1) Another book was *The Return of the Native* by Thomas Hardy. (2) Clym Yeobright first lived and worked in London. (3) He had a very good life and he was also very well educated. (4) He wanted to live in Egdon Heath so he can help the people by opening a school house. (5) His mother disapproved of this very much. (6) She wanted him to stay in London where he was doing much better. (7) His mother Mrs. Yeobright could not get adjusted to this. (8) She also had to adjust herself when he married Eustacia. (9) Mrs. Yeobright didn't like Eustacia because she thought she was evil a witch. (10) She also thought that Eustacia married Clym because she wanted to get out of Egdon Heath and go to London. (11) Mrs. Yeobright had to adjust herself with other people. (12) To get along with them better.

EVALUATION AIDS: PUPIL N

1. State two reasons why N's S1 is not as good as M's S3.

2. S2 contains an error of fact which is repeated in S6 and 10. What is the error?

3. Why does the statement in S11 fail to meet the requirements of the question?

4. Which "sentence" is really a sentence fragment?

5. Locate an error of tense in S4 and another in S10.

Rating: 100%, 80%, or 60%?

Pupil O

(1) In *The Return of the Native,* a novel by Thomas Hardy, Eustacia was not very successful in adjusting to her environment. (2) Eustacia had been raised in the lively seacoast town of Budmouth and had moved to the

Heath when she was still a young woman.   (3) She considered the Heath a lonely, dreary place to live, and she was not content there.   (4) Eustacia thought of ways that she could get away from the Heath, and, when she married Clym, she was sure that it would be a short matter of time before her desire would be fulfilled.   (5) However, her marriage did not result in her leaving the Heath.

(6) Eustacia never really adjusted to the people in the Heath.   (7) She was very different from them in a number of ways.   (8) Because she had more education than the Heath folk, Eustacia was not happy with the dull life led by them.   (9) She never went out of her way to be friendly.   (10) One evidence of her relationship with the people was shown by the fact that she wasn't invited to Clym's party when he came home for Christmas. (11) Almost everybody else was.

(12) One custom of the Heath folk was the lighting of bonfires on Guy Fawkes Day, November 5th.   (13) The people would gather around the fires and have a good time singing and dancing.   (14) Eustacia never joined in these affairs.

(15) Eustacia was not very successful in adjusting to her surroundings in any respect.

EVALUATION AIDS: PUPIL O

1. Compare O's opening sentence with M's and N's. Which is the best of the three? Why?

2. With what environmental factor does O deal in paragraph 1? in paragraph 2? in paragraph 3? What does this suggest about O's knowledge of the novel? about O's ability to organize a composition?

3. What evidence of good reasoning does O offer in paragraph 2? in paragraph 3?

Rating: 100%, 80%, 60%?

QUESTIONS A AND B FROM PART II OF FORMER EXAMINATIONS

Test 1

A. Poets and essayists often appeal to a reader's sense of sight, smell, taste or touch. From the poems and essays you have read, choose a total of *four* selections. In each case, show by definite references that there is in the selection an appeal to one or more of the above senses. Give titles and authors.

B. In literature, as in life, people are confronted by difficult situations. In them, some people act honorably; other people act shamefully. From the novels and full-length plays you have read, choose a total of *two* books. For one book, show by specific references that a person in the book acted honorably in a difficult situation. For a second book, show by specific references that a person in the book acted shamefully in a difficult situation. (Or, you may discuss two persons, each from a different book, who acted honorably *or* two who acted shamefully.) Give titles and authors.

Test 2

A. Often a conversation or a meeting between two people has a significant effect upon the life of one or both of them. From the novels, full-length plays and biographies that you have read, choose a total of two books in which such a conversation or meeting occurs. In each case, describe briefly the gist of the conversation or the circumstances of the meeting. Then show by specific references that the conversation or the meeting had a significant effect on the life of *one* of the two people involved. Give titles and authors.

B. Poets and essayists deal with many aspects of life: beauty, ugliness, honor, dishonor, wisdom, folly, the commonplace, the unusual. From the poems and essays that you have read, choose a total of *four* selections, including at least *one* poem and *one* essay. In each case indicate the aspect of life with which the author is dealing. Then show by specific references the author's feeling or opinion about his subject. [You may use the same aspect for any number of selections.] Give titles and authors.

Test 3

A. In literature, as in life, some people experience aloneness. In some cases, a person lives apart from others. In other cases, the person lives with others, but is, or feels that he is, alone in his ideas, feelings, or circumstances.

From the full-length books (novels, plays, biographies, books of true experience) you have read, choose a total of *two* books in which a person experiences aloneness. For each book, state which of the above types of aloneness the person experiences, *and* show by specific references the effect of the aloneness upon him. Give titles and authors.

B. Poets, short-story writers, and essayists frequently write about such subjects as: war, love, faith, patriotism, injustice. Choose *two* of these subjects. For each subject, choose *two* selections (poems, short stories, essays), each by a different author. For each selection, show by specific references the author's viewpoint toward the subject. Give titles and authors. [*Be sure that in your answer you discuss a total of four selections.*]

Test 4

A. At the end of some short stories we feel like saying, "That's just right. That's how it should have been." At the end of other stories, we are left wishing the stories could have concluded differently. Choose *four* short stories. For *each*, show by specific references that the ending was either satisfactory or unsatisfactory to you, and explain why. Give titles and authors.

B. From the books and full-length plays you have read, choose a total of *two* works. For *each*, show by specific references that a person in the work felt trapped, and show how the person reacted. Give titles and authors.

Test 5

A. Often a novelist or playwright creates one character who contrasts sharply with another character in the same book. From the novels and full-length plays you have read, choose a total of *two* books. For each book, show by specific references that the actions or opinions of one character contrast sharply with those of another in the book. Give titles and authors.

B. In some poems, essays, and short stories, the authors use description to make a person, place, or experience vivid in the reader's mind. From the poems, essays, and short stories you have read, choose a total of *four*. For each selection, show by specific references that its author uses *description* to make a person, place, or experience vivid to you. Give titles and authors.

*Chapter 8   The Literature Test
(Question C. Consisting of C-1 and C-2)

*IMPORTANT NOTICE TO STUDENTS

Skip Chapter 8 and go directly to Chapter 9. *Question C is no longer a part of the test.* Use Chapter 8 only if you wish to review tests given before 1982 reprinted at the back of this book.

THE C-1 TEST (Discontinued as of January 1982)

The ten questions in *C-1* dealt with the following aspects of a passage:

1. *Theme,* or *Main Idea.*

2. *Type of Writing.* There are four main types: narration, description, argumentation, and exposition.

3. *Setting.* This includes the time and place of the action, plus the customs and attitudes of the people.

4. *Mood.* This is the atmosphere, or emotional context, of a passage.

5. *Plot.* The plan, or *plot,* is a series of incidents that create a conflict and lead to the *climax,* or turning point.

6. *Tone.* By this term we mean the author's *attitude* toward his subject—serious, ironic, pessimistic, etc.

7. *Connotation.* The *connotation* of a word or phrase is its suggestive power.

8. *Style.* Among the matters covered by this term are the author's *diction* (choice of words), economy of language, variety of sentence structure, and use of literary devices and figures of speech.

9. *Literary Devices and Figures of Speech.* Here are some of the most common:

Alliteration is the repetition of initial consonant sounds. Example: the repetition of "l" in the following from "We Real Cool" by Gwendolyn Brooks: "We Lurk late."

Exaggeration, also known as **hyperbole,** is overstatement for the purpose of emphasizing something that the author considers important, as in the following description of the folk hero Jesse James by William Rose Benét:
"He could put six shots through a woodpecker's eye . . ."

Irony describes (1) the use of words to express the *opposite* of the intended meaning, as when we refer to a latecomer as being "too early"; also, (2) a situation which is the *reverse* of what was expected, as the killing of the giant Goliath by the boy David.

A **metaphor** is an implied comparison, without the use of "like" or "as." A good example is the second line of "The Highwayman" by Alfred Noyes:
"The moon was a ghostly galleon tossed upon cloudy seas,"
in which the poet compares the moon to a storm-tossed galleon.

Metonymy is the substitution of one noun for another that is closely associated with it. In the following example of *metonymy*, the noun "White House" is substituted for the noun "President":
"The *White House* expects an increase in foreign trade."

Onomatopoeia is the use of words whose sound suggests their meaning.
"The moan of doves in immemorial elms
And the murmuring of innumerable bees."
—*Alfred, Lord Tennyson*

Oxymoron is the use of a noun together with an adjective that seems to contradict its meaning, as in the following line from *Macbeth* by William Shakespeare:
"I know this is a *joyful trouble* to you."
The adjective *joyful* seems to contradict the noun *trouble.*

A **paradox** is a seemingly contradictory statement which is nevertheless true, as in these lines from *Macbeth:*
"And you all know security
Is mortals' chiefest enemy."

Normally, we consider *security* man's friend. Yet, by causing him to relax his vigilance, it may turn out to be his worst *enemy.*

Personification is the giving of human characteristics to objects, ideas, animals, or plants.
> "The mountain sat upon the plain
> In his eternal chair."
> *—Emily Dickinson*

A **pun** is a play on words. It always involves homonyms (words alike in pronunciation but different in meaning), as in *Board* of Education and *bored* of education. In William Shakespeare's *Julius Caesar,* a cobbler (shoemaker) puns when he says, humorously, that he is "a mender of bad *soles,*" knowing that *soles* can be interpreted also as *souls* (people).

Satire is writing that holds up abuses, stupidities, and vices to ridicule. Sinclair Lewis' novel *Arrowsmith* is a *satire* on the medical profession in the early part of the twentieth century.

Simile is a comparison that makes use of "like" or "as."
> "My heart is like a singing bird . . ."
> *—Christina Georgina Rossetti*

Understatement, the opposite of *exaggeration,* is a restrained statement in ironic contrast to what might have been said, as when Mercutio, in Shakespeare's *Romeo and Juliet,* refers to the mortal wound he has received in a sword fight as "a scratch."

ANALYSIS OF A C-1 TEST

C-1 Directions (1–10): The passage below is followed by 10 incomplete statements or questions about the passage. Select the word or expression that best completes the statement or answers the question, and write its *number* in the space provided on the separate answer sheet.

Oberfest

On a morning in early spring, 1873, the people of Oberfest left their houses and took refuge in the town hall. No one knows why, precisely. A number of rumors had raced through the town during recent weeks, and there was a profound uneasiness among the people. Idle talk and
5   gossip were passed on and converted to news; predictions became certainties. On this particular morning, fear turned into terror, and people rushed through the narrow streets, carrying their most precious possessions, pulling their children, and dashing into the great hall. The first to arrive occupied the largest rooms; the others found space in smaller
10   rooms, in hallways, on stairs, in the towers. The doors were nailed shut,

and men took turns watching out the window. Two days passed. Order
was maintained. The unruly, the sick, and the unstable were consigned
to the cellars; the cellar stairs were guarded. When no disaster came,
the fear grew worse, because the people began to suspect that the dan-
15 ger was already within the hall, locked inside. No one spoke to anybody
else; people watched each other, looking for signs. It was the children
who rang the great bell in the first bell tower—a small band of bored
children, unable to bear the silence and having run through all the
halls, slid down all the banisters, climbed all the turrets. They found the
20 bell rope and swung on it—set the bell clanging. This was the traditional signal of alarm, and in a moment the elders were dashing in panic
to all the other bell towers and ringing the bells. For nearly an hour,
the valley reverberated with the wild clangor—and then, a thousand feet
above, the snow began to crack, and the avalanche began; a massive
25 cataract of ice and snow thundered down and buried the town, silenc-
ing the bells. There is no trace of Oberfest today, not even a spire, because the snow is so deep; and, in the shadow of the mountains, it is
very cold.

QUESTION 1

Which word best expresses the main ideas of the
passage?

1 faith	3 nostalgia	5 morning
2 patriotism	4 disaster	

$\left[4 \right]$

ANSWER EXPLAINED

  Careful reading shows that choice 4, *disaster*, is supported by every sentence in the passage.

WRONG CHOICES

1. There was an *absence* of faith. The people abandoned their homes,
fled to the town hall, nailed its doors shut, and suspected one another.

2 and 3. There is no mention or suggestion of *patriotism* (love of country) or *nostalgia* (longing for the past).

5. *Morning* is mentioned in lines 1 and 6, but only as a detail of the
setting.

QUESTION 2

This passage is an example of which type of writing?

1 exposition	3 criticism	5 narration
2 definition	4 persuasion	

$\left[5 \right]$

ANSWER EXPLAINED

  Writing that tells a story is called *narration*. The passage *narrates* (tells)
the story of Oberfest.

1. Writing that explains something—for example, how to give artificial respiration—is known as *exposition*.
2. *Definition* is writing that defines or tells what is meant by a topic, such as an article defining *community college* or *recession*.
3. *Criticism* is a general term for writing that discusses the faults and merits of a work. A book review is one example of such writing.
4. *Persuasion*, also known as *argumentation*, is a form of writing that offers arguments for a particular course of action. Campaign literature and sales letters belong in this category.

QUESTION 3

Which element is especially significant in this passage?
1 dialogue   3 illustrations   5 rhythm
2 setting   4 levels of usage $[2]$

ANSWER EXPLAINED

Setting is the time and place of an action. It includes also the customs and attitudes prevailing at that time and in that place. In some stories, as in this one, setting is very important. If Oberfest were not set in a valley a thousand feet below snow-capped mountains, if it were not early spring, and if the people did not have the customs and attitudes that they had, the disaster might not have occurred.

WRONG CHOICES

The passage contains no dialogue (conversation) or illustrations. Since it is written in formal English, it represents only one level of usage. It has the rhythm of good narrative prose, but this is of little significance for the outcome of the story.

QUESTION 4

Which is the most valid conclusion regarding the *theme* of the passage?
1 It is a minor feature of the passage.
2 It is not related to the plot.
3 It is related to the topic sentence.
4 It is stated, rather than implied.
5 It is implied but not stated. $[5]$

ANSWER EXPLAINED

The *theme* is the main idea, meaning, or moral lesson. Sometimes it is stated directly; often it is *implied* (hinted at or suggested). In this passage the theme—that rumor can set off a chain reaction culminating in disaster—is implied.

WRONG CHOICES

1. The theme is a *major* feature of this passage.
2. It is closely related to the plot.
3. This passage has no topic sentence. If we were to add the theme ("Rumor can lead to disaster") to the beginning of the passage, *that* would be its topic sentence.
4. Nowhere in the passage is the theme stated.

QUESTION 5

In writing this passage, the author uses *mood* to
1 advance the plot   3 play upon words
2 contradict the theme   4 intensify rhythm
         5 characterize the hero $\left[\,\boldsymbol{/}\,\right]$

ANSWER EXPLAINED

The *mood* of a literary work is its atmosphere or emotional context. The mood of this passage is one of fear, suspicion, and foreboding. This mood harmonizes with, and advances, the plot.

WRONG CHOICES

2. The author uses mood to support the theme.
3. There is no pun, or play on words, in the passage.
4 The author employs rhythm to intensify the mood, as when he shifts to a very short sentence (S2 and S8) to create suspense.
5. There is no hero in this passage.

QUESTION 6

That the alarm, sounded to avert danger, became the apparent cause of the avalanche is an example of
1 irony   3 satire   5 exaggeration
2 simile   4 personification $\left[\,\boldsymbol{/}\,\right]$

ANSWER EXPLAINED

Irony is a state of affairs which is the reverse of what would normally be expected. Normally we would expect an alarm to safeguard people from disaster.

WRONG CHOICES

2. A *simile* is a comparison introduced by *like* or *as*: ". . . *like a thunderbolt* he falls" (from "The Eagle" by Alfred, Lord Tennyson).
3. *Satire* is the use of ridicule to expose an abuse. George Orwell's novel *Animal Farm*, for example, is a satire on totalitarianism.
4. *Personification* is the giving of human qualities to animals, things, or ideas: *The river glideth at his own sweet will* (from "Composed Upon Westminster Bridge" by William Wordsworth).

5. *Exaggeration,* also known as *overstatement* or *hyperbole,* is a device for emphasizing something that the author or speaker considers important: *I lov'd Ophelia. Forty thousand brothers/ Could not, with all their quantity of love,/ Make up my sum!* (from *Hamlet* by William Shakespeare).

QUESTION 7

Which characterizes the style of this passage *as a whole?*
1 colorful similes   3 economy of words
2 poor diction   4 constant repetition
                5 vague references $\boxed{3}$

ANSWER EXPLAINED

The author uses words economically (sparingly). He does not, for example, in line 12, write "Those who were unruly . . ." He writes: "The unruly . . ." He gives a maximum of information in a minimum of words: "predictions became certainties" (lines 5–6); "fear turned into terror" (line 6); "Order was maintained" (lines 11–12). He does not waste words.

QUESTION 8

In lines 13–16, the author presents a
1 minor climax   4 figure of speech involving rhythm
2 personal bias   5 flashback to an earlier event
3 new setting $\boxed{1}$

ANSWER EXPLAINED

Usually, in a plot, there is a series of incidents leading to a *climax*—the highest point of interest, or turning point, of the story. Occasionally, before the climax, there is the second highest point of interest, just below the climax in importance. This is the *minor climax;* it occurs in this story in lines 13–16, when the people turn against one another.

QUESTION 9

In this passage, the highest point of the action occurs in lines
(1) 2–4   (3) 16–19   (5) 22–26
(2) 6–8   (4) 19–20 $\boxed{5}$

ANSWER EXPLAINED

The climax, or highest point of the action, to which all the previous incidents have been suspensefully building, comes with the description of the avalanche in lines 22–26.

QUESTION 10

The effect of the last phrase of the passage, "it is very cold" (lines

27–28), depends mainly on

1 rhythm	3 comparison	5 sound
2 rhyme	4 connotation	

[✗]

ANSWER EXPLAINED

It is very cold carries with it the *connotation* (suggestion) of freezing and refrigeration. By ending the passage with this phrase, the author suggests that Oberfest and its people remain frozen in the snow. If he had stated this idea directly, instead of suggesting it through the phrase *it is very cold,* his ending would have been far less stimulating to our imagination—and far less effective.

C-1 TESTS FROM PART II OF FORMER EXAMINATIONS

Each of the passages below is followed by incomplete statements or questions about the passage. Select the word or expression that best completes the statement or answers the question.

A

At dawn, which in summer occurs shortly after bedtime and lasts for several hours, I was awakened by the birds, which were making a dreadful din above me in the trees. I found that four mosquitoes were perched on the netting
5 about fourteen inches from my face—great, hungry fellows, regular eagles. They stared at me till I could have hidden myself for embarrassment. Presently a friend of theirs, bloated with drink, sailed down and sat beside them, singing a triumphant bloodlust song in a harsh, drunken tenor.
10 He was plainly a degenerate going the pace that kills.
They say that if you look a wild animal in the eye he will turn away uneasily. I tried this on Macbeth, the new arrival—I called him Macbeth because he murdered sleep—but he was unabashed. I even spoke to him sternly, told him
15 to go home and take his friends away with him, asked him what sort of place this was for a chap with a family; I appealed to his better self.
Macbeth's only reply was to crawl insolently through a tear in the netting and come straight at me. His song of
20 triumph rose in sharp crescendo till he struck my nose; then it ceased. I was just reaching to kill him, even at the risk of disfiguring myself for life, when suddenly and without

warning the netting gave way completely and fell about
my ears. Can you imagine a worse predicament than to be
25 pinned under so much wreckage with a mosquito that you
personally dislike?

1. Which phrase best expresses the main ideas of this passage?   (1) the
wreckage   (2) the chorus of crescendos   (3) disaster at dawn
(4) the melancholy mosquitoes   (5) the pace that kills
2. The underlying tone of this passage is one of   (1) grim earnestness
(2) vague foreboding   (3) studied indifference   (4) triumphant
praise   (5) wry humor
3. Which statement can best be made about the setting of this passage?
(1) The author establishes it immediately at the beginning of the passage.   (2) The author regards it as more important than the plot.
(3) The author regards it as less important than characterization.
(4) The author establishes it very gradually.   (5) The author with-
holds it until the climax.
4. In writing this passage, the author makes use of which of the following?   (1) exposition   (2) argumentation   (3) narration
(4) order of importance   (5) examples
5. In writing this passage, the author frequently uses   (1) rhetorical
questions   (2) exaggeration   (3) reasons   (4) objectivity
(5) flashback
6. The basis for this passage is   (1) conflict   (2) coincidence   (3)
scientific evidence   (4) mistaken identity   (5) definition
7. Which phrase is most consistent with the connotations of the word
"perched" in line 4?   (1) "four mosquitoes" (line 4)   (2) "hungry fellows" (line 5)   (3) "regular eagles" (line 6)   (4) "bloodlust song" (line 9)   (5) "sharp crescendo" (line 20)
8. Which phrase is most clearly related in idea to the phrase "the pace
that kills" as it is used in line 10?   (1) "awakened by the birds"
(line 2)   (2) "stared at me" (line 6)   (3) "bloated with drink"
(line 8)   (4) "sailed down and sat beside them" (line 8)   (5)
"gave way completely" (line 23)
9. Which statement is true about sentence 7 (lines 12-14)?   (1) It
contains a rhetorical question.   (2) It contains free verse.   (3)
It is written in the second person.   (4) It contains a figure of speech.
(5) It is very simple in structure.
10. The point of view of "I" in this passage is that of   (1) a minor
character   (2) the reader   (3) the observer   (4) the major
character   (5) Macbeth

B

Every Good Boy Does Fine

I practiced my cornet in a cold garage
Where I could blast it till the oil in drums
Boomed back; tossed free-throws till I couldn't move my thumbs;
Sprinted through tires, tackling a headless dummy.

5 In my first contest, playing a wobbly solo,
I blew up in the coda, alone on stage,
And twisting like my hand-tied necktie, saw the judge
Letting my silence dwindle down his scale.

At my first basketball game, gangling away from home
10 A hundred miles by bus to a dressing room,
Under the showering voice of the coach, I stood in a towel,
Having forgotten shoes, socks, uniform.

In my first football game, the first play under the lights
I intercepted a pass. For seventy yards, I ran
15 Through music and squeals, surging, lifting my cleats,
Only to be brought down by the safety man.

I took my second chances with less care, but in dreams
I saw the bald judge slumped in the front row,
The coach and team at the doorway, the safety man
20 Galloping loud at my heels. They watch me now.

You who have always horned your way through passages,
Sat safe on the bench while some came naked to court,
Slipped out of arms to win in the long run,
Consider this poem a failure, sprawling flat on a page.

1. The "I" of the poem probably regards himself mainly as   (1) an athlete   (2) a musician   (3) a loser   (4) a wit   (5) a critic
2. In relation to the content of the poem, its title is an example of   (1) personification   (2) allegory   (3) sensory language   (4) irony   (5) an epithet
3. In line 9, which best describes the function of the phrase "gangling away from home"?   (1) It uses a wornout expression for a picture of the dressing room.   (2) It gives a vivid word picture of the speaker's youth and inexperience.   (3) It uses words whose sounds re-

inforce the idea of the speaker's nervous tension.   (4) It misuses one part of speech to show the speaker's happiness.   (5) It uses judgmental words about the speaker's overconfidence.

4. In line 7, "twisting like my hand-tied necktie" is an example of   (1) a striking contrast   (2) a vague reference   (3) an implied meaning   (4) an overused symbol   (5) a vivid comparison

5. In the second stanza, the poet's purpose most probably is to   (1) show that an event of the first stanza led to an unexpected result   (2) give specific examples of the general statements in the first stanza   (3) show the complexity of the events in the first stanza   (4) generalize from the statements of the first stanza   (5) reinforce the statements of the first stanza

6. What is the relationship of the third stanza to the second stanza?   (1) It contrasts with the second stanza.   (2) It gives cause and effect.   (3) It develops events of the second stanza.   (4) It relates a similar experience.   (5) It indicates chronological order.

7. In lines 14 and 15, the function of the phrase "ran through music and squeals" is to   (1) catalogue several similar expressions about athletic contests   (2) present a favorable image of football playing   (3) dramatize the speaker's momentary elation   (4) compress the speaker's mixed emotions into one phrase   (5) offer the dominant image of the poem

8. In line 20, the sentence, "They watch me now," seems to imply that the early experiences   (1) haunt the speaker   (2) were a result of careless coaching   (3) gave the speaker a split personality   (4) showed the continuing interest of adults in adolescents they have coached   (5) benefited the speaker

9. In which group of words does the poet address the reader directly?   (1) "I practiced my cornet" (line 1)   (2) "In my first contest" (line 5)   (3) "in dreams I saw the bald judge" (lines 17 and 18)   (4) "some came naked to court" (line 22)   (5) "Consider this poem a failure" (line 24)

10. Which contains a pun?   (1) "In my first contest, playing a wobbly solo" (line 5)   (2) "Letting my silence dwindle down his scale" (line 8)   (3) "A hundred miles by bus to a dressing room" (line 10)   (4) "Only to be brought down by the safety man" (line 16)   (5) "I saw the bald judge slumped in the front row" (line 18)

C

The wind had become different. Its steady pressure of sound had changed to a spasmodic violence. Snow was stinging against the northern and western storm windows,

and Mrs. Thayer already knew that the doors on those sides
5 of the cottage were frozen shut. It did not matter. A door
to the outside place where people change bathing suits in
the summer began to bang hard, in irregular patterns. "It
is unhinged," she said with a sly grin. That did not matter,
either. Nothing mattered except to keep herself inside her
10 own skin, and with real sweat she did.

She pulled every trick out of the bagful she had collected
during her long life with neurotics. She brushed her hair
firmly, and all the while her heart kept kicking against her
ribs and she felt so sick that she could scarcely lift her arm.
15 She tried to say some nursery rhymes and the Twenty-third
Psalm, but with no other result than an impatient titter.
She sipped the dreadful sweet milk. She prayed to those
two pills she had swallowed.

1. When Mrs. Thayer said, "It is unhinged" (lines 7-8), she was speaking
to   (1) herself   (2) the author   (3) the neighbors   (4) the
reader   (5) the bathers
2. In line 13, the word "firmly" is more effective than "carefully" would be,
because "firmly" better describes Mrs. Thayer's   (1) fondness for
neat appearance   (2) interest in contemporary styles   (3) attempt
to control anxiety   (4) concern for correct procedure   (5) memories of earlier friendships
3. In line 15, the use of the phrase "nursery rhymes" is more effective than
"poetry" would be, because "nursery rhymes" suggests greater   (1)
beauty   (2) understanding   (3) interest   (4) feeling   (5)
dependency
4. In lines 15-16, the reference to Mrs. Thayer's attempting to say the
Twenty-third Psalm indicates her   (1) devotion and love   (2)
growing tension   (3) passive listening   (4) spiritual rebirth
(5) pleasant childhood memories
5. Which device does the author use at the beginning of each sentence in
the second paragraph?   (1) literary allusion   (2) parallel structure   (3) dramatic irony   (4) assonance   (5) exaggeration
6. In the second paragraph, Mrs. Thayer undergoes a significant change
that can best be described as a movement from   (1) vague uneasiness to relief   (2) humor to tragic awareness   (3) failing confidence to fear   (4) pathetic ignorance to knowledge   (5) terror
to calm acceptance
7. Which phrase contains a paradox?   (1) "spasmodic violence" (line
2)   (2) "every trick" (line 11)   (3) "brushed her hair" (line 12)
(4) "dreadful sweet milk" (line 17)   (5) "those two pills" (lines
17-18)

8. In this passage, the image of the storm is used to   (1) suggest Mrs.
   Thayer's courage   (2) cause an immense amount of damage   (3)
   suggest the fears of summer guests   (4) reflect Mrs. Thayer's loud
   cries   (5) parallel Mrs. Thayer's fears
9. Which phrase best expresses the mood of the passage?   (1) quiet
   desperation   (2) enraged violence   (3) simple faith   (4) pretended terror   (5) useless irony
10. In this passage, the author makes considerable use of (1) anecdotes
    (2) rhetorical questions   (3) suspense   (4) theme   (5) poetic
    license

D

THE CIVIC BANQUET

Pompeians buried by surprise
In parlors, bedrooms, baths and hallways,
At least could breathe their final sighs
As warm as always.
5 But should Americans face doom
I know how we will be positioned:
All frozen in some banquet room
That's air-conditioned.

The frost is on the pumpkin pie,
10 It chilled the soup, congealed the dinner
And kept the butter hard and dry,
The only winner,
While ladies who can see their breath,
In evening dress turn blue and colder,
15 Exposing to the kiss of death
A naked shoulder.

The arctic blasts are filtered clear;
Two thousand diners can't pollute them
Nor can the speakers we must hear
20 And then salute them.

Ah! We will die and make world news
From cold, increasing slow but steady,
While listening to those men whose views
We knew already.

1. In this poem, a phrase that appeals to the sense of sight is   (1) "breathe their final sighs" (line 3)   (2) "As warm as always." (line 4)   (3) "That's air-conditioned." (line 8)   (4) "While ladies who can see their breath," (line 13)   (5) "And then salute them." (line 20)

2. In line 12, "The only winner" most probably refers to   (1) a chilled lady   (2) the dinner   (3) the butter   (4) the poet   (5) a modern invention

3. Which phrase most effectively uses exaggeration for effect?   (1) "In parlors, bedrooms, baths and hallways," (line 2)   (2) "Exposing to the kiss of death" (line 15)   (3) "Nor can the speakers we must hear" (line 19)   (4) "From cold, increasing slow but steady," (line 22)   (5) "We knew already." (line 24)

4. The poet unifies the stanzas of the poem through the use of   (1) refrain and onomatopoeia   (2) rhythm and rhyme   (3) alliteration and assonance   (4) symbol and connotation   (5) simile and metaphor

5. The poet establishes the tone of the poem in the   (1) first stanza   (2) second stanza   (3) third stanza   (4) fourth stanza   (5) title

6. The poet views the dinner guests with   (1) helpless rage   (2) great envy   (3) happy approval   (4) amused pity   (5) vague annoyance

7. Which does the poet use to support her views?   (1) opinions of famous men   (2) criticism of the Pompeians   (3) myths and legends   (4) annual reports   (5) modern references

8. The attitude of the poet is most clearly revealed by her   (1) listing historical references   (2) quoting authorities   (3) describing humorous examples   (4) quoting proverbs   (5) taking a solemn oath

9. The author's intent in stanza 1 seems to be to   (1) suggest contrast   (2) develop characters   (3) establish diction   (4) create conflict   (5) introduce facts

10. The title of the poem refers to the   (1) plot   (2) mood   (3) setting   (4) hero   (5) interpretation

THE C-2 TEST (Discontinued as of January 1982)

The thirty questions in this section, of which you were required to answer *only ten*, tested your knowledge of literature. The correct answers have been inserted in the right-hand column. Cover them up and jot down your own. Then compare.

C-2 Directions (11–40): Choose only *10* of the following, and, in the space provided on the separate answer sheet, write the *number* of the word or expression that best completes the statement or answers the question.

11 Casey Jones achieved fame as a
    1 scuba diver   3 baseball pitcher
    2 railroad engineer   4 heavy eater   11 ..2..

12 The title and theme of *Of Mice and Men* concern the
    1 interrelationships of the arts   3 causes of drug addiction
    2 value of scientific research   4 brotherhood of man   12 ..4..

13 In Shaw's *Pygmalion,* the author chiefly satirizes
    1 social classes   3 the church
    2 the teaching profession   4 business   13 ..1..

14 In the poem "The Unknown Citizen," W. H. Auden expresses the belief that
    1 modern man has lost his faith in God
    2 people have lost their individuality
    3 communes are an answer to the world's problems
    4 citizens must develop greater patriotism   14 ..2..

15 In "On the Duty of Civil Disobedience," Thoreau maintains that the individual is "a higher and [more] independent power" than
    1 authors   3 the government
    2 the family   4 artists   15 ..3..

16 To establish himself at Lonesome Valley School, Jesse Stuart had to
    1 pass an examination in school law
    2 get a high mark in algebra
    3 whip a boy in a fight
    4 produce a winning basketball team   16 ..3..

17 In *Macbeth,* the banquet was disrupted when
    1 Macbeth saw a ghost   3 Lady Macbeth fainted
    2 Macbeth killed Fleance   4 the castle was attacked   17 ..1..

18 In *Giants in the Earth,* what did the settlers hope to find in the new land?
    1 gold   3 happiness
    2 the Fountain of Youth   4 religious freedom   18 ..3..

19 In "God Sees the Truth But Waits," Aksenov receives a pardon just before
    1 Makar confesses   3 he leaves the prison
    2 he dies   4 his wife joins him   19 ..2..

20 The protagonist in Ellison's *Invisible Man* is unusual in that he
    1 becomes a hero
    2 leaves America
    3 is nameless throughout the novel
    4 returns to the South   20 ..*3*..

21 To which tragic figure does the following quotation refer?
      "And as he spoke,
        He struck at his eyes, not once, but many times;"
    1 Creon   3 Teiresias
    2 Oedipus   4 Jocasta   21 ..*2*..

22 In his work, Jacques-Yves Cousteau is most likely to encounter
    1 a rattlesnake   3 an avalanche
    2 a meteorite   4 a killer shark   22 ..*4*..

23 Jem, Scout, and Dill are companions in
    1 *Native Son*   3 *Jubilee*
    2 *The Autobiography of Malcolm X*   4 *To Kill a Mockingbird*   23 ..*4*..

24 *Animal Farm* and *Lord of the Flies* are similar in that they both
    1 use animals as principal characters
    2 deal with violent struggles for leadership
    3 have happy endings
    4 express a belief in man's basic goodness   24 ..*2*..

25 Perhaps the main quality of American music according to
    Leonard Bernstein's "What Makes Music American?" is its
    1 rowdiness   3 sentimentality
    2 objectivity   4 many-sidedness   25 ..*4*..

26 An important event in the life of the main character in James
    Baldwin's *Go Tell It on the Mountain* is
    1 a religious experience
    2 an interview with a movie star
    3 a trip to Paris
    4 his debut as a professional tennis player   26 ..*1*..

27 In *Wuthering Heights,* many of Heathcliff's actions in the
    latter part of the story are motivated by
    1 revenge   3 patriotism
    2 pity   4 humility   27 ..*1*..

28 In *West Side Story,* who is the counterpart of Juliet's nurse
    in *Romeo and Juliet?*
    1 Maria's employer   3 the tomboy Anybody's
    2 Bernardo's fiancée   4 Tony's mother   28 ..*2*..

29 In "A Word," Emily Dickinson believes that after a word is
said it
1 is dead   3 begins to live
2 is forgotten   4 is misquoted   29 ..*3*..

30 Who was slain by Achilles?
1 Patroclus   3 Hector
2 Paris   4 Achates   30 ..*3*..

31 The lines
　　　Whenever I feel afraid,
　　　I hold my head erect
　　　And whistle a happy tune
are from
1 *The King and I*   3 *South Pacific*
2 *Carousel*   4 *Oklahoma!*   31 ..*1*..

32 In William Blake's poem "The Tiger," the principal images
are connected with
1 air   3 fire
2 earth   4 water   32 ..*3*..

33 The quotation, "Only he who attempts the absurd is capable of
achieving the impossible," best expresses the theme of which
play?
1 *The Lion in Winter*
2 *The Prime of Miss Jean Brodie*
3 *A Man For All Seasons*
4 *Man of La Mancha*   33 ..*4*..

34 *The Sea Around Us* contains
1 accounts of long ocean voyages
2 stories of famous shipwrecks
3 explanations of common phenomena in the sea
4 folk tales about early sailors   34 ..*3*..

35 In Maugham's short story "The Verger," the tone of the story's
ending may best be described as
1 satiric   3 ironic
2 melancholic   4 tragic   35 ..*3*..

36 In *Billy Budd,* the essential conflict is between
1 law and justice   3 religion and science
2 man and corporations   4 man and the elements   36 ..*1*..

37 The authors of *Mad, Sad, and Glad* are
1 musicians   3 drama critics
2 policemen   4 teenagers   37 ..*4*..

38 Markham's poem "The Man with the Hoe" closes with a
   1 prayer   3 pun
   2 prophecy   4 psalm   38 ..2..

39 In Ray Bradbury's short story "The Flying Machine," the
   emperor's reaction to the inventor of the machine is to
   1 praise him   3 exile him
   2 have him killed   4 ignore him   39 ..2..

40 In Jack London's "To Build a Fire," the man was most afraid of
   1 losing the boxing championship
   2 running the ship aground
   3 running out of ammunition
   4 getting his feet wet   40 ..4..

ANALYSIS OF THE C-2 TEST

Each question asks you to recognize a detail, such as the following:

1. A detail about the characters. Note that the main character is sometimes called the *protagonist*.

   20 The protagonist in Ellison's *Invisible Man* is unusual in
      that he
      1 becomes a hero   3 is nameless throughout the novel   [3]
      2 leaves America   4 returns to the South

   23 Jem, Scout, and Dill are companions in
      1 *Native Son*
      2 *The Autobiography of Malcolm X*
      3 *Jubilee*
      4 *To Kill A Mockingbird*   [4]

2. A detail about the main idea (theme) or one of the other important ideas.

   12 The title and theme of *Of Mice and Men* concern the
      1 interrelationships of the arts   3 causes of drug addiction   [4]
      2 value of scientific research   4 brotherhood of man

   14 In the poem "The Unknown Citizen," W. H. Auden ex-
      presses the belief that
      1 modern man has lost his faith in God
      2 people have lost their individuality
      3 communes are an answer to the world's problems
      4 citizens must develop greater patriotism   [2]

3. A detail about the plot or the contents.

36 In *Billy Budd,* the essential conflict is between
1 law and justice
2 man and corporations
3 religion and science
4 man and the elements

[*1*]

16 To establish himself at Lonesome Valley School, Jesse Stuart had to
1 pass an examination in school law
2 get a high mark in algebra
3 whip a boy in a fight
4 produce a winning basketball team

[*3*]

34 *The Sea Around Us* contains
1 accounts of long ocean voyages
2 stories of famous shipwrecks
3 explanations of common phenomena in the sea
4 folk tales about early sailors

[*3*]

4. A detail about an author.

22 In his work, Cousteau is most likely to encounter
1 a rattlesnake
2 a meteorite
3 an avalanche
4 a killer shark

[*4*]

5. The tone (author's attitude toward his subject).

35 In Maugham's short story "The Verger," the tone of the story's ending may best be described as
1 satiric
2 melancholic
3 ironic
4 tragic

[*3*]

6. The source of a quotation.

31 The lines
    Whenever I feel afraid,
    I hold my head erect
    And whistle a happy tune
are from
1 *The King and I*
2 *Carousel*
3 *South Pacific*
4 *Oklahoma!*

[*1*]

7. A detail from mythology or folklore.

30 Who was slain by Achilles?
1 Patroclus
2 Paris
3 Hector
4 Achates

[*3*]

11 Casey Jones achieved fame as a
 1 scuba diver   3 baseball pitcher
 2 railroad engineer   4 heavy eater $\left[2\right]$

8. (Not in the above C-2 test, but found in subsequent tests)

A detail about the setting (locality or period of the action).

The setting of Lorraine Hansberry's *A Raisin in the Sun* is a
 1 city apartment   3 Southern resort
 2 small farmhouse   4 neighborhood restaurant $\left[1\right]$

The C-2 test is very reasonable because the details you are asked to recognize are not obscure. If you have read and understood the works, you should have no difficulty in recognizing such details. Besides, you have to answer *only ten* of the thirty questions.

CAUTION: If you answer more than ten questions, only your first ten will be rated.

REVIEWING FOR THE C-2 TEST

1. *Titles, Authors, Characters, Setting, Theme, Plot, etc.*

Skim through the brief annotations in Chapter 9, *Guide to Good Literature*, pages 343–399. They will help you recall works you have studied in class or read on your own.

2. *Quotations*

Quotations are valuable because they can help you recall the essence of a work. Here are some quotations that have appeared in Question C in past examinations:

Quotations From Plays

Julius Caesar by William Shakespeare

"Why, man, he doth bestride the narrow world
Like a Colossus."
                              (spoken by Cassius)

"Yond Cassius has a lean and hungry look;
He thinks too much; such men are dangerous."
                              (spoken by Caesar)

"Cowards die many times before their deaths;
The valiant never taste of death but once."
(spoken by Caesar)

"But 'tis a common proof
That lowliness is young ambition's ladder."
(spoken by Brutus)

"The fault, dear Brutus, is not in our stars,
But in ourselves, that we are underlings."
(spoken by Cassius)

"The evil that men do lives after them;
The good is oft interred with their bones."
(spoken by Antony)

"O, pardon me, thou bleeding piece of earth,
That I am meek and gentle with these butchers!"
(spoken by Antony)

Hamlet by William Shakespeare

"The time is out of joint; O cursed spite,
That ever I was born to set it right!"
(spoken by Hamlet)

"The play's the thing
Wherein I'll catch the conscience of the king."
(spoken by Hamlet)

"Good night, sweet prince."
(spoken by Horatio)

"For the apparel oft proclaims the man."
(spoken by Polonius)

"Alas, poor Yorick! I knew him, Horatio."
(spoken by Hamlet)

"The rest is silence."
(dying words of Hamlet)

The King and I by Richard Rodgers and Oscar Hammerstein II

"Whenever I feel afraid,
I hold my head erect
And whistle a happy tune . . ."

King Lear by William Shakespeare

"How sharper than a serpent's tooth it is
To have a thankless child!"
(spoken by Lear)

Macbeth by William Shakespeare

"Is this a dagger which I see before me?"
(spoken by Macbeth)

"Tomorrow and tomorrow and tomorrow
Creeps in this petty pace from day to day."
(spoken by Macbeth)

"Infirm of purpose!
Give me the daggers."
(spoken by Lady Macbeth)

"Methought I heard a voice cry 'Sleep no more!
Macbeth does murder sleep.'"
(spoken by Macbeth)

"Life's but a walking shadow, a poor player,
That struts and frets his hour upon the stage
And then is heard no more. It is a tale
Told by an idiot, full of sound and fury,
Signifying nothing."
(spoken by Macbeth)

Oedipus Rex by Sophocles

"And as he spoke,
He struck at his eyes, not once, but many times;"

Richard III by William Shakespeare

"A horse! a horse! my kingdom for a horse!"
(spoken by Richard III)

Romeo and Juliet by William Shakespeare

"Parting is such sweet sorrow."
(spoken by Juliet)

"A plague on both your houses!"
(spoken by Mercutio)

"What's in a name? That which we call a rose
By any other name would smell as sweet."
(spoken by Juliet)

The Tempest by William Shakespeare

"We are such stuff
As dreams are made on."
(spoken by Prospero)

Our Town by Thornton Wilder

"A man looks pretty small at a wedding, George. All those good women standing shoulder to shoulder making sure that the knot's tied in a mighty public way."
(spoken by Mr. Webb)

Quotations From Novels

Alice in Wonderland by Lewis Carroll

"Off with their heads!"
(a common expression of the queen)

David Copperfield by Charles Dickens

"Something will turn up."
(a common expression of Micawber)

"Barkis is willin'."
(Barkis' proposal to Peggotty)

A Tale of Two Cities by Charles Dickens

"It is a far, far better thing that I do, than I have ever done."
(Carton's reflection on his way to the guillotine)

Quotations From Poems

Rupert Brooke

"If I should die, think only this of me,
    That there's some corner of a foreign field
That is forever England."
("The Soldier")

Elizabeth Barrett Browning

> "And, if God choose,
>   I shall but love thee better after death."
>   (*Sonnets from the Portuguese*)

Robert Browning

> "If I can rid your town of rats,
>   Will you give me a thousand guilders?"
>   ("The Pied Piper")

William Cullen Bryant

> "The groves were God's first temples."
>   ("A Forest Hymn")

> "To him who in the love of Nature holds
>   Communion with her visible forms"
>   ("Thanatopsis")

Robert Burns

> "My Mary's asleep by thy murmuring stream"
>   ("Flow Gently, Sweet Afton")

> "Wee, sleekit, cow'rin, tim'rous beastie"
>   ("To a Mouse")

> "Still thou art blessed, compared wi' me!"
>   ("To a Mouse")

> "O wad some Pow'r the giftie gie us
>   To see oursels as ithers see us!"
>   ("To a Louse")

> "And I will luve thee still, my dear,
>   Till a' the seas gang dry."
>   ("A Red, Red Rose")

Samuel Taylor Coleridge

> "As idle as a painted ship
>   Upon a painted ocean"
>   ("The Rime of the Ancient Mariner")

Emily Dickinson

> "I like to see it lap the miles."
> > (from the poem of the same name)

> "I never spoke with God,
>   Nor visited in heaven."
> > ("Chartless")

Thomas Stearns Eliot

> "We are the hollow men"
> > ("The Hollow Men")

Ralph Waldo Emerson

> "Tell them, dear, that if eyes were made for seeing,
>   Then Beauty is its own excuse for being."
> > ("The Rhodora")

Robert Frost

> "When I see birches bend to left and right"

> "I'd like to get away from earth a while
>   And then come back to it and begin over"

> "One could do worse than be a swinger of birches."
> > ("Birches")

> "Home is the place where, when you have to go there,
>   They have to take you in."

> " 'Dead,' was all he answered."
> > ("The Death of the Hired Man")

> "Two roads diverged in a wood, and I—
>   I took the one less traveled by"
> > ("The Road Not Taken")

> "Whose woods these are I think I know."

> "But I have promises to keep,
>   And miles to go before I sleep."
> > ("Stopping by Woods on a Snowy Evening")

Oliver Goldsmith

> "And still they gazed, and still the wonder grew
>   That one small head could carry all he knew."
> > ("The Deserted Village")

Thomas Gray

"Far from the madding crowd's ignoble strife"
("Elegy Written in a Country Churchyard")

Robert Herrick

"Gather ye rosebuds while ye may,
  Old Time is still a-flying."
("To the Virgins, to Make Much of Time")

Oliver Wendell Holmes

"Ay, tear her tattered ensign down!"
("Old Ironsides")

Leigh Hunt

"Write me as one that loves his fellow men."
("Abou Ben Adhem")

Ben Jonson

"Drink to me only with thine eyes."
("To Celia")

John Keats

"Heard melodies are sweet, but those unheard
  Are sweeter."

"Beauty is truth, truth beauty."
("Ode on a Grecian Urn")

"When I have fears that I may cease to be"
(from the sonnet of the same name)

"Much have I traveled in the realms of gold."
("On First Looking Into Chapman's Homer")

Francis Scott Key

"The war's desolation"

"Then conquer we must, when our cause it is just."
("The Star-Spangled Banner")

Rudyard Kipling

"Lest we forget!"

(refrain from "Recessional")

Vachel Lindsay

> "It breaks his heart that kings must murder still,
> That all his hours of travail here for men
> Seem yet in vain. And who will bring white peace
> That he may sleep upon his hill again?"
> ("Abraham Lincoln Walks at Midnight")

> "Beat an empty barrel with the handle of a broom."
> ("The Congo")

Henry Wadsworth Longfellow

> "Over the wide and rushing rivers
> In his arms he bore the maiden."
> ("Song of Hiawatha")

> "A boy's will is the wind's will."
> ("My Lost Youth")

> "I heard the trailing garments of the Night
> Sweep through her marble halls."
> ("Hymn to Night")

James Russell Lowell

> "And what is so rare as a day in June?
> Then, if ever, come perfect days."
> ("The Vision of Sir Launfal")

Edwin Markham

> "Bowed by the weight of centuries"
> ("The Man with the Hoe")

John Masefield

> "And all I ask is a tall ship and a star to steer her by"
> ("Sea-Fever")

Edgar Lee Masters

> "Degenerate sons and daughters,
> Life is too strong for you."
> ("Lucinda Matlock")

John McCrea

"We shall not sleep, though poppies grow"
("In Flanders Fields")

Claude McKay

"Like men, we'll face the cowardly, murderous pack,
Pressed to the wall, dying, but fighting back!"
("If We Must Die")

Edna St. Vincent Millay

"The world stands out on either side
No wider than the heart is wide."
("Renascence")

John Milton

"When I consider how my light is spent"

"They also serve who only stand and wait."
("On His Blindness")

"And justify the ways of God to men."
(*Paradise Lost*)

Alfred Noyes

"Come down to Kew in lilac time."
(refrain from "The Barrel-Organ")

"The moon was a ghostly galleon."

"I'll come to thee by moonlight."
("The Highwayman")

Edgar Allan Poe

"I was a child and she was a child,
In this kingdom by the sea."
("Annabel Lee")

"Hear the mellow wedding bells, golden bells."
("The Bells")

Edwin Arlington Robinson

"And he glittered when he walked."
("Richard Cory")

Carl Sandburg

"Come and show me another city with head lifted and singing so proud to be alive."
("Chicago")

William Shakespeare

"But if the while I think on thee, dear friend,
All losses are restored and sorrows end."
("When to the Sessions of Sweet Silent
Thought")

Percy Bysshe Shelley

"Destroyer and preserver; hear, oh hear!"
("Ode to the West Wind")

"Look on my works, ye Mighty, and despair!"
("Ozymandias")

"Music, when soft voices die,
Vibrates in the memory."
("To—: Music, When Soft Voices Die")

"Hail to thee, blithe spirit!
Bird thou never wert."
("To a Skylark")

Robert Southey

"It was a famous victory."
(refrain from "The Battle of Blenheim")

Samuel F. Smith

"From every mountain-side
Let freedom ring."
("America")

Alfred, Lord Tennyson

"Theirs not to reason why."
("The Charge of the Light Brigade")

"I hope to see my Pilot face to face
When I have crost the bar."
> ("Crossing the Bar")

"Follow Christ, the King.
Live pure, speak true, right wrong, follow the King."
> ("Gareth and Lynette")

Louis Untermeyer

"Fling us a handful of stars."
> ("Caliban in the Coal Mines")

William Wordsworth

"Earth has not anything to show more fair."
> ("Composed Upon Westminster Bridge")

"The waves beside them danced, but they
Out-did the sparkling waves in glee."
> ("The Daffodils")

"Our birth is but a sleep and a forgetting."
> ("Ode on the Intimations of Immortality")

"Little we see in Nature that is ours."
> ("The World Is Too Much With Us")

Quotations From Essays

Francis Bacon

". . . for prosperity doth best discover vice, but adversity doth best discover virtue."
> ("Of Adversity")

"Some books are to be chewed and digested."

"Reading maketh a full man."

"Read not to contradict and confute; nor to believe and take for granted; nor to find talk and discourse; but to weigh and consider."
> ("Of Studies")

Winston Churchill

"Never . . . was so much owed by so many to so few."
> (Speech on the Battle of Britain)

John Donne

> "No man is an island, entire of itself; every man is a piece of the continent, a part of the main."
>
> ("Meditation XVII")

Patrick Henry

> "I know not what course others may take; but as for me, give me liberty, or give me death!"
>
> ("Speech in the Virginia Convention")

Thomas Jefferson

> "When in the course of human events"

> "We hold these truths to be self-evident."

> "And for the support of this declaration, with a firm reliance on the protection of Divine Providence, we mutually pledge to each other, our lives, our fortunes, and our sacred honor."
>
> ("The Declaration of Independence")

John F. Kennedy

> "All this will not be finished in the first one hundred days. Nor will it be finished in the first one thousand days, nor in the life of this Administration, nor even perhaps in our lifetime on this planet. But let us begin."
>
> ("Inaugural Address")

Abraham Lincoln

> "Government of the people, by the people and for the people"
>
> ("The Gettysburg Address")

> "With malice toward none, with charity for all."
>
> ("Second Inaugural Address")

Christopher Morley

> "There are degrees of sadness in the closing of doors."
>
> ("On Doors")

Thomas Paine

> "These are the times that try men's souls."
>
> ("The American Crisis")

Quotations From Short Stories

Stephen Vincent Benét

"But even the damned may salute the eloquence of Mr. Webster."
(spoken by Walter Butler in "The Devil and Daniel Webster")

Edward Everett Hale

"He loved his country as no man loved her; but no man deserved less at her hands."
(said of Philip Nolan in "The Man Without a Country")

Shirley Jackson

"Although the villagers had forgotten the ritual and lost the original black box, they still remembered to use stones."
("The Lottery")

Edgar Allan Poe

"During the whole of a dull, dark and soundless day in the autumn of the year, when the clouds hung oppressively low in the heavens"
("The Fall of the House of Usher")

Quotations From the Bible

Old Testament

"Thy people shall be my people, and thy God my God."
(Book of Ruth)

"A time to be born, and a time to die."
(Ecclesiastes)

"He leadeth me beside the still waters."

"The valley of the shadow of death"
(Twenty-third Psalm)

New Testament

"Blessed are the poor in spirit, for theirs is the kingdom of heaven."
(Sermon on the Mount)

3. *Mythological and Biblical Allusions*

The following details about mythology, folklore, and the Bible could have helped you answer Question C in past examinations:

Achilles   Greek hero vulnerable only in his heel. His wrath was incurred when he was forced to give up his prize, the maiden Briseis.

Amazons   tribe of men-hating warrior women dwelling near the Black Sea.

Androcles   legendary Roman slave spared by a lion who remembered him— he had once removed a thorn from the lion's foot.

Antigone   daughter of deposed Theban king. She defied her uncle, King Creon, by daring to give her slain brother decent burial.

The *Argonauts*   sailors who sought the golden fleece.

Atalanta   swift-footed Greek girl who refused to marry unless her suitor should first overcome her in a footrace.

Athena   Greek goddess and protector of Athens, the city named after her because she gave it the olive tree.

Atlas   Elder Greek god sentenced to bear the weight of the heavens.

The *Augean stables,* dirty from housing 3000 oxen for thirty years, were cleaned by Hercules as one of his twelve labors.

Camelot   legendary court of King Arthur.

Cassandra   an accurate Trojan prophetess whom no one would believe.

Cerberus   three-headed dog guarding the gate to the Greek underworld, where dead souls go.

Charon   boatman who ferried the souls of the Greek dead across the river Styx.

Circe   beautiful wily witch who turned Odysseus' men into swine.

Clytemnestra   Greek queen who sought vengeance on her husband Agamemnon because he had sacrificed their daughter Iphigenia.

Cupid   Roman god of love, who married the beautiful Psyche.

Cyclops (also known as *Polyphemus*)   one-eyed man-eating giant outwitted by Odysseus.

Electra   daughter of the murdered Agamemnon, obsessed by a desire to avenge his death.

Excalibur   King Arthur's sword, given to him by the Lady of the Lake.

Frigga   Norse goddess of love and beauty, from whom *Friday* (*Frigga's Day*) is derived.

Goliath   giant Philistine warrior whom the boy David slew with a stone from a sling.

Guinevere   King Arthur's faithless queen. She spent her last years in a convent.

Hector   bravest of the Trojans. Slain by Achilles.

Hercules   Greek hero of superhuman strength.

Hermes   Greek messenger of the gods.

Ixion   punished for treachery and ingratitude by being bound to an endlessly revolving wheel of fire in the Greek underworld.

John Henry   American folk hero of gigantic strength who died of overexertion.

Labyrinth   twisting maze on island of Crete. Once inside, it was impossible to find the way out.

Loki   Norse god of strife noted for his cunning.

The *Lorelei*   maiden dwelling on the shores of the Rhine who, by her singing, lured sailors and fishermen to their deaths in the rapids.

Lot   nephew of Abraham. Lot's wife turned into a pillar of salt because she looked back as they were fleeing Sodom.

Medusa   gorgon (dragonlike monster) who turned all who looked at her into stone. Slain by the Greek hero Perseus.

Mercury   Roman counterpart of Hermes.

Midas   king of Phrygia who had the power to turn everything he touched into gold.

Minotaur   man-eating monster who inhabited a Cretan maze known as the Labyrinth.

Odysseus   Greek hero who confused Polyphemus by calling himself Noman. He was detained on his way home from the Trojan War because he had offended the god Poseidon.

Pandora   first woman created by the Greek gods, she was given a box that she was warned not to open, but out of curiosity, she opened it. Out flew all the sorrows and misfortunes that have since plagued humanity. By the time she closed the lid, the only thing left in the box was hope.

Pegasus   winged horse of the Greek Muses.

The *Phoenix*   legendary bird of Egyptian mythology with the power to be reborn in its dying moment.

Pluto   Greek god, ruler of the underworld.

Prometheus   stole fire from the Greek gods and gave it to man. For this, he was punished by being chained to a rock, with an eagle gnawing at his liver.

Pygmalion   sculptor living on Cyprus who grew enamored of his statue. As a result of his prayers, it was given life and became his wife Galatea.

Scylla and *Charybdis*   Sea monsters in the Straits of Messina. Also, Scylla was a treacherous rock, and Charybdis a whirlpool. To be "between Scylla and Charybdis" is to be in a predicament.

Sherwood Forest   home of Robin Hood, Friar Tuck, and Little John.

Sisyphus   was condemned in the Greek underworld perpetually to roll a heavy stone uphill, only to have it roll back on him—all this for having revealed a secret of Zeus, king of the Greek gods.

Tantalus   was submerged in the Greek underworld up to his chin in a stream whose waters would recede whenever he tried to drink. Above his head was a fruit-laden tree, but just beyond his grasp. He suffered these tortures for having divulged the secrets of the gods to mortals.

Thor   Norse god of thunder. *Thursday* bears his name (*Thor's Day*).

Troilus   a young Trojan slain by Achilles. According to later writers, Troilus loved Cressida.

Valhalla   Norse paradise for brave warriors killed in battle.

The *Valkyries*   twelve maidens of Scandinavian legend who conducted slain heroes to Valhalla.

Woden   chief Germanic god, akin to the Norse *Odin*. *Wednesday* is his day (*Woden's Day*).

C-2 TESTS FROM PART II OF FORMER EXAMINATIONS

Test 1

C-2 Directions (11-40): Choose only *10* of the following, and, in the space provided on the separate answer sheet, write the *number* of the word or expression that best completes the statement or answers the question.

11. In "The Tell-Tale Heart," the madman thought he heard a   (1) watch ticking   (2) man's heart beating   (3) cat mewing loudly   (4) cock crowing

12. In *Peter Pan*, an attempt was made to force Wendy to live with   (1) pirates   (2) gypsies   (3) dwarfs   (4) witches

13. In *The Call of the Wild*, why was Buck, the sled dog, so loyal to Thornton?   (1) Buck was well fed.   (2) Thornton had saved the dog's life.   (3) The dog was lonely in the wilds.   (4) Thornton protected him from the other dogs.

14. In "Concord Hymn," the poet eulogizes a conflict between the   (1) colonists and the Indians   (2) colonists and the British   (3) colonists and the French   (4) British and the French

15. Wordsworth would rather be a "Pagan suckled in a creed outworn," because   (1) he liked ancient religions   (2) he was fond of mythology   (3) the ancients appreciated Nature   (4) he was an atheist

16. A henpecked husband appears in   (1) "Mammon and the Archer"   (2) "The Secret Life of Walter Mitty"   (3) "The Catbird Seat"   (4) "The Last Leaf"

17. "I'll come to thee by moonlight" is the promise of   (1) a highwayman   (2) a disguised noble   (3) Sir Lancelot   (4) Robin Hood

18. In solving his biggest problem, Hamlet got practical help from   (1) his mother   (2) his stepfather   (3) the father of the girl he loved   (4) the traveling actors

19. Which is typical of the images found in Thor Heyerdahl's *Kon-Tiki*?   (1) "lush gardens of bluebells, hyacinths, and violets"   (2) "coral islands . . . like pearls on a string"   (3) "a flare dropping in a bucket of trash on the piazza"   (4) "hardtack, frozen pemmican, and whisky to counteract the height"

20. In *Fiddler on the Roof*, the mother is preoccupied with finding   (1) a new violin teacher   (2) a new house to live in   (3) mates for her daughters   (4) work for her husband

21. In the *Iliad*, a 12-day truce was agreed upon by the warring sides so that   (1) Paris and Menelaus could fight   (2) Hector could see his wife and child   (3) Achilles could pacify the angry river god   (4) both sides could bury their dead

22. Walter Sullivan's *We Are Not Alone* deals with   (1) the work of spies   (2) lost children   (3) campus radicals   (4) life on other planets

23. "Although the villagers had forgotten the ritual and lost the original black box, they still remembered to use stones." This quotation is from a story in which the action takes place during a   (1) funeral   (2) witch trial   (3) lottery   (4) hanging

24. In *Moby Dick,* Captain Ahab was killed by   (1) his ship, the *Pequod*   (2) a harpoon rope   (3) Queequeg's canoe-coffin   (4) fire

25. In *The Light in the Forest,* the conflict is between   (1) industrial giants   (2) cattlemen and settlers   (3) lumbermen and the railroads   (4) Indians and white men

26. In his "Letter from Birmingham Jail," whom does Martin Luther King, Jr. refer to as "an extremist for love, truth, and goodness"?   (1) Malcolm X   (2) Jesus Christ   (3) Thomas Jefferson   (4) W. E. B. Dubois

27. Which book is about boys growing up?   (1) *Arrowsmith*   (2) *1984*   (3) *A Separate Peace*   (4) *The Incredible Journey*

28. Eugene O'Neill's drama, "In the Zone," takes place in a   (1) torrid zone   (2) factory zone   (3) war zone   (4) polar zone

29. In "Birches," Robert Frost states that life is sometimes too much like   (1) a pathless wood   (2) untimely storms   (3) a walking shadow   (4) checkered shade and sunshine

30. In *Great Expectations,* Miss Havisham can best be characterized as being   (1) eccentric   (2) benevolent   (3) frivolous   (4) outgoing

31. In "The Adventure of the Speckled Band," Dr. Roylott murdered his victims by using   (1) an axe   (2) a rope   (3) a gun   (4) a snake

32. *I Never Promised You a Rose Garden* reveals schizophrenia to be   (1) incurable and largely uncontrollable   (2) caused by chemical imbalance in the brain   (3) the result of inherited characteristics   (4) primarily a matter of choice by the patient

33. In *Notes of a Native Son,* James Baldwin describes his father as   (1) an idealist   (2) a stubborn, proud man   (3) a reformer   (4) a strong leader

34. In *Raisin in the Sun,* the Youngers are struggling to   (1) fulfill their dreams   (2) stay in their apartment   (3) integrate the schools   (4) obtain money to go to Europe

35. In the Bible, which person was turned into a pillar of salt? (1) Job's wife (2) Cain's son (3) Ruth's husband (4) Lot's wife

36. The central incident in "The Lifeguard" by James Dickey is (1) a lifesaving drill (2) a tidal wave (3) a fight in the water (4) an attempted rescue

37. Which poet is also well known for an extensive collection of short stories that deal almost exclusively with Harlem life? (1) Langston Hughes (2) Gwendolyn Brooks (3) Mari Evans (4) Don L. Lee

38. Joseph Palmer suffered indignities, harassment, humiliation, and persecution mainly because he (1) left home (2) went away to sea (3) had false teeth (4) wore a beard

39. In Carl Sandburg's "Prairie-Town Boy," the author includes an autobiographical account of (1) army life (2) hobo life (3) overseas life (4) college life

40. Vance Packard's book *The Wastemakers* deals chiefly with the (1) spoils of war (2) built-in obsolescence of commercial products (3) money spent on national defense (4) extravagance of the motion picture industry

Test 2

11. Cyrano de Bergerac writes love letters to Roxane under a false identity because he (1) has alienated her by his previous advances (2) fears reprisals from her other lover (3) enjoys the effect of his joke on her (4) fears that she would reject him in his true identity.

12. In *When the Legends Die,* a legend which people told was that the Devil escaped from Tom Black by turning himself into a (1) bear (2) bronco (3) deer (4) mountain lion.

13. In *The Old Man and the Sea,* Manolin left Santiago to go out in another fishing boat because Manolin (1) was ordered to do so by his father (2) was tired of Santiago's lack of success (3) learned that Santiago had cheated him (4) could no longer stand being ridiculed by the other fishermen.

14. In the poem "Mr. Flood's Party," by E. A. Robinson, Mr. Flood is a (1) rich banker (2) popular socialite (3) lonely old man (4) strange traveler.

15. In *A Doll's House,* the cause of Nora's problem is (1) another woman in her husband's life (2) another man in love with her

(3) her husband's debt to the bank   (4) her husband's idea of the role of women

16. In *Bury My Heart at Wounded Knee,* the Sand Creek massacre is cited because it   (1) caused Custer's attack   (2) proved that the Indian scalped his victims   (3) was the last great Indian attack against the white man   (4) showed the cruelty of the white man

17. Why is Romeo reluctant to fight Tybalt?   (1) Tybalt is Juliet's cousin. (2) Tybalt is a superior swordsman.   (3) Mercutio asks Romeo not to duel.   (4) Romeo is on his way to church.

18. In *The Lord of the Rings,* why are the rings dangerous?   (1) They make the wearer invisible.   (2) They inspire the wearer with a desire for power.   (3) They are claimed by the Orks and the Worgs. (4) They can be turned to fire by the Dark Lord.

19. In H. G. Wells' *War of the Worlds,* the Martians lose because they are unable to withstand   (1) the hydrogen bomb   (2) an artillery bombardment   (3) a dense green gas   (4) the Earth's bacteria

20. In *I Never Promised You a Rose Garden,* the rose garden represents (1) an ideal world   (2) sanity   (3) the world of Yr   (4) inner conflict

21. The only quality left in Pandora's box is   (1) charity   (2) hope (3) faith   (4) humility

22. In attempting to arrive at moral perfection, Benjamin Franklin   (1) found he had fewer faults than he had imagined   (2) found it easy to conquer pride   (3) planned to master one virtue at a time   (4) had impractical schemes for improving Philadelphia

23. The title of the novel *The Learning Tree,* by Gordon Parks, refers to (1) Rufus' childhood in Cherokee Flats   (2) Rufus' desire to be an ecologist   (3) the ship on which Rufus sailed   (4) the tree hut Rufus built

24. In *Future Shock,* Alvin Toffler indicates that most of the "shock" will be caused by   (1) greater use of technology   (2) travel to other planets   (3) increasingly rapid changes   (4) atomic wars

25. Essayist and commentator Eric Hoffer has worked most of his life as a (1) baker   (2) longshoreman   (3) foreman   (4) plumber

26. In *Oliver Twist,* Fagin is the leader of a group of   (1) musicians (2) pickpockets   (3) pirates   (4) militiamen

27. The setting of *The Crucible* is the period of the   (1) Salem witch

hunt   (2) Second World War   (3) Robber Barons   (4) French Revolution

28. The "miracle" for which the boy in Frank O'Connor's "Man of the House" is hoping is that   (1) the medicine bottle will be refilled   (2) his mother will be well when he returns home   (3) he will meet the little Dooley girl again   (4) his truancy will go unnoticed at school

29. In the ballad "Lord Randall," Lord Randall dies when he is   (1) accused of treachery and hanged   (2) sent on a dangerous mission at sea   (3) poisoned by his sweetheart   (4) thrown by his horse

30. In *Black Boy* by Richard Wright, a change in the major character is caused by his   (1) sudden awareness of prejudice   (2) unwitting participation in a murder   (3) becoming a deacon in the Adventist Church   (4) marriage to a white girl

31. The characters in *Spoon River Anthology* are all   (1) mothers   (2) failures   (3) businessmen   (4) dead people

32. In *The Spirit of St. Louis,* the hero is   (1) a manager of a baseball team   (2) an early martyr   (3) an aviator   (4) a priest-poet

33. In "The New Dress" by Virginia Woolf, the dress becomes most clearly identified with   (1) Mrs. Milan's hard work   (2) Charles Burt's indifference   (3) Mrs. Holmes' ailing children   (4) Mabel's feelings of inferiority

34. In "The Leader of the People," Grandfather annoys his son-in-law by   (1) telling stories of the past   (2) leaving work undone   (3) being away for long periods of time   (4) neglecting the farm animals

35. In *A Man for All Seasons,* the Common Man functions as   (1) the narrator of the play   (2) the protagonist of the play   (3) a minor character who is essential to the theme of the play   (4) a participant in, and an observer of, the action of the play

36. The poem "Do Not Go Gentle into That Good Night" shows that Dylan Thomas felt death should be faced   (1) willingly   (2) defiantly   (3) indifferently   (4) fearfully

37. *Yes I Can* is the life story of a   (1) noted black entertainer   (2) determined Washington politician   (3) successful surgeon   (4) major league baseball player

38. The sonnet "If We Must Die" urges black people to   (1) face death quietly and peacefully   (2) react violently to injustice   (3) consider death as only a beginning   (4) refuse to mourn those who die

39. In his writing, Poe wanted above all to   (1) describe odd events   (2) dramatize moral truths   (3) achieve a single effect   (4) depict a specific setting

40. In *The Miracle Worker,* Annie Sullivan succeeds because she   (1) uses diplomacy with Helen's father   (2) follows the advice of Helen's mother   (3) has the wisdom of years of experience   (4) decides not to pity Helen

Test 3

11. The theme of *Lord of the Flies* is suggested in the idea that   (1) evil is present as a destructive influence in man   (2) history does not repeat itself   (3) civilization will eventually be embraced by all men   (4) man has lost his sense of humor

12. In "Ode to the West Wind," Shelley sees the wind as a symbol of   (1) joy   (2) beauty   (3) freedom   (4) triumph

13. Thomas Paine's "Common Sense" urged the American colonies to   (1) unite their strength with the British   (2) continue a shipping trade with England   (3) deserve protection through prayer   (4) develop the continent as an independent nation

14. In "Ulysses," a poem by Tennyson, Ulysses is described as a man who   (1) was satisfied to draw comfort from past experiences   (2) had an unquenchable thirst for adventure and knowledge   (3) deserted his post as King of Ithaca   (4) anticipated death with resignation

15. In mythology, the Minotaur, Medusa, and Cerberus were all   (1) monsters   (2) magicians   (3) heroes   (4) women

16. In Steinbeck's *The Pearl,* which is *not* a result of Kino's finding the pearl?   (1) The pearl dealers conspire against Kino.   (2) Kino kills a man who tries to steal the pearl.   (3) Kino's canoe is broken and his house is burned.   (4) Kino becomes wealthy.

17. In "The Fall of the House of Usher," the predominant mood is one of   (1) nostalgia   (2) disgust   (3) terror   (4) gaiety

18. According to the poem "When I Was One-and-Twenty," one should be most careful before giving away his   (1) love   (2) wealth   (3) secrets   (4) good reputation

19. In the lines "Life's but a walking shadow," the character who speaks reflects his   (1) joy of living   (2) despair at his fate   (3) anxiety for his son   (4) dislike for law and order

20. *One Day in the Life of Ivan Denisovich* describes the experiences of
    (1) a prisoner   (2) a sensitive child   (3) a librarian   (4) an
    unhappy student

21. Which statement is true of the two women in *The Glass Menagerie?*
    (1) One is involved in politics, the other is involved in women's rights.
    (2) One is lost in the past, the other is lost in herself.   (3) One has
    abdicated her responsibilities, the other has assumed them.   (4) One
    needs affection, the other does not.

22. Don Quixote's major purpose as he sets forth from La Mancha is to
    (1) conquer his personal enemies   (2) gain a reputation and acquire
    wealth   (3) right wrongs and defend the oppressed   (4) win a
    title and a place at court

23. In *Billy Budd, Foretopman,* the decision to execute Billy is prompted by
    the captain's   (1) disappointment at Billy's conduct   (2) belief in
    the necessity of law   (3) desire to catch whales   (4) jealousy of
    Claggart

24. In Faulkner's "Barn Burning," Sarty learns that he must   (1) obey
    his elders   (2) yield to authority   (3) face up to military service
    (4) think for himself

25. In *The Andromeda Strain,* the inhabitants of a town are wiped out by
    (1) a powerful virus   (2) an earthquake   (3) an atomic bomb
    (4) a hurricane

26. What are the two basic images in Edna St. Vincent Millay's poem
    "Renascence"?   (1) the rebirth of nature and the poet's death   (2)
    the rebirth of nature and the death of nature   (3) the poet's reawak-
    ening and the rebirth of nature   (4) the poet's reawakening and the
    death of nature

27. In Arthur Miller's *All My Sons,* Chris Keller is disillusioned when he
    finds that his father is guilty of   (1) dope peddling   (2) drunken
    driving   (3) industrial pollution   (4) war profiteering

28. In *1984,* the love affair between Winston and Julia conflicts with the
    government philosophy that insists that   (1) children must be brought
    up collectively   (2) complete loyalty must be professed by all citizens
    (3) all proposed marriages must be approved by Big Brother   (4) the
    individual exists only for the State

29. In "Samantha," the poet William J. Harris immortalizes his   (1)
    friend   (2) cat   (3) mother   (4) sweetheart

30. In *Wuthering Heights,* Cathy refuses to marry Heathcliff because he
    (1) continually ignores her   (2) has no social position   (3) is

above her social station   (4) is very bashful in telling her his feelings

31. In *The Red Badge of Courage,* Henry rationalizes his running away from battle on the basis that   (1) it is a law of nature to run from danger (2) many others in his regiment ran away   (3) he had received a slight wound   (4) the officers were incompetent

32. "Let America Be America Again" by Langston Hughes reemphasizes the (1) spirit of frontier independence   (2) importance of States' rights (3) need for industrial growth   (4) worth of the individual

33. In *Go Tell It on the Mountain,* James Baldwin uses the pervasive violence in his homelife to propel John, the protagonist, to the   (1) safety of school   (2) peace of church   (3) life of the streets   (4) regimentation of the army

34. In the poem by Edwin Arlington Robinson, Miniver Cheevy was a (1) medieval knight   (2) rich banker   (3) suicide   (4) wishful thinker

35. In *Future Shock,* Alvin Toffler indicates that the best preparation education can give students is to increase their   (1) scientific knowledge (2) appreciation of the humanities   (3) sense of curiosity and awareness   (4) grasp of basic skills

36. In *Death Be Not Proud,* according to Johnny Gunther's father, the event that most vividly showed Johnny's will to live was his   (1) accepting the Gerson diet   (2) taking the admission examination for Harvard University   (3) walking up the aisle in the Deerfield Church to get his diploma   (4) sending Professor Einstein his theory concerning the dimensions of the universe

37. In his essay "Symbols," S. I. Hayakawa states that the most advanced form of symbolism is   (1) language   (2) music   (3) painting (4) dance

38. In *The Member of the Wedding,* Frankie's main concern is   (1) her bridesmaid's outfit   (2) the death of John Henry   (3) escaping Bernice's restrictions   (4) living with her brother and his wife

39. A theme of the play *Antigone* that is relevant to contemporary American society is that of   (1) dissatisfaction with military policy   (2) civil disobedience   (3) conflict between the races   (4) urban turmoil

40. Which is a major theme of *The Effect of Gamma Rays on Man-in-the-Moon Marigolds?*   (1) the dangers of radiation   (2) a return to the simple life   (3) hope in the human spirit   (4) the evils of society

Chapter 9   Guide to Good Literature

PURPOSE OF THE GUIDE

This chapter describes about 600 short stories, poems, essays, novels, plays, biographies, and books of true experience commonly studied in class or recommended for outside reading. Below each title is a brief annotation summarizing the work, or emphasizing a significant or interesting detail. The purpose of these annotations is twofold: (1) to arouse interest in worthwhile and enjoyable literature of all types for your future reading, and (2) to help you refresh your memory about works you may already have read.

LITERARY WORKS

A. SHORT STORIES

Aiken, Conrad   "Silent Snow, Secret Snow"
A twelve-year-old boy gradually withdraws into an abnormal secret mental world of his own.

Andersen, Hans Christian   "The Emperor's New Clothes"
Two rogues proceed to weave clothes that they claim will be beautiful, but invisible to anyone stupid or unfit for his office.

Benét, Stephen Vincent   "By the Waters of Babylon"
A visitor from a future, simple civilization visits the deserted ruins of a large Eastern city and finds evidence that its inhabitants were men, not gods.

                              "The Devil and Daniel Webster"
Webster's eloquent pleading saves Jabez Stone's soul from the Devil.

Bennett, Arnold   "The Silent Brothers"
After a quarrel over a girl, two brothers speak neither to each other nor to the girl for ten years.

Bradbury, Ray   "The Flying Machine"
The emperor has the inventor of a primitive airplane executed, fearing its potential for evil.

Buck, Pearl S.   "The Frill"
A colonial officer's wife unashamedly exploits her Chinese tailor.

Bunner, Henry C.   "Zenobia's Infidelity"
An elephant becomes enamored of a physician and pursues him.

Burrage, A. M.   "The Waxwork"
A journalist spends the night in the Murderers' Den of a wax museum to write a story.

Cather, Willa   "Paul's Case"
At a hearing before his principal and teachers, Paul is unable to explain his poor behavior and attitude in class.

Cheever, John   "The Enormous Radio"
The peculiar radio of a couple in a fashionable Manhattan apartment brings in conversation from other tenants in the building, dispelling illusions they have held about their neighbors.

Chekhov, Anton   "The Bet"
An old banker wagers two million that a young lawyer cannot endure prison confinement for fifteen years.

                                              "A Slander"
Akhineyev's attempts to head off a personal scandal backfire amusingly.

Chesnutt, Charles Waddell   "The Wife of His Youth"
After twenty-five years Sam is reunited with 'Liza Jane, who had been his wife before the Emancipation on a Missouri plantation.

Chesterton, Gilbert K.   "The Invisible Man"
Father Brown apprehends a murderer who escapes everybody else's notice because he is so ordinary.

Collins, Wilkie   "A Terribly Strange Bed"
An Englishman who has a fabulous streak of luck at a Parisian gambling establishment is persuaded to sleep there for the night.

Connell, Richard   "The Most Dangerous Game"
On his private island, Zaroff amuses himself by hunting the most intelligent animal, man.

Conrad, Joseph   "The Heart of Darkness"
Mr. Kurtz, a Belgian, works to educate the natives and to obtain ivory in the heart of the Congo.

"The Lagoon"
Arsat, escaping with his sweetheart, fails to come to the aid of his brother, who is covering the lovers' flight.

Crane, Stephen   "The Open Boat"
In sight of shore, four shipwreck survivors must head for the open sea to avoid death in the raging surf.

Dahl, Roald   "Poison"
Harry Pope imagines that a poisonous snake is asleep on his stomach and may bite him.

Daly, Maureen   "Sixteen"
Girl meets boy at skating rink. He walks her home and promises to call. After a few days she realizes he never will.

Daudet, Alphonse   "The Last Class"
Children in an Alsatian village about to be ceded to Germany listen attentively to their last lesson in French.

"The Siege of Berlin"
As the Prussians close in on Paris, a young lady alters the news from the front, for the morale of her ailing, aged grandfather.

Dickens, Charles   "A Christmas Carol"
Miserly old Ebenezer Scrooge sees the ghost of his late partner Jacob
Marley.

Doyle, Arthur Conan   "The Adventure of the Three Garridebs"
A visitor with the odd name of John Garrideb arouses the suspicions of
Sherlock Holmes.

                                           "The Redheaded League"
A beneficiary of the Redheaded League, on hearing of its dissolution,
asks Sherlock Holmes to investigate.

                               "The Adventure of the Speckled Band"
Dr. Grimesby Roylott falls victim to the deadly snake with which he had
intended to kill his stepdaughter.

Dreiser, Theodore   "The Lost Phoebe"
Crazed by loneliness after his wife Phoebe dies, old Henry imagines she
has left him because of a quarrel, and he goes looking for her.

Edmonds, Walter   "The Death of Red Peril"
The crowd is big and the wagers are high at a race between two cater-
pillars, the Horned Demon and Red Peril.

Faulkner, William   "The Bear"
The boy can't shoot at Old Ben, the bear, in their first encounter because
he doesn't have his gun.

                                                      "Two Soldiers"
A nine-year-old tells how he tried to enlist in the U.S. Army to be with
his brother Pete.

Fessier, Michael   "That's What Happened to Me"
To compensate for disappointments and failures, "Bottles" creates an
imaginary world in which he is the hero.

Freeman, Mary E. Wilkins   "A Village Singer"
Candace Whitcomb, the leading soprano in the choir, is dismissed after
forty years of service and replaced by Alma Way.

Galsworthy, John   "The Pack"
People as individuals tend to be kind and considerate, but in groups
they sometimes lose their sense of decency.

"Quality"

The Gessler Brothers were excellent bootmakers, but they took too much time and they did not advertise.

Gogol, Nikolai   "The Overcoat"

This sad tale of an obscure clerk whose overcoat is stolen provides an insight into Russian society of the 19th century.

Hale, Edward Everett   "The Man Without a Country"

In a moment of anger, Philip Nolan expresses a wish that he may never see the United States again.

Hardy, Thomas   "The Three Strangers"

A hangman, en route to his assignment, sings and drinks with a companion who, ironically, is his intended victim.

Harrison, Henry Sydnor   "Miss Hinch"

Miss Hinch, a fugitive from justice, disguises herself as a clergyman.

Harte, Bret   "The Luck of Roaring Camp"

The birth of a baby alters the manners, habits, and spiritual outlook of a rough-and-ready California mining town.

"The Outcasts of Poker Flat"

Banished from Poker Flat, a group of objectionable characters head for Sandy Bar but are caught in a blizzard.

Hawthorne, Nathaniel   "The Ambitious Guest"

A young man stops at a mountainside house and falls in love with the host's daughter, but all are destroyed by a sudden landslide.

"Dr. Heidegger's Experiment"

The experiment shows that, if given a chance to relive their lives, people would commit the same mistakes.

"The Minister's Black Veil"

The black veil Reverend Hooper insists on wearing, despite the pleas of his congregation, is a symbol of the secret sin that we try to conceal—even from ourselves—and that separates us from others.

Hemingway, Ernest   "The Killers"

The occupants of Henry's lunchroom cower as two killers enter and wait for their intended victim to arrive.

"The Short Happy Life of Francis Macomber"
Macomber and his wife are involved in a hunting accident during their African safari.

Henry, O.   "The Gift of the Magi"
Della sells her long hair to buy Jim a watch chain for Christmas, but he has just sold his watch to buy a set of combs for her long hair.

"The Ransom of Red Chief"
Two desperadoes pay a father to take back the mischievous redheaded son they have kidnapped, when he makes life miserable for them.

"The Whirligig of Life"
This humorous tale of marital discord and reconciliation is set in the Cumberland Mountains.

Hughes, Langston   "One Friday Morning"
Denied a prize because of her black color, a talented art student resolves to work hard for the American ideal of "liberty and justice for all."

"Duty Is Not Snooty"
Simple, a philosopher-humorist, explains what would happen if whites had to travel as blacks on just one vacation.

Irving, Washington   "The Devil and Tom Walker"
Tom Walker is not unduly concerned when the Devil makes off with his nagging wife.

Jackson, Margaret Weymouth   "The Stepmother"
As Arthur is given the sportsmanship award at an annual ceremony, he bestows it on his stepmother to show his affection.

Jackson, Shirley   "The Lottery"
In a certain village, every inhabitant participates in an annual lottery. The winner is immediately stoned to death by the other villagers.

Jacobs, William W.   "Keeping Up Appearances"
The appearance of Silas's ghost scares Bill off drink and nearly impoverishes Bill's wife.

"The Monkey's Paw"
A mummified monkey's paw has the power to grant three different persons three wishes each.

Joyce, James   "Eveline"
About to elope with a sailor to Argentina, Eveline suddenly decides to remain with her father in Dublin.

"Araby"
A boy looks with high anticipation to his visit to a bazaar, but his experiences there greatly disillusion him.

Kipling, Rudyard   "Moti Guj, Mutineer"
Moti Guj, the Pearl Elephant, mutinies when his driver Deesa fails to return from vacation on time.

Knight, Eric   "All Yankees Are Liars"
The influence of American movies causes a visitor to be disbelieved when he tells the truth about America in Yorkshire, England.

"Cockles for Tea"
A Yorkshireman revisiting his native village is considered foolish until he bests the villagers in a couple of wagers.

Langdon, John   "The Blue Serge Suit"
Unable to afford a new one, Neal wears Grandpop's blue serge suit to his high school graduation exercises.

Lardner, Ring   "Haircut"
As he gives a newcomer a haircut, a talkative village barber relates an exciting local episode.

"I Can't Breathe"
This is a series of entries from the diary of a teenager who cannot decide which of her boyfriends she prefers.

Lawrence, D. H.   "The Rocking-Horse Winner"
Paul, a child in a house beset with anxiety over money, is able to predict the winners of horse races by wildly riding his wooden rocking horse.

Lederer and Burdick   *The Ugly American*
This collection of stories is based on the successes and failures of United States citizens abroad.

Lewis, Sinclair   "Young Man Axelbrod"
At 65, Knute Axelbrod, a retired Midwest farmer, passes the entrance examinations and is admitted to Yale.

London, Jack   "A Piece of Steak"
  Aging Tom King, an impoverished ex-champion, loses a critical bout to
  a less experienced but younger pugilist.

                                                "To Build a Fire"
  A newcomer is warned by an old-timer not to travel alone in the Klondike
  when the temperature reaches 50° below zero, but he disregards the
  warning.

Mansfield, Katharine   ·   "A Cup of Tea"
  Rosemary Fell's generosity to a starving girl is not exactly an act of
  charity.

                                                "Bliss"
  A young wife's illusion of bliss is shattered when she accidentally learns
  that her prized friend is her rival.

                                                "Her First Ball"
  Leila's first dancing partner, an older man, spoils her evening with his
  depressing remarks about youth's brevity.

                                                "Miss Brill"
  Miss Brill's self-image is shattered when she realizes that her old fur
  piece is a symbol of how others regard her.

Maugham, W. Somerset   "The Outstation"
  Washburton dresses formally for dinner every night in his remote Borneo
  outpost, as if he were in fashionable London.

                                                "The Verger"
  Mr. Foreman, dismissed for illiteracy from his post as verger in a London
  church, goes into business and makes a fortune.

Maupassant, Guy de   "The Little Cask"
  This masterful portrayal of greed pits a crafty French innkeeper against
  an old woman who rivals him in avarice.

                                                "The Necklace"
  A pretty young Frenchwoman's vanity leads to a life of altogether needless drudgery for herself and her spouse.

                                                "A Piece of String"
  "Just for a piece of string," Hauchecorne, victim of a vengeful personal
  enemy, suffers derangement and premature death.

Melville, Herman   "Bartleby the Scrivener"
    Asked to do some simple proofreading, Bartleby startles his employer
    with the reply "I would prefer not to."

O'Flaherty, Liam   "The Sniper"
    In a gun battle from Dublin rooftops, a Republican kills a Free-Stater
    who turns out to be his own brother.

Patterson, Norma   "The Whoffing Gods"
    The "whoffing gods" are road construction machines that come to repave
    the roadway in front of Mrs. Battle's orphanage.

Poe, Edgar Allan   "The Cask of Amontillado"
    Insulted by Fortunato, Montresor lures him into an underground crypt
    where he exacts revenge.

                                                          "The Gold Bug"
    The solution of a coded message leads William Le Grand to a fortune
    buried by Captain Kidd.

                                            "The Masque of the Red Death"
    Prince Prospero and a thousand lords and ladies retire to a castle to
    avoid the plague, but the "Red Death" overtakes them.

                                            "The Murders in the Rue Morgue"
    C. Auguste Dupin, an amazing detective, solves a murder mystery that
    baffles the Paris police.

                                                    "The Purloined Letter"
    The Prefect of the Paris police calls on Dupin for assistance in recover-
    ing a letter stolen from the royal apartments.

                                                    "The Tell-Tale Heart"
    A deranged murderer mistakes the ticking of a watch, which he had not
    removed from the corpse, for the beating of the victim's heart.

Porter, Katherine Anne   "Noon Wine"
    A stranger, by his years of faithful labor, brings prosperity to a Texas
    farm until he is found to be an escaped maniac.

Richter, Conrad   "Early Marriage"
    A girl of seventeen and her younger brother leave their father's trading
    post in a wagon and travel 170 miles to meet her bridegroom.

Runyon, Damon   "A Piece of Pie"
Miss Violette Shumberger, coached by Nicely-Nicely, defeats Joel Duffle
in an eating contest.

Saki (H. H. Munro)   "The Lumber-Room"
The central character is a witty, mischievous boy named Nicholas.

                                                "The Open Window"
A witty, mischievous young girl devises an ingenious scheme to get rid
of a bore.

                                                "The Storyteller"
Three children reject their aunt as a storyteller, but listen to a stranger's
tale about a little girl who was "horribly good."

Salinger, J. D.   "For Esmé—With Love and Squalor"
An American soldier reminisces about a child who befriended him in wartime London just before the Normandy invasion.

Saroyan, William   "Locomotive 38, the Ojibway"
When his donkey is killed in an accident, a wealthy American Indian by
the name of Locomotive 38 buys an expensive limousine.

Steele, Wilbur D.   "Footfalls"
Blind Boaz wreaks vengeance on his son's murderer after recognizing
him by his footfall.

Steinbeck, John   "Flight"
After killing a man who had called him insulting names, Pepé tries to
hide out in the mountains.

                                        "The Leader of the People"
Grandfather, a former wagon-train leader, bores everyone except his
grandson with the telling and retelling of his exploits.

Stevenson, Robert Louis   "The Bottle Imp"
Each of the successive owners of a magic bottle must sell it for less than
he paid, or burn in hell forever.

                                                          "Markheim"
Markheim enters a shop, ostensibly to buy a Christmas gift for his fiancée,
and commits a dreadful crime.

"The Sire de Maletroit's Door"
The Sire's cunning and treacherous nature explains why he treats his niece so strangely when he suspects she is in love.

Stockton, Frank   "The Lady or the Tiger?"
For daring to fall in love with the King's daughter, a youth is condemned to open one of two fateful doors.

"The Remarkable Wreck of the *Thomas Hyke*"
An unusual construction feature prevents the *Thomas Hyke* from sinking.

Stuart, Jesse   "Split Cherry Tree"
After Dave is given detention, his father, armed with a gun, calls on the teacher. The scene is the Kentucky backcountry.

Thomas, Dorothy   "The Car"
Mrs. Barton teaches her family a lesson when each of them insists on having the family car for Sunday.

Thurber, James   "The Secret Life of Walter Mitty"
Mitty meekly follows his domineering wife's orders, but in his daydreams he is the admired hero of many perilous adventures.

Tolstoi, Leo   "God Sees the Truth, but Waits"
Aksënov, falsely accused of murder, is condemned to Siberia where, years later, he meets the real murderer.

Twain, Mark   "The Celebrated Jumping Frog of Calaveras County"
Jim Smiley lays a wager on the jumping ability of his frog Dan'l Webster.

Welty, Eudora   "A Worn Path"
The path old Phoenix Jackson traverses into Natchez with the aid of her cane at Christmastime, like life itself, is thorny, difficult, and occasionally somewhat easier.

West, Jessamyn   "The Pacing Goose"
A hired farmhand, out of regard for his employer's wife, fails to "count correctly."

Williams, Ben Ames   "They Grind Exceeding Small"
A ruthless, coldblooded individual learns the consequences of his meanness when the vengeful gods strike at his only son.

Wood, Frances Gilchrist   "Turkey Red"
   Turkey-red calico curtains symbolize the courage of the pioneers in the
   desolate Dakota Territory in the days before the railroad.

Vonnegut, Kurt, Jr.   "Report on the Barnhouse Effect"
   By "dynamopsychism" (force of mind), Professor Barnhouse is able to
   roll ten consecutive sevens in dice.

Yezierska, Anzia   "Children of Loneliness"
   Just back from college, a daughter objects to the table manners of her
   immigrant parents.

B. POEMS

Anonymous   *Beowulf**
   The monster Grendel ravages the mead hall of Hrothgar, King of the
   Danes, until Beowulf slays it.

                                     "Robin Hood and Little John"
   John Little, seven feet tall, is rechristened Little John and initiated into
   Robin Hood's band.

                                              "Sir Patrick Spens"
   Sir Patrick, on orders of the King, sails at a bad time of year and is lost
   at sea with all his men.

Auden, W. H.   "The Unknown Citizen"
   The "average" modern man has lost his individuality because his ideas,
   attitudes, and habits are steeped in conformity.

Benét, Stephen Vincent   *John Brown's Body*
   Using both historical and fictional characters, the poet recreates the fighting and suffering of the Civil War.

                                     "The Mountain Whippoorwill"
   Poor, unknown Hill-Billy Jim wins out over the most famous and the
   greatest in a fiddlers' contest at a Georgia county fair.

Benét, William Rose   "Jesse James"
   This tall tale celebrates the exploits of an outlaw who has become an
   American folk hero.

---

* In this section and in those that follow, italics are used for the titles of full-length
works.

Blake, William   "The Tiger"
In describing the tiger, who like the lamb is a creature of God, Blake
uses images connected principally with fire.

Brooke, Rupert   "The Soldier"
A World War I soldier, anticipating death on the battlefield, expresses
love for his native England.

Brooks, Gwendolyn   "We Real Cool"
Some think "they real cool" because "they quit school." The poet does
not agree.

Browning, Robert   "My Last Duchess"
A Renaissance duke, about to remarry, reveals his character as he reminisces about his last duchess.

                                              "Pippa Passes"
"God's in his heaven," writes Browning, optimistically. "All's right with
the world!"

                                            "Rabbi Ben Ezra"
The poem celebrates old age. God planned a whole of which youth is
but half; old age, still to come, is "the best."

Bryant, William Cullen   "Thanatopsis"
The poet's view of death, based on Nature's teachings, is comforting and
inspiring.

                                            "To a Waterfowl"
The same Power that guides the waterfowl in his migratory flight will
guide the poet through life.

Burns, Robert   "Flow Gently, Sweet Afton"
"My Mary's asleep by thy murmuring stream,
Flow gently, Sweet Afton, disturb not her dream."

                                    "A Man's a Man for A' That"
The honest man, though poor, is superior to those sustained only by titles
and wealth.

                                              "To a Louse"
At church, Miss Jenny attracts notice not for her beauty and clothes, as
she supposes, but for the louse crawling on her bonnet.

"To a Mouse"
The poet commiserates with a fieldmouse that he routed from its winter quarters while plowing.

Byron, Lord   "The Prisoner of Chillon"
After being in prison for many years for his beliefs, Bonnivard loses his desire for personal liberty.

Carroll, Lewis   "The Jabberwocky"
This humorous poem contains a number of nonsense words, such as "slithy," a compound of "slimy" and "lithe."

Chaucer, Geoffrey   Prelude to *The Canterbury Tales*
Twenty-nine 14th-century pilgrims assemble at the Tabard Inn on their way to the shrine of St. Thomas à Becket at Canterbury.

Chesterton, Gilbert K.   "Lepanto"
Don John of Austria defeats the Turks in the naval battle of Lepanto.

Coleridge, Samuel Taylor   "Kubla Khan"
This unfinished poem describes the Khan's palace in Xanadu, suggests that war is impending, and then ends abruptly.

The Rime of the Ancient Mariner
The Mariner senselessly shoots the albatross with his crossbow and does penance for the rest of his life.

Crane, Stephen   "I Saw a Man"
Those who fanatically persist in a folly will not trust anyone who shows them they are wrong.

Cullen, Countee   "From the Dark Tower"
The poet asserts that black people "were not made eternally to weep" and that black, too, is beautiful.

"Incident"
A racial epithet spoils a visit to Baltimore for an eight-year-old boy.

cummings, e.e.   "anyone lived in a pretty how town"
This poem describes a town where
   "Women and men (both little and small)
   cared for anyone not at all"

"in Just-"
The world is "mud-luscious" and "puddle-wonderful" in "Just-spring."

Dickey, James   "The Lifeguard"
A lifeguard agonizes over his failure to perform the miracle expected of him—to save a child from drowning.

Dickinson, Emily   "A Book"
Books take us inexpensively to distant lands and ages.

"Because I Could Not Stop for Death"
The poet depicts Death as a courtly gentleman in a carriage who calls to take her out for a drive.

"Chartless"
Though she has never spoken with God or visited Heaven, the poet is absolutely certain that God and Heaven exist.

"A Word"
Once a word is said, it is dead, some say. Not so, says the poet: it has just begun to live.

Donne, John   "Death Be Not Proud"
"One short sleep past, we wake eternally,
And Death shall be no more; Death, thou shalt die!"

Dunning, Stephen (ed.)   *Mad, Sad, and Glad*
Imaginative poems by teenagers who won *Scholastic* Writing Awards.

Eberhart, Richard   "The Groundhog"
The speaker periodically revisits a field where he saw a groundhog lying dead. After three years, there is no trace of the groundhog.

Eliot, T.S.   "The Hollow Men"
The poet complains of the spiritual paralysis and sterility of twentieth-century man, likening him to a scarecrow.

Frost, Robert   "The Death of the Hired Man"
An unreliable hired man returns in his final illness to a farm couple.

"Mending Wall"
The annual practice of repairing the fence between them brings together two New England neighbors of different temperaments.

"Out, Out—"
A Vermont boy is fatally injured by a buzz saw. The title is an allusion to the "Out, out, brief candle" speech in Shakespeare's *Macbeth*.

"The Road Not Taken"
At the crossroads, the poet takes the lonelier road, but regretfully.

"Stopping by Woods on a Snowy Evening"
The conflict in this poetic masterpiece is between man's enjoyment of beauty and his responsibility to others.

"The Tuft of Flowers"
Turning mown grass, the poet sees some flowers the mower had spared. The poet, too, appreciates their beauty.

Gilbert, William S.   "The Yarn of the *Nancy Bell*"
In this tall tale of cannibalism, the cook is also the captain, mate, bo'sun, midshipmite, and crew of the captain's gig.

Gray, Thomas   "Elegy Written in a Country Churchyard"
Among those at rest in the churchyard are some who might have risen to greatness, but they never had the opportunity.

"Ode on a Distant Prospect of Eton College"
The ode ends ". . . where ignorance is bliss, / 'Tis folly to be wise."

Guiterman, Arthur   "Dorlan's Home-Walk"
Safe at first on a close play, Dorlan walks to second, third, and home, while the opposing team feuds with the umpire.

Hardy, Thomas   "The Man He Killed"
An ex-soldier is haunted by the memory of a man he killed and with whom he might have been friends if there had been no war.

Hay, John   "Jim Bludso of the *Prairie Belle*"
The engineer of a burning Mississippi River steamboat saves the passengers and crew at the cost of his life.

Henley, William E.   "Invictus"
Stoically facing extreme hardship, the poet thanks "whatever gods may be" for his "unconquerable soul."

Herrick, Robert   "To the Virgins, to Make Much of Time"
Youth, says the poet, is the best age and should not be wasted, as life is
short.

Holmes, Oliver Wendell   "The Ballad of the Oysterman"
In this humorous tale, a fisherman reacts violently when he learns that
an oysterman is wooing his daughter.

Homer   *The Iliad*
Agamemnon leads the Greeks against Troy to recover the abducted Helen,
wife of his brother Menelaus.

                                                        The Odyssey
After the Trojan War, Odysseus suffers and wanders for ten years on his
way home to his native Ithaca.

Hood, Thomas   "The Song of the Shirt"
The poet protests the long monotonous hours of toil in a shirt factory
where women sew amid poverty, hunger, and dirt.

Housman, A. E.   "Reveillé"
Precious mornings and days must not be spent in slumber. ". . . when
the journey's over / There'll be time enough to sleep."

                                                    "Eight O'Clock"
A prisoner about to be hanged hears the bell in the steeple toll away
the last seconds of life.

                                        "To an Athlete Dying Young"
The young athlete is complimented on his early departure from a world
where fame is so short-lived.

                                        "When I Was One-and-Twenty"
A wise man cautions a youth not to fall in love, but he pays no attention.

Hughes, Langston   "Brass Spittoons"
A black man does menial, degrading work to be able to buy shoes for
the baby, pay rent, and go to church on Sunday.

                                        "The Negro Speaks of Rivers"
A Negro speaks of rivers associated with his heritage: the Euphrates,
the Congo, the Nile, and the Mississippi.

Hunt, Leigh   "Abou Ben Adhem"
Because he loves his fellow men, Abou ranks first in the favor of the Almighty.

Johnson, James Weldon   "The Creation"
God created the world because he was desirous of companionship: "I'm lonely— / I'll make me a world."

Keats, John   "Ode to Autumn"
Autumn, "season of mists and mellow fruitfulness," is a time of harvest and great natural beauty.

"Ode on a Grecian Urn"
To Keats, truth and beauty are inseparable: "Beauty is truth, truth beauty."

"On First Looking Into Chapman's Homer"
Keats is enthusiastic about Chapman's translation of Homer, which introduces him into a rich new world of literature.

Kipling, Rudyard   "Boots"
After weeks of marching up and down Africa, a British infantryman cannot endure the sight of boots.

"Danny Deever"
The whole regiment is turned out to witness the hanging of Danny Deever, who has shot a sleeping comrade.

"Gunga Din"
A native water carrier tends the wounded under fire and earns the tribute "You're a better man than I am, Gunga Din!"

Lieberman, Elias   "I Am an American"
An immigrant boy whose ancestors were persecuted in Russia pledges allegiance to his adopted land.

Longfellow, Henry Wadsworth   *Evangeline*
When the people of Acadia are expelled from their homes on King George II's orders, Evangeline is separated from her betrothed.

Lovelace, Richard   "To Althea, From Prison"
"Stone walls do not a prison make,
Nor iron bars a cage."

"To Lucasta, on Going to the Wars"
"I could not love thee, Dear, so much
Lov'd I not Honour more."

Lowell, Amy   "Patterns"
A lady is notified by special messenger that her fiancé has died in action
in Flanders.

Lowell, James Russell   "The Vision of Sir Launfal"
As he sets out in quest of the Holy Grail, Sir Launfal finds a leper
crouched at the gate.

Markham, Edwin   "The Man With the Hoe"
Markham warns the "masters, lords and rulers" that someday the laborers
they have exploited will rise up against them.

Masefield, John   "Cargoes"
By depicting three ships, each of a different epoch, Masefield catches
the spirit of three different civilizations.

"A Consecration"
Masefield dedicates himself to writing about the nameless, ordinary people who do the work and fight the battles.

"Sea-Fever"
A sailor feels an irrepressible longing to return to the sea, to "the flung
spray and the blown spume and the seagulls crying."

Masters, Edgar Lee   "Anne Rutledge"
The alleged sweetheart of young Abe Lincoln speaks from her tomb
about her love.

"Lucinda Matlock"
The departed Lucinda, who lived a difficult but useful life, reproaches
the younger generation for being too soft.

Millay, Edna St. Vincent   "God's World"
Autumn's winds, mists, woods, and skies make the poet exclaim: "O
world, I cannot hold thee close enough!"

"Lament"
Left alone to fight poverty and illness on the death of her husband, a
mother laments to her little ones: "Life must go on; / I forget just why."

"Renascence"
Anguished by the suffering in the world, the poet craves death. Then, hearing the raindrops on her tomb, she longs to live again.

Milton, John   *Paradise Lost*
The true cause of man's loss of Paradise is Satan, who had been expelled from Heaven for revolting against God.

Nash, Ogden   "The Purist"
Told his bride had just been eaten by an alligator, the purist corrected his informant with a smile. "You mean," he said, "a crocodile."

Noyes, Alfred   "The Highwayman"
Bess, the landlord's daughter, dies trying to save her lover, the highwayman, from King George's men.

Parker, Dorothy   "One Perfect Rose"
A sentimental lover sends "one perfect rose," but his materialistic sweetheart wonders why no one has sent her yet "one perfect limousine."

Poe, Edgar Allan   "Annabel Lee"
Upon the death of the beautiful Annabel, the poet is consoled by his conviction that their souls can never be separated.

"The Bells"
By its onomatopoeia, the poem enables the reader to hear sleigh bells, wedding bells, "alarum" bells, etc.

"The Raven"
The sleepy poet, mourning his lost Lenore, hears a mysterious tapping on his window at midnight.

Robinson, Edwin Arlington   "The House on the Hill"
Nobody knows about the people who once lived in the abandoned house. "They are all gone away."

"Miniver Cheevy"
Miniver, an alcoholic, blames his misfortunes on Fate rather than himself.

"Mr. Flood's Party"
Eben Flood climbs a hill in the moonlight, has a few drinks, sings "Auld Lang Syne," and recalls the many friends he once had in the town below.

"Richard Cory"
Richard Cory apparently had everything. He was envied. Yet one night he put a bullet through his head.

Roethke, Theodore   "Night Journey"
As his train heads west, the poet, instead of sleeping, stares into the night to see the land he loves.

Sandburg, Carl   "Chicago"
Freely conceding Chicago's wickedness and crime, the poet nevertheless admires its youth, power, and industry.

"Clean Curtains"
New tenants in a slum put up clean curtains. Soon the dust from factories and trucks forces them to take down the curtains.

"Four Preludes on Playthings of the Wind"
Time has reduced to a ruin a proud city that once boasted: "We are the greatest city . . . nothing like us ever was."

"Grass"
The grass "covers all" so well that man quickly forgets how terrible war is.

Sassoon, Siegfried   "Dreamers"
The "dreamers," World War I soldiers in the trenches, hopelessly long for the pleasures and comforts of home as the firing begins.

Scott, Walter   "Lochinvar"
Young Lochinvar interrupts a wedding at Netherby Hall to rescue his sweetheart from an unfortunate marriage.

Seeger, Alan   "I Have a Rendezvous With Death"
A World War I soldier prophetically senses that when spring returns, and the world is beautiful again, he will be killed.

Service, Robert W.   "The Cremation of Sam McGee"
This tall tale of the Arctic features two prospectors in the Klondike Gold Rush. One of them is from warm Tennessee.

Shakespeare, William   "The Marriage of True Minds"
True love never alters, regardless of circumstances or the passing of time.

"When in Disgrace"
Despite his lack of worldly success, the poet finds such solace in his love that he would not change places with a king.

Shapiro, Karl   "Auto Wreck"
A witness to a highway accident reflects on the senseless slaughter caused by the automobile.

Shelley, Percy Bysshe   "Ozymandias"
All that remains of the empire of boastful Ozymandias is the wreck of his statue sunk in the desert sands.

Spender, Stephen   "The Express"
Nature cannot match the music of the steam locomotive as it passes through metropolis and countryside to its mysterious destination.

Teasdale, Sara   "Barter"
                    "Life has loveliness to sell . . .
                    Spend all you have for loveliness
                    . . . and never count the cost."

Tennyson, Alfred Lord   "The Charge of the Light Brigade"
Tennyson memorializes the gallant but futile charge by the six hundred men of the Light Brigade at Balaclava in the Crimean War.

"Crossing the Bar"
Because of his unshakable confidence in God, death will be no sad occasion for the poet.

"The Lady of Shalott"
The Lady of Shalott is under a curse that compels her to learn of the world in her mirror rather than by direct observation.

"Ulysses"
After many years of toil and wandering, the restless Ulysses finds he cannot stay home, for he still hungers for new knowledge.

Thayer, Ernest L.   "Casey at the Bat"
Mudville loses the game when its batting star, the mighty Casey, strikes out.

Thompson, Francis   "The Hound of Heaven"
This spiritual autobiography tells of man's flight from God and the unrelenting pursuit of man's soul by God's love.

Whitman, Walt   "As Toilsome I Wandered Virginia's Woods"
The poet cannot forget the simple, moving inscription he encountered
on the grave of a Civil War soldier.

"I Hear America Singing"
Whitman reflects the spirit of a young, happy America to which crafts-
men, mothers, and young people contribute harmoniously.

"O Captain! My Captain!"
The captain of the ship of state (Abraham Lincoln) lies cold on the deck
at the very moment that the "fearful trip" (Civil War) is over.

"When I Heard the Learn'd Astronomer"
Bored by the astronomer's complicated charts and figures, the poet leaves
the lecture hall to gaze at the night sky and the beautiful stars.

"When Lilacs Last in the Dooryard Bloom'd"
Whitman mourns Abraham Lincoln, who died when lilacs were in bloom.

Widdemer, Margaret   "The Factories"
The poet rouses the reader's conscience against the inhumanity of child
labor in factories.

Wordsworth, William   "The Daffodils"
The daffodils afford pleasure not only when first seen, but also when
recollected in tranquillity.

"The World Is Too Much With Us"
We are so preoccupied with earning a living and spending for material
things that we overlook the beauties of nature.

"Composed Upon Westminster Bridge"
Viewed from the bridge at sunrise on September 3, 1802, the city of
London is beautiful and inspiring.

Yeats, William Butler   "The Lake Isle of Innisfree"
The speaker yearns to leave the city's "pavements gray" for Innisfree,
where he may live alone and enjoy peace and nature.

"The Wild Swans at Coole"
The wild swans that delight the poet's eyes each autumn remind him, too,
that he is growing older.

C. ESSAYS

Adamic, Louis   "The Making of Americans"
A naturalized citizen writes of the diversity and contributions of America's immigrants.

Addison, Joseph   "Sir Roger de Coverley in Church"
The amusing relationships of a country squire with his tenants and chaplain recreate a bit of 18th-century England.

Andrews, Roy Chapman   *Heart of Asia*
A noted American explorer and scientist recounts twelve true tales of the Far East.

Bacon, Francis   "Of Friendship"
". . . this communicating of a man's self to his friends . . . redoubleth joys, and cutteth griefs in halves."

                                                    "Of Adversity"
". . . for prosperity doth best discover vice, but adversity doth best discover virtue."

                                                    "Of Studies"
"Some books are to be tasted; others to be swallowed; and some few to be chewed and digested."

                                                    "Of Truth"
"There is no vice that doth so cover a man with shame as to be found false and perfidious."

Baldwin, James   *The Fire Next Time*
In a "Letter to My Nephew on the One Hundredth Anniversary of the Emancipation," Baldwin tells what it is like to be black in America.

Benchley, Robert   *Chips Off the Old Benchley*
This is a posthumous collection of humorous essays on the homeliest of topics.

                "The Tooth, the Whole Tooth, and Nothing but the Tooth"
A timid patient develops a fondness for the dentist ("a splendid fellow, really") once the filling is completed.

Benedict, Ruth   *Patterns of Culture*
An anthropologist comments on taboos and customs she found in native tribes.

Bennett, Arnold   "The Daily Miracle"
The "miracle" is our fresh supply of twenty-four hours each day, the "most precious of possessions."

Broun, Heywood   "The Fifty-First Dragon"
The case of the hapless Gawaine proves that a magic word is no substitute for genuine self-confidence.

Carson, Rachel   *The Sea Around Us*
The author presents fascinating scientific knowledge about the oceans and the earth.

Silent Spring
The topic is the potentially disastrous effects of man's indiscriminate use of insecticides.

Chesterton, Gilbert K.   "On Lying in Bed"
The essayist has a word of caution "for those who can do their work in bed (like journalists), still more for those whose work cannot be done in bed (as, for example, the professional harpooner of whales)."

"On Running After One's Hat"
A man running after his hat is not half so funny as a man running after a wife.

Cooke, Alistair   "On Discovering the United States"
An experienced traveler offers suggestions about what to see and how to go in touring the United States.

Cousins, Norman   "The First Citizens of the Atomic Age"
The citizens of Hiroshima, having regained faith in humanity, hope their suffering will avert future Hiroshimas.

Donne, John   "Meditation XVII"
"Any man's death diminishes me, because I am involved in mankind. And therefore never send to know for whom the bell tolls; it tolls for thee."

Du Bois, William E. B.   *The Souls of Black Folk*
Du Bois eloquently opposes those who think they can achieve civil and
political rights through submission and silence.

Emerson, Ralph Waldo   "Civilization"
"Hitch your wagon to a star," advises Emerson.

                                                            "Self-Reliance"
The reader is urged to be a leader, rather than a follower; to rely on his
own powers, rather than to conform.

Faulkner, William   "Nobel Prize Acceptance Speech"
The author ponders the role of a writer in a world endangered by imminent atomic destruction.

Forster, Edward M.   "Tolerance"
A famous novelist of the 20th century talks about how to rebuild a war-
torn world.

Gallico, Paul W.   *Farewell to Sport*
A sports writer reminisces about some outstanding athletes and both
the gallantry and ugliness of the sports world.

Galsworthy, John   "Holiday"
This provocative essay may make the reader regret how he has misspent
past vacations and holidays.

Hemingway, Ernest   *Death in the Afternoon*
The author is deeply fascinated with bullfighting in Spain.

Henry, Patrick   "Speech in the Virginia Convention"
Henry's concluding words—"give me liberty, or give me death"—were a
powerful appeal to rebellion.

Hersey, John   *Letter to the Alumni*
Adults can go far astray, says the author, if they generalize about college
youth.

Hubbard, Elbert   "A Message to Garcia"
Lt. Rowan's fulfillment of a dangerous mission in the Spanish-American
War is a memorable example of perseverance.

Hudson, William H.   "The Death of an Old Dog"
The idea of death has an emotional impact on an inquiring, sensitive
boy of six.

Huxley, Thomas   "A Liberal Education"
Life is a game of chess in which the world is the chessboard, the phenomena of the universe the pieces, and the laws of nature the rules of
the game.

"The Method of Scientific Investigation"
Without realizing it, people use the method of induction (reasoning
from the particular to the general) in everyday life.

Irving, Washington   *The Legends of the Alhambra*
The Alhambra is a fortress and palace built by the Moors in the 13th
century in Granada, Spain.

Jefferson, Thomas   "The Declaration of Independence"
Among man's inalienable rights are "life, liberty, and the pursuit of
happiness."

Johnston, Eric   "A Warning to Labor and Management"
In the interests of a strong America, the author appeals to labor and
management to refrain from monopolistic practices.

Keller, Helen   "Three Days to See"
A gifted blind and deaf lady explains how she would spend her time if
she could see for three days.

Kennedy, John F.   "Inaugural Address"
"Let us never negotiate out of fear. But let us never fear to negotiate."

King, Martin Luther, Jr.   *Stride Toward Freedom*
Dr. King recounts the success of nonviolent resistance in the Montgomery
bus boycott.

"I Have a Dream"
The author wants to see black and white Americans live together in
peace.

"Letter From Birmingham Jail"
In reply to fellow clergymen opposed to his methods of protesting injustice, the author recalls "Jesus Christ was an extremist for love, truth,
and goodness . . ."

Where Do We Go From Here: Chaos or Community?
In a series of essays, Dr. King discusses the logic of nonviolence as the way to achieve freedom and dignity for all men.

Lamb, Charles   "A Dissertation Upon Roast Pig"
The carelessness of Bo-bo, a lubberly shepherd boy of ancient China, leads to the discovery of a rare delicacy—roast pig.

"Dream Children: A Reverie"
A bachelor who devotes his life to caring for his invalid sister talks of the imaginary children that people his unfulfilled dreams.

"Old China"
Lamb concludes that material things are not too necessary for true happiness.

Leacock, Stephen   "A, B, and C—The Human Element in Mathematics"
Leacock pokes fun at the practice of having A come off best in math problems, while poor B and C fare much worse.

Lippmann, Walter   "Education vs. Western Civilization"
Unless it studies the traditions of the past, each generation is doomed to repeat the errors of its predecessors.

"The Rivalry of Nations"
Lippmann investigates the problem of why we keep on winning the wars but losing the peace.

Miller, Clyde R.   "How to Detect and Analyze Propaganda"
Miller explains seven of the techniques commonly employed by the propagandist.

Morley, Christopher   "Ingo"
The essayist expresses his wartime concern for a lad he had once befriended in a now enemy country.

"On Doors"
The opening and closing of doors are associated with matters of the greatest importance in a person's life.

"On Unanswering Letters"
According to Morley, there is something queer about people who answer letters the same day they receive them.

"What Men Live By"
The art of conversation requires a setting aside of pet prejudices and a willingness to face truth.

Packard, Vance O.   *The Hidden Persuaders*
Advertising uses psychological research to make people buy certain products and to influence their voting for political candidates.

The Status Seekers
Packard discusses the efforts of certain groups to achieve social status in contemporary American life.

Sandburg, Carl   "A Lincoln Preface"
The essay sums up Lincoln's statesmanship and humanity and reads almost like a poem.

Steffens, Lincoln   "I Get a Colt to Break In"
Young Steffens teaches his colt to walk over his sisters, but his father doesn't like the idea.

Steinbeck, John   *Travels With Charley*
With his French poodle Charley, Steinbeck tours 34 states in a pickup truck to learn about the American people.

Stevenson, Robert Louis   "An Apology for Idlers"
Stevenson wittily attacks the error of "all work and no play" and emphasizes the "duty of being happy."

Strunsky, Simeon   "Romance"
One day Wesley breaks his routine of going home on the 5:15 downtown subway and takes the uptown train instead.

Struther, Jan   "One of the Best"
The author satirizes the tendency toward the use of superlatives in describing mediocre people.

Sullivan, Frank   "A Garland of Ibids for Van Wyck Brooks"
Sullivan pokes fun at the overuse of footnotes and, incidentally, at some distinguished New Englanders.

Swift, Jonathan   "A Modest Proposal"
With savage satire, Swift dramatizes the problem of starvation in Ireland by "proposing" that babies be eaten.

Thoreau, Henry D.   "Civil Disobedience"
The individual, according to Thoreau, should non-violently resist government policy that is contrary to his principles.

"Where I Lived and What I Lived For"
Thoreau explains why he went to live by himself in a cabin he had built
in the woods.

Thruelson and Kobler   *Adventures of the Mind*
These essays from the *Saturday Evening Post* deal with science, philosophy, the arts, government, economics, etc.

Thurber, James   "The Macbeth Murder Mystery"
A lady who reads detective stories offers an unusual opinion as to the
identity of the third murderer in *Macbeth*.

"The Night the Bed Fell"
Thurber satirizes unreasonable fears, such as those of his eccentric Aunt
Gracie Shoaf.

Tomlinson, H. M.   *The Sea and the Jungle*
The voyage began in Wales and took the author 2000 miles up the
Amazon River into the Brazilian jungle.

Tunis, John R.   "The Great Sports Myth"
Tunis attacks organized sports and comes out for genuine amateur sports.

Twain, Mark   "Fenimore Cooper's Literary Offenses"
Twain satirizes Cooper's novel *The Deerslayer*, which he claims violates
18 of the 19 rules of literary art.

"Personal Recollections of Joan of Arc"
Joan's triumph despite overwhelming odds makes her "the most extraordinary person the human race has ever produced."

White, William Allen   "Mary White"
A father writes an editorial on his talented sixteen-year-old daughter
killed in a freak riding accident.

Woolf, Virginia   "How Should One Read a Book?"
"The only advice, indeed, that one person can give another about reading
is to take no advice, to follow your own instincts . . ."

Wylie, Philip   "Science Has Spoiled My Supper"
   Marketers have developed foods that are attractive, easy to ship, and
   resistant to spoilage, but also flavorless.

D. NOVELS

Austen, Jane   *Pride and Prejudice*
   A mother's remarks and a younger sister's behavior almost ruin the marriage prospects of two fine girls.

Baldwin, James   *Go Tell It on the Mountain*
   John Grimes, a fourteen-year-old Harlem youth, is troubled by many
   conflicts.

Bellamy, Edward   *Looking Backward*
   In the year 2000, the problems of poverty, war, ignorance, and equality
   have been solved. An ideal society exists.

Boulle, Pierre   *The Bridge Over the River Kwai*
   Colonel Nicholson typifies the military officer who rigidly and unthinkingly adheres to outworn rules.

Brontë, Charlotte   *Jane Eyre*
   The day she is supposed to marry Edward Rochester, Jane learns he has
   an insane wife secluded at Thornfield Hall.

Brontë, Emily   *Wuthering Heights*
   The thwarted love of Heathcliff, a gypsy orphan, for Catherine, his benefactor's daughter, entails terrible consequences.

Buck, Pearl   *The Good Earth*
   Wang Lung and his wife O-lan prosper when they cultivate the soil, but
   their sons do not prize the good earth.

                                                          The Sons
   In this sequel to *The Good Earth,* Wang Lung's sons sell the land and
   seek their fortunes in other endeavors.

Bulwer-Lytton, Edward   *The Last Days of Pompeii*
   A blind flower girl guides two lovers to safety as Vesuvius destroys the
   city of Pompeii in 79 A.D.

Camus, Albert   *The Stranger*
Meursault, a young Algiers resident not prone to violence, kills a man
who he thinks is about to attack him.

Cather, Willa   *My Ántonia*
An immigrant girl and her family endure many hardships as pioneer
settlers in Nebraska.

Death Comes for the Archbishop
Fathers Latour and Vaillant struggle to build a cathedral in the wilderness of the Southwest.

A Lost Lady
Neil, who has a high regard for Mrs. Forrester, is hurt by her association
with people he does not respect.

Clark, Walter Van Tilburg   *The Ox-Bow Incident*
Three men suspected of cattle rustling are hanged by a lawless posse.
The men are innocent.

Conrad, Joseph   *Lord Jim*
Jim devotes his life to atoning for one mistake: in a moment of panic,
he had abandoned a seemingly doomed ship.

Crane, Stephen   *The Red Badge of Courage*
After joining the Union Army, Henry Fleming worries about how he will
behave in his first battle.

Crichton, Michael   *The Andromeda Strain*
A frightening situation develops when deadly extraterrestrial bacteria
invade man's environment.

Cronin, A. J.   *Beyond This Place*
An innocent man rots in jail as a convicted murderer until his son, grown
to manhood, secures his release.

Dickens, Charles   *Great Expectations*
Pip learns that his secret benefactor is Magwitch, an escaped prisoner
he had once aided.

David Copperfield
David grew up in an environment that included a harsh stepfather (Mr.
Murdstone) and a cruel schoolmaster (Mr. Creakle).

Oliver Twist
Oliver, an orphan, creates a sensation in the workhouse by having the audacity to ask for a second helping of porridge.

Pickwick Papers
Mr. Pickwick and his traveling companions (Mr. Tupman, Mr. Winkle, Mr. Snodgrass, and Sam Weller) have many amusing adventures.

A Tale of Two Cities
Sydney Carton goes to the guillotine for the sake of a woman he had loved but could not hope to win.

Dostoevski, Fyodor   *The Brothers Karamazov*
Dmitri is torn between his obligations to his fiancée Katerina and his passion for Grushenka.

Crime and Punishment
Driven nearly insane by poverty, Raskolnikov murders an elderly lady pawnbroker.

Douglas, Lloyd   *The Robe*
A young Roman soldier wins possession of Christ's robe after the crucifixion.

Dumas, Alexandre   *The Count of Monte Cristo*
Edmond Dantes yearns for revenge against four men responsible for his long and unjust imprisonment.

Du Maurier, Daphne   *Rebecca*
The second Mrs. de Winter eventually solves the mystery of her late predecessor, the beautiful Rebecca de Winter.

Eliot, George   *Adam Bede*
An intelligent young English carpenter eventually recovers from his love for a silly, vain beauty.

Silas Marner
Accused of a crime his best friend had committed, Silas becomes a social outcast.

Ellison, Ralph   *Invisible Man*
An unnamed black man struggles to find his true self.

Fast, Howard   *April Morning*
  Fifteen-year-old Adam Cooper tells what happened in Lexington and
  Concord on April 19, 1775.

Faulkner, William   *Intruder in the Dust*
  A proud, elderly black man is cleared of murder charges by the heroic
  efforts of a boy of 16 and a woman of 70, both white.

                                                                      Sartoris
  Young Bayard Sartoris, obsessed by the death of his twin brother in
  World War I, seeks dangerous work as a test pilot.

Ferber, Edna   *Cimarron*
  Yancey Cravat and his wife Sabra are the contrasting main characters
  in this story of the Oklahoma land rush.

Fitzgerald, F. Scott   *The Great Gatsby*
  Jay Gatsby achieves wealth and social status as a racketeer in the 1920's.

Forbes, Esther   *Johnny Tremain*
  A young apprentice takes part in the stirring events culminating in the
  Boston Tea Party and the Battle of Lexington.

Forester, C. S.   *Captain Horatio Hornblower*
  A resourceful British naval officer fights pirates and outwits enemy fleets.

Frank, Pat   *Alas, Babylon*
  The novel presents a vivid picture of the effects of a nuclear war on a
  group of people in central Florida.

Gipson, Fred   *Old Yeller*
  Set in the Texas hill country, this novel is about a fourteen-year-old boy
  and his big, ugly dog.

Golding, William   *Lord of the Flies*
  A group of children are stranded on an island in an atomic war. Some
  of them revert to savagery.

Green, Hannah   *I Never Promised You a Rose Garden*
  Deborah Blau, a sixteen-year-old schizophrenic, can as a matter of choice
  retreat from reality into her private fantasy world of Yr.

Hardy, Thomas   *The Return of the Native*
Clym Yeobright turns his back on the attractions of Paris to become a
teacher on his native Egdon Heath.

Tess of the D'Urbervilles
On her wedding night Tess' husband refuses to forgive her for a past
misfortune in which she was totally blameless.

Hawthorne, Nathaniel   *The House of the Seven Gables*
About to be executed for witchcraft, Matthew Maule pronounces a curse
on Colonel Pyncheon that lasts for generations.

The Scarlet Letter
Roger Chillingworth is determined to learn the identity of Hester
Prynne's lover in order to take revenge on him.

Hemingway, Ernest   *For Whom the Bell Tolls*
Robert Jordan, an American, fights on the side of the Loyalists in the
Spanish Civil War.

The Old Man and the Sea
After eighty-four days without a single catch, Santiago hooks the biggest
marlin he has ever seen.

Hersey, John   *A Bell for Adano*
Major Joppolo risks the displeasure of his superior officers by helping the
people of Adano in World War II.

The Wall
The men and women of the Warsaw ghetto heroically resist the full
might of the Nazi forces.

Hesse, Hermann   *Steppenwolf*
Harry Haller leads a hermitlike, solitary existence, like a lone wolf from
the steppes.

Siddhartha
Though his worthy teachers have taught him all they know, Siddhartha
feels restless and remote from wisdom, and there is no joy in his heart.

Heyward, Du Bose   *Porgy*
Porgy, a crippled beggar, and Crown, a stevedore, compete for the love
of Bess.

Hilton, James   *Goodbye, Mr. Chips*
Chips, at 85, recalls the many boys he taught in his long career at Brookfield, including those killed in World War I.

                                                              Lost Horizon
Conway, kidnapped and brought to Shangri-La, is interviewed by the High Lama, who is 250 years old.

Howells, William D.   *The Rise of Silas Lapham*
A newly rich paint manufacturer fails to win social acceptance by the aristocratic families of Boston.

Hudson, W. H.   *Green Mansions*
Mr. Abel falls in love with Rima, a mysterious, birdlike girl of the South American jungle.

Hugo, Victor   *Les Misérables*
Ex-convict Jean Valjean becomes a mayor and aids humanity but is ruthlessly hounded by Inspector Javert.

Huxley, Aldous   *Brave New World*
It is 632 A.F. (After Ford). Human beings are mass-produced. There is no individuality.

Johnson, James Weldon   *The Autobiography of an Ex-Colored Man*
The light-colored hero successfully passes as a white man, but at times he feels guilty for deserting his people.

Kantor, MacKinlay   *Andersonville*
This novel depicts conditions at Andersonville, a Civil War prison for Yankee soldiers in Sumter County, Georgia.

Kipling, Rudyard   *Kim*
Kim, orphaned son of an Irish color-sergeant stationed in India, becomes a disciple of a Tibetan lama and an agent for the British Secret Service.

Knowles, John   *A Separate Peace*
A New England prep school student is obsessed by guilt feelings over the death of his friend Finney, a school athlete.

Lane, Rose W.   *Let the Hurricane Roar*
Charles and Caroline, a young married couple, face the problems of pioneer life in the Dakotas in the 1870's.

Lee, Harper   *To Kill a Mockingbird*
A band intent on lynching an innocent man is foiled by the sudden arrival of three children.

Lewis, Sinclair   *Arrowsmith*
Martin Arrowsmith encounters numerous difficulties in his attempts to serve humanity in this satire on the medical profession.

Main Street
Carol Kennicott rebels against the cultural barrenness of Gopher Prairie in this satire on small-town life.

Llewellyn, Richard   *How Green Was My Valley*
Huw Morgan, near the end of his life, recalls memories of his boyhood in a Welsh mining family.

London, Jack   *The Call of the Wild*
Buck, a husky, intelligent dog, performs remarkable feats for the love of his master John Thornton.

White Fang
Transplanted from the Yukon to California, a wild wolf-dog adjusts to civilized ways.

McCullers, Carson   *The Heart Is a Lonely Hunter*
John Singer, a deaf-mute, helps an adolescent girl, a black physician, and several others in a small Southern town.

The Member of the Wedding
Twelve-year-old Frankie, who insists on accompanying her brother and his bride on their honeymoon, is heartbroken when left behind.

MacLean, Alistair   *The Guns of Navarone*
A British sabotage team is assigned to blow up a vital Nazi target in the eastern Mediterranean.

Malamud, Bernard   *The Fixer*
In this novel about anti-Semitism in Tsarist Russia, Yakov Bok, falsely accused, imprisoned, and tortured, gains courage as he is at last brought to trial.

Marquand, John P.   *The Late George Apley*
George Apley's life is a satire on the Boston aristocracy of the late 19th and early 20th centuries.

Maugham, W. Somerset   *The Moon and Sixpence*
  Charles Strickland deserts his family to paint. Like the artist Gauguin, whose life the novel parallels, he goes to Tahiti.

Of Human Bondage
  Philip Carey, sensitive about his clubfoot, attempts to find himself as he grows to manhood.

Melville, Herman   *Moby Dick*
  Captain Ahab seeks a second encounter with a ferocious white whale, to whom he has already lost a leg.

Billy Budd, Foretopman
  Billy, popular with all of his shipmates, cannot understand why Claggart, the master-at-arms, dislikes him.

Mitchell, Margaret   *Gone With the Wind*
  Scarlett O'Hara escapes from besieged Atlanta, determined to rebuild the family estate ravaged by Sherman's troops.

Nathan, Robert   *Portrait of Jennie*
  Eben Adams, an artist struggling to find himself, meets a remarkable little girl in Central Park one winter evening.

Nordhoff, Charles B.   *The Pearl Lagoon*
  The novel deals with the South Seas adventures of Charlie Selden, a young Californian.

Nordhoff and Hall   *Mutiny on the Bounty*
  Fletcher Christian leads a part of the crew in a mutiny against harsh Captain Bligh of H.M.S. *Bounty*.

Norris, Frank   *The Octopus*
  The "octopus" is the Pacific and Southwestern Railroad, chief opponent of the California wheat farmers.

The Pit
  Curtis Jadwin, a speculator, manages to corner the world's wheat market.

O'Connor, Edwin   *The Last Hurrah*
  At 72, Frank Skeffington, longtime mayor of an Eastern metropolis, declares his intention of running for another term.

Orczy, Baroness   *The Scarlet Pimpernel*
A mysterious Englishman known as the Scarlet Pimpernel helps aristo-
crats escape from revolutionary France.

Orwell, George   *Animal Farm*
Through animal counterparts, Orwell portrays some of the leading figures
of the Russian Revolution.

Nineteen Eighty-Four
The totalitarian state of the future deprives the individual of freedom
and dignity through the telescreen, propaganda techniques, and thought
control.

Paton, Alan   *Cry, the Beloved Country*
Arthur Jarvis, Jr., is slain by a man whose people he was trying to
liberate.

Portis, Charles   *True Grit*
Fourteen-year-old Mattie Ross persuades a U.S. marshal to help her track
down her father's murderer.

Priestley, John B.   *The Good Companions*
Leaving his nagging wife, Jess Oakroyd roams about England and becomes involved with an actors' troupe, "The Good Companions."

Rawlings, Marjorie K.   *The Yearling*
Jody's experience with his pet fawn matures him rapidly in this tale of
the Florida scrub country.

Richter, Conrad   *The Light in the Forest*
Johnny Butler, reared as an Indian from age 4, is forcibly returned to
his white parents at age 11.

Roberts, Kenneth   *Northwest Passage*
Major Robert Rogers leads an expedition against an Indian town in
the French and Indian War.

Rölvaag, O. E.   *Giants in the Earth*
Per Hansa, a Norwegian immigrant, does everything he can to make life
on the lonely prairie bearable for his wife Beret.

Sabatini, Rafael   *Scaramouche*
This historical novel of the French Revolution has some of the stock ingredients of romance: a noble hero in disguise, a beautiful lady, and
dueling.

Saroyan, William   *The Human Comedy*
Marcus Macauley, killed in World War II, lives on in the hearts and
minds of his family and Army buddy.

Schaefer, Jack   *Shane*
The hero is extremely reticent about his past. The setting is Wyoming
in 1889.

Scott, Walter   *Ivanhoe*
Hard pressed in a tournament, Ivanhoe receives help from the Black
Knight, who is King Richard the Lion-Hearted in disguise.

Shute, Nevil   *On the Beach*
With radiation spreading after a nuclear war with cobalt bombs, a group
of survivors sense that their days are numbered.

Sienkiewicz, Henryk   *Quo Vadis?*
The pagan Vinicius, a guard of the Emperor Nero, falls in love with
Lygia, a beautiful Christian.

Smith, Betty   *A Tree Grows in Brooklyn*
Francine Nolan, oldest child in an impoverished family, struggles to
survive and to get an education.

Steinbeck, John   *The Grapes of Wrath*
The Joads, unable to make a living in drought-ridden Oklahoma, drive
to California in search of farm work.

The Moon Is Down
The Germans execute Mayor Orden in a futile reprisal for the continuing resistance in a country they have invaded.

Of Mice and Men
George faithfully tries to protect Lennie, his simpleminded but physically
powerful friend.

The Pearl
The rare pearl that Kino finds excites envy and brings tragedy to his family.

Stephens, James   *The Crock of Gold*
The angry Leprechauns try to recover their gold from Meehawl Mac-Murrachu, who has stolen it on the advice of the Philosopher.

Stevenson, Robert Louis   *Kidnapped*
Young David Balfour escapes a deathtrap set by his miserly uncle, who then has the lad kidnapped and sent abroad.

Treasure Island
Unaware of the treacherous nature of the crew, Jim and his friends set sail in the *Hispaniola* to secure a buried pirate treasure.

Stone, Irving   *The Agony and the Ecstasy*
Michelangelo, the great sculptor and painter of Renaissance Italy, is the subject of this fictionalized biography.

Lust for Life
This is the fictionalized biography of Vincent van Gogh, painter of sunflowers and the bridge at Arles.

Swift, Jonathan   *Gulliver's Travels*
On his fourth voyage, Gulliver comes to a land where horses (Houyhnhnms) rule over human creatures (Yahoos).

Tarkington, Booth   *Seventeen*
Willie Baxter is captivated by the charming Miss Pratt, a summer visitor of the Parchers.

The Turmoil
The Sheridans stand for business and industry, and the Vertrees for genteel aristocracy. Bibbs and Mary unite the two families happily.

Taylor, Kamala   *Nectar in a Sieve*
Constantly threatened by poverty and starvation, a devoted peasant couple in southern India confronts life with courage and dignity.

Thackeray, William M.   *Vanity Fair*
Scheming, flirtatious Becky Sharp is determined to get ahead. One of the main events in the novel is the Battle of Waterloo.

Tolkien, J. R. R.   *The Hobbit*
This novel is about an adventure of Bilbo Baggins, a hobbit. Hobbits are small people, about half our size, who wear no shoes and live in comfortable holes in the ground.

Twain, Mark   *The Adventures of Huckleberry Finn*
Huck, a refugee from his cruel father, and Jim, a runaway slave, hide out on a raft in the Mississippi.

The Adventures of Tom Sawyer
Tom and his friend Huck Finn are eyewitnesses to a murder when they visit a cemetery one night.

Uris, Leon   *Exodus*
This historical novel portrays the suffering of European Jews and their struggle to establish the state of Israel.

Verne, Jules   *Twenty Thousand Leagues Under the Sea*
An electric submarine takes Captain Nemo on adventure-packed cruises long before the actual invention of the submarine.

Vonnegut, Kurt   *Slaughterhouse Five*
An ex-GI describes the death and destruction inflicted by the fire-bombing of Dresden in the closing days of World War II.

Wallace, Lew   *Ben Hur*
After escaping from the galleys, Ben Hur ruins his enemy Messala by beating him in a chariot race.

Wells, H. G.   *Tono-Bungay*
George Ponderevo makes a fortune by selling a worthless patent medicine called "tono-bungay."

Werfel, Franz   *The Song of Bernadette*
The Blessed Virgin appears to Bernadette, a fourteen-year-old girl of Lourdes, France.

West, Jessamyn   *The Friendly Persuasion*
Though Josh Birdwell is a Quaker, he goes to fight when Morgan's raiders approach his Indiana home in the Civil War.

Wharton, Edith   *Ethan Frome*
In a bleak New England community, Ethan Frome, married to the nagging Zeena, falls disastrously in love with Mattie Silver.

Wilder, Thornton   *The Bridge of San Luis Rey*
  Five travelers perish when a bridge in Peru collapses. Was it fate or the
  hand of God? Their life stories provide a clue.

Wister, Owen   *The Virginian*
  The cowboy hero, who lacks formal education but has a fine character,
  eventually marries a schoolteacher from the East.

Wright, Richard   *Black Boy*
  A change occurs in the major character of this autobiographical novel
  when he suddenly becomes aware of racial prejudice.

                                                        Native Son
  Bigger Thomas panics when he realizes he has accidentally caused the
  death of his employer's daughter.

E. PLAYS

Anderson, Maxwell   *Elizabeth the Queen*
  Elizabeth I desires peace, while her lover, the Earl of Essex, is ambitious
  for military fame.

                                                         High Tor
  A young man escapes from modern civilization to High Tor, a mountain
  overlooking the Hudson.

                                                         Winterset
  Mio seeks to avenge his dead father, executed for a crime he did not
  commit. The play is based on the Sacco-Vanzetti case.

Barrie, James M.   *The Admirable Crichton*
  Crichton, the perfect servant in Lord Loam's London home, becomes
  the respected leader when the Lord's party is stranded on a tropical
  island.

                                                       Dear Brutus
  The characters learn that they themselves, not fate, create their own
  unhappiness.

                              "The Twelve-Pound Look" (one-act play)
  A woman wins her independence from a pompous husband by learning
  how to type.

What Every Woman Knows

Maggie's father and brothers agree to finance John's education on condition that he propose to her after five years.

Besier, Rudolf   *The Barretts of Wimpole Street*
The love of the English poets Elizabeth Barrett and Robert Browning triumphs over the tyranny of a Victorian father.

Bolt, Robert   *A Man for All Seasons*
Sir Thomas More (1478–1535) goes to his death rather than give an oath that is against his conscience.

Capek, Karel   *R.U.R.*
Rossum's Universal Robot Factory produces mechanical men that have no feelings or desires and think of nothing but work.

Chekhov, Anton   *The Cherry Orchard*
An upper-class Russian family in financial straits rejects a sensible way out because it means cutting down their famous cherry trees.

Drinkwater, John   *Abraham Lincoln*
This historical play portrays some of the outstanding episodes of Lincoln's life.

Dunsany, Lord   "The Lost Silk Hat" (one-act play)
A fashionable 20th-century Londoner dreads being seen in public without a hat.

"A Night at an Inn" (one-act play)
Cockney sailors and a gentleman who have stolen a precious stone from an idol are pursued by Hindu priests.

Eliot, T. S.   *Murder in the Cathedral*
Sir Thomas à Becket, Archbishop of Canterbury, is assassinated by the agents of King Henry II.

Galsworthy, John   *Justice*
Justice does not deal fairly with William Falder, who committed forgery to help a woman escape her husband's cruelty.

Loyalties
Feelings of class consciousness and religious prejudice are aroused when De Leirs accuses Captain Dancy of theft.

Strife

A captain of industry and a labor leader cross swords in a prolonged strike that ends in tragedy for both sides.

Gibson, William   *The Miracle Worker*
The "miracle worker" is Anne Sullivan, the teacher of Helen Keller.

Gilbert, W. S.   *The Mikado*
Disguised as a minstrel, Nanki-Poo, son of the Mikado, seeks the hand of Yum-Yum, ward of the Lord High Executioner.

Glaspell, Susan   "Trifles" (one-act play)
A woman has killed her husband, but under highly extenuating circumstances.

Goetz, Ruth and Augustus   *The Heiress*
An heiress discovers the man courting her is interested only in her money. The play is based on Henry James' novel *Washington Square*.

Goldsmith, Oliver   *She Stoops to Conquer*
Since Marlow is bashful with ladies but not with serving-girls, Miss Hardcastle assumes the latter role to win his heart.

Gregory, Lady   "Spreading the News" (one-act play)
False reports and exaggeration result in an apparently tragic but humorous situation.

Hallard and Middlemass   "The Valiant" (one-act play)
A convicted murderer awaiting electrocution refuses to disclose his identity.

Hansberry, Lorraine   *A Raisin in the Sun*
Walter tries to persuade Mama to let him invest his late father's insurance money in a liquor store.

Hart, Moss and Kaufman, George   *You Can't Take It With You*
This comedy deals with the Vanderhofs and the Kirbys, two families with very different life-styles.

Howard, Sidney   *The Late Christopher Bean*
Nobody appreciated Bean's genius, except Abby, a servant girl. After his death, there is a mad scramble for his paintings.

Ibsen, Henrik   *A Doll's House*
Nora Helmer commits forgery for the sake of her sick husband, but
without his knowledge, and becomes the victim of blackmail.

An Enemy of the People
Dr. Stockmann faces persecution because he has the courage to tell the
truth about a serious problem in his town.

Kingsley, Sidney   *Dead End*
The setting is a dead-end street in a New York slum not far from a
luxury-apartment district.

Men in White
A surgeon finds himself torn between professional responsibilities and
romance.

Laurents, Arthur   *Home of the Brave*
A World War II soldier loses the ability to walk as a result of psychological shock. His cure is a lesson in the evils of prejudice.

Laurents and Bernstein   *West Side Story*
This musical about two rival street gangs is patterned after Shakespeare's
Romeo and Juliet.

Lerner and Loewe   *My Fair Lady*
A speech professor transforms a Cockney flower girl into a lady in this
musical comedy based on G. B. Shaw's play *Pygmalion*.

Lindsay and Crouse   *Life With Father*
This comedy of late 19th-century upper-middle-class life is based on
autobiographical sketches by Clarence Day, Jr.

MacLeish, Archibald   *Air Raid* (radio play)
The terror and destruction of an air raid are portrayed in free verse.

Miller, Arthur   *The Crucible*
The setting is the Salem witch-hunt. John Proctor refuses to lie to save
himself and is hanged.

Death of a Salesman
Salesman Willy Loman destroys himself and his family by his blind worship of false ideals common today.

O'Neill, Eugene   *Beyond the Horizon*
Farming is the wrong occupation for Robert Mayo. This mistake ruins the lives of the three principal characters.

The Emperor Jones
The tom-tom beats terrify Jones, as he is pursued by exploited West Indian natives seeking vengeance.

The Hairy Ape
Yank, a stoker on a transatlantic liner, meets a bizarre fate in a zoo.

"Ile" (one-act play)
An Arctic whaler captain takes his wife along on a two-year voyage during which she is depressed with loneliness.

"In the Zone" (one-act play)
Wartime hysteria leads to strange actions on a ship in the war zone.

Rattigan, Terence   *The Winslow Boy*
A father believes in the innocence of his son, expelled from the Royal Naval College for stealing. The play is based on a famous lawsuit.

Rodgers, Richard and Hammerstein, Oscar II   *The King and I*
This musical comedy, based on Margaret Landon's *Anna and the King of Siam,* deals with the experiences of an English governess at the Siamese court in the early 1860's.

Rose, Reginald   *Twelve Angry Men*
This television play deals with the conflicts in a jury responsible for bringing in a verdict in a murder case.

Rostand, Edmond   *Cyrano de Bergerac*
Cyrano of the monstrously long nose helps another to court Roxane, though he loves her himself.

Schary, Dore   *Sunrise at Campobello*
This play about a critical period in Franklin D. Roosevelt's life shows how his personal suffering affected his character.

Shakespeare, William   *As You Like It*
Banished from the court, Rosalind, disguised as a boy, escapes to the Forest of Arden, where she meets Orlando.

Hamlet

Hamlet seeks revenge on his uncle Claudius who he has learned is the murderer of his father.

Julius Caesar

Brutus, "the noblest Roman of them all," allows himself to be misled into participating in Caesar's assassination.

King Lear

Cordelia is disinherited when she refuses to imitate her sisters' hypocritical protestations of love for their vain father, King Lear.

Macbeth

Macbeth, once a person of fine character and a national hero, destroys himself by his unbridled ambition.

Othello

Othello allows his mind to be poisoned against his wife Desdemona by Iago, a treacherous subordinate.

Romeo and Juliet

The love of Romeo and Juliet is thwarted by a feud between their families, the Montagues and the Capulets.

The Tempest

Through magic, Prospero, deposed Duke of Milan, causes the shipwreck of his enemies.

Shaw, George Bernard   *Major Barbara*

Sir Andrew Undershaft, a munitions manufacturer, and his daughter Barbara, a major in the Salvation Army, are the main characters.

Man and Superman

Jack Tanner is the "man"; Ann Whitfield is the "superman." Once she has determined to marry him, he cannot escape.

Pygmalion

To prove a theory, Professor Higgins tries to impose Oxford diction on Eliza Doolittle, a Cockney flower girl.

Sheridan, Richard B.   *The Rivals*

Lydia's interest in the lover she rejected revives when she learns of his impending duel with a rival for her hand.

The School for Scandal
Victimized by scandal in her youth, Lady Sneerwell dedicates herself
to ruining the reputation of others.

Sherwood, Robert E.   *Abe Lincoln in Illinois*
President-elect Lincoln addresses his Springfield neighbors from the rear
platform of the train, as he leaves for Washington.

Sophocles   *Antigone*
Antigone is condemned to death when, in defiance of the ruler of Thebes,
she gives her brother's corpse decent burial.

Oedipus Rex
Oedipus, King of Thebes, blinds himself when he learns that he has un-
wittingly fulfilled the awful prophecy he has sought to avoid.

Stoppard, Tom   *Rosencrantz and Guildenstern Are Dead*
Two of Hamlet's schoolfellows, involved against their will in the conflict
between the King and Hamlet, feel powerless in the grip of the circumstances in which they are trapped.

Synge, John M.   *Playboy of the Western World*
Christy Mahon is treated as a hero for allegedly killing his tyrannical
father, until the father appears on the scene.

"Riders to the Sea" (one-act play)
Maurya is left with but one son, Bartley, but he, too, is drowned, like
his brothers.

Thurber and Nugent   *The Male Animal*
By reading Vanzetti's letter to his class as an example of eloquent broken
English, a professor sets off a university crisis.

Van Druten, John   *I Remember Mama*
The Hansons are very poor, but Mama gives the children a sense of security by pretending there is a family bank account.

Vane, Sutton   *Outward Bound*
The passengers learn that their mysterious vessel is "outward bound"
to the next world.

Vidal, Gore   *Visit to a Small Planet*
From outer space, Kreton arrives in Virginia to visit with the family of
a television celebrity.

Wilder, Thornton *Our Town*
George's wife Emily dies in childbirth in this poignant drama of life in a small New Hampshire town.

Williams, Emlyn *The Corn Is Green*
An idealistic schoolteacher coaches Morgan Evans, a talented young Welsh miner.

Williams, Tennessee *The Glass Menagerie*
Laura's one and only gentleman caller reveals at the end of the evening that he is already engaged.

Zindel, Paul *The Effect of Gamma Rays on Man-in-the-Moon Marigolds*
Despite her depressing home environment, Tillie takes first prize in the school science fair with her experiment in growing marigolds from seeds previously exposed to varying degrees of atomic radiation.

F. BIOGRAPHIES AND BOOKS OF TRUE EXPERIENCE

Adamson, Joy *Born Free*
The author and her husband, a game warden, raise a lion cub as a pet in Kenya, East Africa.

Andrews, Roy Chapman *Under a Lucky Star*
A noted explorer and zoologist tells his life story.

Baldwin, James *Notes of a Native Son*
After his father's death the author realized they had hardly ever spoken to each other. Both were stubborn and proud.

Beebe, William *Half Mile Down*
The author descends in a diving bell to the ocean floor to study undersea life.

High Jungle
In the "high jungle" of Venezuela, Beebe examines strange specimens in their natural habitat.

Boswell, James *Life of Samuel Johnson*
Dr. Johnson, a leading 18th-century English intellectual, is portrayed by Boswell, his observant friend.

Bowen, Catherine D.   *Yankee From Olympus*
The "Yankee" is Supreme Court Justice Oliver Wendell Holmes, Jr.

Braithwaite, E. R.   *To Sir, With Love*
A black teacher from British Guiana (now Guyana) wins the respect
and love of hostile white adolescents in a London slum school.

Bridgeman and Hazard   *The Lonely Sky*
A test pilot flies a top-secret experimental plane.

Brown, Dee   *Bury My Heart at Wounded Knee*
This is a documented account of the white man's barbarity toward the
American Indian from the time of Columbus to the Massacre at Wounded
Knee, South Dakota, in 1890.

Buck, Pearl   *The Exile*
The author's mother serves as a missionary in China and, at the same
time, raises a family.

Catton, Bruce   *Glory Road*
The author recounts the bloody Civil War battles of Fredericksburg,
Chancellorsville, and Gettysburg.

This Hallowed Ground
The title of this Civil War history is from Lincoln's "Gettysburg Address."

Cottler and Jaffe   *Heroes of Civilization*
Lister, the Wright Brothers, Darwin, Mendel, Newton, Koch, and similar
"heroes of civilization" are the subjects of this volume.

Cousins, Norman   *Dr. Schweitzer of Lambaréné*
The author interviews Dr. Schweitzer on his humanitarian work and gets
his views on critical world problems.

Cousteau, Jacques-Yves   *The Silent World*
As menfish, the author and his diving companions explore the sea depths,
photographing undersea life and sunken ships.

Day, Clarence, Jr.   *Life With Father*
Clarence Day, Sr., is the eccentric father in this humorous account of a
New York family in the late 19th century.

De Kruif, Paul   *Microbe Hunters*
The "microbe hunters" are Pasteur, Leeuwenhoek, Spallanzani, and other
geniuses of bacteriological research.

De Mille, Agnes   *Dance to the Piper*
American dancer and choreographer Agnes De Mille writes about her
training and her early disappointments and achievements.

                                           And Promenade Home
Miss De Mille tells of her wartime romance and her successes as choreographer of *Oklahoma!*, *Carousel*, and other Broadway musicals.

Donovan, Robert J.   *PT-109*
This work deals with John F. Kennedy's experiences as a PT boat commander in the South Pacific.

Duggan, Alfred L.   *My Life for My Sheep*
This is the life story of Thomas à Becket, a 12th-century courtier, soldier,
statesman, and churchman.

Eadie, Thomas   *I Like Diving*
A professional deep-sea diver discusses the raising of a sunken submarine.

Eisenhower, Dwight D.   *Crusade in Europe*
The Supreme Commander of the Allied Expeditionary Forces in Europe
in World War II tells how victory was achieved.

Farrow, John   *Damien the Leper*
Father Damien dedicates his life to easing the suffering of the lepers on
Molokai, in the Hawaiian Islands.

Forbes, Esther   *Paul Revere and the World He Lived In*
This is the prize-winning portrayal of a hero of the American Revolution
and the Boston of his time.

Frank, Anne   *Diary of a Young Girl*
A girl of thirteen, hiding from the Nazis in an Amsterdam attic with her
family, records her day-to-day hopes and fears.

Franklin, Benjamin   *Autobiography of Benjamin Franklin*
The work does not go beyond 1757, but by that time Franklin had been
a printer, publisher, philosopher, inventor, scientist, legislator, and
diplomat.

Gilbreth and Carey   *Cheaper by the Dozen*
This is the entertaining account of a family of twelve children and their
extraordinary parents.

Graham, Frank   *Lou Gehrig: A Quiet Hero*
The first baseman of the New York Yankees becomes "the iron man of
baseball."

Grenfell, Wilfred T.   *Adrift on an Ice-Pan*
A humanitarian serving the natives of the Far North is trapped on floating
ice.

Griffin, John Howard   *Black Like Me*
A white man darkens his skin to learn at first hand of the discrimination
suffered by black people.

Gunther, John   *Death Be Not Proud*
A distinguished reporter writes about his teen-age son's inspiring struggle
with illness.

Hart, Moss   *Act One*
In this autobiography, Hart discusses in detail his collaboration with
George S. Kaufman in writing plays.

Hersey, John   *Hiroshima*
The author interviews victims of the atomic attack on Hiroshima and
records its impact in their words.

Hertzler, Arthur E.   *The Horse and Buggy Doctor*
A country physician writes about his career and the progress of medical
science.

Herzog, Maurice   *Annapurna*
The author leads an expedition that successfully scales the higher of
the two peaks of Annapurna.

Heyerdahl, Thor   *Kon-Tiki*
By their 101-day voyage on a balsa raft, the author and five companions
prove that it would have been possible for the ancient Peruvians to mi-
grate to Polynesia, 4300 miles across the Pacific.

Hilary, Edmund   *High Adventure*
Tenzing Norgay and the author are the first to reach the summit of the world's highest mountain, Mt. Everest.

Holt, Rackham   *George Washington Carver*
A child of slave parents gains international fame for his agricultural research.

Hubbard, Bernard   *Cradle of the Storms*
Father Hubbard describes his expedition to Alaska and the Aleutian Islands.

James, Marquis   *The Raven*
This is a biography of Sam Houston, a Virginian who became governor of Tennessee but won his greatest fame in Texas.

Johnson, James Weldon   *Along This Way*
A Negro lawyer and poet tells the story of his life.

Keller, Helen   *The Story of My Life*
A severely handicapped girl triumphs over her afflictions with the aid of her gifted teacher.

Kennedy, John F.   *Profiles in Courage*
These sketches portray courageous American statesmen who at moments of crisis refused to yield to the pressures of the majority.

Kugelmass, J. Alvin   *Ralph J. Bunche, Fighter for Peace*
A victim of poverty and discrimination struggles for an education and becomes a peacemaker in a troubled world.

Kuhn, Irene   *Assigned to Adventure*
A roving woman journalist discusses her exciting career.

Lindbergh, Charles   *We*
The author describes his career from his early barnstorming days to the epic nonstop transatlantic flight to Paris.

Lord, Walter   *Incredible Victory*
Outnumbered and outclassed U.S. naval forces gain an unbelievable victory at the Battle of Midway in World War II.

MacDonald, Betty   *The Egg and I*
This is a humorous autobiographical narrative by a woman who raised
chickens.

McGinley, Phyllis   *Sixpence in Her Shoe*
This book on the American housewife is based largely on the author's
own experiences.

McKenney, Ruth   *My Sister Eileen*
This is an entertaining account of the adventures of two sisters.

Merton, Thomas   *The Seven Storey Mountain*
The author becomes a Trappist monk to find peace of soul.

Morison, Samuel Eliot   *Christopher Columbus, Mariner*
A recognized authority on Columbus discusses the life of the great
navigator.

Nader, Ralph   *Unsafe at Any Speed*
An outspoken consumer advocate exposes the designed-in dangers of the
American automobile.

Pepys, Samuel   *Diary*
Among the entries is an eye-witness account of the Great Fire of London
of September 2, 1666.

Riis, Jacob A.   *The Making of an American*
An immigrant from Denmark becomes a reporter and wages war on the
New York City slums.

Roos, Ann   *Man of Molokai*
Serving the lepers of Molokai, Father Damien discovers one day that
he, too, has contracted the disease.

Roosevelt, Eleanor   *This I Remember*
The widow of Franklin D. Roosevelt recalls men and events associated
with an extraordinary President.

Saint-Exupéry, Antoine de   *Wind, Sand, and Stars*
After crashing in the desert on a Paris-to-Saigon flight, the author and
his companion fight thirst and mirages.

Sandburg, Carl   *Abraham Lincoln: The Prairie Years*
This part of Sandburg's monumental biography deals with Lincoln's life before his coming to the White House.

Schweitzer, Albert   *Out of My Life and Thought*
An unusually gifted and versatile person dedicates himself wholly to the service of the unfortunate.

Scott, Robert L.   *God Is My Co-Pilot*
One of the Flying Tigers of World War II fame discusses his experiences in the China-Burma-India theater.

Stefansson, Vilhjalmur   *My Life With the Eskimos*
A noted Arctic explorer describes his experiences in the polar regions.

Steffens, Lincoln   *The Autobiography of Lincoln Steffens*
A crusading reporter uncovers political corruption in America's principal cities.

Strachey, Lytton   *Eminent Victorians*
Four leading figures of the Victorian Age are portrayed: Cardinal Manning, Florence Nightingale, Doctor Arnold, and General Gordon.

Queen Victoria
On becoming Queen, Victoria removes her mother from "every vestige of influence, of confidence, of power."

Stuart, Jesse   *The Thread That Runs So True*
A writer recalls his earlier career as a teacher in Kentucky and Ohio.

Teale, Edwin Way   *Wandering Through Winter*
A naturalist records his observations as he travels thousands of miles through the American winter from the Southwest to the Northeast.

Toffler, Alvin   *Future Shock*
We are suffering—and will be suffering even more—from "future shock," a disease caused by our inability to adapt to the increasingly rapid changes in our society.

Toland, John   *The Last 100 Days*
The author recounts the events of the last 100 days of World War II.

Toor, Frances   *Three Worlds of Peru*
The author recounts her experiences and illuminates the life and customs of the natives.

Tuchman, Barbara   *The Guns of August*
The topic is August, 1914. The author describes the political background and opening battles of World War I.

Twain, Mark   *Life on the Mississippi*
The author describes his training as a Mississippi River steamboat pilot and the mystery and romance of that river.

Waite, Helen   *How Do I Love Thee?*
Elizabeth Barrett asserts her independence from her tyrannical father by eloping with Robert Browning, a fellow poet.

Waksman, Selman A.   *My Life With the Microbes*
The discoverer of the drug streptomycin tells his life story.

Washington, Booker T.   *Up From Slavery*
Born a slave, the author becomes a national leader in the struggle to educate the black people.

Werner, Morris R.   *P. T. Barnum*
The author relates amusing anecdotes about Barnum's showmanship and his sensational publicity stunts.

White, Theodore H.   *The Making of the President: 1972*
This account of Richard M. Nixon's successful campaign for reelection to the Presidency deals also with the Watergate Affair.

White, W. L.   *They Were Expendable*
Motor Torpedo Boat Squadron Three plays a gallant and heroic role in the Philippine campaign in World War II.

Woodham-Smith, Cecil B.   *Lonely Crusader*
This is the life story of Florence Nightingale, founder of modern nursing.

Woodward, Grace S.   *The Man Who Conquered Pain*
William Thomas Green Morton pioneers in the development of anesthesia.

Yablonsky, Lewis   *The Tunnel Back: Synanon*
Ex-drug addicts help narcotics users to return to normal lives.

PART III OF THE EXAMINATION

Chapter 10   The Composition Test

IMPORTANCE OF COMPOSITION ABILITY

Composition ability—the ability to organize your thoughts and express them effectively in writing—is a basic requirement for a high school diploma. As you grow in composition skill through study and practice, you will discipline yourself to think and to communicate more clearly. This chapter will help you to achieve these goals.

The Board of Regents underscores the importance of the composition test by assigning more value to it than to any other part of the examination—thirty credits.

PURPOSE OF THE COMPOSITION TEST

The composition test measures your ability to collect your thoughts on a topic and to organize them under main headings into an effective plan. It further measures your ability to introduce your topic interestingly, to connect your thoughts on the topic logically from sentence to sentence and paragraph to paragraph, and to come to a rational conclusion. Note that in writing a composition you will be putting into practice most of the skills tested earlier in the examination, such as vocabulary, spelling, punctuation, capitalization, and grammar.

The pages that follow will give you practical assistance with the thinking and planning required for a good composition.

NEED FOR CAREFUL REVISION

Keep in mind the following statement printed in bold type in the heading of the examination: **"No paper seriously deficient in English composition will be accepted for Regents credit."** This means that a paper passing in subject matter may nevertheless be rejected if it contains "several serious errors in composition, such as faulty sentence structure or gross illiteracy in grammatical expression or many minor errors." (Reprinted from *Suggestions on the Rating of Regents Examination Papers in English,* New York State Education Department.)

From experience we know that many careless errors can in a first draft be detected and eliminated by patient rereading. Therefore:

Carefully revise your composition—and literature-discussion essay, too— before handing in your paper.

TYPICAL COMPOSITION TEST

Answer *A* or *B* or *C.*   [30]

A   Write a composition of 250 to 300 words on one of the topics below.

I love New York	My favorite magazine
To err is human; to really foul things up requires a computer	The popularity of pro basketball
	Pass/fail
Transplants	Early one morning
	I'm not everybody: I'm me
Garden on a windowsill	Mirrors

B   Today, more than ever before, young people are asking questions and demanding answers about matters that concern them deeply. In a composition of 250 to 300 words, give *two* specific questions that have been asked or need to be asked by young people, *and* in each case give reasons why an answer must be sought.

C   Write an account of about 250–300 words on a famous American historical event as if you were an eyewitness reporter.

The composition test offers you the choice of answering question A or B or C. Regardless of which you choose, you will have to write a 250–300 word composition.

ANALYSIS OF THE COMPOSITION TOPICS

The topics in A, B, and C may be grouped into two categories: *general topics* and *specific topics.*

1. **General topics** are those that fall within the experience of practically everyone taking this examination.

The following topics in A may be considered general topics:

I love New York
Pass/fail
Early one morning
I'm not everybody: I'm me
Mirrors

Two questions that concern young people, the topic discussed in B, also belongs in this category.

You should be able to get sufficient material for a composition on a general topic by recalling personal experiences or using your imagination.

2. **Specific topics** are those that require exact information about a particular subject. You cannot, for example, write an *eyewitness account of a famous American historical event* unless you are sure of the basic facts of that event. Similarly, you cannot develop the topic *To err is human; to really foul things up requires a computer* if you do not know of some common computer foul-ups, such as repeated requests for payment of a bill already paid, or repeated inquiries about why you have ignored summonses for traffic violations you never committed. Here are the remaining specific topics and the special knowledge that they require:

Transplants
(familiarity with kidney, heart, eye, or garden transplants)
Garden on a windowsill
(familiarity with houseplants)
My favorite magazine
(acquaintance with a particular magazine)
The popularity of pro basketball
(familiarity with professional basketball)

CHOOSING A TOPIC

People write best about the things they know. Therefore you should avoid specific topics for which you do not have the necessary information.

If there is no specific topic offered on which you are qualified to write, choose a general topic that you can develop by using your imagination or recalling past incidents.

Caution: If you select a topic on which you present inadequate material, you will be charged with *meager development of topic,* a common reason for failure in the composition test.

PLANNING THE COMPOSITION

The following discussion is intended to help pupils who have had difficulty in organizing a composition. It is based on a four-paragraph approach. In four paragraphs it should not be too difficult to meet the minimum length requirement of 250 words. Do not hastily conclude, though, that a Regents composition should be limited to four paragraphs. If you write well, you may (and should) have five or even six paragraphs.

1. Composition Length. Deductions will be made for compositions noticeably below 250 words. If you write only 200 words, the maximum your composition can earn is 24 points (instead of 30). If you write only 150, the maximum drops to 18. No deduction, on the other hand, will be made for length beyond 300 words if it is not excessive and helps to develop the composition.

2. Providing for Four Paragraphs. Naturally you will want one paragraph as an introduction and another as a conclusion. This means that in the body (paragraphs 2 and 3) of your 250- to 300-word composition you will in most cases have room to discuss *two* main ideas or phases of your topic.

3. General Plan

PARAGRAPH 1. Introduce the topic in an interesting way.

PARAGRAPH 2. Discuss one main idea or phase of the topic.

PARAGRAPH 3. Discuss another main idea or phase of the topic.

PARAGRAPH 4. Arrive at a conclusion that stresses your chief point.

4. The Main Problem: Paragraphs 2 and 3. If you know what you will discuss in paragraphs 2 and 3, you should have no difficulty in writing a suitable introduction and conclusion. The main problem, however, is: "What are you going to discuss in paragraphs 2 and 3?"

5. Five Ways to Develop Paragraphs 2 and 3. The following are not the only ways to develop the key paragraphs of your composition. You will, however, find them useful if you have had difficulty in planning.

1. DEVELOPMENT BY ADVANTAGES AND DISADVANTAGES

Discuss the advantages, or good aspects, of your topic in paragraph 2, and the disadvantages, or bad aspects, in paragraph 3, or vice versa.

TOPIC	IN PARAGRAPH 2 DISCUSS	IN PARAGRAPH 3 DISCUSS
I love New York	Admitted disadvantages of living in N.Y.	Overwhelming advantages
Pass/fail	Advantages of the pass/fail marking system	Disadvantages of this system
Transplants	Good aspects of transplant operations	Harmful aspects of these operations

2. DEVELOPMENT BY COMPARISONS

Compare and contrast one phase of your topic with another.

I love New York	Living in some other city or state	Living in the city or state of New York
Mirrors	The image I have of myself in my mind	The image of myself as seen in the mirror
Pass/fail	How the traditional marking system works	How pass/fail operates
To err is human; to really foul things up requires a computer	Complaints about billing errors to firms that are not computerized	Complaints about such errors to firms having computerized billing

3. DEVELOPMENT BY REASONS OR CAUSES

Discuss one reason or cause of your topic in paragraph 2, and another in paragraph 3.

The popularity of pro basketball	One cause of the popularity of professional basketball—for example, the high caliber of the players	Another cause of its popularity —for example, the excitement of the game

I love New York	One reason—the people	Another reason—the cultural opportunities
Garden on a windowsill	One reason for having such a garden—for example, its beauty	Another reason —for example, the pleasure of watching things grow
My favorite magazine	One reason why magazine X is my favorite	Another reason
Two questions that concern young people	Reason(s) why an answer must be sought to the first question	Reason(s) why an answer must be sought to the second question

4. DEVELOPMENT BY EXAMPLES

Discuss one example of your topic in paragraph 2, and another in paragraph 3.

I'm not everybody: I'm me	One example of how I am different from others	Another example
Mirrors	One type of person who fusses before mirrors	Another type
Transplants	One example of a transplant operation— a heart transplant	Another example —a kidney transplant
Garden on a windowsill	One type of plant that does well in such a garden— for example, a cactus	Another type— for example, ivy
To err is human; to really foul things up requires a computer	One example of a foul-up: repeated requests for payment of bills already paid	Another example: repeated inquiries about summonses never issued to you

5. DEVELOPMENT BY CHRONOLOGICAL ORDER

Discuss one chronological phase of your topic in paragraph 2, and another in paragraph 3.

Early one morning	What happened early that morning	What happened later
Transplants	Transplants of human organs now being performed successfully	Transplants that may be attempted in the future
Garden on a windowsill	First steps in making a windowsill garden	Later steps
Eyewitness account of a famous American historical event	Washington's crossing of Delaware, Christmas night, 1776	His capture of 918 Hessians next morning at Battle of Trenton

ORGANIZING THE WHOLE COMPOSITION

Suppose that, after carefully examining all the topics, you decide that the best topic for you to write about is *I love New York.* Here are some practical suggestions about what to do next.

Step One

List your thoughts about the topic on scrap paper exactly as they occur to you. Example:

I Love New York

1. I love New York.
2. New York is not perfect.
3. It has crime.
4. A large percentage of its young people still have no jobs.
5. It has traffic congestion.
6. The cost of living is very high in New York.
7. It has air pollution.
8. New York is not the only place with these problems.
9. New York has some good points.
10. It has people from all parts of the world.
11. It has people of all races and creeds.
12. These people enrich New York with their culture.
13. They make life in New York interesting.
14. They make life in New York exciting.
15. It is the entertainment capital of the world.

16. It used to be the capital of the United States.
17. It has excellent museums.
18. It has large department stores.
19. It has never turned away poor people from other sections or foreign countries.
20. It has tried to do more for them than any other American city.
21. It has nearly bankrupted itself in the attempt.
22. It is a beautiful city.
23. The Manhattan skyline is a thrilling sight.
24. Above all, it is a city with a heart.
25. That is why I love New York.

Step Two

Cross out any thoughts that are off the topic or that repeat a previous idea. Examples:
Item 14 is practically a repetition of item 13. Cross out item 14.
Item 16 has nothing to do with the topic. Get rid of it.

Step Three

Find the main headings under which your thoughts can be grouped. Example:
One fairly obvious heading is "Disadvantages of living in New York." Items 3–8 can be grouped under this heading to provide the material for paragraph 2 of your composition.
Another fairly obvious heading is "Advantages of living in New York." Items 9–13, 15, and 17–24 can be grouped under this heading to provide the material for paragraph 3.

Under these headings you will be able to develop the body of your composition as suggested in Section 1 on page 404: "In paragraph 2, discuss the admitted disadvantages of living in New York. In paragraph 3, discuss the overwhelming advantages."

Now all you need is material for an introduction (paragraph 1) and a conclusion (paragraph 4). These paragraphs should be brief.
Items 1 and 2 convey the idea that "I love New York despite its faults." These items are sufficient material for paragraph 1.
Item 25, "That is why I love New York," sums up the composition. It can stand by itself as paragraph 4.
Your outline, then, will be as follows:

I Love New York

I. I love New York despite its faults (items 1, 2).
II. I admit there are disadvantages to living in New York (items 3–8).

    III. However, the advantages of living in New York are overwhelming (items 9–13, 15, and 17–24).

    IV. That is why I love New York (item 25).

Step Four

Write the composition, following your outline. Do not feel compelled to include every single item in your outline. For example, in writing the final composition from the above outline, the student made no mention of items 4, 6, and 15–18 because she felt she had more than enough material for a composition of 250–300 words. On the other hand, feel free to include some important items not in your outline if these occur to you as you are writing the composition, as they often do. Also, you do not have to discuss your supporting items in the numerical order of the outline. Change the order when necessary for the best effect.

Let us now examine the composition that a student wrote from the outline just discussed. The student wisely left herself enough time to revise her first draft. As a result she was able to eliminate some obvious errors and make some minor improvements. This is the composition as finally submitted:

I Love New York

I love New York not because it is a perfect place to live—far from it—but because the advantages it offers greatly outweigh its faults.

New York, I admit, has a high crime rate, as do other large cities. Crime is everywhere in modern life. Some of the worst crimes reported these days are committed in suburban areas and quiet rural communities. Another charge against New York is its traffic congestion. If you have tried to go crosstown in Manhattan recently by bus, taxi, or auto, especially during the rush hours, you know what I mean. But New York does not have a monopoly on traffic problems; we run into them in all parts of the country. Last month it took us more than two hours to go a mile and a half on a road leading out of Fort Lauderdale. And then, there is the fact of air pollution in New York, except of course on windy days. New York has greatly improved its air quality in the past few years. At any rate, its air is far cleaner than that of Los Angeles.

But consider New York's advantages. First, there are its people. If you go to China, you will see Chinese, in Nigeria you will meet Nigerians, and in Peru Peruvians. But if you stand on a corner in midtown New York, you will encounter people of all races and creeds from all parts of the globe. These people contribute their talents and culture to New York, making it a truly cosmopolitan city and an exciting place to live. Consider, too, the beauty of the city. The Manhattan skyline, as seen from one of New York's many beautiful bridges, or from the Brooklyn side of the East River, is one of the world's most awesome sights. Whenever I see it, I am proud I am a New Yorker. Lastly, consider New York's heart. It has never rejected the poor and the unfortunate who have come to it from other sections of the country, or from foreign lands. It has spent more in trying to help them—in fact, in so doing, it has nearly bankrupted itself—than any other American city, though admittedly this help has not been enough to wipe out slums and poverty.

That is why I love New York.

SERIOUS ERRORS IN COMPOSITION TECHNIQUE

1. POOR INTRODUCTION

Your introduction may be considered poor if it fails to achieve two goals: (1) to start discussing the topic and (2) to arouse the reader's interest. Study the following introductions from pupil compositions:

The Popularity of Pro Basketball

Poor Introduction: Pupil A

In the society that we live in, much stress is put on the activities of our leisure time. It is apparent that the physical activities of each individual are essential for proper growth. The topic of pro basketball reflects this condition.

Better Introduction: Pupil B

A graceful, high-arching jump shot, a twisting, gravity-defying lay-up, a leaping, consummately timed block—these commonplace occurrences in the average professional basketball game are part of the explanation for the ever-increasing popularity of the sport.

Pupils A and B Compared

Pupil A fails to introduce his topic. His first two sentences deal with leisure and physical activities, and are therefore irrelevant. His third sentence vaguely suggests a connection between physical fitness and pro basketball, but this is still far from the topic, which is the *popularity* of pro basketball. Pupil A bores the reader by his overuse of words. His first seven words can be condensed to three: "In our society." The message of his first two sentences can be summed up in four words: "physical activities are important." Pupil A has made a painfully slow, weak, and uninteresting start.

Pupil B introduces his topic interestingly by briefly describing three exciting plays that make the sport of pro basketball popular. He gets to his topic at once. He wastes no words.

2. POOR THOUGHT COHERENCE

Your thought coherence is poor if your sentences and paragraphs do not follow logically one from the other. Study the thought coherence in these two later excerpts from the compositions of Pupils A and B:

The Popularity of Pro Basketball

Poor Thought Coherence: Pupil A

Of course, at times the play of the game is sloppy. That is what holds the interest of a fan at any game. It is the satisfaction of a devoted fan to see an opponent, after playing continuously well throughout the game, miss an easy basket or make a foolish mistake.

Pro basketball in itself is nothing to be laughed at. It renders the best of each player. It is a tremendous body builder for the mind and soul.

Analysis: Many of Pupil A's thoughts do not cohere ("stick together") with what comes before and after:

"Pro basketball in itself is nothing to be laughed at" is a surprising, illogical statement; nothing that precedes or follows it suggests that pro basketball should be "laughed at," i.e., is not important. A look at Pupil A's context shows that he would have achieved coherence between his two paragraphs if he had written instead: "Pro basketball excites not only the fans but also the players."

"It renders the best of each player" is another illogical statement because Pupil A has just finished describing the "sloppy" play, including the missing of "easy" shots and "foolish mistakes" that the fans enjoy. He would have been logical if he had written: "Each player tries to render the best account of himself."

"It is a tremendous body builder for the mind and soul" is, of course, illogical. Do the mind and soul have bodies? But there is an even more serious error in the sentence because by "It" Pupil A means *pro basketball. Basketball,* not pro basketball, is a "tremendous body builder." Pupil A should have written: "It (pro basketball) contributes to physical fitness by stimulating more and more people to play basketball."

Good Thought Coherence: Pupil B

At present two major professional basketball leagues exist. The fledgling American Basketball Association was born in the late 1960's, while the National Basketball Association dates from the 1940's. The ABA's struggle for parity with the NBA has been hampered by consistent desertions of its star athletes to the older league. A pending merger of the two leagues, should Congress and the Players' Association permit it, would remedy this problem and help satisfy America's growing appetite for quality basketball. If the nation's school yards continue to produce college and professional players in sufficient quantities, a serious dilution of talent in the pro ranks will be averted, and the sport can only gain a still greater following.

Analysis: Pupil B's thoughts flow logically from sentence to sentence and paragraph to paragraph. There are no gaps or irrelevancies to vex the reader.

3. POOR SENTENCE STRUCTURE

Your sentence structure must be considered poor if you write (1) run-on sentences or (2) sentence fragments. These errors entail heavy deductions. Learn to avoid them by studying the following:

1. A **run-on sentence** results from running together two or more sentences.

> TYPICAL RUN-ON: Cooperatives take nothing for *granted, they* act only with the approval of the majority of the members.

> RUN-ON CORRECTED: Cooperatives take nothing for *granted. They* act only with the approval of the majority of the members.

> EXPLANATION: Since *granted* ends the first sentence, it must be followed by a period. Since the next word starts a new sentence, it should begin with a capital (*They*).

2. A **sentence fragment** results from writing a piece (fragment) of a sentence as if it were a whole sentence.

> TYPICAL SENTENCE FRAGMENT (from the end of a sentence): There are many problems. *Which arise when you move into a new neighborhood.*

> SENTENCE FRAGMENT CORRECTED: There are many problems *which* arise when you move into a new neighborhood.

> EXPLANATION: "Which arise when you move into a new neighborhood" is merely a piece (fragment) of the previous sentence. Therefore (1) there must be no period before *which,* and (2) *which* must start with a small letter.

TYPICAL SENTENCE FRAGMENT (from the beginning of a sentence): *When they leave their old home.* They have the difficult task of saying goodby.

SENTENCE FRAGMENT CORRECTED; When they leave their old *home, they* have the difficult task of saying goodby.

EXPLANATION: "When they leave their old home" is merely a piece (fragment) of the next sentence. Therefore (1) the period after *home* must be replaced by a comma, and (2) the next word (*they*) must start with a small letter.

4. POOR PARAGRAPHING

Here are some reasons why paragraphing may be considered poor:

1. Including material that is irrelevant (off the topic of the paragraph).

2. Failing to support the general statement (topic sentence) of the paragraph by specific facts, details, examples, etc.

3. Failing to begin a new paragraph at the point where a new unit of thought begins.

Study the paragraphing in these two excerpts from pupil compositions:

Pass/Fail

Poor Paragraphing: Pupil C

The main advantage of this system is that it relieves pressure. This may be the only advantage of the system. Students are often very competitive and want to be on top. Quite often, when I take an important test, I feel the pressure. This may cause me to freeze up. With the pass/fail system, this feeling will be eliminated. I'll take an exam and do the best I can, but the mark won't matter as long as I pass. I see many more disadvantages with the pass/fail system than advantages. The main disadvantage is that there would be a loss of incentive to work. If a student can get the same mark for "C" work as for "A" work, why should he bother working for an "A"? Some students would do the work even if there were no marks, but I think the majority would not strive to do well.

Better Paragraphing: Pupil D

The main advantage of pass/fail is that it eliminates competition. Students have been conditioned to study for that "A," no matter what. By cramming until 2 A.M., they get that "A," but by the next week they have forgotten three-fourths of the subject matter. The main reason for wanting the "A" is that in the future that "A" will beat out any "B" for a job. The student with the "B" might remember more of what he learned, but grades do not convey that.

The main disadvantage of pass/fail is that it downgrades the superior student. Straight "passes" come nowhere near to looking as good as straight "A's." However, he may balance this loss by taking up extra courses and activities. With the time saved from not having to cram, a really brilliant student can enrich his background by doing independent study.

Pupils C and D Compared

Pupil C has good material but has crammed both the advantages and disadvantages of the pass/fail system into one lengthy paragraph. Pupil C's writing would have been clearer and more effective if he had started a new paragraph with the sentence beginning "I see many more disadvantages . . ."

Pupil D has dealt with essentially the same material more clearly and more effectively by discussing the advantages and disadvantages in separate paragraphs.

5. LACK OF UNITY

Your composition should contain *only material directly related to the topic.* Otherwise it will be considered to lack unity.

Study the following excerpt from a pupil composition.

Transplants

Lack of Unity: Pupil E

The gift of life is the greatest gift in the world. With the many medical discoveries and modern scientific techniques, man is being given a new lease on life.

Pneumonia and tuberculosis were once terrible killers. However, since the discovery of antibiotics and sulfa drugs, the death rate from these diseases has gone down very sharply. Infantile paralysis used to be one of the most dreaded diseases, but with the discovery of anti-polio vaccines it has practically disappeared.

One of the most amazing developments in twentieth-century medicine is the success of organ transplant operations. Many surgeons are now able to replace defective parts of a person's body with healthy organs from another person.

A few years ago, Dr. Christian Barnard, now a world-famous heart surgeon, performed the first human heart transplant and gave an ailing man, Louis Waskkansky, a chance to live longer. Complications arose, and a few days later the patient died of pneumonia, but medical science had made an important advance. A few months later Dr. Barnard performed a similar operation on Philip Blaiberg, who lived for almost two years. Since then several other surgeons have attempted heart transplants, some successfully and some not.

Kidney transplants are now very common . . .

Restoring Unity: Pupil E. Pupil E's second paragraph spoils the unity of her composition because it is *not directly related* to the topic. The second paragraph deals with antibiotics, sulfa drugs, and anti-polio vaccines, but the topic of this composition is "Transplants." (Pupil E's second paragraph would have been appropriate if the topic of her composition were "Medical Advances of the Twentieth Century.")

To restore unity, Pupil E must leave out her entire second paragraph.

6. POOR CONCLUSION

Your conclusion may be judged poor for these reasons: (1) failure to sum up, briefly but interestingly, the main points you have made, or (2) failure to stress the main point that you wish to leave with your reader.

Study the following conclusions from pupil compositions:

Two Questions That Concern Young People

Poor Conclusion: Pupil F

In conclusion, we can readily see that both of these questions need to be answered now, or in the near future. The answers, when they are found, cannot hurt us. They can only help us.

Better Conclusion: Pupil G

With nuclear arms in the hands of so many nations, we must realize that the next war we become involved in may spell the end of civilization. For this reason the United States should learn to live without war.

Pupils F and G Compared

Pupil F merely wants to end his composition. His first sentence is mechanical; it involves no profound thought. His second sentence says something so obvious that it is hardly worth saying. Pupil F leaves no deep impression.

Pupil G, on the other hand, brings his composition to a climax in his final paragraph by introducing a very important point that he wishes to impress on the reader—the possibility of nuclear destruction of the world. This point commands our attention and interest.

ANALYZING PUPIL COMPOSITIONS

One valuable way to improve your ability to write a composition is to analyze the compositions of other pupils. The following are all on the same topic: "Garden on a windowsill."

Notice that each sentence has been numbered. This will help you locate the writing strengths and weaknesses discussed in the evaluation that follows each composition.

Pupil H

Garden on a Windowsill

(1) A child can learn about responsibility through caring for his very own garden on a windowsill. (2) Although an ordinary indoor plant is simple to care for, the parent can make it seem like a great responsibility.

(3) First, the proper routine must be explained to the child. (4) My first plant was a cactus that needed watering once every three days. (5) I would mark off on a calendar the days I was to water my plant. (6) In this way I learned the names and order of the days and months. (7) See how a child can gain knowledge of other subjects through the simple watering of a plant?

(8) The special day arrived when my mother asked me, "Wouldn't it be nice if you had your own watering can to use, instead of the bathroom cup?" (9) I was thrilled! (10) That same day my mother and I walked to the department store. (11) I spent what seemed to be hours searching the garden equiptment section before my eyes fell upon the perfect watering can. (12) I chose the little can with the ballerinas on it, and I couldn't wait until the following Wednesday when I would be able to use it.

(13) I still have the plant on my windowsill, a decade later. (14) All these years I had been waiting for the cactus to bloom. (15) A few weeks ago, a mysterious stem appeared. (16) It grew higher and higher until it reached the height of the other stalks. (17) The next morning a beautiful white flower, resembling a lily, appeared. (18) Unfortunately it lasted only a few days.

(19) I shall keep waiting, however, even for another decade, for the cactus that grew up with me to bloom again.

EVALUATION: PUPIL H

1. *General Plan:* Very clear. The opening paragraph (S1 and 2) makes the generalization that a child can learn responsibility by taking

care of an indoor plant. The rest of the composition supports this generalization by describing three specific incidents, each in a separate paragraph: the explanation of the routine of caring for the plant (S3–7); the purchase of the watering can (S8–12); and the blooming (S13–18). The concluding paragraph (S19) looks ahead to the next blooming. Pupil H develops her composition by the method of chronological order (page 406).

2. *Thought Coherence:* Excellent. Notice how Pupil H signals the different time divisions by key words at the beginning of her paragraphs: *First* (S3); The *special day arrived* (S8); I *still* have the plant (S13); I *shall keep waiting* (S19). The thought flows smoothly from sentence to sentence and paragraph to paragraph, with no gaps or irrelevancies.

3. *Sentence Variety:* Superior. One way by which Pupil H makes her writing interesting is by varying her sentence length. For example, compare the length of S8 and S9. Another way is by varying her sentence type, as in S7 (an interrogative sentence) and S9 (an exclamatory one). Also, by quoting the exact words of her mother, Pupil H makes her writing more dramatic.

4. *Vocabulary:* Very good. Note, for example, the effective use of *ballerinas* (S12), *decade* (S13), and *stalks* (S16).

5. *Spelling:* Accurate, except for one word in S11: it should be *equipment.*

Rating: 29 (out of 30) or 97%

Pupil I

Garden on a Windowsill

(1) My grandfather loved plants. (2) Wherever he lived, he had plants in all rooms, but especially on the windowsills, where they could get sunlight and air.

(3) Plants always seem to grow for my grandfather. (4) They were like children to him. (5) I watched him plant tiny seedlings that developed into big towering trees. (6) He gave each grandchild a tree of their own and, as the grandchildren grew, so did the trees. (7) Around our summer home were windowboxes filled with flowers of every assortment and color. (8) It was so beautiful that, when people approached the house, this is what they noticed first, and they would remark about it. (9) My grandfather would smile a slight smile and try to hide his pride.

(10) For a year and a half before my grandfather died he was very ill. (11) We felt that it would help his morale if he were brought to the summer home. (12) This helped immensely, but something was missing. (13) My grandfather wanted to garden. (14) He wanted to get his hands in the soil and watch things grow. (15) One day my step-grandmother entered the room carrying a small windowbox. (16) She placed it on the windowsill right by my grandfather's bed. (17) My grandfather could now have his "garden on a windowsill." (18) This delighted him; he now felt useful again. (19) His plants needed him, and he needed to be needed.

(20) I truly beleive that this idea helped keep my grandfather alive for several more months than the doctors dreamed possible. (21) Each morning he would look forward to waking up and tending to his plants.

EVALUATION: PUPIL I

1. *General Plan:* Very good. The opening paragraph (S1 and 2) introduces grandfather's attachment to plants. The body of the composition is developed by the method of chronological order. The second paragraph (S3–9) presents one chronological phase of the topic—grandfather and his plants before his illness. The third paragraph (S10–19) deals with another phase—grandfather and his plants during his illness. The concluding paragraph (S20–21) states the writer's belief that plants prolonged his grandfather's life.

2. *Thought Coherence:* Good, except for S21, which logically should follow S19. Pupil I should make S21 the last sentence of his third paragraph. His last paragraph, then, will consist only of S20, which is more fitting as the concluding sentence than S21.

3. *Vocabulary:* Some needless repetition: *big* (S5) should be eliminated because it is implied in *towering; smile a slight smile* (S9) should be condensed to *smile slightly; help* (S11) should be replaced by a word like *boost* because *helped* appears in the next sentence, S12; *now* (S18) is unnecessary because it was mentioned in the previous sentence, S17.

4. *Usage:* Good, except for *their* (S6), which should be replaced by *his* (He gave each grandchild a tree of *his* own). See page 167.

5. *Spelling:* Perfect until S20, in which Pupil I misspelled *truly* and *believe.*

Rating: 25½ (out of 30) or 85%

Pupil J

Garden on a Windowsill

(1) Who can get more pleasure from plants and flowers, country people or those who live in a city and keep a garden on there windowsill. (2) I think I know the answer.

(3) In many familys in the country or the suburbs people do not take proper care of plants. (4) They do not prevent their children from running through the flower beds. (5) Do they ever stop to watch the grass grow or the flowers bloom? (6) The beauty of growing things is wasted on these people. (7) Many people who see to much of flowers and plants take it for granted. (8) They think these things will allways be there when they decide to look at them.

(9) If you are not fortunate enough to live in the country, what is more beautiful than flowers on a windowsill. (10) Those small pots of love deserve to get enough water and sunlight. (11) What satisfaction you get when you see the first flower, or the bud to a tomatoe plant. (12) Later on you can pick that flower or tomatoe off of the plant. (13) What adds more beauty to a plain windowsill than plants and flowers? (14) As you sit there by your window you can see what is going on in the street. (15) Maybe the barber is having an argument with a customer, or women are talking together outside the grocery store. (16) Maybe the kids on the block are having a stickball game. (17) It is fasinating to watch what is going on in the world.

(18) So next time don't say, "look at that poor person with only those plants in a big city of concrete." (19) People with gardens on there windowsills realize their beauty and value. (20) They never take it for granted.

EVALUATION: PUPIL J

1. *General Plan:* Good. The opening paragraph (S1 and 2) raises a question, and the rest of the composition answers it. The body of the composition is developed by the method of comparison (page 404). The second paragraph (S3–8) discusses the attitude of some country people with regard to plants. The third paragraph, in S9–13, compares this with the attitude of a city person. The final paragraph (S18–20) settles the question as far as the writer is concerned.

2. *Unity:* Some irrelevant material. (S14–17 are off the topic and should be removed from this composition.)

3. *Punctuation:* There are three errors. Both S1 and S9 are questions and should end with question marks (page 186). S11 is an exclamation and should end with an exclamation point (page 187).

4. *Capitalization:* In S18, *look* should be replaced by *Look* because it is the opening word of a direct quotation (page 192).

5. *Usage:* There are three errors. In S7 the singular pronoun *it* should be changed to the plural pronoun *them* because its antecedent (*flowers and plants*) is plural. In S20 the same correction should be made for the same reason. In S12 the preposition *of* is unnecessary (pages 181–182).

6. *Spelling:* Several errors.

SENTENCE	ERROR	CORRECT SPELLING
1 and 19	"there"	**their**
3	"familys"	**families**
7	"to"	**too**
8	"allways"	**always**
11 and 12	"tomatoe"	**tomato**
17	"fasinating"	**fascinating**

Rating: 21 (out of 30) or 70%

Pupil K

Garden on a Windowsill

(1) There's a garden on my windowsill and the rays of sunshine are bringing life to it. (2) The leafs of my flowers are penetrating the sun. (3) Which starts photosynthesis. (4) Without sun my garden couldn't live. (5) I water my garden every day, some of the flowers need more water than the others. (6) The water helps the flowers to grow and blossom. (7) My garden is consisted of many kinds of flowers. (8) At one end of the windowsill are seeds for red, red roses. (9) I'm aware that I cant keep them on my windowsill once they grow, but I can transplant them to the garden in my back yard. (10) At the other end is a small yellow daisy that my boyfriend picked special for me. (11) It has a certain glow to it that shines over all the other flowers. (12) In the middle I have pansys, they are very pretty and add a lot of color to my garden. (13) Pansys spred over a period of time and soon they will be all over my garden. (14) Every garden needs grass, and that is exactly what my garden has, plenty of grass. (15) Grass has that extrordinary touch.

(16) It spreds happiness throughout a garden. (17) When people come to my room and look at my garden. (18) They always tell me how beautiful it is. (19) I'm very proud to own a windowsill garden. (20) It gives me a sence of responsibility. (21) I know its all mine. (22) Noone can take it away from me.

Evaluation: Pupil K

1. *Factual Correctness:* Leaves do not penetrate the sun, as Pupil K carelessly states in S2. The sun's rays penetrate leaves.

   In S8, Pupil K refers to "seeds for red, red roses." Roses are not grown from seeds.

   In S14, Pupil K claims that "every garden needs grass." This is not necessarily true even of outdoor gardens. In a windowsill garden consisting of the plants Pupil K has previously mentioned, grass would be an unattractive weed, crowding those plants and robbing them of nourishment. It is difficult to see how Pupil K's windowsill garden can contain "plenty of grass" (S14) and be considered "beautiful" (S18).

2. *General Plan:* At first it seems that Pupil K did not plan her composition, for it consists of one long paragraph. On closer examination we can see that there is a definite organization in her thinking. She could have made her organization clearer to us and improved her composition if she had divided it into the following paragraphs:

   Paragraph 1 (How my garden grows): S1–6.
   Paragraph 2 (What my garden consists of): S7–16.
   Paragraph 3 (Why I enjoy my garden): S17–22.

3. *Sentence Structure:* Poor.

   S3 is a sentence fragment. It should be combined with S2 as follows: *The leaves of my flowers are penetrated by the sun, which starts photosynthesis.*

   S5 is a run-on sentence. There are three ways to correct it:
   a. *I water my garden every day. Some of the flowers need more water than the others.* or
   b. *I water my garden every day; some of the flowers need more water than the others.* or
   c. *I water my garden every day because some of the flowers need more water than the others.*

S12, too, is a run-on sentence. It may be corrected as follows:
a. *In the middle I have pansies. They are very pretty and add a lot of color to my garden.* or
b. *In the middle I have pansies; they are very pretty and add a lot of color to my garden.* or
c. *In the middle I have pansies that are very pretty and add a lot of color to my garden.*

S17 is a sentence fragment. It should be combined with S18 as follows: *When people come to my room and look at my garden, they always tell me how beautiful it is.*

4. *Vocabulary:* In S2, 5, 6, and 7 Pupil K has carelessly used *flower* instead of *plant*. In S7 instead of "My garden *is consisted* of," Pupil K should have written:

a. *My garden consists of . . .* or
b. *My garden is composed of . . .*

5. *Usage:* In S10, Pupil K should replace the adjective *special* with the adverb *specially* (pages 170–171).

6. *Spelling:* Weak.

SENTENCE	ERROR	CORRECT SPELLING
2	"leafs"	leaves
9	"cant"	can't
12 and 13	"pansys"	pansies
13	"spred"	spread
15	"extrordinary"	extraordinary
16	"spreds"	spreads
20	"sence"	sense
22	"Noone"	No one

Rating: 18 (out of 30) or 60%

EXERCISE

See how accurately you can evaluate the next three compositions. They all deal with the same topic: "Mirrors." Before assigning a rating to a composition, carefully consider its main strengths and weaknesses. Make use of the evaluation aids that have been inserted below each composition.

(The teachers who graded these compositions rated them 90%, 75%, and 55%. Can you tell which is which?)

Pupil L

Mirrors

(1) I may very well turn out to be the instigator of a petition to break all existing mirrors and ban all future ones. (2) You look puzzled? (3) You don't understand? (4) Well, let me give you an example.

(5) Pretend you are walking down the boulevard in your new blue dress pants with the high waistband and the cute little buttons, and you are wearing your new high platform shoes and a hugging angora sweater. (6) You feel cool, huh? (7) You think you look sharp, right? (8) As you pass a shop, you accidently catch a glimpse of yourself in a full-length mirror, and now, instead of that blasted glass, you are shattered. (9) Your image of yourself has been burst, and you are forced to accept the picture of yourself as the fat, clumsy elephant you really are. (10) The strawberry sundae you have at lunch every day doesn't help matters very much either.

(11) Don't think I don't see you fellows over there smirking and laughing. (12) How about you? (13) Do you still feel that mirrors serve a positive function? (14) Now it's your turn to hear a story. (15) Remember, after your steamy shower last Friday, you got the feeling that something was wrong? (16) Your hair just didn't seem to feel as thick as it used to. (17) "Oh," you told yourself, "its probably that barber. (18) He must have layered my hair to give it the 'mod' look." (19) Wise up, buddy. (20) That haircut was over three weeks ago. (21) Wipe the steam off of the sweet little glass and examine your scalp more closely. (22) See that place you used to start your part at? (23) You don't have to reach quite that far back now, do you?

(24) So? (25) Are you with me? (26) Men? (27) Women? (28) Okay. (29) Raise those hammers. (30) One, two, three . . .

EVALUATION AIDS: PUPIL L

1. What is your opinion of Pupil L's general plan for organizing her composition?

2. One technique for achieving interest is to vary sentence length and type. What evidence can you find that Pupil L has, or has not, used this technique?

3. How well does Pupil L's final paragraph meet the requirements of a good conclusion (page 414)? Why?

4. What error can you locate in S8? S17? S21?

Rating: 55%, 75%, or 90%?

Pupil M

Mirrors

(1) It's seven years of bad luck. (2) It helps you brush your teeth. (3) It let's you know who is near you on the expressway. (4) Yes, the mirror plays a role somehow every day of our lives. (5) We get up and groom ourselfs in the looking glass. (6) We almost never stop to think how useful mirrors are or how many their are in our surrounding. (7) I would guess that in a room of one hundred women there would be at least one hundred mirrors.

(8) There are mirrors everywhere. (9) In dinning rooms, in bedrooms, inside of cars, outside of cars, in busses, and in basements.

(10) The uses of mirrors are so common and useful. (11) If there were no mirrors, ladies would not put on their make-up correctly. (12) Changing lanes at 50 m.p.h. on the expressway would mean sudden death, men would shave their faces off along with their beards.

Evaluation Aids: Pupil M

1. Consider the length of Pupil M's composition. See page 403.

2. Carefully examine the structure of S9 and S12.

3. What changes, if any, need to be made in S1? S10?

4. Check the spelling in S3, 5, 6, and 9.

Rating: 55%, 75%, or 90%?

Pupil N

Mirrors

(1) Most people use mirrors to comb their hair, brush their teeth, and wash their faces. (2) I use the mirror for these purposes, too. (3) But the mirror also serves a more important function for me. (4) I use it to escape into a dream world.

(5) This morning as I was combing my hair something came over me. (6) I starred into the mirror and saw my huge chest muscles jutting out like a cliff. (7) I saw my massive shoulders and pulverizing arms. (8) My eyes then caught sight of my slim muscular stomach. (9) My sturdy legs were next to come to my attention.

(10) I then remembered that I was a middle linebacker for the NFL in the All-Star Game. (11) It was the first play of the game. (12) The AFL were in their offensive huddle, and we were waiting in our positions. (13) The huddle was broken. (14) They had their strategy mapped out. (15) I knew what I was suppose to do. (16) My job was to blitz. (17) This was my first All-Star Game. (18) I was extremely nervous. (19) The quarterback gave the signals. (20) The center snapped the ball. (21) I broke from my position. (22) I met the center and right guard head on. (23) I wouldn't let no one stop me. (24) I continued passed my human obsticles. (25) I saw the quarterback. (26) He was fading back to pass. (27) I pursued him. (28) I then landed a tremendous tackle with the force of lightning striking a tree. (29) The quarterback reeled. (30) The ball sprang loose. (31) At this point I heard my mother call Anthony hurry up you'll be late.

(32) I was out of my dream world. (33) Wasn't it wonderful to leave the harsh realities of life for a few minutes. (34) The mirror had served it's purpose. (35) I finished combing my hair and then I ate my breakfast and left. (36) The moment I had this morning is still with me. (37) I have a smile on my face and I'm grateful for my mirror.

EVALUATION AIDS: PUPIL N

1. Compare Pupil N's general plan with Pupil M's. Which is better? Why?

2. In which is Pupil N more proficient, vocabulary or spelling? Examine his spelling in S6, 15, 24, and 34. Note his use of vocabulary in S7, 20, 26, and 33.

3. Check the punctuation in S31 and S33.

4. Which sentence contains a double negative (pages 174–175)?

Rating: 55%, 75%, or 90%?

QUESTIONS FROM PART III OF FORMER EXAMINATIONS

Test 1

Answer A, or B, or C   [30]

A. Write a well-organized composition of 250–300 words on *one* of the following topics:

Freedom is a car	A person whose life I envy
I belong to myself	A river is dying
Handbook for the 80's	It's only hair
What have we done to our heroes?	Call of the open road
Movies Hollywood never should have made	Nightmares

B. Young children are very curious about the origins of things. They ask why people have five toes, why stars twinkle at night, or how popcorn came to be popular at the movies.

In 250–300 words, write a story for a preschooler in which you tell the origin of one of the things mentioned above, or of any other real or imaginary thing.

C. I wonder why somebody doesn't do something. Then I realize, I am that somebody.

Choose a situation in your life when you realized that you had to do something because there was no one else who could or would respond.

Write a monologue of 250–300 words in which you relate the event that aroused your response. Write the monologue as though you were talking to a friend, and state what you did or wished you had done.

Test 2

Answer either A or B   [30]

A. Write a well-organized composition of 250–300 words on *one* of the topics below:

Something truly amazing	Jobs
Modern pioneers	A conversation with —
Prisoners	Modern medicine and prolonging life
Women will!	On the bus

B. Choose *one* of the two situations below:

1. Some critics feel that violence plays an all-too-important role in today's sports. Choose a sport and write a letter of about 250–300 words to the editor of a local newspaper. In the letter, assume the role of a person either attacking or defending the violence in sports. The salutation *Dear Editor:* is the only heading needed for the letter.

2. Pretend that you have come home two hours late from a date. Your mother is waiting up for you. As soon as you come into the house, she says, "Why are you so late? What have you been doing?" Your mother does not interrupt you while you explain, but you can see that she is greatly concerned. Write an explanation of 250–300 words, giving specific reasons for your lateness.

Directions for the Listening Section:

1. The teacher will read a passage aloud. Listen carefully. DO NOT WRITE ANYTHING.
2. Then the teacher will tell you to open your test booklet to page 2 and to read questions 1 through 10. At this time you may mark your tentative answers to questions 1 through 10 if you wish.
3. Next, the teacher will read the passage aloud a second time. *As you listen to the second reading*, WRITE THE NUMBER of the answer to each question in the appropriate space on the answer sheet.
4. After you have listened to the passage the second time, you will have up to 5 minutes to look over your answers.
5. The teacher is not permitted to answer questions about the passage.
6. After you have answered the listening questions on page 2, go right on to the rest of the examination.

Part I
Listening   [10]

1. By his word choice, the speaker suggests that the French buy cowboy outfits in order to
   (1) enjoy a fantasy world
   (2) express strong anti-Indian feelings
   (3) have a better concept of the American West
   (4) relive their own past glory
2. Which are the major sources of the popular frontier image?
   (1) American myths   (3) travel brochures
   (2) mass media   (4) historical accounts
3. In this speech, the depiction of sinister characters is best described as
   (1) accurate   (3) stereotyped
   (2) conflicting   (4) vague
4. According to this speech, most Indians in Western stories are portrayed as
   (1) bad   (3) glamorous
   (2) passive   (4) oppressed
5. The speaker compares the position of the cowboy to that of
   (1) a TV programmer   (3) a famous actor
   (2) an Israeli soldier   (4) a chivalrous knight
6. According to the projected image of the Old West, justice was handled by
   (1) the sheriff   (3) the good guys
   (2) each person   (4) no one
7. According to the speaker, the main reason for the allure of this Western imagery is that the
   (1) past provides relief from the present
   (2) present is very similar to the past
   (3) past serves as a model for the present
   (4) achievement of the present outweighs that of the past
8. Throughout this description of the West, a recurring difference from modern-day life that is expressed is the
   (1) cowboy's knowledge of self-defense   (3) individual's control of life
   (2) chance to fight evil   (4) opportunity to become famous
9. This speech suggests that the projected image of the West is best described as
   (1) realistic   (3) changing
   (2) understated   (4) romantic
10. According to this speech, the largest group that accepts the projected image of the West is
    (1) modern ranchers   (3) the American public
    (2) movie viewers   (4) people around the world

Directions (11–30): In the space provided on the separate answer sheet, write the *number* of the word or phrase that most nearly expresses the meaning of the word printed in heavy black type. [10]

11. **defame**   (1) slander   (2) depress   (3) outwit   (4) arouse
12. **retaliation**   (1) recommendation   (2) list   (3) revenge   (4) victory
13. **zeal**   (1) boredom   (2) enthusiasm   (3) compassion   (4) trust
14. **unilateral**   (1) one-wheeled   (2) unanticipated   (3) similar   (4) one-sided
15. **gratuity**   (1) tip for service   (2) tool for printing   (3) medal for achievement   (4) thank-you note
16. **bewitch**   (1) repel   (2) fascinate   (3) satisfy   (4) fear
17. **desist**   (1) cause   (2) change   (3) help   (4) stop
18. **bigotry**   (1) invention   (2) obstruction   (3) intolerance   (4) belief
19. **somber**   (1) gloomy   (2) gentle   (3) lively   (4) careful
20. **redemption**   (1) power   (2) sale   (3) religion   (4) deliverance
21. The **eccentric** old lady loved her cats, her hats, and her tumbledown house.   (1) moody   (2) lovable   (3) strange   (4) friendly
22. The author was totally displeased with the **abridged** version of his novel.   (1) televised   (2) shortened   (3) translated   (4) censored
23. He made the statement **assertively**.   (1) reluctantly   (2) hastily   (3) positively   (4) honestly
24. Because of his **inertia**, he seldom achieves his goal.   (1) temper   (2) laziness   (3) stupidity   (4) carelessness
25. The executive believes that people must be **ruthless** in order to succeed in business.   (1) powerful   (2) dishonest   (3) reckless   (4) merciless
26. The actress was described as having **mediocre** talent.   (1) ordinary   (2) uncommon   (3) excellent   (4) inferior
27. The **gaudy** dress is trimmed with pearls.   (1) elegant   (2) worn-out   (3) pretty   (4) flashy
28. The class **extolled** the virtues of their teacher.   (1) listed   (2) praised   (3) apologized for   (4) explained
29. The child was both **gregarious** and hardworking in school.   (1) comfortable   (2) prompt   (3) sociable   (4) happy
30. Many **credulous** people are influenced by television advertisements to buy certain products.   (1) believing   (2) uneducated   (3) clever   (4) logical

Directions (31–40): In each of the following groups of words, only one of the words is misspelled. In *each* group, select the misspelled word and spell it correctly in the space provided on the separate answer sheet. [5]

31. lengthen   region   solidly   gases   inspecter
32. imediately   forbidden   complimentary   aeronautics   identical
33. continuous   paralel   opposite   definite   receptive
34. Antarctic   Wednesday   Febuary   Hungary   Pittsburgh
35. transmission   exposure   pistol   customery   telescope
36. juvinile   implore   martyr   deceive   collaborate
37. unnecessary   repetitive   cancellation   quantity   airey
38. patent   transit   availible   objection   galaxy
39. ineffective   believeable   arrangement   compass   aggravate
40. possession   progress   reception   predjudice   criticism

Directions (41–60): Below each of the following passages, there are one or more incomplete statements or questions about the passage. For each, select the word or expression that best completes the statement or answers the question *in accordance with the meaning of the passage*, and write its *number* in the space provided on the separate answer sheet. [20]

Passage A

Many archeologists assume that Ice Age animal images represent only a form of hunting magic. The hunter, so the theory runs, made an animal image and "killed" it, then went out and hunted with the power of magic on his side. Still other archeologists theorize that the animals were totems—figures of ancestor animals from which different human groups or
5 clans supposedly descended. The animals have also been interpreted as sexual symbols, with certain species representing the male principle and others the female. I was now to ask new questions.

When I put the Vogelherd horse under the microscope, I discovered that its ear, nose, mouth and eye had been carefully and accurately carved, but that these features had been
10 worn down by long handling. The figure had obviously been kept by its owner and used for a considerable period. Clearly, it had not been created for the purpose of being "killed" at once.

But in the shoulder of the horse was engraved one unworn angle that I took to represent a dart or wound. Apparently some time late in the use of this figure, it *had* been killed.
15 But why? Was the killing intended as hunting magic? Perhaps. But if Cro-Magnon was as sophisticated as I was beginning to find he was, could the killing not have been for some other symbolic purpose, such as initiation, the casting of a spell, the curing of illness, a sacrifice for the coming of winter, or the celebration for the coming spring?

Whatever the meaning, here was an indication that Ice Age images, like notations and
20 certain tools, were made to be kept and used over a long period for specific purposes.

—Adapted from *National Geographic*, January 1975

41. In line 4, the dash is used to   (1) take the place of a semicolon   (2) set off a definition
    (3) introduce a list   (4) indicate that something has been left out
42. According to this passage, figures such as the Vogelherd horse may have been used by Ice
    Age   (1) individuals as some kind of symbol   (2) tribes as currency   (3) tribes as objects of worship   (4) hunters as trophies for big kills
43. The author's purpose in examining the Vogelherd horse was to   (1) discover its origin
    (2) analyze its construction   (3) question its significance   (4) determine its age
44. What does this passage imply about the author?   (1) He is not familiar with Cro-Magnon
    man's hunting strategies.   (2) He has personally examined numerous Ice Age artifacts.
    (3) He has found new evidence about Cro-Magnon man from recent diggings.   (4) He
    has known about the significance of the Vogelherd horse for a long time.
45. Which sentence best summarizes the main idea of this passage?   (1) "Many archeologists
    assume that Ice Age animal images represent only a form of hunting magic." (lines 1 and 2)
    (2) "I was now to ask new questions." (lines 6 and 7)   (3) "Clearly, it had not been created for the purpose of being 'killed' at once." (lines 11 and 12)   (4) "Whatever the
    meaning, here was an indication that Ice Age images, like notations and certain tools, were
    made to be kept and used over a long period for specific purposes." (lines 19 and 20)
46. The overall tone of this passage may be best described as   (1) argumentative   (2) questioning   (3) suspenseful   (4) humorous

Passage B

The theater is a jungle in which the playwright, the actor, and the director struggle for supremacy. Sometimes the fight goes one way and then, for a time, another. I have lived through the reign of each in turn, and now it seems to me the playwright is once more supreme. Pinter, Stoppard, and Gray stalk unchallenged by Olivier and Peter Brook. Once
5 more the audience is invited not only to look and listen but to think as they once thought with Shaw and Galsworthy. There is a rich heritage in the British theater, but it is not, alas, the heritage of the actor, still less of the director. The playwright must in the final battle always prove the winner. His work, imperishable; his fame, enduring. I write "alas" because although I have tried my hand at both directing and playwriting, I am in essence one of
10 those of whom Shakespeare wrote that we were destined to strut and fret an hour upon the stage and then be heard no more.

My generation of actors was trained to entice our prey. We kept an eye open, a claw sharpened, even when we professed to slumber. However deep the tragedy or shallow the farce, we never forgot to face front. Nowadays, the relation between player and public
15 tends to be more sophisticated. Together they share a mutual experience of pain and sorrow. Sometimes the actor seems able to dispense with his audience—to no longer need it. He may choose or chance to perfect his performance on a wet afternoon in Shrewsbury, with hardly anyone watching, and thereafter the repetition for him may stale. For me this never happens. I never perfect a performance, though obviously I am sometimes
20 better or worse, but I have learned that without a perfect audience, my struggle to the summit is impossible. I am aware as the curtain rises of the texture of the house.

—Adapted from "The Play's Still the Thing"
by Robert Morley, *Saturday Review*, June 11, 1977

47. According to this passage, Pinter, Stoppard, and Gray are involved with the theater as (1) theater owners (2) actors (3) playwrights (4) directors
48. Which image is presented in lines 1 through 8? (1) Producing a play is like a battle. (2) The playwright is like a god. (3) The director is a hunter who attempts to capture and tame the actors. (4) Actors are like murderers and directors are their victims.
49. In lines 8 through 11, what reason does the author give for using the word "alas" in line 8? (1) He believes that playwrights have too much power. (2) He believes that directors have too much power. (3) He feels he has been ignored. (4) He realizes he has limited abilities.
50. What relationship usually exists between the modern actor and his audience? (1) The actor ignores the audience completely. (2) The actor merely presents the playwright's ideas to the audience. (3) The audience enters into the experience with the actor. (4) The audience must be perfect, or the actor will not be successful.
51. In lines 12 through 14, the actors of the author's generation are pictured as (1) hypocrites (2) predators (3) perfectionists (4) sophisticates
52. The author personally believes that the audience (1) is vital (2) is a necessary evil (3) is largely irrelevant (4) would rather not think
53. According to this passage, what is the author's usual occupation in the theater? (1) playwright (2) director (3) actor (4) reviewer

Passage C

Love Poem

My clumsiest dear, whose hands shipwreck vases,
At whose quick touch all glasses chip and ring,
Whose palms are bulls in china, burs in linen,
And have no cunning with any soft thing

5 Except all ill at ease fidgeting people:
The refugee uncertain at the door
You make at home; deftly you steady
The drunk clambering on his undulant floor.

Unpredictable dear, the taxi drivers' terror,
10 Shrinking from far headlights pale as a dime
Yet leaping before red apoplectic streetcars—
Misfit in any space. And never on time.

A wrench in clocks and the solar system. Only
With words and people and love you move at ease.
15 In traffic of wit expertly maneuver
And keep us, all devotion, at your knees.

Forgetting your coffee spreading on our flannel,
Your lipstick grinning on our coat,
So gayly in love's unbreakable heaven
20 Our souls on glory of spilt bourbon float.

Be with me darling early and late. Smash glasses—
I will study wry music for your sake.
For should your hands drop white and empty
All the toys of the world would break.

—John Frederick Nims

54. The woman in this poem may be clumsy at washing dishes, but is probably very skillful at
(1) fixing clocks   (2) serving coffee   (3) driving a car   (4) talking to shy people
55. The poet's attitude toward the woman in this poem is one of   (1) tolerance   (2) disbelief   (3) ridicule   (4) endearment
56. The effect of using the words "hands" and "palms" as subjects of the clauses "whose hands shipwreck vases" (line 1) and "Whose palms are bulls in china" (line 3) is to   (1) help separate the woman's clumsiness from the woman herself   (2) establish her ineptness   (3) emphasize her great responsibility   (4) make her appear to be ignorant
57. The woman in this poem is the "taxi drivers' terror" (line 9) most likely because she   (1) frightens taxi drivers whenever she rides with them   (2) is an unpredictable pedestrian   (3) is afraid of taxi drivers   (4) jumps off buses
58. The phrase "For should your hands drop white and empty" (line 23) refers to the woman's   (1) dropping everything   (2) being clumsy   (3) injuring her hands   (4) dying
59. What is the theme of this passage?   (1) Loving others is more important than being graceful.   (2) Learning to be on time is important.   (3) Clumsy people must be loved despite their faults.   (4) Unpredictable people are misfits in society.
60. The last line of the poem most likely means   (1) all material things would be destroyed   (2) accidents would occur by themselves   (3) there would be no more joy in the world   (4) his childish entertainment would end

Directions (61–66): Choose only *5* of the following questions. Each question refers to the dictionary entry below. For each question you choose, select the answer that best completes the statement or answers the question and write its *number* in the space provided on the separate answer sheet. [5]

of·fi'cious *(o-fish'us), adj.* [F. or L.; F. *officieux*; fr. L. *officiosus.*] 1. *Obs.* Kind; obliging; dutiful. 2. Volunteering one's services where they are neither asked nor needed; meddlesome. 3. *Diplomacy.* Of an informal or unauthorized nature; unofficial; as, an *officious* conversation. –of·fi'cious·ly, *adv.* –of·fi'cious·ness, *n.* Syn. Impertinent, imprudent, saucy, pert, cool

61. The expression "1. *Obs.* Kind; obliging; dutiful" means that (1) at one time "officious" meant "kind" (2) "officious" has a slang meaning (3) a common meaning of "officious" is "kind" (4) an important meaning of "officious" is "impertinent"
62. The vowel sound of the last syllable in "officious" is the same as the vowel sound in (1) cute (2) loot (3) rub (4) ought
63. The expression "2. Volunteering one's services where they are neither asked nor needed; meddlesome" gives (1) a meaning of "officious" as a verb (2) a second meaning of "officious" (3) an unusual meaning of "officious" (4) an unauthorized meaning of "officious"
64. The expression "3. *Diplomacy.* Of an informal or unauthorized nature; unofficial; as, an *officious* conversation" gives a meaning of "officious" that is (1) authoritative (2) colloquial (3) official (4) specialized
65. This entry suggests that today "officious" (1) has a positive connotation (2) can be used to mean "official" (3) has almost no shades of meaning (4) has a negative connotation
66. Which sentence best makes clear to a reader a current meaning of "officious"? (1) How can you be so officious? (2) He is a very officious person. (3) Only an officious person would be so concerned with others' business. (4) His kindness stamps him as one of the most officious people I know.

Part II

Directions: Write a well-organized essay of at least 200–250 words on *A* or *B*, or answer *both* parts of *C*. [20]

A. Often in literature, situations reach a "point of no return," a point after which the life of a character in the work can never be the same. From the novels, full-length plays and biographies you have read, select *two* in which a point of no return exists. Describe this turning point and explain why the characters can never resume life as it was before. Use specific references. Give titles and authors.
B. Imagine that characters from short stories will be interviewed on a TV talk show. Choose *four* characters, each from a different short story, that you would like to see interviewed. For each character:
  Explain why you would choose that character.
  Point out the importance of the character in the story in which he or she appears.
  Indicate two or three questions you would like the interviewer to ask *each* character.
  Give titles and authors.
C. Answer *both C-1* and *C-2*, which appear on pages 7–10.

Answer C-1 and C-2 *only* if you choose Part IIC.

C-1. Directions (1–10): The passage below is followed by 10 incomplete statements or questions about the passage. For *each*, select the word or expression that best completes the statement or answers the question, and write its *number* in the space provided on the separate answer sheet.

Filling Out a Blank

High School Profile—Achievement Form
for D. Wagoner, 1978 . . . Item 8
Job Preferences: 1) chemist 2) stage magician
3) _____

My preference was to be
The shrewd man holding up
A test-tube to the light,
Or the bowing charlatan
5 Whose inexhaustible hat
Could fill a stage with birds.
Lying beyond that,
Nothing seemed like me.

Imagining the year
10 In a smock or a frock coat
Where all was black or white,
Idly I set about
To conjure up a man
In a glare, concocting life
15 Like a rich precipitate
By acid out of base.

What shivered up my sleeve
Was neither rabbit nor gold,
But a whole bag of tricks:
20 The bubbling of retorts
In sterile corridors,
Explosions and handcuffs,
Time falling through trapdoors
In a great cloud of smoke,

25 But the third guess leaves me cold:
It made me draw a blank,
A stroke drawn with my pen
Going from left to right
And fading out of ink
30 As casually as a fact.
It came to this brief line,
This disappearing act.

—David Wagoner

1. In line 3, the phrase, "A test-tube to the light," and in line 23, the phrase, "Time falling through trapdoors," are examples of (1) alliteration (2) onomatopoeia (3) pun (4) oxymoron
2. The effect of the second stanza is to (1) explain the speaker's background (2) present additional choices for the speaker (3) tell the requirements for each profession (4) combine elements of two choices
3. Which image helps to unify the first three stanzas? (1) a test-tube (2) an inexhaustible hat (3) a bag of tricks (4) a stage full of birds
4. By denotation, "Where all was black or white" (line 11) refers to the smock or frock coat. By connotation, the line also refers to (1) moral choices (2) test-tube and hat (3) intellectual problems (4) acid and base
5. Assonance is the repetition of vowel sounds. In this poem, an example of assonance is (1) "Or the bowing charlatan" (line 4) (2) "smock or a frock coat" (line 10) (3) "Explosions and handcuffs" (line 22) (4) "fading out of ink" (line 29)
6. Which literary technique is used in lines 15 and 16? (1) onomatopoeia (2) personification (3) simile (4) understatement
7. The mood at the end of this poem is (1) optimistic (2) pessimistic (3) sarcastic (4) apathetic
8. The effect of ending this poem with the same images it began with serves to (1) suggest uncertainty (2) contrast the symbols (3) unify the poem (4) suggest conflicts
9. In the context of the entire poem, the title "Filling Out a Blank" suggests (1) fulfilling one's roles in life (2) accepting one's fate (3) filling a void in one's experiences (4) completing the form
10. In which poetic form is this poem written? (1) Spenserian stanzas (2) blank verse (3) sonnet form (4) free verse

C-2. Directions (11-40): Choose only *10* of the following questions, and, in the space provided on the **separate answer sheet, write the *number* of the word or expression that best completes the statement or answers the question.**

11. In "The Bear" by William Faulkner, the boy does *not* shoot the bear because the (1) boy has too much sympathy for all of nature (2) bear is old and sick (3) bear has taught him something about human virtue (4) boy has not yet reached manhood
12. Robert Hayden's poem "Frederick Douglass" suggests that, when true freedom is realized, Douglass will be remembered most appropriately with (1) "legends and poems and wreaths of bronze" (2) "lives grown out of his life" (3) "statues' rhetoric" (4) "the gaudy mumbo-jumbo of politicians"
13. In "Year's End" by Richard Wilbur, the snow and ice represent the (1) ever-present approach of death (2) cyclic recurrence of the winter season (3) frigidity and indifference of modern society (4) fearful coming of old age
14. In Liam O'Flaherty's short story "The Sniper," the main character kills his brother during a (1) demonstration (2) jailbreak (3) civil war (4) parade
15. In his essay "The Spreading 'You Know'," James Thurber writes humorously about the (1) tendency to "pass the buck" (2) inadequacies of encyclopedias (3) wider range of studies in modern schools (4) misuses of language
16. In Betty Greene's *Summer of My German Soldier*, Patty Belsen is imprisoned because she had been (1) hiding a fugitive (2) accused by her father (3) brought up by a Jewish family (4) unjustly convicted by mob pressure
17. The major theme of Harold Borland's *When the Legends Die* is that people (1) have the ability to believe that they are infallible (2) tend to become alienated from themselves and their environment (3) have the power to adapt to and conquer any environment (4) cannot adapt to their environment

18. When Julia Fields writes "I wear you in my heart" and concludes "—Silent forever The Heart. So quiet the lovely Song," she is referring to (1) Countee Cullen (2) Charles Cooper (3) Langston Hughes (4) Malcolm X

19. In his essay "Civil Disobedience," Henry David Thoreau argues that the only place for a just man in an unjust society is in (1) government office (2) jail (3) a teaching position (4) a commune

20. According to Langston Hughes in "The Negro Speaks of Rivers," the chief importance of great rivers is that they (1) serve as a connecting link between the territories through which they flow (2) force mankind to keep individual segments of civilization confined by natural barriers (3) are personified and often considered gods by those who live along their shores (4) add depth to the souls of those who become closely involved with them

21. In Greek mythology, which pair suffer tragedy on their wedding day? (1) Orpheus and Eurydice (2) Pygmalion and Galatea (3) Zeus and Hera (4) Odysseus and Penelope

22. In Greek mythology, the messenger of the gods is (1) Apollo (2) Hera (3) Hermes (4) Dionysus

23. According to mythology, Icarus is so taken with the ecstasy of flight that he (1) loses his way among the stars (2) flies too near the sun (3) crashes into Mount Olympus (4) loses his respect for earthbound creatures

24. The biblical story of Job emphasizes (1) God's wrath (2) Satan's treachery (3) Job's faithfulness (4) humanity's indecision

25. In A Raisin in the Sun by Lorraine Hansberry, a representative of the Clybourne Park Improvement Association visits the Youngers to try to (1) buy their house (2) enlist their aid in a campaign to save the elm trees (3) get Mrs. Younger to join the Association (4) keep them out of the neighborhood

26. In Tennessee Williams' play The Glass Menagerie, Amanda Wingfield repeatedly recalls (1) her Southern girlhood (2) her late husband's prosperity (3) the births of her children (4) her son's desertion

27. In Shakespeare's play Romeo and Juliet, the line "Wisely and slow; they stumble that run fast" is (1) Friar Laurence's gentle warning to Romeo (2) Mercutio's ominous prediction for Tybalt (3) the Nurse's advice to Juliet (4) the Duke's warning to the Montagues and Capulets

28. In Euripides' play The Trojan Women, the chorus represents the (1) royal family of Troy (2) Greek army (3) ordinary women of Troy (4) spirits of the dead Trojans

29. In Sarah Jewett's short story "A White Heron," Sylvia refuses to reveal the location of the heron's nest because she (1) dislikes the young ornithologist (2) senses the sacredness of nature (3) does not need the money (4) fears for the ornithologist's life

30. The main theme of the short story "The Open Boat," by Stephen Crane, is (1) the sea's beauty (2) man's pollution of the sea (3) man's indifference to danger (4) nature's indifference to man

31. In Edgar Lee Masters' poem "Lucinda Matlock," what is Lucinda's attitude toward life? (1) Life has little meaning for old people. (2) Life is demanding but rewarding. (3) Life today is more complicated than years ago. (4) Life should be lived through one's children.

32. In Richard Eberhart's "The Groundhog," the speaker's repeated visits to the animal's remains represent (1) his preoccupation with death (2) the certainty of death (3) the passage of time (4) his love for life

33. In Walt Whitman's poem "When I Heard the Learn'd Astronomer," the listener learns most from (1) the astronomer's lecture (2) the questions from the audience (3) the astronomer's charts and diagrams (4) his own observations of the stars

34. In Fedor Dostoevski's novel The Brothers Karamazov, Dmitri is accused of (1) arson (2) robbery (3) murder (4) extortion

35. Which term best describes the style of the opening section of Ralph Ellison's *Invisible Man*? (1) objective   (2) surrealistic   (3) journalistic   (4) chronological
36. In Charles Dickens' novel *Great Expectations*, the motive of Pip's benefactor in providing for Pip's education is the desire to   (1) repay a kindness once done to him   (2) have someone indebted to him   (3) help poor but deserving young people   (4) receive praise and recognition for his charity
37. In Ernest Hemingway's novel *A Farewell to Arms*, Frederic Henry faces final disillusionment as a result of   (1) his own severe wound   (2) the disintegration of the Italian Army   (3) Rinaldi's depression   (4) Catherine's death in childbirth
38. The novel *The Ox-Bow Incident* by Walter Clark develops the theme that   (1) direct action is the only way to solve some problems   (2) justice triumphs in the end   (3) no one can predict the consequences of every action   (4) the apple never falls far from the tree
39. In "By the Waters of Babylon," Stephen Vincent Benét warns against   (1) defying taboos   (2) acquiring knowledge too quickly   (3) seeking new experiences   (4) looking backwards
40. In the essay by Heywood Broun, the Fifty-first Dragon escapes because Gawaine   (1) forgets the word "Rumplesnitz"   (2) loses interest in killing   (3) lets it go   (4) loses his confidence

Part III

Directions: Answer *A* or *B* or *C* or *D*.   [30]

A. Write a well-organized composition of 250–300 words on one of the following topics:

Should women be drafted?	They are driven
Where have all our heroes and heroines gone?	Schools are more than classrooms
If I were a designer	My road
Wheels of all different sizes	Seconds can make the difference

B. During the last year, your senior class has been raising money to pay for a trip to Washington, D.C. Last month, the high school marching band went to Gettysburg, Pennsylvania, for a weekend. On that trip, several students started a fight and caused damage to their hotel. Your principal, therefore, is considering canceling your class trip to Washington, D.C. He suggests the money raised be used to hold a senior class dance instead.

Write a letter of 250–300 words in which you persuade your principal that she or he should *or* should not cancel the trip. Be sure to state your opinion clearly and give *three* reasons to support your opinion. *Write only the body of the letter.*

C. Leaving home for the first time in order to become independent is painful for most people.

Write a letter of 250–300 words to a close friend explaining why you have decided to "strike out" on your own despite the emotional difficulty it is causing you and your family. *Write only the body of the letter.*

D. Your local newspaper has lately been emphasizing crime and its prevention. The cartoon on page 11 has been reproduced on the editorial page of your newspaper.

Write a letter of 250–300 words to the editor in which you react to the ideas depicted as well as to the way in which specific visual clues reinforce the ideas. *Write only the body of the letter.*

© Uluschak, Edmonton Journal, Canada (Rothco)

"Life imprisonment...and I hope the parole board doesn't let you out for at least three years!"

Directions for the Listening Section:

1. The teacher will read a passage aloud. Listen carefully. DO NOT WRITE ANYTHING.
2. Then the teacher will tell you to open your test booklet to page 2 and to read questions 1 through 10. At this time you may mark your tentative answers to questions 1 through 10 if you wish.
3. Next, the teacher will read the passage aloud a second time. *As you listen to the second reading,* WRITE THE NUMBER of the answer to each question in the appropriate space on the answer sheet.
4. After you have listened to the passage the second time, you will have up to 5 minutes to look over your answers.
5. The teacher is not permitted to answer questions about the passage.
6. After you have answered the listening questions on page 2, go right on to the rest of the examination.

Part I
Listening   [10]

1. To the speaker, the end of summer represents
   (1) the end of a routine
   (2) a new beginning
   (3) a continuation of her schedule
   (4) an end to childhood
2. To the speaker, summer appears to represent
   (1) growth
   (2) responsibility
   (3) efficiency
   (4) freedom
3. To the speaker, fall appears to represent
   (1) peace
   (2) competition
   (3) routine
   (4) maturity
4. The speaker's thoughts are not said aloud to her children because she
   (1) finds no time in their busy schedule
   (2) realizes it would make no difference
   (3) fears rejection
   (4) has too much to say
5. Which statement best expresses the speaker's advice to her audience?
   (1) Do not think of the future.
   (2) Try to avoid disappointments.
   (3) Listen to experienced people.
   (4) Enjoy the present.
6. The speaker compares childhood to a coat because they both can be
   (1) altered to fit
   (2) put aside
   (3) stored
   (4) worn
7. According to the speaker, the positive aspect of disappointments is that they
   (1) are short-lived
   (2) build character
   (3) reveal true friends
   (4) make people humble
8. The speaker's feelings about her own ability to help her children can best be described as
   (1) uncertain
   (2) unrealistic
   (3) sophisticated
   (4) matter-of-fact
9. What is the main idea of this speech?
   (1) Children need some pain in order to become strong.
   (2) Only adults appreciate life.
   (3) People should learn to appreciate all stages of life.
   (4) Competition and responsibility are only for adults.
10. A characteristic of the speaker's style in this speech is that she
    (1) depends on humor to make her point
    (2) makes the same point in different ways
    (3) uses sentimental appeal to please her audience
    (4) uses irony to emphasize her theme

Directions (11–30): In the space provided on the separate answer sheet, write the *number* of the word or phrase that most nearly expresses the meaning of the word printed in heavy black type. [10]

11. larceny   (1) criminal   (2) burning   (3) name-calling   (4) theft
12. simulate   (1) delay   (2) supply   (3) pretend   (4) deny
13. lucid   (1) clear   (2) colorful   (3) lawful   (4) old
14. remorse   (1) anger   (2) regret   (3) apology   (4) coldness
15. laden   (1) optimistic   (2) refined   (3) burdened   (4) worried
16. turbulence   (1) control   (2) interruption   (3) renewal   (4) disorder
17. incessantly   (1) instantly   (2) brilliantly   (3) respectfully   (4) continually
18. chronic   (1) diseased   (2) constant   (3) aged   (4) unsafe
19. tepid   (1) lukewarm   (2) eager   (3) tearful   (4) sharp
20. consensus   (1) survey   (2) contract   (3) association   (4) agreement
21. Have you ever heard the saying "To be **wary** is to be wise"?   (1) thrifty   (2) healthy   (3) careful   (4) industrious
22. Sherlock Holmes was noted for his superb power of **deduction**.   (1) imagination   (2) reasoning   (3) extrasensory perception   (4) concentration
23. The manager encouraged the staff to try to add to the store's **clientele**.   (1) goodwill   (2) profits   (3) customers   (4) variety of merchandise
24. The student was **disconcerted** when she saw her test score.   (1) upset   (2) assured   (3) pleased   (4) surprised
25. An automobile can be a **lethal** machine.   (1) expensive   (2) deadly   (3) essential   (4) magnificent
26. The general promised to **annihilate** the enemy's troops.   (1) pursue   (2) destroy   (3) capture   (4) surround
27. She is the owner of a **lucrative** construction company.   (1) small   (2) reliable   (3) local   (4) profitable
28. After Joan had completed her investigation, she realized that her **premise** was incorrect.   (1) assumption   (2) conclusion   (3) methodology   (4) information
29. During the campaign, the politicians often engaged in **acrimonious** debate.   (1) meaningless   (2) brilliant   (3) bitter   (4) loud
30. There is no value in this **sordid** film.   (1) boring   (2) vile   (3) experimental   (4) inferior

Directions (31–40): In each of the following groups of words, only one of the words is misspelled. In *each* group, select the misspelled word and spell it correctly in the space provided on the separate answer sheet. [5]

31. ridiculous   comparable   shield   merciful   cotten
32. amendment   candadate   accountable   recommendation   bacteria
33. antebiotic   stitches   lengthen   pitiful   sneaky
34. diploma   commission   dependent   luminious   paternal
35. likelihood   blizzard   machanical   momentum   suppress
36. commercial   releif   disposal   endeavor   pronounce
37. talented   avocado   recruit   tripping   probally
38. operate   bronco   excaping   grammar   cafeteria
39. orchard   collar   addiction   embarass   distant
40. sincerely   possessive   weighed   waist   metallic

Directions (41–60): Below each of the following passages, there are one or more incomplete statements or questions about the passage. Select the word or expression that best completes the statement or answers the question *in accordance with the meaning of the passage*, and write its *number* in the space provided on the separate answer sheet.   [20]

Passage A

Those who save money are often accused of loving money; but, in my opinion, those who love money most are those who spend it. To them money is not merely a list of dead figures in a bankbook. It is an animate thing, spasmodically restless like the birds in a wood, taking wings to itself, as the poet has said. Money, to the man who enjoys spending,
5 is the perfect companion—a companion all the dearer because it never outstays its welcome. It is responsive to his every mood. . . . Age, alas, has blotted out half that world of passionate delight in which I once lived, and to many of the things I once loved I have grown indifferent. The love of money, however, remains. So much do I love it that I feel almost a different person when I have money in my pocket and when I have none. Let me have
10 but money, and, for the time being, I am back among the ardent attachments and illusions of the nursery.
From all this I am inclined to conclude that the love of money is a form of infantilism. The man who loves money is the man who has never grown up. He has never passed from the world of fairy tales into the world of philosophy (for philosophy, which is the wisdom
15 of the grown man in contrast to the wonder of the child, is as contemptuous of money as it is of jam, sweets, and bedknobs). Money, according to the philosophers, is dross, filthy lucre, an impediment rather than an aid to true happiness. Those who retain the nursery imagination throughout life, however, cannot be persuaded of this. Money they regard as the loveliest gift ever bestowed on a mortal by the wand of a fairy godmother. They are
20 like boys dreaming of a Treasure Island; and their moneybags become almost as dear to them as—sometimes, dearer than—their country.

—Adapted from *Searchlights and Nightingales* by Robert Lynd

41. According to the first paragraph, money has the quality of   (1) changing a personality   (2) causing restlessness   (3) outstaying its welcome   (4) inspiring greed
42. During the author's lifetime, many things have changed for him except his   (1) love of money   (2) fear of old age   (3) contempt for philosophy   (4) desire to return to his childhood
43. Which expression in the second paragraph describes the characteristics of men who like money?   (1) "I am inclined to conclude" (line 12)   (2) "the wisdom of the grown man" (lines 14 and 15)   (3) "Money . . . is dross, filthy lucre" (lines 16 and 17)   (4) "like boys dreaming of a Treasure Island" (line 20)
44. The author implies that "the ardent attachments and illusions of the nursery" (lines 10 and 11) include   (1) bankbooks and checkbooks   (2) animals and birds   (3) jams, sweets, and bedknobs   (4) parents and companions
45. According to the author, philosphers view money as   (1) a throwback to childhood   (2) a necessary evil   (3) a reward for good living   (4) an obstacle to happiness
46. Some people who love money see its source as   (1) magical   (2) destructive   (3) fateful   (4) philosophical
47. In the author's view, the love of money may even compete with   (1) justice   (2) patriotism   (3) ambition   (4) wisdom

Passage B

Mamie

Mamie beat her head against the bars of a little Indiana town and
    dreamed of romance and big things off somewhere the way the rail-
    road trains all ran.
She could see the smoke of the engines get lost down where the streaks
5   of steel flashed in the sun and when the newspapers came in on the
    morning mail she knew there was a big Chicago far off, where all
    the trains ran.
She got tired of the barber shop boys and the post office chatter and the
    church gossip and the old pieces the band played on the Fourth of
10   July and Decoration Day
And sobbed at her fate and beat her head against the bars and was going
    to kill herself
When the thought came to her that if she was going to die she might as
    well die struggling for a clutch of romance among the streets of
15   Chicago.
She has a job now at six dollars a week in the basement of the Boston
    Store
And even now she beats her head against the bars in the same old way
    and wonders if there is a bigger place the railroads run to from Chi-
20   cago where maybe there is
        romance
        and big things
        and real dreams
        that never go smash.

                —Carl Sandburg

48. What do the "bars" in line 1 symbolize?　　(1) a way of showing how small Mamie's town is　　(2) the moral conventions of small-town life　　(3) a contrast of hope and fear　　(4) Mamie's feeling of being trapped

49. The words "chatter" in line 8 and "gossip" in line 9 both indicate that　　(1) the people had nothing to do　　(2) conversation in Mamie's town is limited　　(3) Mamie liked to talk to people　　(4) people got excited over bad news

50. Which phrase best expresses Mamie's attitude toward her town?　　(1) "the morning mail" (lines 5 and 6)　　(2) "where all the trains ran" (lines 6 and 7)　　(3) "the barber shop boys" (line 8)　　(4) "a clutch of romance" (line 14)

51. Which expression is an example of figurative language?　　(1) "beat her head against the bars" (line 1)　　(2) "where all the trains ran" (lines 6 and 7)　　(3) "the post office chatter" (line 8)　　(4) "if she was going to die" (line 13)

52. In which line is there a definite shift in the tone of the poem?　　(1) line 8　　(2) line 11　　(3) line 16　　(4) line 22

53. Mamie's lack of success in finding romance in Chicago is indicated by the word　　(1) "dollars" (line 16)　　(2) "basement" (line 16)　　(3) "dreams" (line 23)　　(4) "smash" (line 24)

54. The poem suggests that if Mamie were to go somewhere other than Chicago, her dreams would　　(1) not be fulfilled　　(2) most likely come true　　(3) reflect her homesickness　　(4) become more realistic

Passage C

Portrait of a Literary Critic

The madness grew from week to week. With every revolution of the clock, the Chaos of the Cultures grew. But through it all the soul of Dr. Turner kept its feet. Turner hewed true and took the Middle Way. To all things in their course, in their true proportion, he was just.

5   True, he had lapses. In culture's armies he was not always foremost to the front. But he caught up. He always caught up. If there were sometimes errors in his calculations, he always rectified them before it was too late. If he made mistakes—like the man he was, he gallantly forgot them.

It was inspiring just to watch his growth. In 1923, for instance, he referred to *Ulysses* of
10 James Joyce as "that encyclopaedia of filth which has become the bible of our younger intellectuals"; in 1925, more tolerantly, as "that bible of our younger intellectuals which differs from the real one in that it manages to be so consistently dull"; in 1929 (behold this man!) as "that amazing *tour de force* which has had more influence on our younger writers than any other work of our generation"; and in 1933, when Justice Woolsey handed
15 down the famous decision that made the sale of *Ulysses* legally permissible throughout these United States (in a notable editorial that covered the entire front page of the *Fortnightly Cycle*), as "a most magnificient vindication of artistic integrity . . . the most notable triumph over the forces of bigotry and intolerance that has been scored in the Republic of Letters in our time."

—Thomas Wolfe

55. The statement "In culture's armies he was not always foremost to the front" (line 5) indicates that Dr. Turner   (1) was never swayed by public opinion   (2) fought to preserve old values   (3) was sometimes slow to recognize change   (4) had his own unique ideas

56. Which statement does the author make about Dr. Turner?   (1) He admitted making mistakes.   (2) He corrected "errors in his calculations."   (3) He was truly objective in his judgments.   (4) He enjoyed "the most notable triumph."

57. In the words "behold this man!" (lines 12 and 13), the author expresses   (1) admiration for Turner   (2) awe at Joyce's *Ulysses*   (3) approval of Justice Woolsey's decision   (4) amazement at Turner's shifting opinions

58. According to this passage, the reader could most reasonably conclude that *Ulysses*   (1) was not known in the United States for several years after it was published   (2) was universally applauded when it was first published   (3) could not be sold legally in the United States before 1933   (4) was James Joyce's first book

59. Which statement concerning the author's attitude toward the "younger intellectuals" is most nearly correct?   (1) They are too rash.   (2) They are receptive to new ideas.   (3) They are looking to the critics for guidance.   (4) They are disillusioned with the past.

60. The author's statements about Turner are supported by   (1) hints   (2) generalities   (3) quotations   (4) analogies

Directions (61–65): In each group of sentences below, the same idea is expressed in four different ways. For *each* group, select the way that is best, and write its *number* on the separate answer sheet. [5]

61. (1) Each time one of her cubs was threatened, the mother lion was ready to attack. (2) Each time one of her cubs were threatened, the mother lion got ready to attack. (3) Ready to attack, the cubs were protected from every threat by the mother lion. (4) Protected from every threat, the mother lion was ready to defend her cubs every time one of them were threatened.

62. (1) Seatbelts, while unquestionably a good idea, it's sometimes a nuisance to use them. (2) Seatbelts, while unquestionably a good idea, are sometimes a nuisance. (3) Seatbelts are unquestionably a good idea and also they are sometimes a nuisance. (4) Seatbelts, while it's unquestionably a good idea to have them, it's sometimes a nuisance to have them.

63. (1) While trimming the hedges, a bird's nest was discovered. (2) He discovered a bird's nest trimming the hedges. (3) Trimming the hedges, a bird's nest was discovered. (4) As he was trimming the hedges, he discovered a bird's nest.

64. (1) Each person applying for a job must fill out a card listing his or her previous places of employment. (2) Applying for a job, each person must fill out a card listing their previous places of employment. (3) Listing his or her previous places of employment on a card, each person must do this when applying for a job. (4) Each person, by filling out a card on which they list their previous places of employment, can apply for a job.

65. (1) A man, who's successful sets reasonable goals for himself. (2) A man whose successful sets reasonable goals for himself. (3) A man who's successful sets reasonable goals for himself. (4) A man, whose successful, sets reasonable goals for himself.

Part II

Directions: Write a well-organized essay of at least 200–250 words on *A* or *B*, or answer *both* parts of *C*.

A. From among the novels, full-length plays, and books of true experience you have read, choose *two* prominent characters, each from a different work, who change significantly. For each character: (1) Discuss at least *one* major change that occurs. (2) By making specific references to the work, indicate what reasons the author provides to explain each change. (3) State why you feel the change is believable or not.
   Give titles and authors.

B. People can experience loneliness when they live alone, but they can also be lonely if their ideas, feelings, or circumstances are different from those around them. From the short stories and poems you have read, choose *four* selections that deal with loneliness. For *each* work, show by specific references in what way the central character is lonely and explain how he or she deals with that loneliness. Give titles and authors.

C. Answer *both* C-1 and C-2, which appear on pages 7–9.

Answer C-1 and C-2 *only* if you choose Part IIC.

C-1 Directions (1-10): The passage below is followed by 10 incomplete statements or questions about the passage. For *each*, select the word or expression that best completes the statement or answers the question, and write its *number* in the space provided on the separate answer sheet.

> Oh, oh, you will be sorry for that word!
> Give back my book and take my kiss instead.
> Was it my enemy or my friend I heard,
> "What a big book for such a little head!"
> 5 Come, I will show you now my newest hat,
> And you may watch me purse my mouth and prink!
> Oh, I shall love you still, and all of that.
> I never again shall tell you what I think.
> I shall be sweet and crafty, soft and sly;
> 10 You will not catch me reading anymore:
> I shall be called a wife to pattern by;
> And some day when you knock and push the door,
> Some sane day, not too bright and not too stormy,
> I shall be gone, and you may whistle for me.

> —Edna St. Vincent Millay

1. The tone of this poem is   (1) happy   (2) sad   (3) indignant   (4) amused
2. What effect does the author achieve by the repetition of "Oh, oh . . ." in line 1?   (1) It attracts the reader's attention.   (2) It employs the device of onomatopoeia.   (3) It signals the symbol that will follow.   (4) It shows the speaker's shock after hearing "that word."
3. The implication of line 4, "What a big book for such a little head!" is that   (1) young people should not read lengthy books   (2) women are not bright enought to read significant books   (3) the book is meant for men   (4) the speaker thinks too highly of herself
4. What change of mood occurs in line 5?   (1) dismay changes to outward compliance   (2) acceptance changes to rebellion   (3) hate changes to love   (4) enthusiasm changes to dispair
5. What literary device is found in line 9, "I shall be sweet and crafty, soft and sly"?   (1) metaphor   (2) hyperbole   (3) assonance   (4) alliteration
6. Lines 8 through 11 suggest that the speaker is   (1) sorry for past actions   (2) developing a strategy for the future   (3) happy about the whole experience   (4) still confused
7. Which statement most clearly reflects the implication in lines 12 through 14?   (1) If you whistle for me, I will return.   (2) Some day I will become independent.   (3) When things become dull, I will leave.   (4) I will leave when you want me to.
8. Which line best demonstrates the speaker's understanding of the role she is expected to fill?   (1) line 5   (2) line 2   (3) line 7   (4) line 11
9. Which best describes the poetic function of the phrases "some day" and "Some sane day" in lines 12 and 13?   (1) The phrases reinforce the rhyme scheme.   (2) The phrases emphasize the indecision of the speaker.   (3) The phrases move from the general to the specific.   (4) The phrases employ figurative language.
10. In line 14, the speaker uses the word "whistle" to suggest that   (1) he has treated her more like a pet than a person   (2) she will not return until he searches for her   (3) she expects him to chase after her   (4) he will still find her attractive

C-2 Directions (11–40): Choose only *10* of the following, and, in the space provided on the separate answer sheet, write the *number* of the word or expression that best completes the statement or answers the question.

11. In James Baldwin's essay "The Fire Next Time," the author attacks   (1) school boards   (2) racial prejudice   (3) communism   (4) atheism

12. In Mark Twain's novel *A Connecticut Yankee in King Arthur's Court,* who is the chief opponent of the "Boss"?   (1) Merlin   (2) King Arthur   (3) Clarence   (4) Morgan le Fay

13. Corrie Ten Boom's autobiographical account *The Hiding Place* tells of her family's experiences during World War II of hiding Jews in a secret compartment in her father's   (1) church   (2) bookstore   (3) watch shop   (4) clothing store

14. The unknown citizen in Auden's poem of the same name is unknown because he   (1) is a stranger in the city   (2) has assumed the name of another person   (3) is an unidentified corpse   (4) has been robbed of his identity

15. In Milton's sonnet containing the lines "They also serve who only stand and wait," the poet expresses his attitude toward   (1) his betrayers   (2) the King   (3) his library   (4) his handicap

16. In Arthur Miller's *Death of a Salesman,* Biff finally comes to the realization that he   (1) has too much power   (2) has overestimated himself   (3) can beat the system   (4) lacks a sense of humor

17. In Edgar Allen Poe's short story "The Pit and the Pendulum," the prisoner gets away from the pendulum when   (1) the rats chew his bonds   (2) he falls into the pit   (3) he finds the secret entrance   (4) the pendulum breaks

18. The Greek goddess of wisdom is   (1) Athena   (2) Aphrodite   (3) Hera   (4) Artemis

19. The short story "Two Soldiers" by William Faulkner is told from the point of view of   (1) Pete   (2) Old Man Killgrew   (3) Pete's brother   (4) the lieutenant

20. In his soliloquy "To be or not to be," Hamlet decides not to commit suicide because he   (1) is too much in love with Ophelia to part with her   (2) believes suicide is against the law of God   (3) has been cautioned against suicide by his father   (4) is more afraid of the afterlife than the world he knows

21. In the short story "The Rocking Horse Winner" by D. H. Lawrence, Paul wanted   (1) good luck   (2) a new sister   (3) a girl friend   (4) his own horse

22. In Joseph Conrad's "The Secret Sharer," the young captain   (1) is a silent partner in a trading venture   (2) gives refuge to someone who has killed a man   (3) refuses to tell where the treasure is hidden   (4) revels in the self-assurance accompanying his first command

23. In Samuel Beckett's play *Waiting for Godot,* the two main characters are   (1) soldiers   (2) students   (3) hoboes   (4) patients

24. What does Nathaniel Hawthorne suggest is a cause of Chillingworth's death in the novel *The Scarlet Letter?*   (1) Hester encouraged him to go to sea.   (2) The Puritan townspeople convicted him.   (3) Dimmesdale confessed his sin and died.   (4) Pearl refused to accept him.

25. In Carson McCullers' novel *The Member of the Wedding,* the title symbolizes Frankie's   (1) wish to grow up   (2) love for weddings   (3) hope to marry   (4) desire to belong

26. In Willa Cather's novel *My Ántonia,* young Ántonia's life is made more difficult by   (1) Jim Burden's antagonism   (2) her father's suicide   (3) her mother's cruelty   (4) her brother's jealousy

27. In the final scene of Ibsen's play *Hedda Gabler,* Hedda   (1) leaves George   (2) decides to marry Eilert   (3) commits suicide   (4) shoots Judge Brack

28. In the poem "Chicago," Carl Sandburg compares the city to (1) a boastful, undefeated fighter (2) a sly tomcat (3) an evil, unfeeling woman (4) a robot
29. In Robert Frost's poem "The Death of the Hired Man," Silas's refusal to go to his brother's home reveals Silas's (1) ignorance (2) cruelty (3) pride (4) hate
30. In Shakespeare's *Henry IV, Part I*, Falstaff's cowardice is revealed during a (1) tavern brawl (2) fake robbery (3) battle against the French (4) mock duel with Prince Hal
31. In his sonnet "Death Be Not Proud," John Donne says that death must be pleasurable because (1) life is full of uncertainty (2) death is an adventure (3) death ends earthly misery (4) sleep and rest are pleasurable
32. By the end of Jonathan Swift's novel *Gulliver's Travels*, Gulliver feels most comfortable in the company of (1) his family (2) his horse (3) the Lilliputians (4) the Yahoos
33. *The Thread That Runs So True* is Jesse Stuart's autobiographical account of his years as a (1) schoolteacher (2) foreman in a steel mill (3) sharecropper (4) long-distance runner
34. In Hal Borland's novel *When the Legends Die*, Tom's favorite animal and "brother" is a (1) deer (2) bear (3) raccoon (4) mountain lion
35. In Charles Dickens' novel *Great Expectations*, Miss Havisham encourages Estella to be (1) indifferent to worldly values (2) suspicious of other women (3) cruel to any man who loves her (4) rebellious toward her father
36. Charles Lamb is best known for his (1) essays (2) translations (3) sonnets (4) biographies
37. In John Steinbeck's novel *The Grapes of Wrath*, the plight of the Joads is symbolized in (1) the turtle's crossing the highway (2) the character of Jim Casy (3) Tom's having been in jail (4) the description of the truckdrivers
38. In Robert K. Massie's *Nicholas and Alexandra*, many Russians resent the fact that Alexandra was born in (1) the United States (2) Germany (3) Austria (4) France
39. The overall theme of *Bury My Heart at Wounded Knee* by Dee Brown is that the (1) Indians deserved their treatment at Wounded Knee because they had massacred Custer (2) Indians only want payment for their land (3) sacred mountain at Wounded Knee should be returned to the Osage Indians (4) ancient rights and ceremonies of the Indians should be safeguarded
40. The situation in Theodore Roethke's poem "My Papa's Waltz" arouses in the boy feelings of (1) hope and anticipation (2) jealousy and need (3) fear and love (4) horror and excitement

Part III

Directions: Answer *A* or *B* or *C* or *D*. [30]

A. Write a well-organized composition of 250–300 words on one of the following topics:

Schools are not just classrooms	Getting it into the picture
Forward leaps in science	The high price of sports
Modern miracles	The importance of understanding
The biggest change	one's roots
Why now is the time that matters	

B. You like your job with a fast-food chain. The manager, however, has begun to schedule you for exceptionally long hours during the week. Since this seriously interferes with your schoolwork, you have repeatedly asked the manager to reduce your hours. When the same kind of scheduling continues, you decide to contact the area supervisor. Write a letter of 250–300 words in which you state your problem. Be sure to include the reasons you want to work and the reasons why your hours should be shortened. *Write only the body of the letter.*

C. Imagine that the Senior Council has designated you to write to the commencement speaker for the June 1982 exercises at your school. Your task is to write a letter of 250–300 words to the speaker suggesting at least *four* topics that would be appropriate for the audience and the occasion, and explain why you think they would be appropriate. In your explanation, you may wish to include relevant information about your class. *Write only the body of the letter.*

D. As a member of the editorial staff of your school newspaper, you have been selected to write an editorial of 250–300 words on the topic of what young people feel are priorities for the new administration in Washington, D.C. Since everything cannot be done at once, explain why you think these particular problems or projects should receive immediate attention, and why attention to certain other problems or projects could be postponed.

Directions for the Listening Section:

1. The teacher will read a passage aloud. Listen carefully. **DO NOT WRITE ANYTHING.**
2. Then the teacher will tell you to open your test booklet to page 2 and to read questions 1 through 10. At the time you may mark your tentative answers to questions 1 through 10 if you wish.
3. Next, the teacher will read the passage aloud a second time. *As you listen to the second reading,* **WRITE THE NUMBER** of the answer to each question in the appropriate space on the answer sheet.
4. After you have listened to the passage the second time, you will have up to 5 minutes to look over your answers.
5. The teacher is not permitted to answer questions about the passage.
6. After you have answered the listening questions on page 2, go right on to the rest of the examination.

Part I
Listening   [10]

1. The mother clearly realizes that her son
   (1) wants a lot of money for himself
   (2) is too young to understand the situation
   (3) is jealous of his sister
   (4) would rather have fun than have responsibility

2. The mother most likely holds this conversation with her son because she
   (1) wants no more arguments   (3) was asked to by the father
   (2) is unsure of his response   (4) needs to feel better about herself

3. The father's attitude toward his daughter's education could best be described as
   (1) uninformed   (3) negative
   (2) questioning   (4) indifferent

4. The mother supports her idea that times are changing by referring to
   (1) Madame Curie   (3) motion pictures
   (2) her own marriage   (4) science

5. Which word best describes how the mother felt about her own marriage?
   (1) disappointed   (3) satisfied
   (2) resentful   (4) accepting

6. The example of the son's friend in the machine shop supports the idea that machines
   (1) will not last very long   (3) must be integrated into our world
   (2) must be used for peaceful purposes   (4) are not being accepted

7. The mother firmly believes that in the future her daughter will
   (1) make a contribution to humanity   (3) be the subject of a movie
   (2) be like Madame Curie   (4) marry a scientist

8. Which word best describes the mother's attitude toward her son?
   (1) protective   (3) sympathetic
   (2) approving   (4) apathetic

9. Compared with the father's thinking, the mother's thinking in this scene from the play could best be described as
   (1) judgmental   (3) biased
   (2) progressive   (4) faulty

10. Which statement best describes the mother's approach to life?
    (1) Plan for the future.   (3) Take life one day at a time.
    (2) Remember the past.   (4) Question your own decisions.

Directions (11-30): In the space provided on the separate answer sheet, write the *number* of the word or phrase that most nearly expresses the meaning of the word printed in heavy black type. [10]

11. **intuition** (1) payment (2) faith (3) introduction (4) insight
12. **compel** (1) lengthen (2) help (3) force (4) distract
13. **vent** (1) discharge (2) omit (3) entertain (4) worship
14. **cohort** (1) commander (2) companion (3) candidate (4) craftsman
15. **ordeal** (1) alternate route (2) logical sequence (3) important duty (4) severe trial
16. **fabrication** (1) addition (2) remedy (3) analysis (4) creation
17. **unwitting** (1) ordinary (2) unaware (3) unnecessary (4) inadvisable
18. **zealot** (1) sharp tool (2) worthy cause (3) eager person (4) extinct animal
19. **indulge** (1) spoil (2) surprise (3) direct (4) compare
20. **hamper** (1) offer (2) confuse (3) order (4) restrict
21. The first settlers in America faced a cold winter in the **vast** wilderness. (1) unknown (2) untamed (3) enormous (4) empty
22. Her very presence at the party **nettled** the other guests. (1) embarrassed (2) irritated (3) puzzled (4) quieted
23. The attorney was eager to **disclose** her evidence. (1) examine (2) reorganize (3) report (4) reveal
24. When the brakes failed, the bus nearly went off the road into a **chasm**. (1) gorge (2) field (3) river (4) wall
25. I avoid that restaurant because of its **insipid** food. (1) spicy (2) tasteless (3) overcooked (4) expensive
26. A **malicious** person is usually unpopular. (1) conceited (2) selfish (3) spiteful (4) stingy
27. He was able to **elude** the soldiers for only a short time. (1) escape (2) train (3) aid (4) restrain
28. The man **denounced** his neighbor because of her political activities. (1) avoided (2) ridiculed (3) spied on (4) condemned
29. The grapegrowers in California employ many **transient** workers. (1) immigrant (2) youthful (3) temporary (4) experienced
30. The money has been **allocated** for new school buses. (1) set aside (2) raised (3) spent (4) borrowed

Directions (31-40): In each of the following groups of words, only one of the words is misspelled. In *each* group, select the misspelled word and spell it correctly in the space provided on the separate answer sheet. [5]

31. parallel   aluminum   calendar   dedicated   eigty
32. magazine   expository   imitation   permenent   careless
33. microbe   ancient   supposed   autograph   existance
34. plentiful   skillful   amoung   fiery   capsule
35. erupt   quanity   opinion   competent   exempt
36. excitement   discipline   luncheon   regreting   definite
37. ferosious   machinery   precise   stimulate   magnificent
38. curiosity   conceive   narritive   separation   management
39. muscular   witholding   pickle   glacier   radiation
40. vehical   mismanage   correspondence   dissatisfy   mockery

Directions (41–60): Below each of the following passages, there are one or more incomplete statements or questions about the passage. For each, select the word or expression that best completes the statement or answers the question *in accordance with the meaning of the passage,* and write its *number* in the space provided on the separate answer sheet. [20]

Passage A

The football is oval in shape, usually thrown in a spiral, and when kicked end over end may prove difficult to catch. If not caught on the fly, it bounces around erratically.

The apparent intent of the game is to deposit the ball across the opponent's goal line. Any child with a ball of his own might do it, six days a week and most of Sunday morning,
5 but the rules of the game specify it must be done with members of both teams present and on the field. Owing to large-scale substitutions, this is often difficult.

In the old days people went crazy trying to follow the ball. The players still do, but the viewing public, who are watching the game on TV, can relax and wait for the replay. If anything happens, that's where you'll see it. The disentanglement of bodies on the goal line
10 is one of the finer visual moments available to sport fans. The tight knot bursts open, the arms and legs miraculously return to the point of rest, before the ball is snapped. Some find it unsettling. Is this what it means to be born again?

All ball games feature hitting and socking, chopping and slicing, smashing, slamming, stroking, and whacking, but only in football are these blows diverted from the ball to the
15 opponent. And the more the players are helped or carried from the field, the more attendance soars. This truly male game is also enjoyed by women who find group therapy less rewarding. The sacking of the passer by the front four is especially gratifying. Charges that a criminal element threatens the game are a characteristic, but hopeful, exaggeration. What to do with big, mean, boyish-hearted men, long accustomed to horsing around in good clean
20 dormitories, unaccustomed to the rigors of life in the Alaska oilfields, was, until football, a serious national dilemma.

—Adapted from "Odd Balls" by Wright Morris, *Atlantic,* June 1978

41. Which audience would most likely find the greatest enjoyment in this passage? (1) young boys who plan to play football   (2) women who love sports   (3) nonathletic Americans (4) professional football players
42. The purpose of the second paragraph is to suggest that football   (1) has very strict rules (2) is a simple game made unnecessarily complicated   (3) can be played anywhere and anytime   (4) is best played on a regulation field
43. According to this passage, football is unlike other sports in that it   (1) is played with a ball that is difficult to catch   (2) is being infiltrated by criminals   (3) relies on instant replay as a vital part of the game   (4) directs violence at the players rather than at the ball
44. The author of this passage most likely believes that   (1) football is overrated   (2) most women want to play football   (3) sports are to be played rather than watched   (4) too many injuries occur in football
45. One of the ironies of football is that   (1) the players cannot follow the ball as well as the viewers   (2) children can play the game   (3) the game is played by men acting like children   (4) both men and women love the game
46. The author describes football players as   (1) lovers of violence   (2) overgrown boys (3) members of organized crime   (4) oilfield workers
47. The tone of this passage can best be described as   (1) argumentative   (2) questioning (3) suspenseful   (4) satiric

Passage B

The Whipping

The old woman across the way
is whipping the boy again
and shouting to the neighborhood
her goodness and his wrongs.

5 Wildly he crashes through elephant ears,
    pleads in dusty zinnias,
while she in spite of crippling fat
    pursues and corners him.

She strikes and strikes the shrilly circling
10   boy till the stick breaks
in her hand. His tears are rainy weather
    to woundlike memories:

My head gripped in bony vise
    of knees, the writhing struggle
15 to wrench free, the blows, the fear
    worse than blows that hateful

Words could bring, the face that I
    no longer knew or loved . . .
Well, it is over now, it is over,
20   and the boy sobs in his room,

And the woman leans muttering against
    a tree, exhausted, purged—
avenged in part for lifelong hidings
    she has had to bear.

—Robert E. Hayden

48. The whipping occurs in a   (1) garden   (2) street   (3) driveway   (4) bedroom

49. The poet views the whipping as   (1) an unusual punishment for the boy   (2) inappropriate punishment for the boy   (3) acceptable as a punishment by the boy   (4) helpful in correcting the boy's errors

50. From lines 13 through 15, it is evident that the   (1) boy in the poem was fighting to get away   (2) poet had also suffered beatings   (3) old woman held the boy's head between her knees   (4) boy's head was held in a vise

51. In lines 17 and 18, the poet "no longer knew or loved" the face because it most likely   (1) had become a strange face to him   (2) had aged suddenly   (3) was twisted with rage   (4) was the face of a criminal

52. In the final stanza, the woman feels cleansed because she has   (1) released her own frustrations   (2) done her duty in punishing the boy   (3) tired herself out   (4) succeeded in catching the boy

53. In lines 21 through 24, the poet's attitude toward the woman is one of   (1) spitefulness   (2) indifference   (3) fear   (4) understanding

54. Lines 23 and 24 suggest that the woman has   (1) an easy life   (2) sympathy for the boy   (3) unpleasant memories   (4) a deep hatred for the boy

Passage C

She walked along the river until a policeman stopped her. It was one o'clock, he said. Not the best time to be walking alone by the side of a half-frozen river. He smiled at her, then offered to walk her home. It was the first day of the new year, 1946, eight and a half months after the British tanks had rumbled into Bergen-Belsen.

5   That February, my mother turned twenty-six. It was difficult for strangers to believe that she had ever been a concentration camp inmate. Her face was smooth and round. She wore lipstick and applied mascara to her large dark eyes. She dressed fashionably. But when she looked into the mirror in the morning before leaving for work, my mother saw a shell, a mannequin who moved and spoke but who bore only a superficial resemblance to her real
10 self. The people closest to her had vanished. She had no proof that they were truly dead. No eyewitnesses had survived to vouch for her husband's death. There was no one living who had seen her parents die. The lack of confirmation haunted her. At night before she went to sleep and during the day as she stood pinning dresses she wondered if, by some chance, her parents had gotten past the Germans or had crawled out of the mass grave into
15 which they had been shot and were living, old and helpless, somewhere in Poland. What if only one of them had died? What if they had survived and had died of cold or hunger after she had been liberated, while she was in Celle dancing with British officers?

She did not talk to anyone about these things. No one, she thought, wanted to hear them. She woke up in the mornings, went to work, bought groceries, went to the Jewish Com-
20 munity Center and to the housing office like a robot.

—Adapted from *Children of the Holocaust* by Helen Epstein

55. The policeman stopped the author's mother from walking along the river because   (1) the river was dangerous   (2) it was the wrong time of day   (3) it was still wartime   (4) it was too cold
56. The author states that her mother thought about her parents when she   (1) walked along the river   (2) thought about death   (3) danced with the officers   (4) was at work
57. When the author mentions her mother's dancing with British officers, she implies that her mother   (1) compared her dancing to the suffering of her parents   (2) had clearly put her troubles behind her   (3) felt it was her duty to dance with them   (4) felt guilty about dancing
58. The mother did not discuss her concerns about her loved ones with anyone because she   (1) thought no one was interested   (2) felt it was no one's business   (3) was too shy   (4) did not know anyone
59. The author's ability to detail her mother's thoughts suggests that the author   (1) has lived through the same experience   (2) has antiwar sentiments   (3) is sympathetic and attentive   (4) is religious and thoughtful
60. The author's purpose in writing this passage is most likely to   (1) inform people about atrocities in the concentration camp   (2) explain the long-range effects of a traumatic experience   (3) enlist active participation in refugee affairs   (4) encourage people to prosecute former concentration camp guards

Directions (61–66): Choose only 5 of the questions below. For each question you choose, select the answer that best completes the statement or answers the question, and write its number in the appropriate space on the separate answer sheet. [5]

61. Which of the following is the *most* specific in meaning?   (1) athlete   (2) girl   (3) Tracy Austin   (4) student
62. A writer's expressions of approval or disapproval of something are best regarded as   (1) inferences   (2) reports   (3) allusions   (4) judgments
63. One way a modern screen actor differs from a stage actor is that the screen actor   (1) has

had more thorough training   (2) relies more on subtle facial expressions   (3) needs to have a better memory   (4) depends more upon exaggerated physical gestures
64. Which literary technique is used in the title "Schools, Subsidies, and Segregation"?   (1) alliteration   (2) allegory   (3) parable   (4) personification
65. In the card catalog, cross-reference cards are used primarily to   (1) locate a book on the shelves   (2) determine the author of a certain work   (3) locate additional information on a subject   (4) find other books by an author
66. How are novels arranged on a library shelf?   (1) alphabetically by subject   (2) alphabetically by author's last name   (3) numerically by Dewey Decimal number   (4) alphabetically by title

Part II

Directions: Write a *well-organized* essay of *at least* 200–250 words on *A* or *B*.   [20]

A. Many authors deal with a special relationship between members of the older and younger generations. From the novels, plays, or short stories you have read, choose *two* in which there is a special relationship between members of different generations. For *each* work, identify the two characters, and, using specific references, describe their relationship and explain how the relationship benefits one or both of the characters or how it harms one or both of the characters. Give titles and authors.

B. Imagery and symbolism are devices that authors frequently employ. From the poems, short stories, essays, or one-act plays you have read, choose *four* in which an image or symbol is effectively used. Using specific references, describe an image or symbol in *each* selection and explain how it works in the context of the selection as a whole. Give titles and authors.

Part III

Directions: Answer *A* or *B* or *C* or *D*.   [30]

A. Many places can be very different at two distinctly different times. Think of such a place that is familiar to you. Write a 250–300 word composition in which you describe this place at *two* distinctly different times. Include vivid details that point up the differences. You may, for example, describe a place you knew as a child and revisited as a young adult, a familiar street during rush hour and early in the morning, or a beach in summer and in winter. You may use these suggestions or you may use your own ideas provided you keep to the assigned topic.
B. Arriving late to school and cutting class have become serious problems in your school. As editor-in-chief of the school newspaper, you have decided to write an editorial in which you address the problem. Write an editorial of 250–300 words in which you discuss the problem and offer possible solutions.
C. Your local movie theater is sponsoring an all-request film festival. The manager of the theater is offering prizes for the best suggestions recommending previously shown films to be revived during the festival. Write a letter of 250–300 words in which you recommend *two* films for the manager's consideration. Make your reasons for selecting the particular films as specific and convincing as possible. *Write only the body of the letter.*
D. Write a well-organized composition of 250–300 words on one of the following topics:

Showoffs	My battle with inflation
A time for remembering	Living in a computer world
Where's the justice?	Music speaks for an era

Directions for the Listening Section:

1. The teacher will read a passage aloud. Listen carefully. DO NOT WRITE ANYTHING.
2. Then the teacher will tell you to open your test booklet to page 2 and to read questions 1 through 10. At this time you may mark your tentative answers to questions 1 through 10 if you wish.
3. Next, the teacher will read the passage aloud a second time. *As you listen to the second reading*, WRITE THE NUMBER of the answer to each question in the appropriate space on the answer sheet.
4. After you have listened to the passage the second time, you will have up to 5 minutes to look over your answers.
5. The teacher is not permitted to answer questions about the passage.
6. After you have answered the listening questions on page 2, go right on to the rest of the examination.

Part I
Listening   [10]

1. The speaker talks as if she were a
   (1) defendant on trial
   (2) chairperson of a committee
   (3) legislator arguing for a new law
   (4) judge ruling at a trial
2. The speaker broadens her appeal to her audience by showing how her case could affect all
   (1) existing laws
   (2) United States citizens
   (3) women
   (4) uneducated persons
3. The speaker quotes the preamble to the Constitution in order to
   (1) impress the audience with her intelligence
   (2) share common knowledge with her audience
   (3) point out which part of the preamble needs to be changed
   (4) add force to her argument
4. According to this speech, one reason for forming the Union was to
   (1) establish an aristocracy
   (2) limit the powers of the states
   (3) insure domestic harmony
   (4) draw up a Constitution
5. According to the speaker, who formed the Union?
   (1) only one-half of the people
   (2) the whole people
   (3) white male citizens, only
   (4) only the male citizens of all races
6. When the speaker says that the blessings of liberty are forever withheld from women and their female posterity, she means that
   (1) women of the present and the future will suffer
   (2) all classes of women are discriminated against
   (3) women of the past have been victimized
   (4) female children of the poor will be the only ones affected
7. The speaker argues that a government that denies women the right to vote is not a democracy because its powers do not come from the
   (1) Constitution of the United States
   (2) rights of the states
   (3) consent of the governed
   (4) vote of the majority
8. According to this speech, an oligarchy of sex would cause
   (1) women to rebel against the government
   (2) men to desert their families
   (3) poor women to lose hope
   (4) problems to develop in every home
9. In this speech, a citizen is defined as a person who has the right to vote and also the right to
   (1) change laws
   (2) acquire wealth
   (3) speak publicly
   (4) hold office
10. The speaker argues that state laws that discriminate against women are
    (1) being changed
    (2) null and void
    (3) helpful to the rich
    (4) supported only by men

Directions (11–30): In the space provided on the separate answer sheet, write the *number* of the word or phrase that most nearly expresses the meaning of the word printed in heavy black type. [10]

11. **resurrection** (1) reassurance (2) encouragement (3) fascination (4) revival
12. **recede** (1) take over (2) show off (3) hold out (4) move back
13. **fissure** (1) opening (2) path (3) mountain (4) landslide
14. **delectable** (1) carefree (2) elaborate (3) delightful (4) deliberate
15. **oblivious** (1) understated (2) unmindful (3) untrue (4) unappetizing
16. **inevitable** (1) unable (2) forceful (3) certain (4) plain
17. **paradox** (1) incomplete response (2) sharp comment (3) obvious truth (4) seeming contradiction
18. **cataclysm** (1) disaster (2) deception (3) denial (4) debate
19. **sanction** (1) stop (2) expel (3) approve (4) refund
20. **assiduously** (1) decidedly (2) diligently (3) randomly (4) correctly
21. The judge ordered that **restitution** be provided for the robbery victims. (1) apologies (2) recognition (3) publicity (4) compensation
22. The trumpets announced the **imminent** arrival of the dignitary. (1) approaching (2) delayed (3) unexpected (4) distant
23. The shopper was **indignant** at the treatment given him by the clerk. (1) embarrassed (2) pleased (3) angry (4) surprised
24. The cook in the old diner had a **slatternly** appearance. (1) dreary (2) sloppy (3) homey (4) strange
25. The **nebulous** argument that he presented failed to explain the main issue. (1) careful (2) complex (3) vague (4) idealistic
26. The prisoner longed for the life of a **vagabond**. (1) wanderer (2) millionaire (3) celebrity (4) journalist
27. The entire neighborhood came out to see the **celestial** display. (1) artistic (2) fantastic (3) unusual (4) heavenly
28. Because the shopkeeper was upset, we were unable to **glean** the details of the robbery. (1) connect (2) gather (3) tell (4) comprehend
29. The problem rests not with her beliefs but with her excessive desire to **propagate** them. (1) spread (2) live up to (3) protect (4) justify
30. The young athlete tried to **emulate** his high school coach. (1) obey (2) assist (3) imitate (4) deceive

Directions (31–40): In each of the following groups of words, only one of the words is misspelled. In *each* group, select the misspelled word and spell it correctly in the space provided on the separate answer sheet. [5]

31. irresistible   varius   destination   mutual   refrigerator
32. chocolate   instrument   volcanoe   cardboard   shoulder
33. amateur   distinguish   rehearsal   poision   surrender
34. ancestry   obscure   intention   morality   ninty
35. biased   ommission   precious   amazing   coordinate
36. artical   bracelet   beggar   hopeful   memorized
37. calculated   enthusiasm   yoke   sincerely   parashute
38. tournament   sponsor   perpendiclar   dissolve   derivation
39. salvation   sentry   materials   incredable   budget
40. yeild   physician   computer   greasiest   admitting

Directions (41–60): Below each of the following passages, there are one or more incomplete statements or questions about the passage. Select the word or expression that best completes the statement or answers the question *in accordance with the meaning of the passage*, and write its *number* in the space provided on the separate answer sheet.   [20]

Passage A

I turned on my back and floated, looking up at the sky, nothing around me but cool clear Pacific, nothing in my eyes but long blue space. It was as close as I ever got to cleanliness and freedom, as far as I ever got from all the people. They had jerrybuilt the beaches from San Diego to the Golden Gate, bulldozed superhighways through the mountains, cut down
5 a thousand years of redwood growth, and built an urban wilderness in the desert. They couldn't touch the ocean. They poured their sewage into it, but it couldn't be tainted.

There was nothing wrong with Southern California that a rise in the ocean level wouldn't cure. The sky was flat and empty, and the water was chilling me. I swam to the kelp-bed and plunged down through it. It was cold and clammy like the bowels of fear. I came up
10 gasping and sprinted to shore with a barracuda terror nipping at my heels.

I was still chilly a half-hour later, crossing the pass to Nopal Valley. Even at its summit, the highway was wide and new, rebuilt with somebody's money. I could smell the source of the money when I slid down into the valley on the other side. It stank like rotten eggs.

The oil wells from which the sulphur gas rose crowded the slopes on both sides of the
15 town. I could see them from the highway as I drove in: the latticed triangles of the derricks where trees had grown, the oil-pumps nodding and clanking where cattle had grazed. Since 'thirty-nine or 'forty, when I had seen it last, the town had grown enormously, like a tumor.

—Adapted from *The Drowning Pool* by Ross MacDonald

41. In the first paragraph, the ocean is the symbol of nature's   (1) inability to adapt   (2) resistance to humanity's endeavors   (3) submission to a mechanized society   (4) attack on technology
42. What is the narrator's attitude toward people as expressed in the first paragraph?   (1) They are like the cool clear Pacific.   (2) He is indifferent toward them.   (3) Nature is nothing without them.   (4) Freedom is preferable to an association with them.
43. The tone of lines 7 and 8 can best be described as   (1) sarcastic   (2) optimistic   (3) nostalgic   (4) cautious
44. What are the prevailing images in lines 8 through 10?   (1) light and dark   (2) cold and heat   (3) terror and fear   (4) death and defeat
45. In this passage, the narrator apparently is trying to   (1) appeal to legislators for environmental action   (2) inform readers of what Southern California looks like   (3) indicate his disapproval of what has been done   (4) show the potential beauty of the area
46. In the last paragraph, the main idea is developed through the use of   (1) cause and effect   (2) contrast   (3) analogy   (4) incident
47. In the last paragraph, the narrator feels that the growth of the town is   (1) detrimental   (2) inevitable   (3) progressive   (4) hasty

Passage B

First Lesson

Lie back, daughter, let your head
be tipped back in the cup of my hand.
Gently, and I will hold you. Spread
your arms wide, lie out on the stream
5 and look high at the gulls. A dead-
man's float is face down. You will dive
and swim soon enough where this tidewater
ebbs to the sea. Daughter, believe
me, when you tire on the long thrash
10 to your island, lie up, and survive.
As you float now, where I held you
and let you go, remembering when fear
cramps your heart, what I told you:
lie gently and wide to the light-year
15 stars, lie back, and the sea will hold you.

—Philip Booth

48. The statement "Spread your arms wide, lie out on the stream and look high at the gulls" (lines 3 through 5) suggests that the father (1) understands that his daughter can now float (2) realizes that his daughter does not fear the water (3) need not teach his daughter any longer (4) asks his daughter to gain self-confidence
49. The statement "You will dive and swim soon enough" (lines 6 and 7) most likely indicates that the father (1) resents the daughter's impatience (2) looks forward to the daughter's swimming alone (3) imagines the daughter facing life alone (4) will teach the daughter diving and swimming
50. By saying "Daughter, believe me" (lines 8 and 9), the father is really offering her his (1) warning (2) support (3) fear (4) philosophy
51. By saying to his daughter, "when you tire on the long thrash to your island, lie up, and survive" (lines 9 and 10), the father most likely means a time when she (1) is floundering in deep water (2) feels discouraged (3) suffers pain (4) needs to be alone
52. In line 10, the word "island" symbolizes a (1) goal (2) dream (3) rejection (4) new home
53. The father's final advice to his daughter (lines 14 and 15) may be summed up as (1) float through life (2) avoid fearful situations (3) trust both yourself and life (4) be open to all experiences

Passage C

A Hook, a Worm, and Thou

In the archives of Smith College's Library there exists a delightful letter from George Washington Cable to his friend Harry Norman Gardiner. "Dear Mr. Gardiner," the letter begins, "Will you go fishing again this afternoon to the same place, the watery graveyard of the oarlock and the rod-tip? You will have only your own equipment to provide and we will 5 take a basket of lunch along, and stay to our heart's content, and come home to a fresh bite spread just for us. And there will be the fruit of the vine in the basket, and we will angle for that pickerel. . . . O come, come away! When shall we start?"

This genteel and lyrical invitation, dated July 13, 1901, shows just how far we've drifted from the simple joys of fishing. I mean, of course, the unspeakable rod-and-gun columns
10 and magazines, the big money "pro-am fishout" contests to catch the biggest fish, and the lure-of-the-month mentality, all of which have threatened in recent years to transform fishing from a Tom Sawyer expedition to a NATO maneuver.

In a sense, fishing, which is by very far the most popular sport in the country, has become a kind of subsidiary enterprise of the great propaganda machines that sell war, sex, and
15 automobile technology to the American male and his adolescent sons. The fish is no longer incidental to the experience of fishing, nor to the friendship of a Cable for a Gardiner.

No, the fish has become an enemy, still another threat to our self-image, to be pursued, subdued, and vanquished. It's the awful way of our culture to swamp every activity with volumes of complicating instruction which keep us from feeling true emotion. We are losing
20 the right to say, as Hemingway does in *Big Two-Hearted River*, "Nick's heart tightened as the trout moved. He felt all the old feeling."

—Jonathan Evan Maslow

54. Which statement best expresses the main idea of this passage? (1) Fishing is the most popular sport in the United States. (2) Fishing has been changed by advertising interests. (3) Fishing no longer unites friends. (4) Fishing is essential for survival.
55. The author's attitude toward the letter from Cable to Gardiner can best be described as (1) admiring (2) amused (3) bored (4) flippant
56. In line 9, the word "unspeakable" reveals the author's attitude toward (1) fishermen (2) modern sports (3) NATO maneuvers (4) sports propaganda
57. In lines 13 through 16, the reader can infer that the author's attitude toward modern-day fishing is (1) concerned (2) critical (3) interested (4) indifferent
58. In line 14, the phrase "the great propaganda machines" refers to the (1) mass media (2) Federal Government (3) fishing industry (4) automobile industry
59. In lines 17 and 18, the author implies that the fish has become the enemy because (1) people no longer like to fish (2) fish have learned to outwit people (3) fishing has become a symbol of mastery (4) fishing has too many regulations
60. The author's main purpose in writing this passage most likely is to (1) train fishermen (2) entertain with tales of the past (3) promote the fishing industry (4) mourn the passing of simple joys

Directions (61–65): In each group of sentences below, the same idea is expressed in four different ways. For *each* group, select the way that is best, and write its *number* in the space provided on the separate answer sheet. [5]

61. (1) I don't like hiking as much as I like cross-country skiing. (2) I don't like to hike as much as I like cross-country skiing. (3) I don't like hiking as much as I like to ski cross-country. (4) I don't like to hike as much as I like going cross-country skiing.
62. (1) I wouldn't of gone if I had known about Emily. (2) I wouldn't have gone if I had known about Emily. (3) I wouldn't have went if I had known about Emily. (4) I wouldn't of went if I had known about Emily.
63. (1) She planned a trip to the beach, a visit with her grandmother, and to take a long walk with her cousin. (2) She planned to go to the beach, a visit with her grandmother, and a long walk with her cousin. (3) She planned a trip to the beach, a visit with her grandmother, and a long walk with her cousin. (4) She planned a trip to the beach, visiting with her grandmother, and to take a long walk with her cousin.
64. (1) It is better to, I think, tell the truth than to lie. (2) It is better to, I think, tell the truth than lying. (3) Telling the truth, I think, is better than to lie. (4) It is better, I think, to tell the truth than to lie.

65. (1) He was not only a fine student but also a superior athlete.   (2) Not only was he a fine student but a superior athlete, also.   (3) He was not only a fine student but a superior athlete also.   (4) Also, he was not only a superior athlete, but a fine student.

Part II

Directions: Write a well-organized essay of *at least* 200-250 words on either *A* or *B*.   [20]

A. Sometimes a literary character is afflicted with a physical or psychological handicap. From the novels, full-length plays, and biographies you have read, choose *two* in which a character suffers from a physical or psychological handicap. For *each* work, identify the character. Using specific references, show how the character's handicap affects his or her adjustment to life. Give titles and authors.

B. Some literary characters have inspired readers to model their own lives after the character. From the novels, poems, short stories, plays, or books of true experience you have read, choose *two* in which a character appears whom some young people might consider a worthy model for their own lives. For *each* work, identify the character, and by specific references, explain why that character provides a good example on which to model one's life. Give titles and authors.

Part III

Directions: Answer *A* or *B* or *C* or *D*.   [30]

A. Write a well-organized composition of 250-300 words on *one* of the following topics:

Rain	Is there life after high school?
The life of the "rich"	Killing time
Whatever happened to . . .?	Junk food addicts

B. The editor of your school literary magazine has asked you to write a short fictional narrative for next month's edition describing how an experience or a circumstance changed the life of the person involved. You have decided to use an accident, real or imagined, as the basis for a 250-300 word fictional narrative showing how that accident changed the life of the person involved.

C. Imagine that you have been looking through an old photograph album as part of an assignment for a unit on local history. One picture especially fascinates you, but no one has any information about the person(s) in the photograph. In a 250-300 word composition that you will share with your class, describe the photograph, present a theory about who the individual(s) might be, and suggest why the photograph may have been taken.

D. You are a student representative on a school committee that is considering the possibility of abolishing final examinations. Each committee member has been asked to write a 250-300 word letter to the chairperson of the committee stating his or her opinion about eliminating final examinations. In your letter, state your point of view and fully develop a persuasive argument to support your opinion. *Write only the body of the letter.*

Directions for the Listening Section:

1. The teacher will read a passage aloud. Listen carefully. DO NOT WRITE ANYTHING.
2. Then the teacher will tell you to open your test booklet to page 2 and to read questions 1 through 10. At this time you may mark your tentative answers to questions 1 through 10 if you wish.
3. Next, the teacher will read the passage aloud a second time. *As you listen to the second reading*, WRITE THE NUMBER of the answer to each question in the appropriate space on the answer sheet.
4. After you have listened to the passage the second time, you will have up to 5 minutes to look over your answers.
5. The teacher is not permitted to answer questions about the passage.
6. After you have answered the listening questions on page 2, go right on to the rest of the examination.

Part I
Listening   [10]

1 The speaker gains the attention of the audience at the beginning of the speech through the use of a

  1 rhetorical question   3 patriotic appeal
  (2) comparison   (4) personal example

2 The speaker believes that those who are truly responsible for the growth of social service programs are the

  1 worthy recipients who receive help
  2 powerful lobby groups who demand action
  3 government bureaucrats who are protecting their jobs
  (4) individuals who refuse to accept social responsibility

3 According to the speaker, government has been a "soft touch" because it has

  1 developed too many programs for too many problems
  (2) been too lenient in developing program guidelines
  3 shown more concern for the needs of recipients than the needs of taxpayers
  4 been spoiled by the willingness of the public to fund worthwhile programs

4 According to the speaker, fewer State and Federal programs should be developed in the future because
  1 less money might be available for programs
  2 the number of needy people is decreasing
  3 existing programs are becoming more effective
  4 problem solving should become a community responsibility

5 The speaker believes that doubling the amount of money spent on crisis management would be
  1 justifiable
  2 unappreciated
  3 ineffective
  4 wise

6 According to this speech, fewer government services would be necessary if
  1 problems were handled more efficiently in their early stages
  2 public officials were held more accountable for the programs
  3 stricter eligibility requirements were used to define need
  4 costly duplication of services was eliminated

7 Marginally effective programs are those programs which the speaker feels
  1 treat only the visible signs of a crisis
  2 show the greatest cost savings
  3 work to reduce the number of people serviced by the program
  4 provide a minimum of services to a maximum of people

8 According to the speaker, present government programs tend to encourage the public's
  1 responsibility
  2 anger
  3 dependency
  4 despair

9 According to the speaker, the reduction of government services is
  1 a dream that will never be achieved
  2 a painful necessity that must be attempted
  3 a cruel approach to dealing with a problem
  4 an impossible task for a responsive government

10 The speaker's attitude might be considered somewhat surprising since his position is that of a
1 political reporter
2 candidate for office
3 head of a government agency
4 leader of a lobbying organization

Directions (11–30): In the space provided on the separate answer sheet, write the *number* of
the word or phrase that most nearly expresses the meaning of the word printed in heavy black
type. [10]

11 **abduct**
   1 ruin   3 fight
   2 aid   4 kidnap

12 **demerit**
   1 outcome   3 prize
   2 fault   4 notice

13 **mutinous**
   1 silent   3 rebellious
   2 oceangoing   4 miserable

14 **negligent**
   1 lax   3 cowardly
   2 desperate   4 ambitious

15 **contest**
   1 disturb   3 detain
   2 dispute   4 distrust

16 **query**
   1 wait   3 show
   2 lose   4 ask

17 **insidious**
   1 treacherous   3 internal
   2 excitable   4 distracting

18 **palpitate**
   1 mash   3 throb
   2 stifle   4 pace

19 **animosity**
   1 hatred   3 silliness
   2 interest   4 amusement

20 **egotism**
   1 sociability   3 self-confidence
   2 aggressiveness   4 conceit

21 Bob's account of the accident **incriminated** others.
   1 annoyed   3 ignored
   2 involved   4 helped

22 When Jack left his position as chief of staff, he was
completely **demoralized**.
   1 satisfied   3 liberated
   2 frenzied   4 disheartened

23 The architect designed a modern **edifice** of wood and red glass.
   1 framework   3 structure
   2 platform   4 false front

24 The speaker kept the meeting interesting with her **facetious** remarks.
   1 amusing   3 personal
   2 informal   4 factual

25 The new ruling set a **precedent** for all similar cases that would be tried in court.
   1 direction   3 regulation
   2 standard   4 test

26 The botanist wanted a picture of the tree because it was so **gnarled**.
   1 old   3 fruitful
   2 unusual   4 deformed

27 Harriet's **ostentatious** display of wealth is upsetting to her friends.
   1 frequent   3 showy
   2 thoughtless   4 unnatural

28 The answer was too **oblique** to receive full credit.
   1 indirect   3 disorganized
   2 repetitive   4 brief

29 The magician did the sleight-of-hand trick with remarkable **dexterity**.
   1 swiftness   3 charisma
   2 assurance   4 skill

30 The principal had no **qualms** about suspending the three boys for fighting.
   1 comments   3 arguments
   2 misgivings   4 regrets

Directions (31-40): In each of the following groups of words, only one of the words is misspelled. In *each* group, select the misspelled word and spell it correctly in the space provided on the separate answer sheet. [5]

31 banana
   trafic → *traffic*
   spectacle
   boundary
   prescription

32 commentator
   abbreviation
   battaries → *batteries*
   monastery
   urgently

33 *annonymous*
   envelope
   transit
   variable → *rarible*
   stereotype

34 originate
   petroleum
   bigoted
   meager
   resistence → *resistance*

35 *practically* → *practicaly*
   advise
   measured
   pursuade
   laboratory → *labortory*

36 *fatigueing* → *fatiguing*
   invincible
   strenuous
   ceiling
   migrant

37 cafeteria
   propeller
   reverence
   piecemeal
   underneth → *underneath*

38 permissible
   indictment
   fundamental
   nowadays
   parliamentary → *parlimenta*

39 thief
   bargin
   nuisance → *nuisance*
   vacant → *racc*
   awkward

40 technique
   vengeance
   aquatic
   heighth
   category → *category*

Directions (41-60): Below each of the following passages, there are one or more incomplete statements or questions about the passage. For each, select the word or expression that best completes the statement or answers the question *in accordance with the meaning of the passage,* and write its *number* in the space provided on the separate answer sheet. [20]

Passage A

She came forward, all in black, with a pale head floating towards me in the dusk. She was in mourning. It was more than a year since his death, more than a year since the news came; she seemed as though she would remember and mourn forever. She took both my hands in hers and murmured, "I had heard you were
5 coming." I noticed she was not very young—I mean not girlish. She had a mature capacity for fidelity, for belief, for suffering. The room seemed to have grown darker, as if all the sad light of the cloudy evening had taken refuge on her

forehead. This fair hair, this pale visage, this pure brow, seemed surrounded by an ashy halo from which the dark eyes looked out at me. Their glance was guile-
10   less, profound, confident, and trustful. She carried her sorrowful head as though she were proud of that sorrow, as though she would say, I—I alone know how to mourn him as he deserves. But while we were still shaking hands, such a look of awful desolation came upon her face that I perceived she was one of those crea-tures that are not the playthings of Time. For her he had died only yesterday.

—Adapted from *Heart of Darkness*
by Joseph Conrad

41 The narrator suggests that the woman appears ma-ture because of her
  1 consciousness of age
  2 acceptance of responsibility
  3 worldly manner
  4 capacity for suffering

42 The woman's forehead seemed to be a resting place for
  1 her inner anxieties
  2 the darkness of the room
  3 the mournful light of the evening
  4 her trust

43 The narrator noticed that the woman appeared espe-cially grief-stricken when
  1 they were shaking hands
  2 he entered the room
  3 he first looked into her eyes
  4 she came forward to greet him

44 When the narrator observes that the woman is not one of the "playthings of Time" (line 14), he proba-bly means that she
  1 is too young to look so old
  2 does not believe in wasting her life
  3 welcomes approaching old age
  4 is not affected by the passage of time

45 The narrator states that the woman will probably
grieve for a long time because she
1 acts as if the man had just died
2 had known the dead man for a long time
3 is so very young
4 is a sensitive person

46 The author's purpose in writing this passage is most
probably to
1 describe the character of the visitor
2 show the extent of one person's mourning
3 explain the woman's need for compassion
4 demonstrate the relationship between the woman
and the dead man

Passage B

America

Although she feeds me bread of bitterness,
And sinks into my throat her tiger's tooth,
Stealing my breath of life, I will confess
I love this cultured hell that tests my youth!
5   Her vigor flows like tides into my blood,
Giving me strength erect against her hate.
Her bigness sweeps my being like a flood.
Yet as a rebel fronts a king in state,
I stand within her walls with not a shred
10   Of terror, malice, not a word of jeer.
Darkly I gaze into the days ahead,
And see her might and granite wonders there,
Beneath the touch of Time's unerring hand,
Like priceless treasures sinking in the sand.

          —Claude McKay

47 Lines 9 and 10 imply that the poet is
1 frightened and nervous
2 proud and revengeful
3 calm and self-contained
4 angry and defiant

48 Which quote from this poem is *not* an example of
   figurative language?
   1 "bread of bitterness" (line 1)
   2 "tiger's tooth" (line 2)
   3 "like tides" (line 5)
   ④ "days ahead" (line 11)

49 The poet expresses his feeling toward America as
   one of
   ① love   3 terror
   2 malice   4 indifference

50 Which group of words most vividly uses exaggeration
   for effect?
   1 "she feeds me bread of bitterness" (line 1)
   ② "sinks into my throat her tiger's tooth" (line 2)
   3 "I will confess" (line 3)
   4 "her might and granite wonders" (line 12)

51 The poet views the greatest of all forces as
   1 America   ③ time
   2 the tides   4 civilization

52 The poet expresses a paradox in stating that America
   both
   1 flows and ebbs
   2 rebels and rules
   ③ nourishes and destroys
   4 grows and dies

53 The poet views his relationship with America as one
   of
   1 child and parent
   2 prisoner and warden
   3 pupil and teacher
   ④ rebel and authority

Passage C

Some new religious groups answer the need young people feel today for a way of life not based on accumulation and competition. Others promise an experience of the holy, undiluted by the accommodations Christianity and Judaism have made to consumer culture. Thus, minority religious movements can also be seen
5 as symptoms of a hunger seemingly too deep for our existing religious institutions to feed.

I doubt if many people will ultimately find answers in these movements. Most of those who try an Oriental path will eventually find it too exotic for the Western psyche. They will then turn, as some are doing already, to the neglected spiritual
10 and critical dimensions of our own traditions. Meanwhile, minority movements need protection, in part because they help us to see what is missing in our own way of life.

American culture has an enormous capacity to domesticate its critics. It is not unique in that respect. Christianity was once an exotic cult, providing a way of life
15 visibly different from the jaded society around it. After a short period of persecution, it accommodated to the culture so well it was eventually accepted as Rome's only legitimate religion. Christians then quickly turned to the persecution of other religions. The same thing could happen to today's "cultists."

A new test of America's capacity for genuine pluralism is under way. We could
20 flunk it by driving unconventional religious movements into accommodation before their message can be heard. I hope not. It is important to preserve freedom of religion, not only for the sake of the minority immediately involved but also because the majority needs to hear what the minority is saying.

—Adapted from "Playing the Devil's
Advocate, As It Were" by Harvey
Cox, Dolan J. Paul, and Edward
Quinn

54 The purpose of the first paragraph is to
1 present reasons for the existence of religions
② explain the rise of minority religious movements
3 suggest how major religions can survive
4 criticize the increasing popularity of cults

55 According to this passage, young people will not be satisfied by minority Oriental religious movements because those movements contain beliefs that will
① ultimately seem too foreign
2 be as prejudicial as major religions
3 soon become commonplace
4 neglect important traditions

56 According to this passage, those people who try Oriental religions will later
1 drop all religious beliefs
2 start American cults
③ turn to traditional Western religions
4 protect minority religions

57 According to the authors, in its early days, Christianity was an
① escape from a corrupt way of life
2 answer to the demands of a complex society
3 intermingling of two different cultures
4 offshoot of the popular beliefs

58 The authors support the existence of minority religious movements primarily because they
1 are protected by the Constitution
2 help fight immorality
3 eventually become major religions
④ provide varied points of view

59 The predominant tone of this passage is
1 hostile   ③ objective
2 passive   4 pessimistic

60 Which statement best expresses the main idea of this passage?
1 Young people need new religions.
② Religious freedom is essential.
3 Cults can be dangerous.
4 Minority religious movements are not the answer.

Directions (61–66): Choose only 5 of the questions below. For each question you choose, select the answer that best completes the statement or answers the question, and write its number in the appropriate space on the separate answer sheet. [5]

61 The items in a bibliography are arranged in
① alphabetical order according to the author's last name
2 chronological order according to date of publication
3 alphabetical order according to the first word in the title
4 alphabetical order according to name of publisher

62 Which would *not* be likely to appear on the editorial page of a newspaper?
 1 readers' reactions 3 syndicated columns
 2 masthead 4 classified ads

63 In filmmaking, the term "dissolve" refers to the
 1 splicing of two different shots
 2 disintegration of the film
 3 merging of one shot into another
 4 speed of film projection

64 Which reference source would contain the most complete information on the British game of cricket?
 1 *The World Almanac*
 2 *Skeat's Etymological Dictionary*
 3 *Readers' Guide to Periodical Literature*
 4 *Encyclopedia Britannica*

65 In the theater, what is the definition of an "aside"?
 1 a stage direction in the script
 2 a comment made by a character for the audience alone to hear
 3 a painted piece of scenery
 4 a long speech made by a character alone on stage

66 Which pair of prefixes has the same meaning?
 1 sub and ultra 3 intra and circum
 2 ante and pre 4 hyper and tele

Part II

Directions: **Write a well-organized essay of *at least* 200–250 words on either *A* or *B*.** [20]

A Dignity, pride, and understanding the needs and feelings of other people are among the positive human qualities frequently praised in literature. From the novels, full-length plays, and poems you have read, choose *two* in which a positive human quality is presented. For *each* work, describe the positive quality and use specific references to show how the author praises that quality. Give titles and authors.

B   Sometimes pressure from other people can force a person to take an action that person might not have taken on his or her own. From the short stories, biographies, and books of true experience you have read, choose *two* works. From *each* work select one character who was forced to take action because of pressure from some other character or group. Using specific references, explain the intentions of those who were exerting the pressure and the effect this pressure had on each character. Give titles and authors.

Part III

Directions: Answer *A* or *B* or *C* or *D*.   [30]

A   You have been given the opportunity to nominate an individual for *TIME* magazine's "Man or Woman of the Year." In a 250–300 word letter to the editors of *TIME*, state whom you would nominate as "Man or Woman of 1982" and discuss why you consider the individual to be worthy of this honor. *Write only the body of the letter.*

B   A well-known American educator has stated that every college-bound student should spend a year in the armed services before beginning college study. Write an editorial of 250–300 words for your school newspaper, giving your opinion as to whether or not a year spent this way would be worthwhile to you and other young people. Support your point of view with specific details.

C   A local group called Parents for Better Reading has proposed that all books be reviewed and approved by a committee of parents before being placed in the school library. In a 250–300 word letter to the editor of your local newspaper, state your opinion of the proposal and explain your reasons for holding that opinion. *Write only the body of the letter.*

D   Write a well-organized composition of 250–300 words on *one* of the following topics:

The best invention ever	The destruction of our idols
Emergencies that weren't	The school politician
Instant success	Blaming others

COMPREHENSIVE EXAMINATION IN ENGLISH—JUNE 1983 (1)

Directions for the Listening Section:

1. The teacher will read a passage aloud. Listen carefully. DO NOT WRITE ANYTHING.
2. Then the teacher will tell you to open your test booklet to page 2 and to read questions 1 through 10. At this time you may mark your tentative answers to questions 1 through 10 if you wish.
3. Next, the teacher will read the passage aloud a second time. *As you listen to the second reading,* WRITE THE NUMBER of the answer to each question in the appropriate space on the answer sheet.
4. After you have listened to the passage the second time, you will have up to 5 minutes to look over your answers.
5. The teacher is not permitted to answer questions about the passage.
6. After you have answered the listening questions on page 2, go right on to the rest of the examination.

Part I
Listening   [10]

1 The speaker emphasizes the age of the store by re-marking on the
   1 smells of the spices
   2 smoothness of the floorboards
   3 availability of penny candy
   4 presence of a coffeegrinder

2 What was the speaker's first reaction when Mr. Hance gave him a stick of Yucatan gum?
   1 suspicion   3 delight
   2 pride   4 amazement

3 One characteristic which Mr. Hance and Aunt Wilma shared was
   1 an enthusiasm for religion
   2 an ability to calculate swiftly
   3 the alertness of their eyes
   4 a sense of humor

4 Aunt Wilma thought that many people in church were
   1 praying to become better persons
   2 thinking unworthy thoughts
   3 sleeping during the sermon
   4 looking to her as a model

5 From this passage, the listener can most safely assume that when the speaker was in church he often
  1 looked at the other worshipers
  2 disagreed with the sermon
  3 whispered to others
  4 fell asleep

6 The speaker's amusement at the clashes between Mr. Hance and Aunt Wilma was shared by
  1 his neighbors
  2 fellow church members
  3 his family
  4 other customers

7 The relationship between Aunt Wilma and Mr. Hance was characterized by their
  1 suspicion of each other's honesty
  2 respect for each other's intelligence
  3 dislike of each other's personality
  4 distrust over each other's arithmetic

8 Aunt Wilma thought the ability to do arithmetical calculations quickly was
  1 dishonest   3 unholy
  2 magic   4 lucky

9 What was the speaker's attitude toward Aunt Wilma?
  1 affectionate   3 confused
  2 disapproving   4 proud

10 In this passage, the speaker demonstrates his ability to
  1 create suspense
  2 recall people
  3 communicate opinions
  4 describe action

Directions (11-30): In the space provided on the separate answer sheet, write the *number* of the word or phrase that most nearly expresses the meaning of the word printed in heavy black type. [10]

11 **stow**
  1 pack
  2 report
  3 interest
  4 beg

12 **irrepressible**
  1 unrestrainable
  2 impatient
  3 unknowable
  4 impractical

13 **grimace**
  1 important development
  2 point of view
  3 expression of disgust
  4 act of spite

14 **promenade**
  1 limp
  2 walk
  3 jog
  4 race

15 **indicative**
  1 defensive
  2 attractive
  3 disruptive
  4 suggestive

16 **medley**
  1 game
  2 entertainment
  3 discussion
  4 mixture

17 **jaunty**
  1 mighty
  2 dirty
  3 lively
  4 petty

18 **undue**
  1 genuine
  2 wavy
  3 faultless
  4 inappropriate

19 **visage**
  1 appearance
  2 vividness
  3 prospect
  4 valor

20 **avid**
  1 eager
  2 easy
  3 dry
  4 flat

21 That **bestial** act marked him for life.
  1 unkind
  2 insensitive
  3 brutal
  4 spiteful

22 The professor was regarded as an **erudite** teacher.
  1 rigid
  2 scholarly
  3 demanding
  4 reasonable

23 We could see the **knolls** from our window.
  1 rounded hills
  2 groups of trees
  3 high waves
  4 marshes

24 As the nurse prepared the shot, I **winced** in anticipation.
  1 moaned aloud
  2 stared ahead
  3 lay still
  4 shrank back

25 The president said that he would not **countenance** such policies.
  1 order
  2 implement
  3 approve
  4 introduce

26 The lawyer proved that the witness was a **prevaricator**.
  1 murderer
  2 liar
  3 thief
  4 fraud

27 The explorers followed the **tributary** to its origin.
  1 stream
  2 lake
  3 trail
  4 valley

28 She always comes to school **impeccably** groomed.
  1 carelessly
  2 conservatively
  3 stylishly
  4 flawlessly

29 Mrs. Royce **discreetly** answered all the questions asked about her neighbor.
  1 precisely
  2 tactfully
  3 honestly
  4 positively

30 The actor's **feigned** southern accent was praised by the critics.
  1 pretended
  2 acquired
  3 unusual
  4 low-pitched

Directions (31-40): In each of the following groups of words, only one of the words is misspelled. In *each* group, select the misspelled word and spell it correctly in the space provided on the separate answer sheet. [5]

31 assortment
segregate
excessivly
territory
obstacle

32 unnecessary
monopolys
harmonious
irrigation
privilege

33 sinthetic
intellectual
gracious
archaic
vestibule

34 beneficial
fulfill
patent
sarcastic
disolve

35 umbrella
dominant
sentimental
inefficent
psychiatrist

36 noticable
knapsack
librarian
meant
ingredient

37 conference
upheaval
vulger
humidity
odor

38 surmount
pentagon
calorie
inumerable
statistics

39 classifiable
mistreated
moisturize
monitor
assesment

40 investigate
thermastat
corrupting
approach
thinness

Directions (41-60): Below each of the following passages, there are one or more incomplete statements or questions about the passage. For each, select the word or expression that best completes the statement or answers the question *in accordance with the meaning of the passage,* and write its *number* in the space provided on the separate answer sheet. [20]

Passage A

I saw him look that last look away beyond me into a sky so full of light that I could not follow his gaze. The little breeze flowed over me again, and nearby a mountain aspen shook all its tiny leaves. I suppose I must have had an idea then of what I was going to do, but I never let it come up into consciousness. I just
5　reached over and laid the hawk on the grass.
He lay there a long minute without hope, unmoving, his eyes still fixed on that blue vault above him. It must have been that he was already so far away in heart that he never felt the release from my hand. He never even stood. He just lay with his breast against the grass.

10   In the next second after that long minute he was gone. Like a flicker of light, he had vanished with my eyes full on him, but without actually seeing even a premonitory wing beat. He was gone straight into that towering emptiness of light and crystal that my eyes could scarcely bear to penetrate. For another long moment there was silence. I could not see him. The light was too intense. Then from
15 far up somewhere a cry came ringing down.
    I was young then and had seen little of the world, but when I heard that cry my heart turned over. It was not the cry of the hawk I had captured; for, by shifting my position against the sun, I was now seeing further up. Straight out of the sun's eye where she must have been soaring restlessly above us for untold
20 hours, hurtled his mate. And from far up, ringing from peak to peak of the summits over us, came a cry of such unutterable and ecstatic joy that it sounds down across the years and tingles among the cups of my quiet breakfast table.

—Loren Eisley

41 In line 1, "that last look" suggests that the hawk
  1 has been blinded
  2 expects to be rescued
  3 believes his death is near
  4 cannot comprehend what is happening

42 In line 4, the clause "I never let it come up into consciousness" suggests that the freeing of the hawk is
  1 premeditated   3 impossible
  2 impulsive   4 accidental

43 In line 4, the pronoun "it" refers to the
  1 narrator's plan of action
  2 captured hawk
  3 mate of the hawk
  4 act of trapping the hawk

44 In line 6, the minute is "long" to the narrator because he
  1 is thinking of changing his mind
  2 is young and inexperienced
  3 regrets the action he is taking
  4 is not sure what the hawk will do

45 By the end of this passage, the hawk's gaze is probably focused on
  1 the light   3 the blue sky
  2 mountain peaks   4 his mate

46 Throughout this passage, the natural phenomenon
the narrator seems most impressed by is the
1 deathlike silence   3 steady breeze
2 intense light   4 blue sky
47 The narrator's most lasting memory is of the
1 hawk's eyes   3 complete stillness
2 bright light   4 joyous call

Passage B

Sickness is a crime.
For habitual offenders
the penalty is death.
In the doctor's waiting room
5   we study one another
slyly, like embezzlers.
In the hospital
even those who love us
seem afraid of what
10 we might do to them.
(The sick have no friends.
Here there are only strangers,
brothers and lovers.)
Anyone who can walk
15   erect without swaying
is my superior.
Astonishing how soon
one learns the tricks
the weak use
20 against the strong.
For almost the first time
I have become
a credible flatterer. Next
I will learn to whine
25 —already I find myself
struggling against it.
The orderly who sneered
at the fat bearded man
in the Mother Hubbard—
30 would I have done differently
or only been more clever,
deceiving myself
that what I felt was pity.

—Alden Nowlan

48 In lines 5–6, "we study one another/slyly, like embezzlers," implies that sick people
1 sympathize with each other
2 envy the fate of people who are healthy
3 are secretly curious to know the illnesses of others
4 do not really care about other people

49 Which group of words from the poem is the best example of exaggeration?
1 "Sickness is a crime." (line 1)
2 "Here there are only strangers," (line 12)
3 "Anyone who can walk erect without swaying" (lines 14–15)
4 "I find myself struggling against it." (lines 25–26)

50 In lines 17 through 26, which statement best expresses the poet's opinion about sick people?
1 They ought to be pitied.
2 They want the sympathy of friends and relatives.
3 They dislike having orderlies tend to them.
4 They sometimes take advantage of healthy people.

51 Which group of words is used figuratively?
1 "we study one another slyly, like embezzlers" (lines 5–6)
2 "even those who love us seem afraid" (lines 8–9)
3 "I have become a credible flatterer" (lines 22–23)
4 "The orderly who sneered" (line 27)

52 The tone of this poem is best described as
1 objective   3 cynical
2 arrogant   4 indifferent

53 The poet's purpose in writing this poem most likely is to
1 criticize the medical profession
2 present a picture of the mind of a sick person
3 condemn the artificiality of hospital visits
4 present an autobiographical account of his illness

Passage C

The secret of Billy the Kid's greatness as a desperado lay in a marvelous coordination between mind and body. He had not only the will but the skill to kill. Daring, coolness, and quick thinking would not have served unless they had been combined with physical quickness and a marksmanship which enabled him to pink
5 a man neatly between the eyes with a bullet, at, say, thirty paces. He was not pitted against six-shooter amateurs but against experienced fighters themselves adept in the handling of weapons. The men he killed would have killed him if he had not been their master in a swifter deadliness. In times of danger, his mind was not only calm but also singularly clear and nimble, watching like a hawk for
10 an advantage and seizing it with incredible celerity. He was able to translate an impulse into action with the suave rapidity of a flash of light. While certain other men were a fair match for him in target practice, no man in the Southwest, it is said, could equal him in the lightning-like quickness with which he could draw a six-shooter from its holster and with the same movement fire with deadly ac-
15 curacy. It may be remarked incidentally that shooting at a target is one thing and shooting at a man who happens to be blazing away at you is something entirely different; and Billy the Kid did both kinds of shooting equally well.

—Walter Noble Burns

54 The main idea of the sentence, "While certain other men . . . with deadly accuracy," (lines 11 through 15) is that
1 other men could beat Billy in target practice
2 Billy did not aim before he fired
3 Billy could shoot another person faster than anyone else
4 Billy did most of his shooting in the Southwest

55 In lines 12 and 13, the words "it is said" suggest that the author is basing his conclusion on
1 oral tradition   3 historical evidence
2 radio accounts   4 first-hand experience

56 Billy the Kid's quickness is compared to that of a
1 swooping hawk   3 speeding bullet
2 flash of light   4 blink of an eye

57 According to this passage, Billy the Kid's secret of greatness was that he was
1 an experienced fighter   3 an ideal desperado
2 a wonder of coordination   4 a good marksman

58 The author seems to excuse Billy's murderous ways because Billy
   1 shot men and targets equally well
   2 was so cool and daring
   3 was so quick and accurate
   4 fought only experienced fighters

59 This passage is developed principally by
   1 order of importance   3 chronological order
   2 relevant details   4 definition

60 The tone of this passage is
   1 spiteful   3 conversational
   2 satiric   4 argumentative

Directions (61–65): In each group of sentences below, the same idea is expressed in four different ways. For *each* group, select the way that is best, and write its *number* in the space provided on the separate answer sheet. [5]

61 1 Either Janice wanted to be student council president or valedictorian of her class.
   2 Janice either wanted to be student council president or class valedictorian.
   3 Janice wanted either to be president of student council or class valedictorian.
   4 Janice wanted to be either student council president or class valedictorian.

62 1 John having left school was without his fathers' permission.
   2 John left school without his fathers' permission.
   3 John left school without his father's permission.
   4 John having left school was without his father's permission.

63 1 Jane is the girl, who's purse was stolen.
   2 Jane is the girl whose purse was stolen.
   3 Jane is the girl who's purse was stolen.
   4 Jane is the girl, whose purse was stolen.

64 1 It's too bad that people are not more compassionate.
   2 Its to bad that people are not more compassionate.
   3 Its too bad that people are not more compassionate.
   4 It's to bad that people are not more compassionate.

65 1 The character who suffered the most was Laura.
  2 The character, which suffered the most, was Laura.
  3 The character which suffered the most was Laura.
  4 The character, who suffered the most, was Laura.

Part II

Directions: Write a well-organized essay of *at least* 200–250 words on either *A* or *B*. [20

A In many literary works, characters search for a different or better way of life. From the nove
biographies, full-length plays, or books of true experience which you have read, choose t
works in which an important character searches for a different or better way of life. For ea
work, identify the character. Using specific references, explain what change *each* character
hoping to achieve in his or her way of life and discuss the ways in which each character tries
bring about that change. Give titles and authors.

B The setting of a piece of literature may be an important factor which influences the actions
the characters. From the short stories, one-act plays, and poems you have read, select t
works in which the setting plays an important role. Using specific references, describe
setting in *each* work and explain how it influences the actions of the characters. Give titles a
authors.

Part III

Directions: Answer A or B or C or D. [30]

A An area television station is preparing a local segment for the "I Love New York" campaign
order to attract more people to your community or region. The segment will consist of fi
footage of your community accompanied by the voice of a narrator describing the places sho
in the film. You have been asked to prepare the script for this segment. Write a 250–300 wc
script describing some of the attractive features of your community and explain why they wo
be of interest to potential residents or vacationers.

B You have an opportunity to apply for a scholarship to attend a summer school course in the a
or the sciences—music, painting, drama, dance, film, photography, writing, physics, chemist
biology. Write a 250–300 word letter in which you persuade the selection committee to choc
you for the course you are interested in attending. Be sure to include any information that v
help you get the scholarship. *Write only the body of the letter.*

C Someone has said: "People can be divided into three groups: those who make things happe
those who watch things happen, and those who wonder what happened." Write a 250–3
word article for your school newspaper in which you apply these categories of behavior
students in your school. Use specific examples and details to support your analysis.

D Write a well-organized composition of 250–300 words on *one* of the following topics:

The world that I inherit   New equals good—or does it?

In defense of rules   A chance to begin again

Losing a friend   Letting off steam

INDEX

2